FOLKLORE AND THE SEA

HORACE BECK

Photographs throughout by
JANE BECK

Folklore
AND THE Sea

BY *Horace Beck*

CASTLE BOOKS

This edition published by Castle Books, 1999.
A Division of Book Sales, Inc.
114 Northfield Avenue
Edison, NJ 08837
By arrangement with Penguin Putnam Inc.

Copyright © 1973 by
The Marine Historical Association, Incorporated.
Reprinted by arrangement with The Stephen Green Press,
an imprint of Penguin Putnam Inc.

Stephen Greene Press 1983

This book is manufactured in the United States of America.

Library of Congress Cataloging in Publication Data

Beck, Horace Palmer, 1920 –
Folklore and the sea.

Reprint. Originally published: Middletown, Conn.:
Published for the Marine Historical Association by
Wesleyan University Press, 1973.
Bibliography: p.
Includes index.
1. Ocean – Folklore.   2. Seafaring life – Folklore.
I. Title.

ISBN: 0-7858-1119-2

To Tommy and Rowan — the young shipmates

CONTENTS

ACKNOWLEDGMENTS

WITHOUT the help and friendship of many people in many walks of life this book could never have been written. In fact, I feel my role has been that of a directed compiler more than a creator. To all those who have had a part in the development of this book I would like to express my gratitude, but to some, to whom my debt is great in ways both personal and scholarly, I should like to express especial thanks.

Out of hundreds of informants there loom from the Old World the following: Captains James Buchan, Paddy O'Halloran, David Tait and Bob Roberts. From other walks I would like to express my gratitude to Neal Cameron, the McLennan family of South Uist, Michael Loughney, John Robinson Park, the McBrides of Fanny's Hole, Ireland, and the filé, Michael Guheen.

From the United States and Canada, I cannot fail to mention Captains Charles Ross of Halifax, Archie Spurling and Del Raines of Matinicus; and from the West Indies, Captains Charlie Bristol, Dean McFarlane, Athneal Ollivierre, the Harpooner and his brother Louis. Again from other walks are "Bobbles" Alexis, Verney Lewis, Horace Charlemagne, Carleton Maglorie, Octon (Micoud) Benjamin, Norman Phillips and, last but by no means least, Alexander Charles.

Once the material was collected it had to be put into workable shape, and here the scholarly process began. Before I had finished, I had sent out cries of help to colleagues all over the Western hemisphere, and they responded with all kinds of assistance and advice. Kenneth Goldstein in Philadelphia and Herbert Halpert in Newfoundland not only allowed me the use of their libraries but were helpful in the mechanics of the book.

John Lorne Campbell of Scotland, Sean O'Sullivan and Seamus O'Duilearga of Ireland not only gave critical analysis of the material in their areas but were instrumental in providing informants and sources of reference that would otherwise have been unknown to me. To these I would add James Osborne, shipmate and researcher who accompanied us through about ten thousand miles of collecting.

I am indebted for the music for all the songs in Chapter VI to Mrs. Mary H. Henkels, Fort Washington, Pennsylvania, who has very kindly and painstakingly transcribed them over the years. And to Middlebury College, Middlebury, Vermont, for allowing me a leave of absence to pull the book together. I must also give thanks for the help afforded by the Egbert Starr Library, and especially by Helen Davis, who ferreted out rare and hard-to-find volumes from the four corners of the United States.

After all these people had worked in my behalf and the book had grown to the point where it began to be discernible, Reginald L. Cook painstakingly read every word and offered invaluable advice as to style and order. Such efforts should ensure his entrance through the celestial gates.

After all these I must express some feeling of gratitude to my own family, to Thomas and Rowan who beguiled their way into homes and hearts of informants everywhere, and to my scholarly wife Jane, alias "Muck Ruhr," who attacked me on every point, did the unpleasant tasks attendant on writing a book, and generally served to keep me at it, to keep me honest, and preserved what semblance of sanity I possessed.

Last but not least come thanks to John Barleycorn in his many aliases, from Guinness to Jack Iron, who smoothed troubled waters on many occasions and was generally helpful when called upon with moderation.

INTRODUCTION

FOR folklore to survive and flourish it requires a very special climate. It feeds on isolation, illiteracy and tradition—tradition stretching backward into the dimmest, most musty corners of antiquity. It is bred in unknowing and in violence. It survives because in some way it is functional. Environment plays a large part in its creation, shaping and preserving. Few areas of the world are better suited to the preservation and creation of folklore than the sea.

Since before the dawn of history man has been a voyager. He has traveled along the coasts, fished in the estuaries and bays, been driven offshore in some gales and onshore in others. Some men have sunk and some have burned and some have won home to end their days on the beach dreaming of the other days. Others, still before the dawn of history, have fared forth over the edge of the world to the place where the sun set in the seething waters. Some came back, some drowned and a few found haven in new strange lands. Those who returned told stories about their adventures, and those who came home no more themselves became the topics of speculation and of stories.

Yet man is never at home, completely, on the sea. Even the most hardy and dedicated sailor has his qualms about his occupation at times, and although some, like *Moby-Dick*'s Bulkington, are easy only in deep water, it is because they are forced there by dangers ashore that present even greater hazards. Because man is not indigenous to the sea, neither is folklore entirely indigenous. Rather the majority of this material comes from the land

and is adjusted to fit the aquatic climate. That which is native to the sea has been created after the manner of terrestrial lore.

In brief, the folklore of the sea is the flotsam and jetsam of folklore from many lands, from many peoples over many centuries, that has been immersed in the brine of the oceans and has become a product as different from the original as is the resin that is soaked in seawater and becomes amber.

Were one to attempt to discuss, compile and evaluate all this great mass of material it would take more than a lifetime even with the aid of a computer, and the result would be a dictionary of sea language, terms, superstitions, beliefs, customs, songs and legends, rather than a book on maritime folklore.

Instead, my purpose here is to examine this vast body of material, sample it, ask and perhaps assume how it came to be; what value, if any, it possesses or did possess; establish, if possible, rules about the formation of sea folklore, its dispersion and durability. Various aspects of the sea culture will be treated and examples selected to illustrate the points made—examples chosen on the basis of interest, longevity, wide diffusion or unique qualities within the material itself. But first let me examine the sea and then seafaring.

To some the mountains are beautiful, to others ugly, but many view them with indifference. Indifference is not a term often used to describe man's connection with the sea. In the first place it is more volatile than the land. All mountains are mountains; clouds may cast shadows upon them, fog make them hazy, snow turn them white, but they remain mountains— large lumps in a known location. Oliver Wendell Holmes called them pachyderms and declared them harmless. The ocean Holmes likened to a feline creature or a reptile. The sea, he said, was lethal. At one instant it is calm and blue and so still that one can look across it and imagine the rim of the earth. An hour later it is gray, the fog slips silently across it and it vanishes in dank gloom. A breeze picks up and it is covered with whitecaps and breaks upon the shore. On a still bright day, great swells roll up out of its depths and march grimly on the land, to break with a roar and retreat with the rattle of rocks in the undertow. Gulls sweep inland and fine cirrus clouds appear overhead. By midnight there is a gale blowing and huge seas sweep the shore with a sound heavier than artillery. At noon the water laps the rocks, but by evening the sea has withdrawn into itself like a coiled snake and left the shore bare, covered with shells, with mud and with wreckage from far-off lands and the mute testimony of disaster upon the coast. All kinds of life are trapped in the pools, and yet no man may drink their water and long survive. This is but the view from a single vantage point on the shore, in only one season. Add to this the gales of spring and fall, the snows and ice of winter, the great tides of the equinox ("full dreen tide" in New England), and the magnitude of the phenomenon called Ocean begins to be better understood.

Go offshore in a small vessel and the picture becomes even more clear. Suddenly you are in the great deep; the lead is cast and no bottom. Out of the deep rise islands, over it float icebergs. Strange currents run counter to your course and you are carried far away. The color of the water changes; it is blue, green, opaque, clear. Shoals of porpoise pass by, flying fish take the air. Whales and seals loom ahead, giant squid bask in the moonlight. At one moment you are in a gale, at another you lie becalmed, a painted ship upon a painted ocean, for days, weeks. You find yourself in an area where the wind blows always from the same direction. You see strange birds that soar on motionless wings above your vessel day and night without rest, without effort. You pass through acres of seaweed and at night the ship leaves a phosphorescent wake. Off the great capes you meet terrible seas and vicious currents at the mouths of bays and around headlands. And always at your shoulder disaster hovers patiently, ready to strike in fog, in fire, through ice, storm or collision, by starvation or by drowning. All these things combine to create problems and mysteries that the mind of man is unwilling to accept.

These are but surface manifestations of the ocean. What lies beneath? Even today there are vast areas of the sea wastes uncharted, creatures within it unidentified, currents unknown. All of these things lead to mystery; and the mind of man is repelled by mystery, and he must solve it through either religion, folklore or science.

These mysteries are added to by the character of the ships that go to sea and what happens to them. Every vessel built reacts in its own way to wind and wave, propeller or sail, helm or oar. One pitches heavily, another rolls; one will run before the breeze like a whippet, while another can reach or beat to windward. One can be steered with one hand while another can't be controlled with two men at the helm. Some appear to be lucky, others unlucky. Some bring rich returns and safe passages while others never show a profit, drown their crews or are lost. Vessels, well found, sail from home on a pleasant day, slip over the horizon and never return. What has happened? Sometimes the answer is as mysterious as the loss. Let us illustrate with a modern example.

A number of years ago an English newspaper sponsored a single-handed race around the world. Prizes were cash. Among the contestants was a man named Crowhurst. He was not an exceptionally skilled yachtsman but he needed the money and he had a plan. After an appropriate lapse of time a yacht reported her position and came pounding home, an undisputed winner. On her heels came Crowhurst in second place. And the gods moved. The winner's boat was wrecked and Crowhurst was in first place! Crowds gathered to greet him but he never came in. Search planes eventually found his vessel abandoned at sea—kettle on the stove and no sign of panic or disaster.

Eventually the riddle was solved. From a perusal of logs and documents it was discovered that while the rest of the fleet was bashing its way around the world, Crowhurst sailed out into the Atlantic and waited until it was certain that a winner was assured. He then put up his helm and bore away for home to win second place. When he suddenly found himself in first place, the enormity of his situation struck him. Unable to confess his deceit or live with his lie, he did the only thing he could. He jumped overboard.

Sometimes, perhaps most often, we never learn the answer. The *Home Sweet Home* was in the midst of reporting her position to Bermuda radio when her broadcast abruptly ended. To date no traces of vessel or crew have been found.

The sailor is well aware of these hazards. He is also well aware of the awesome depths and the unknown creatures that lurk in the cold pressurized dark of the great deeps. He is aware of the hazard of storm and wrack and ruin that await all who persist in following the sea. For ages he has tried to explain and identify the unknown, without benefit of science. He has tried ways and means to guide his ship, to live in harmony in close wet quarters with his fellow man, to read and control the weather. He has tried without the craft of letters to preserve the memory of events that took place at sea—sometimes to commemorate a great hero, sometimes to demonstrate the ways of folly. This is all folklore. Because the sea is violent, the lore of the sea is frequently violent. Where normal acts are heroic, heroic acts are beyond the pale of credibility.

The life of marine folklore is like the life of a breaker. The sea gathers together, swells, crests and rushes ashore to break, withdraw and re-form. So folklore stems from little incidents to which others accrete for a while and then the mass breaks apart, but the pieces re-form again in another shape and the act is repeated.

As one studies this body of material a number of things become apparent. Some aspects of marine folklore are old, so old that their beginnings may lie in the murky regions beyond history. Because people lack gills or other equipment to allow them to live upon the sea, man is always essentially a stranger to its surface, and the devices he employs to survive upon it are generally land born and adjusted or implemented to fit the marine scene. Much of the maritime lore of the British Isles appears to have its origin in Celtic or Germanic belief. Most of the New World maritime tradition seems to have its basis in English-Scottish-Irish lore with an overlay of African tradition. Onto this core have been grafted traditions from about every nationality who ever went to sea.

The following pages attempt to record examples of the various aspects of maritime folklore. An effort has been made to trace the material toward a source, to give reasons for its acceptance by seamen, to postulate a few rules about maritime folklore and to preserve for a few more years at least, customs, beliefs and traditions that may be closer to extinction than we know. In a sense this book is a sort of folk-eye history of the sea.

Many of the stories told have been paraphrased, many others have been told verbatim. To the purist, to tamper with a text is a heinous crime. But the folklorist uses folklore for many purposes. Mine has an element of the aesthetic in it, and although the linguist and the psychologist may derive information from the informant's lack of memory, from the attendant sounds of barking dogs, wailing children, coughing, spitting and sneezing informants, these things often detract from the artistry of the anecdote. The telling of a legend or a folktale is a high art, but it is not an art that transfers readily to the printed page, for writing is a different art. Whenever a story has been paraphrased, the changes have been mostly in the area of punctuation and attendant distractions. The story rhythm has been preserved and the vocabulary largely adhered to. Whenever salient points or expressions were made or used they have been preserved. The stories told verbatim were generally ones that had the felicity of adaptation to print.

Certainly this collection of material and the interpretations derived from the collectanea will not please everybody, but it is hoped that a marine nosegay has been put together wherein most readers will be able to find at least one forget-me-not to call their own.

FOLKLORE AND THE SEA

SHIPBUILDING

I wish to have no connection with any ship that
does not sail fast for I intend to go in harm's way.
—John Paul Jones[1]

WITH a little luck almost anything will float and even make considerable passages at sea. A German recently came across the Atlantic in a kayak, and an American sailed a twelve-foot boat from North America to Europe (England to be exact). There is little doubt that a considerable voyage could be accomplished in a bathtub with the plug driven in, if the weather remained moderate. Indeed, there is still a legend current in Ireland that a saint made a voyage across the Irish Sea to England on a tombstone, while in Newfoundland two boys were said to commute to the island of Jersey each weekend on a stove grate.[2]

The folk, however, are not so sure that anything will go to sea and come back. They believe that certain designs and rigs are better suited than others for sea voyages. Essentially, folk design seems to aim at one of three properties: to build a boat so strong that no gale can overwhelm her, so buoyant that she can climb over the wildest seas or so swift that she can elude the storm. Which of these ideas a particular folk group adopts depends in part on the prevailing conditions in which they operate and in part on the employment to which they put their vessels. That a vessel designed for one purpose and kind of condition can function equally well in another is borne out by the fact that Captain James Cook embarked on his famous voyage of discovery in an English collier![3]

There are, furthermore, several other factors which serve to modify these three basic concepts of ship design. These are prevailing sea conditions in the area, the size and depth of harbors, and the materials at hand

Opposite: Rabbeting the keel, Fanny's Hole, Ireland

for ship construction. In the Baltic and throughout Scandinavia, where ice is prevalent throughout the winter months, it is not uncommon to find the bows and the entire hull along the water line sheathed in ironwood. Where harbors are deep and large, large vessels will be built, while at places like the Isles of Shoals in New Hampshire or No Mans Land, Massachusetts, where harbors were nonexistent, the vessels were small and constructed with an eye to being hauled out by hand or with oxen after use. No one would quibble that teak, mahogany, cedar and pitch pine make the finest planking, and the Ark was fortunate to be built where cedar grew. Where these woods were unknown, unavailable, or too dear, the folk made do with the best local materials and usually found reasons for justifying their choice of "the very best lumber."

To the folk, life at sea is uncertain and they try in every way they can to convince themselves of the safety of their own craft, and employ every device they can think of to reduce the hazard of a seafaring life. To this end, every folk group that goes to sea will tell you that the particular type of craft they use is the best, and they will tell stories to prove it. Indeed, such an attitude should be expected; what right-thinking sailor would go to sea in a poor ship if a better one were available? For that matter, who would be willing to build an inferior vessel?

For example, there is a story on Block Island, Rhode Island, about their cowhorn dories—large, clinker-built vessels with two pole masts that could be hauled up on shore after fishing, for Block Island, years ago, had no decent harbor. According to legend these dories were a match for the wildest weather and no Block Islander had ever been lost in one.

Some time in the 1890s, thirteen cowhorns were fishing on Cox's Ledge (a favorite fishing ground for the islanders) when a great gale blew up. The boats scattered across the sea, but eventually the weather abated and they, one by one, returned until after several days twelve were back at the island. The thirteenth never returned and the islanders concluded the crew had been blown far to sea, then made port somewhere and decided to stay there. They had not been lost.

This tale has an interesting conclusion.

Times changed and the cowhorns gradually became obsolete and vanished from the scene, except for one that was purported to have been cut in half, set upright and used as a smokehouse. From this boat a yachtsman named Loring took drawings and built a cowhorn in Narragansett Bay. He and a friend then set sail for Block Island. On the way a dense fog set in and they missed the island and when the weather cleared they came in toward it from the south.

Old-timers on the island have a habit of watching shipping from the old South Light and when the fog cleared they saw coming toward them a cowhorn dory. When Loring made port a considerable contingent of the island population was at the wharf to welcome home those who had vanished years before.[4]

Most modern vessels are designed by naval architects, tested in a tank at Stevens Institute or elsewhere and constructed in shipyards adjacent to transportation, to water and to a labor force. For the most part, at least in the United States, a large percentage of the people building them know nothing of shipbuilding. They are merely welders, plumbers or electricians working on an object. In folk society it was not this way. Everything was done by tradition and with ritual.[5]

In Jamaica today the native fishermen fashion dugouts from silk cotton trees. Some of these canoes are over forty feet in length. Even before the tree can be cut certain ceremonies have to be performed. Among other things libations of blood, rice and rum are made to propitiate the three kinds of duppies (spirits) that are thought to inhabit these particular trees. Once the ceremony has been performed—the spirits laid to rest—the tree is felled, split, hollowed out with chisels and gouges and, after more ceremonies have been performed is considered safe to venture on the sea.[6]

Formerly before a vessel could be built in most folk communities, from Buckie in Scotland to Carriacou in the West Indies, a site was chosen for the construction that seemed propitious and the ground was carefully consecrated. If the site of the stocks was adjacent to a launching place and to timber, it was fortunate, but the location was chosen for reasons other than convenience. The ground was then sanctified by either a priest or a clergyman. Care was taken to keep the area clear of evil influences and building was not begun until the signs were auspicious. For instance, in Scotland it was thought good to commence construction on a fair day on a good tide and a westerly wind. It was hoped that omens would be about —sheep feeding on a hill, gulls over the harbor, porpoises playing on the bay and so on. In Christian times Wednesday was "the best day of all"— and we should recall that in pagan times Wednesday was the day of Woden, the supreme god who lived in the forest, who would look with favor upon acts begun on his day. The moon should be full or "on the make," and again we are reminded of the pre-Christian beliefs in the power of the moon and her effect upon the sea and things that went into it. Then and only then would the shaman or cleric appear to render prayers and/or sacrifice live creatures, while the keel (of special wood) was laid by those deemed worthy enough for the job.

If these were good times to build there were poor times as well. No one wanted to begin on the thirteenth of the month, a day connected with the infamous Judas and bearing a magical—i.e., indivisible—number; on Thursday (Thor's day, for he was god of storms); or especially on Friday (named for Freya, leader of the Valkyries and thought a witch by early Christians). An east wind, a heavy surf, no birds, all were considered to portend harm to the ship. So too it was hoped that women (especially virgins), pigs, rabbits, flat-footed people and cross-eyed men would be kept from the site. Demented persons, witches—in short, anyone not considered "normal" by the community—were kept away lest somehow evil spirits enter the growing hull, for in folk communities all abnormalities were looked upon as emanating from evil spirits.

Although ships in folk communities are built largely to traditional shapes and designs—so much so that the modern curragh of Ireland looks to the untrained eye surprisingly like the ancient skin boats of Wales in Roman times—there is variation in design from community to community. Each seaport had its master builder who laid out the plans and oversaw the building. These men gained renown for building a more seaworthy, a faster or a more comfortable vessel than anyone else in the community. Their fame did not always rest on their modification of design or skill in joinery, however. As an illustration of this, Professor George Carey told me an interesting tale he had collected on the Eastern Shore of Maryland:

Many years ago in Scotland, near a town called Inverness, a man was walking along the shore when he heard strange lamentations. Looking around, he saw a mermaid sitting on a rock. The tide had gone out and the poor creature was stranded and scorching in the sun. The man approached the lady with a tail and inquired the trouble. If he would only put her back in the water, she said, she would grant him any wish he wanted. After some thought the man said, "I want to build boats that will never sink and from which no man will be lost." The mermaid agreed and was returned to the sea. This was over a century ago, and to this day no boat built by that man or his descendents has ever been lost nor has a man drowned in them.

Inverness lies at the head of the Moray Firth, and I asked Captain Buchan of St. Coombs, also on the Moray Firth, if he had ever heard anything like this. The captain replied he had not heard this story, but he did know that for over a hundred years no boats or men in them had been lost from the town of Buckie, where a family named Jones owned the shipyard. These boats were in demand on the entire Firth. Buckie, it might be pointed out, is only about fifty sea miles from Inverness. Indeed "a Buckie boat and a Gardner engine" are the epitome of desire of most Scots fishermen.[7]

Until modern times, man had little or no knowledge of why or how a boat actually performed. Designs were usually modified through trial and error, using material available. The method by which the vessel would be propelled and the kind of work she would be engaged in would act as design controls. Wood can be used only in ships of limited length or the vessel will break in two; vessels to be rowed had to be low for the oarsmen to get at the water; vessels carrying bulky cargoes on long voyages had to be broad with extra storage space; ships that were to lie afloat could be "long-legged" (deep draft) while those designed to "dry out" to unload usually had flattish, extra strong bottoms.

In sailing vessels the hull was commonly considered a platform to support the sails. At first it was thought that the wider the platform, the less likely the vessel was to turn over or bury herself in the sea, but gradually the hulls were narrowed, the larger sails were placed further aft, and the vessel deepened. In this manner more speed and stability were obtained, and the final results were the great clippers of the mid-nineteenth century and the schooners at the end of that century and the beginning of this one.

Perhaps the two greatest fears the shipmaster had was that he would "bury" (run the bows under and sink) or that he would be "pooped" (have a large sea break in over the stern). To prevent this, the bow and stern were raised very high, until by the end of the Middle Ages we find a bow and stern "castle" on ships to keep out the water and also to serve as platforms from which spears, stones and arrows could be hurled in case of enemy attack.

These changes took place gradually over centuries and resulted largely from the change in propulsion from oars to sail, from the development of harbors where vessels could lie afloat in security, and from the desire to make more distant passages with larger cargoes. With the advent of what Del Raines of Matinicus Island, Maine, called the "eternal combustion engine," the modifications of folk design were greatly accelerated. As a result, one can observe the rather rapid evolution in design of lobster boats on Cranberry Island, Maine, as a microcosmic example of the whole larger process.

As stated earlier, when alterations were made they were not made by just anyone but by the master builder in the community, who altered his molds partly, at least, to please or placate the prospective owner and partly to satisfy his own curiosity and aesthetic sense—always, of course, working within the larger traditional plan. Such a man was Arthur Spurling (locally known as "Capt'n Archie") the master drafter-builder on Cranberry Island, who spent the major part of his life building boats for his neighbors. I have in my possession a half model whose alterations bear out the following description of how a lobster boat developed.

One day one of Capt'n Archie's neighbors wanted a lobster boat. In his workshop Spurling carved out a model of a peapod dory from a piece of spruce, using a scale of one-half inch to the foot. To the designer the model looked perfect, but the prospective buyer complained that the hull would be too wet. Spurling considered for a while and then glued a piece on the bow. The owner being satisfied by the modification, Spurling made a template of the model's lines using a piece of soft lead and expanded them to full size on the loft floor. From these expanded drawings he built the boat.

His next customer wanted a boat that would beat the one just built. Knowing that a narrow sailboat is faster than a beamy one, the designer retained the bow but narrowed the hull. After trying her, the owner reported that although she was dry she rolled horribly and was no faster than the first boat. Therefore, before he built his next boat, Archie examined his model and considered all he knew. He couldn't raise the bow and have her "look right." Instead he hollowed the bow out. Reasoning that a skiff rolled less than a peapod, he flattened the bilges somewhat and deepened the keel. The new boat proved faster, drier and far more stable than her prototypes. Indeed the boat was such a success that a number were built from this model, each modified slightly from the other. Finally Spurling made another half model. Instead of a canoe (pointed) stern this one had a transom which sloped inboard, for Spurling feared what a sea would do against a square stern. This model proved twice as fast as its predecessors, but because he considered the stern ugly and found, further, that the sea did not bother it, he gradually straightened it until he eventually produced a design we would consider conventional today. Each modification had enhanced both the vessel's beauty and efficiency; for beauty and efficiency seem to go hand in hand in boat design. The result was an extremely able, handsome craft.[8]

Formerly much of the building was done by rule of thumb. In New Bedford, Massachusetts, half a century ago, lived an old Portuguese who had a great reputation for building fishing smacks. His real name has been lost in the past, but according to Al Buffington of Tiverton, Rhode Island, he went by the name of Captain Scup and he had a helper named Louie. The old man would constantly wander around the vessel squinting at her. From time to time he would say, "Hit 'er again, Louie, she's a too plumb." Louie would obligingly belt the offending timber with a maul and construction would continue.

Even today much of the mystery of design is carried in the head of the local designer. Rather than resort to the complicated formulas employed by naval architects to determine the waterline of a vessel, the local shipbuilders in Nova Scotia and the West Indies spend some time wandering, aimlessly, around the hull. They then draw in the waterline by eye, and when the craft is launched it requires only a minimum of adjustment of internal ballast to make her "float to her lines."[9]

What has been said of the master builder could also be said of his crew. Certain men were responsible for certain jobs, and they often inherited the position from their fathers. They made or inherited their own tools and would allow no one else to use them. Some were joiners, carpenters, riggers, caulkers; some were ship carvers who made figureheads, trail boards and decorated the knightheads in larger ships. In Fairhaven, Massachusetts, there was an old man called "Spiler Pete" who did nothing but mark out the shape of the planks to be put into vessels, as his father had done before him.

Over the years very careful nomenclature has grown up about each and every part of a vessel, until almost every plank and timber in her has a name and each type of construction is identified. Starting at the bottom we have keel, keelson, false keel, stern, horn timber, garboard, sheer plank, devil boards, batter boards, dead wood, stopwaters and treenails. Some are hard chine boats, some are round bilged and so on. The interesting thing is that many of these parts are constructed out of special materials.

In the book of Genesis we are told with considerable detail that the Ark was built out of many cords of cedar. We know that boats in Egypt were made out of papyrus thousands of years ago. In fact, just about every kind of material including cement has been used for ship construction, but careful scrutiny of the material will reveal that wood for ship construction is not chosen wholly for structural reasons or because it is handy to the construction site—although these undoubtedly bear weight in determining the kind used. There is more to it than that. Why not any old cedar for the Ark instead of that which came from Lebanon?

The four most popular woods today used in planking are mahogany, teak, cedar and pitch pine. Cedar, which is light and will swell, resists insect

life. Teak does not swell and is impervious to water and bugs. Mahogany
is light and strong and comes in wide widths which are indispensable when
shaping planks to fit a curving hull. Pine is cheap and tough and water resistant. But cedar is knotty and soft, teak heavy and easily shattered,
mahogany hard to work and soft, and pine rough and heavy.

Let us look at a typical vessel built in one folk area in America. Assuming the materials are available, the stern, keel and frames will be of
white oak. The horn timber will be hornbeam (sometimes called ironwood), knees of apple, carlings ash, clamp and shelf spruce, decks fir and
the planking pine. If wooden fastenings (treenails) are used, they will be
of locust, while the stopwaters are made of soft pine. Sometimes the sheer
plank is of oak, and the decorative carving will be done in holly if it is
available.

If you ask the shipwright about these materials he will give you practical reasons for their use. The wood is tough, it resists water, it has a
natural curve, it is extremely light and so on. The shipwright will also tell
you he is using the same materials that his father's grandfather used to
build boats. He is using traditional materials. Close scrutiny of these various
woods will reveal that in the past they were thought to possess supernatural
qualities. Apple and holly were associated with faeries; oak and pine were
trees of special import to pagan dieties. Lest one think this is reaching too
far, let us take a single example of ship construction from Chesapeake Bay
as an illustration.

Black walnut is a rich, easily worked wood that is resistant to water.
It grows straight and tall, and the trees are often three or four feet in
diameter. Sometimes planks thirty feet long could be milled from the log
and show scarcely a single knot. Although it is now scarce, it was at one
time common along the shores of Chesapeake Bay. In fine, it would seem
to be an ideal wood for the shipwright, but it was and is not.

An old waterman once bought a very handsome skiff there for five
dollars. From the day he bought it he had nothing but trouble. It sank,
broke loose, was stolen, leaked; and whenever he went out in it, things
went wrong. He caught no fish, lost oars, a storm came up. Finally he decided to repaint it and stripped off some of the paint. The skiff was made of
black walnut! He did the only thing he could do—sold it to a tourist.[10]

So bad is the reputation of black walnut in this area that the whole
boat need not be made of the stuff to bring trouble. One man fashioned a
seat out of it and was plagued with misfortune. A crank boat was set aright
when it was discovered that a squirrel had stashed some black walnuts

aboard. Then there is a story of a skipper on one of the islands bound to Annapolis with cargo. An old lady asked him to take her along. He agreed and she came aboard with a paper bag. Scarcely had they got out into the bay when a violent gale sprang up. No matter which way the captain tried to go, the wind hauled against them and the sea grew wilder until it looked as if they would swamp. The captain knew that something was wrong and in desperation asked the old woman what she had in the bag. "Black walnuts." Instantly the skipper seized the bag and heaved it overboard. The storm abated and they landed safely in Annapolis a few hours later.[11]

To the folk, the black walnut is a tree of ill omen. On the beach it is said to draw lightning, kill cattle and burn houses. The bark and the nuts stain your hands permanently. Somehow it is associated with the devil. The reasons for much of this lies in the tree. The wood is odd-colored—purplish—and heavier than many other woods. Because of its nature it grows tall and often in isolation. As a result, it is particularly subject to being hit by lightning. Since cows have a way of standing under trees in thunderstorms and these trees offer the most shelter, many a critter has been electrocuted under them. When near a house, lightning often is deflected from the tree and into the building. Just as a dog with a bad name gains the reputation of being a sheep killer, so does the black walnut become the scapegoat for every miserable boatbuilder and lubberly sailor in the area.

Essentially from the initial planning to the final launch, nothing that could be done to assure the success and safety of the ship and her crew was overlooked. To this end, the supernatural and the practical went hand in hand; traditional methods and materials were maintained but modified by the practical considerations of the times and geography to produce, in the folk view of things, the best ship possible. This is illustrated in a curious way by a tale current in Lunenburg, Nova Scotia, about the building of the famous fishing schooner *Bluenose* earlier in this century.

The plans for this vessel were drawn by the well-known Nova Scotia marine architect Billy Roue, and she was laid down in Lunenburg, the province's most prominent fishing port. When she was about half built the master builder became greatly distressed and went to the yard owner. The vessel was not long enough for her beam and draft and must needs be lengthened to meet the specifications the fishermen felt made for good sailing qualities. The master builder prevailed and several feet were added to the ship (some say the addition was to the bow, others say she was sawed in two and the extension made amidships). At any rate she was launched, and established a fabulous record for speed under Captain "Bucky" Walters.

Eventually she was sold out of the country and lost at sea. The Canadian government, which had already inscribed her picture on its currency, decided to build a duplicate vessel. They had Roue's design, and the new *Bluenose* builders scrupulously followed the plans. The *Bluenose II* was launched. Captain Walters was hauled out of retirement to sail her, but the new ship has been able to establish herself only as "a dull sailor" whose performance in no way approaches the original vessel's. "It's because of them extra feet b'ye," the fishermen will tell you—but let us return once more to the building process.

Everything and everyone assembled, the keel would be blessed—in Christian times by a minister or priest, who would say appropriate prayers. In Ireland, he would also sprinkle holy water on the timber or set a vial of the precious liquid on the beam (as is still done in Mulroy Bay in the north of Ireland) before the actual shaping of the wood was begun.[12]

Whenever possible the keel would have been laid in a north-south direction. Although "hollow superstition" could be ascribed as the reason for this act, it actually—like most folk customs—served a useful purpose. In the first place, most vessels, even wooden ones, develop a certain amount of magnetic attraction when building which necessitates compass adjustments. When built in a north-south direction the ship's magnetism lined up with the fore-and-aft direction and did not cause the compass deviation problems it otherwise would. Moreover, since vessels were usually built out-of-doors, if they were lined up north and south the sun would affect both sides of the ship more evenly than if they were lined up in an east-west direction.

Not only were prayers said and holy water placed on the keel at the outset of construction, but throughout the building, various other precautions were taken to assure the vessel's long life, well-being and general prosperity. These precautions were many and varied. In New England, bins were fashioned between the frames and filled with salt "to keep the bilges sweet" and prevent dry rot. In Scotland, after the blessing and the proper directional alignment had been attended to, it was the duty of the master builder to secrete a gold coin "for luck" somewhere in the splicing of the keel, its exact whereabouts known only to the owner and himself.[13] And not only was a gold coin placed in the keel but sometimes a sovereign was fastened to the main beam of the deck (according to a Scots informant).

It is highly possible that the memory of this act has been retained in a kind of horseplay inflicted on green hands in American naval ships who are sometimes told to go below and "polish the golden rivet" located in the most inaccessible part of the keel.

Somewhat analogous to this matter of a gold coin is a story told on the island of Inishbofin by Captain Paddy O'Halloran.

St. Leo was supposed to be in Shark and I don't know what happened to his bell, but they took the bell away out of Shark, too. They landed in Shark one time. I suppose they could be pirates or Northmen or whatever they were but they took the bell out of Shark, brought it aboard and they had to throw the bell out that night, too. A storm got up and they threw out the bell and the bell was back in Shark in the morning again and I remember well to hear the old people tell it. In fact I saw one of the boats. It was built here in the island but she was a small boat you see, small row-boat, maybe about a ton-and-a-half or two-ton boat you know? And they used to break little bits off the bell and they would put it in between the timbers, between the timber, the sheathing and the frame of the boat when they would be building the boat and nothing ever happened to any of the boats that had a bit of the bell in. They were never drowned or anything. They had great belief in the bell anyhow and they wouldn't get a new boat made without putting a bit of the bell into them, just a little teeny bit. I saw one of the boats, the remains of one of the boats that was built here.[14]

Michael Loughney of Kilcummin Roads told a story about another important ingredient to be added to the growing hull.

Years ago a cow went down to the beach and began to lick a box cast up on the shore. For three days the cow returned and licked the box until a woman became curious and opened it. Inside was a tiny baby, which she brought home and raised as her own. One day when the lad was in his teens he was working for a farmer when a flock of crows descended on the field and began eating the grain. The farmer was very distressed and re-marked to the boy, "If only we could drive off the crows we could save the crop." But the crows couldn't be driven off, and the farmer went home to lunch in despair. When he returned all the crows were gone. "Where are the crows?" "I locked them all in the church." Investigation revealed that the crows were indeed there. In fact there were so many of them that the church was full. As a result of this act the people began to think the boy had certain otherworld attachments, and so it proved. He became St. Cummin, a very holy man, performed miracles and created a holy well that cured many diseases. To this day both well and church can be seen and are considered shrines by the natives.

Eventually he died and was buried near the church, but as St. Cummin his benevolence to mankind was not yet over. Providing a woman of the Loughney family gather it, clay from this grave will preserve the bearer from drowning, and if a pinch is placed in a boat it will never sink. My informant's sister was the woman who currently could procure the precious clay, and apparently this practice has been believed in and acted upon now for almost fifteen hundred years.[15]

At Tory Island on the northwest coast of Ireland there is another kind of clay that is very valuable to boatbuilders—or, at least, owners.

According to James Dixon, many years ago this little island was visited by the holy man Cholm Cille, on his way to Iona. Word of his whereabouts reached Scandinavia, and a boat containing five sons of the king of Norway and one woman set out from there to see him. Unfortunately the voyage proved more hazardous than they had expected and all hands died on the trip. The boat, however, drifted on with the corpses and was eventually washed ashore on the island. The people took up the bodies and buried them, but the woman refused to stay underground and seven times she came to the surface. The seventh time she came up, Cholm Cille, who had performed many miracles on the island—among them exterminating all the rats—ordered that the woman be buried separately from the rest. It was done and she remained underground. (In another version of the same story she was said to be a nun and refused to stay buried until "she buried herself.") At any rate, her grave became a very holy place and since that time tons of dirt have been taken from it and placed in boats far and near. Any vessel carrying a pinch of this clay, it is said, will always remain free from rats.[16]

A more popular tradition than those listed heretofore is the placing of statues of saints in specially prepared niches on vessels belonging to Roman Catholics. The saint was generally of the same name as the vessel and it was hoped that the icon would protect the ship from harm—especially storms. To this end, during gales votive candles were lit before the shrine, prayers said and sometimes libations of food or wine offered. Should the storm continue, the captain would berate the statue, and if this proved of no avail the icon would be dragged from its niche, a line affixed and it would be towed astern. Should this, too, fail and the storm was extreme, the captain would sometimes cut the line.[17]

As the vessel sprang from her chips and shavings like the phoenix from her ashes, wood-carvers were at work both on the vessel and elsewhere on decorative objects, catheads, bitts, bollards, trail boards and especially the figurehead. Although they came to be decorative, originally these figures were believed to be possessed of magical protective qualities that would shield the vessel, her crew and cargo from harm.

Lion heads (symbolic of strength), sea birds, mermaids and dolphins were all popular motifs to be found in some profusion on objects about the vessel. It was felt that these carvings would in some cases propitiate malevolent creatures such as mermaids and krakens who might harm the ship, or would scare away denizens of the deep of a lesser nature. In fact the entire ancient Norse longship was designed to look like a sea serpent, with the head at the bow, tail at the stern and the oars like legs amidships. Whether the sea monsters found this apparition pleasing or terrifying is a moot question, but there can be little doubt that the ship itself did nearly as much to strike terror to the enemy as the hairy horde aboard.

Later on, in the time of Samuel Pepys, the number of these carvings grew to such proportions as to raise a scandal in England and the treasury cut back allotments to ships for decoration so sharply that hordes of ship carvers found themselves out of work and spent their days decorating English homes. In the United States, ship carving reached a high point with the building of the U.S. frigate *President*, decorated with a figurehead and trail boards depicting sheaves of corn, wheat, fruit, deer, Indians, bows and arrows, and a few Greek figures to fill in any blank places.[18]

Of greatest importance and antiquity was the figurehead. Ships from China to Norway, ships of civilized peoples such as the Greeks and the French, of primitive people like the Indians of the northwest coast and the Solomon Islanders, attest to the worldwide popularity of this device. Like so many old-world items, the figurehead appears to have reached Europe from the Arabs who decorated their otherwise scruffy dhows with elaborate occuli.[19] From the Arabs they moved across the Mediterranean and thence over Europe. The Arab occuli were not figureheads in the normal sense but huge eyes carved or painted on the bows of the vessel.

Nothing could better testify to man's belief in animism than these figureheads, which were carved in the likeness of the vessel's name and character with great emphasis upon two things, action and the bulging thyroidal eyes. Thus the *Quaker Maid* had a demure little bug-eyed Quaker miss leaning forward into the sea. The *Grand Turk* had a Turk with a scimitar, the *Highlander* a braw Scot plus dirk, and the *Indian Chief* showed a wild-eyed Indian with headdress and a tomahawk held poised in his brawny fist. A figurehead of an "unknown" ship is a plump ogling goose with wings half spread, and it is a shrewd guess that the vessel she adorned may have been the *Wild Goose* or the *Barnacle Goose*—a bird of legendary fame.

The idea behind the occuli and the figurehead is, briefly, that because of the pecularities of a ship, her movement, her internal noises, and her vagaries in handling, seamen believed her to be animate or at least quasi-animate. If her bow were adorned with a representative carving equipped with eyes, albeit of wood, the vessel herself could always be on the lookout for danger and perhaps able to avoid it unaided. Without occuli or a figurehead, the vessel would be forced to go it blind despite the lookout.

In the United States, figurehead carving developed to a high folk art during the latter part of the eighteenth and the first half of the nineteenth century. Working on balks of wood, the sculptors were able in some cases to catch the ripple of flesh beneath the clothing and to portray expression and anatomy to an amazing degree. It was out of these ship carvers that American sculpture grew, for one William Rush of Philadelphia, a carver of figureheads and signboards for many years, opened the first sculpture school in the United States in the eighteenth century.[20]

Not only was carving important to the ship for her strength and safety, but the color of the vessel was also important. Speaking in general terms, light, bright colors are to be encountered along the coasts of Spain, Portugal, France and the Mediterranean. In fact, in the temperate and subtropical areas of the world, these light hues seem to be predominant, while in the more northern latitudes darker colors are the fashion. Around the Aran Islands, on the west coast of Ireland, boats and sails were formerly black. This custom has been perpetuated to the present day in the Galway hookers, which look like funeral vessels as they sail along—black sails, black hulls and even the crew dressed in black. In Scotland and the rest of Ireland, vessels are usually painted black, dark green or red or sometimes blue. Occasionally, too, they appear in natural wood, heavily oiled. On the other hand white, gray, black and yellow (in southern waters) seem to be favorite colors for ships in the United States and Canada. It is also interesting to note that in certain areas of North America, Maine for example, seamen refuse to paint vessels either blue or green—the colors of the sea— believing that they are sure to bring bad luck.

In most cases the upper works of ships are painted different colors than the hulls—usually lighter, the whole being planned with an eye to giving a pleasing design and to improving the silhouette of the ship, which generally seems to mean lowering the aspect of the vessel on the water and accentuating the height of bow and stern.

For centuries ships have been built of wood, but nowadays metal has replaced oak and pine to a considerable degree. In spite of this, there is a good deal of effort made to disguise the metal and give it the appearance of wood. In Scotland, where the fishermen keep the sea in any weather and where "good days" are considered unfit to go out in elsewhere in the world, the deck works have long since been constructed of steel to prevent their being torn off by the seas. Before one of these vessels will go to sea, skilled painters are hired to paint the deck works to look like pine planking. The process is called graining, and consumes a very considerable amount of time and money, but the result is to make the outside of the pilot house look like the inside of a brand-new knotty pine rumpus room.

It has long been my contention that folk customs are invariably based on some utilitarian function or idea, although the function may have become lost to the present-day practioner—if it were ever fully understood. In the case of paint motifs, several things may help to explain the use of colors. Dark colors draw heat, heat dries and shrinks planks and also makes the interior of a boat like a furnace. In the lower latitudes where the rays of the sun are more direct, darker hulls would suffer more from sun than lighter ones. Although the folk in Maine argue that green and blue are bad luck, it is a known fact that these two colors, plus black, are very hard to maintain and in hot weather will blister. Finally, we are faced with a problem of visibility. In northern latitudes certain colors can be seen further than they can in southern climes, and it may be that this is another subconscious control over the paints used.

Not only is color important to a folk group (all the fishing vessels in a harbor in Scotland will be painted in only one or two hues) but the color of a vessel is of particular importance to owners. Years ago, according to Captain Morris of Tenants Harbor, Maine, two men joined forces to build a small coasting schooner. All went well until it came to the color. One man wanted her white, the other black. Black was finally agreed upon; the vessel was painted, rigged and made ready for sea. A "whole load" of potatoes was consigned to her and one of the owners took her to Boston, where he sold the potatoes at a good profit. While he was waiting for another cargo, the black vessel began to upset him. Rather than thinking that black was beautiful the skipper decided he was master of a hearse and, using his share of the profits, he changed the color to white.

When the vessel returned to Tenants Harbor the other owner was standing on the dock. As soon as he saw the color he flew into a towering rage, and one word led to another. The United States marshal was summoned, the vessel impounded. Litigation followed and one year dragged into another. Meanwhile the vessel, sails, gear, cargo and cutlery lay at the wharf. The railroads expanded and began to eat into the coasting trade, which grew less profitable. Eventually, still with her cargo aboard and sails bent, the schooner went to pieces alongside the wharf and sank. According to my informant, her bones were still to be seen in the mud at low tide in the early 1960s.

Of all the things that pertain to the building of a ship, the two most important events are the selection of her name, and the launching. The magic of a name is to human beings, both sophisticated and primitive, very real. Even today highly cultured people agonize over the selection of names for the child. If the offspring is of Roman Catholic parents a saint's name should be included, a family name and so on. Actually, it would be much more satisfactory to give the child in our computerized society its Social Security number and call it "Fifty-seven" as a nickname, but such a thought at the moment is so abhorrent that even the most dedicated bureaucrat would be reluctant to suggest it publicly. This whole problem of onomastics has engaged the scholarly mind for years and only a few ideas can be included here.

Over the ages certain concepts appear to have ruled the naming of vessels. Names have been determined partly by the vessel's occupation and partly by the time, each epoch having popular ships' names. Usually the name, within the confines of these two restrictions, was selected either to protect the ship from harm and further her business, or to avoid offending various spirits that could bring harm or danger to the vessel.

In the seventeenth and eighteenth centuries there was a world of difference between names for British and American warships and humble merchantmen. *The Terrible, Victory, Nonesuch, Tiger* and *Ferret* were names common to warships, while *Pretty Pinnance Virginia, Watch and Wait, Sparrow, Prudence, Quaker Maid*, and *Pyed Cow* (the vessel that brought the first sawmill to North America in 1624) were the kind of names that identified the plodding cargo carriers. During the American Revolution and the War of 1812, American privateers went under such names as the *Teaser, Hawk, Eagle, Weasel, Yankee, Loyal Sam, Thinks I to Myself Thinks I*, and *Poor Sailor*.

Today one can usually tell simply by reading the name of a ship not only what kind it is, but often its nationality. The United States names battleships for states, cruisers for cities, aircraft carriers for battles and submarines for large voracious fish. Merchantmen are called the *American Farmer, American Liberty, Texaco Star, Torrey Canyon*, and by these names we learn that they are cargo carriers, like the first two, or tankers like the last. Sailing yachts go under names like *Queen Mab, Thunderhead, Chanty-man* or *Morning Watch*, while very often American power boats are the *Margie-Jo, Zip Zap, Zoom, Me an' You* or *Happy Daze*. This tendency to give vessels names according to types has long been common. One recalls that as early as the eighteenth century English colliers were often named for a duke, earl or lord.

In contemporary times there still remains a marked difference in names for British and American vessels, both yachts and commercial craft. English yachts are often named in phrases like *Myth of Malham, Helen of Howth, Ahwilda of Rhu*, or with names like *Scimitar, Excalibur* or *Griffon*. English and Scottish fishing vessels are frequently identified with the owners' family as *Girl Vivien*, or carry such names as *The Golden Harvest, The Gleaner, Silver Star, Fern, Golden View, Spray, Harvest* and so on. American vessels carry family names, often saints' names, names of places like *Sankaty Head*, and sometimes names like *Kelpie, Sea Horse, Flying Fish* or—humorously—*Cigar Joe* or *The Crowd from Crotch Harbor*. In America, where custom and superstition have weakened, such names are acceptable but would never be tolerated abroad, where to challenge objects or scorn elements is still thought highly chancy.

One is tempted, and indeed it would be possible, to continue making lists of vessels ad infinitum and comparing them, but the real problem is still to be faced—why these kinds of names? There are, of course, a myriad of reasons for giving or for not giving a boat a particular name. A vessel with a certain name came to harm, was a dull sailor, hard to handle. The personality of the ship—to the folk—is somehow linked to her name and therefore it would simply tempt fate to name a new vessel for a ship of ill fortune. On the other hand, if a ship had good fortune others might be named after her. While careening, *The Great Harry* had her guns break loose and go through her leeward side. She went down with such terrible loss of life that "By the Lord Harry" is still a popular epithet. The *Vasa* capsized and sank with all hands on her initial voyage. So far as I know, no vessels have been given those names since the disasters, whereas the H.M.S. *Victory*, and the U.S.S. *Saratoga*, because of initial successes, are still popular names. In certain areas, too, names have properties attached to them that make them taboo, while in other areas where no taboos exist the names are used. In Scotland no one would name a boat *Seal*, for there are superstitions about seals that have been forgotten in America where the name is now fairly common. To try to record all these reasons would entail a separate volume.

There is, however, one popular and universal belief that bears a little scrutiny. In California recently the author saw an advertisement, "Learn to Impress People with Your Money." This is antithetical to the problem of ship onomastics. It was long explicitly believed that one should take great care never to give a ship an impressive name. A humble name was more likely to pass unnoticed by the elements and a haughty one was bound to land one in trouble. One did not name ships for the larger denizens of the deep, for the oceans, for winds, storms and other cataclysmic events. Indeed one did not even dare use an audacious word (this word was itself taboo) lest as the Bible succinctly points out, the mighty be brought low.

In the eighteenth century there was a vessel named the *Celeste*. She sailed on a Friday. She nearly sank and had to be repaired. She sailed again and a rabbit was found aboard. Rats left her. Smallpox broke out. Her log was found floating on an empty sea with the last entry only an hour old. [One might add that during the present century the *Mary-Celeste* was found drifting along with all sail set and the table laid for dinner, but what became of her crew is still unknown.][21] When the *Atlantic* went down, a poet warned that the ocean said, "There shall not two 'Atlantics' be." For those who have a will to believe in such things I point out that the *Titanic* struck an iceberg, the *Squalus* dove to dive no more and the *Angel Gabriel* went to wrack and ruin off the coast of Maine. To these could be added other audacious names—and a host of humble ones including the aforementioned *Sparrow*.

At any rate, it was not until vessels had reached the thousand-ton size of the American clippers during the 1850s that names like *Herald of the Morning, Typhoon, Hurricane, Witch of the Wave* and *Sovereign of the Seas* became popular. Again it might be remembered that of all these mighty clippers only the *Cutty Sark* remains intact. Of the others, some were wrecked, some burned, some sank and others were broken up under the wrecker's hammer after serving ingloriously as barges or hulks.

One last point to be made about names is one that seems to have some variation from place to place. In America it is looked upon as ill luck to change a vessel's name, while in Scotland such a change is not considered unusual. In Loch Boisdale in the Hebrides, a Mr. Macauley told me that sometimes changing the name would change a ship's luck for the better, and in Frazerburgh on the Moray Firth, David Tait planned to change the *Girl Vivien* to another name when he "found a good one" because he had "no girl Vivien." In Ireland such practices are not countenanced, and there are numerous stories in the United States about what happens to vessels whose names are changed. There has always been a good deal of magic connected with names, and I am inclined to believe that the cavalier attitude expressed toward names by various informants in the British Isles is a modern example of deteriorating folklore rather than a reflection of traditional belief.

All the yard work completed, painted, and with figurehead in place, the ship was now ready for the most crucial moment in its development —the launch with the attendant christening. Over the years and in different places this event has changed markedly, but whatever the ritual, it is imperative that it be strictly conformed to, else the results of months of effort could turn out to be a failure, for it is at the launch that seamen can first tell whether they have a lucky or an unlucky vessel. To insure that all go well, great effort was made by everyone in the community.

The first consideration, and one over which man had some control, was the choice of an auspicious date and time. To this would be added good signs among the elements.

If care and precautions were taken during the building, they were as nothing compared to those that attended the launch. Amongst the seafaring folk no event, barring human birth, was more carefully watched or noted. In fact even today the launching of a great ship is attended with fanfare beyond all logical reason. Bands are hired, champagne is served; often a banquet is held; a man of the cloth is present and great thought goes into the selection of the person designated to christen the vessel— usually a female who has demonstrated political, economic or patriotic worth. But even today there is a trace of folklore to be found in the act, for some effort is made to find a person with the aforementioned qualifications who in some way is connected with the ship. When the destroyer *Halsey Powell* was christened, the widow of the captain for whom the ship was named officiated, and when the destroyer *Kane* was launched, it was that officer's niece who broke the bottle on her bow.

Often with large ships the king, queen, president, governor, mayor or other important figures are present at the launch and a local holiday is usually declared. However, these are largely sophisticated and somewhat meaningless accretions sprouting on an old folk stem.

Until the advent of the computer a ship was the most nearly animate object that man could create. It rolled, wiggled, pitched, and had its own peculiarities that could never be duplicated even in a sister ship. Unlike a building, from which men could escape, it was essential to the crew's welfare. Ships still remain the largest movable objects designed by man.

No matter how banal a modern ship launch may appear, it has roots that go back thousands of years to days before Homer, and much of the ritual was deadly serious. Unlike numerous pagan customs, a great deal of the lore of launching has been changed over the years until sometimes age and Christianity have actually inverted folk custom. A single example should suffice.

The Vikings are said to have tied slaves to the rollers under the newly built ship. When the vessel rolled into the water the slaves popped like plump sausages and bespeckled the vessel with blood and other debris. Later on, these human sacrifices were replaced by animal sacrifices, and these in turn gave way to ritualistic ones. However, in the more remote areas of the English-speaking world, animal sacrifices are still performed. Such a place is the island of Carriacou in the West Indies—a spot locally famous as a shipbuilding center.[22]

Because of the peculiar pattern of building and launching a ship in the West Indies a few words must be added to the above, for in many ways the process is to us today as archaic as the practices of the ancient Norse.

When the time is right and building is about to start, after a sufficient amount of the various timbers have been collected—keel, frames, fastenings and some planking—the shipwright and owner (if he is someone other than the builder) will hold a fête, called a "setting up ceremony." A large feast is prepared, a priest is called and the proceedings are blessed. Sacrifices of various animals are made, and the large crowd that has been invited falls to on the meal and the liquor. The keel is laid, the stern and horn timber put in place and the "ribbons" that outline the hull are secured.

Once the work is completed—and most of it is done with hand saws, block planes, adzes, hammers and pod augers—preparations for the most important event of all, the launch and the attendant "Saraca," are begun. A great anchor is carried out into deep water and dropped overboard with a block attached through which a hawser is run, with one end fast to the ship and the other brought ashore. To insure success in launching, a bull-dozer is hired and invitations to attend the coming feast are sent to every-one in any way connected with the ship or the owners.

The banquet consists of every kind of food available in the area pre-pared in as many different ways, and is accompanied with "lots of liquor, mon, lots of liquor—and Jack Iron" (a kind of local rum consisting, as near as I can judge, of 99 percent pure alcohol; it is traditionally drunk at a gulp and the flames of hell that erupt in the belly are partially extinguished by swallowing a glass of water).

Besides the food and the drink, other entertainment is provided, but the levity is tempered with tremendous religious overtones. Along with the steel band and the more modern musical equipment there is usually the "big drum." Big drum consists of three men who beat special rhythms on goatskin drums and their importance in West Indian religion cannot be overemphasized, for it is through the playing of big drum, through prayer and the pouring of libations of blood and Jack Iron, that the spirits of the dead, the jumbies, are raised to communicate with the quick or are propitiated.

On board the vessel, which has been decked with flags and bunting and is ready for sea in all things save ballast and rigging, a Jumbie Plate is set out. On it are portions of all the food prepared for the guests, and this plate is guarded through the night to make sure that it is not stolen, for it is there to feed the ancestors. It is fervently hoped that the plate will be consumed before daybreak, thus assuring the gathering that the spirits look with favor upon the launch and, since all hands including the guards are liberally supplied with Jack Iron, it generally is.

Prior to the launch the vessel is blessed, and prayers and sacrifices are made. Frizzle fowl (a peculiar-looking chicken without feathers on its neck and whose other feathers grow backwards), a white cock, goats and sheep are sacrificed. Their throats are cut, blood is allowed to drip over the decks and some is scattered to the four winds and some to the water.

The vessel is then "cut down," i.e., the wooden supports that hold her upright are cut through and she is allowed to fall on a bed of prepared rollers, usually greenheart logs. The bulldozer pushes at the bow, the revelers tail onto the hawser and begin to heave her seaward to the tune of chanties, one of which is *Yado*.[23] Frances Kay reiterates what has been said here and includes details omitted.

When the *Sea Laura A* was launched a few years ago, it was noted that the ceremony began at ten in the morning. First, a black he-goat was killed and the decks sprinkled with his blood. Then a priest said prayers and sprinkled the vessel with holy water. A drum began to beat and flags were unfurled from two makeshift masts. Hordes of people came aboard and danced. They then got off and the boat was launched while an island official led a cheer. Once launched, men went aboard and danced and then swam ashore to attend a feast of meat, vegetables and rum and danced the rest of the day.

All of this is, however, far more sinister than it appears. In Dominica there is a certain great tree which is known as the Lagarou tree. Here it is said that the Lagarou, a kind of West Indian vampire, come to school to learn their trade. Local people are disinterested in approaching the tree after dark and report that they often see lights flitting from branch to branch. They say that if one will procure timbers from that tree—in odd numbers from one to seven—and incorporate them in the building of the vessel, she will be a very fast sailer. Unfortunately, vessels containing timbers from this tree are also supposed to be extremely susceptible to capsizing and sinking with the crew, so the builder must juggle eventualities before incorporating this wood into the hull.

As may be surmised from the preceding material, for a boat to be successful in the West Indies it must somehow be in favor with the other world and it is not surprising to learn that it is popularly believed that a boat must have a soul, a human one, in order to function properly. I was first made aware of this one day when I overheard two seamen discussing a vessel hove down for repairs. "Maybe now she be good vessel," one said. Thinking that perhaps she had been damaged, I inquired why, and learned that while hove down one of the crew had drowned so the vessel now had a soul—something she had lacked formerly.

Further interrogation revealed that a man in her had indeed died. One account said it was from a fit, another said a heart attack, still another said he had been clubbed, robbed and thrown overboard and a final one claimed he had been stabbed. All agreed that the schooner in question had not been a success, and all expressed hope that she would now prove a more satisfactory cargo carrier. Still further investigation turned up the dead man's relatives, who said he had been killed.

Once this curious bit of lore had been revealed, I pursued it throughout the area and discovered that it was a popular belief. Moreover, it was thought that the younger the soul the longer the vessel would be a success. I have been informed that within the present decade a small girl had vanished just prior to a launch and was never seen again, and in another instance two children were reportedly stoned to death just before a launch.

This whole idea was given even more credence when I was told a story about "the fastest vessel in the islands." Shortly before she was to be launched a mine came ashore and her owner—not knowing what it was—

wanted to unscrew a piece of brass from it to use as a ring for some part of his new schooner. He enlisted the aid of a number of his friends and they set to with chisels and hammers. The mine blew up and killed fifty-odd people, but the vessel survived. This happened very shortly before the schooner was launched and she became the fastest boat in the islands, which record she retained until she was sold to owners outside the island where she was built, whereupon she immediately foundered.

Of course it is not always necessary to go to such lengths to insure success for one's vessel. Occasionally the deity lends a helpful hand. On one island the population was somewhat concerned over the future of a certain vessel. The night before the launch a highly respected and liked woman on the island died of natural causes. The next day the vessel was launched cheerfully because it had Mrs. ——'s soul. The vessel was a large one, and when she rolled over a slight rise all her weight came down on one greenheart roller which promptly exploded and burst into flame—thus giving added proof that she would be a success. I have seen the vessel in question and she has indeed had a useful and successful career.[24]

Over the years in other regions the idea has grown up that any launch attended by death or injury to anyone involved made the vessel unlucky. Instead of blood the vessel was christened in red wine, then white, then with champagne (encased in a silver mesh to prevent injury from flying glass) and during the unhappy days of prohibition in this country with ginger ale. But even in sophisticated society it is considered bad luck not to christen the vessel with a shower of mild spirits, and numerous devices including loaded bottles, sharp objects attached to the bow and a sur-reptitious hammer have all been employed to make sure the precious liquid spurts at the proper instant.

In commercial yards today the location of the shipyard and the size of the ship dictate how it will be launched—bow first, stern first or sideways. In former times, in the seaports of English-speaking peoples, most vessels were launched either stern first or bow first. The one exception to this rule that I know of was reported by an informant who assured me that New Bedford whaleships were built on a rise and rolled over three times before hitting the water sideways, to make sure they were strong enough for the trade and would be able to right themselves no matter what happened to them at sea.[25]

As stated earlier, good signs were looked for to assure a successful launch. No man would think of launching on a Friday or on the thirteenth of the month. Wednesday was usually "the best day of all," and a full moon would be auspicious. High tide was good and the morning a lucky time. To see fish or porpoise playing, gulls working, a clear day with the wind from the right quarter—all heralded success. To make sure gulls were working and fish about, I was told both in Nova Scotia and in Maine, people would often throw out "chum" (bits of cut-up fish) to attract gulls, porpoises, etc. One could not control the weather, but where possible the other contingencies could be taken care of.

In many places when the vessel was ready to launch, long poles were laid down into the water, the vessel jacked up and rollers put under the cradle and above the poles. The cradle was weighted so it would not float and a retrieving line attached to it. Sometimes the cradle would be rolled to the water without the poles, and for very large ships a pair of iron or wooden tracks took the place of the poles and the cradle trundled along on wheels.

The things most feared at the launch were that the vessel would kill or injure someone as she went down the ways or that she would "stick," i.e., stop or hesitate as she took the water. To insure that she did not stick, the skids or ways were thickly coated with tallow. In case there was no tallow, substitutes were used—in one instance bananas replaced tallow in New England, and at Lunenburg, Nova Scotia, it was said that a vessel was launched over a juicy roadway of clams! It is significant to note that lard is not mentioned as a lubricating agent, for lard is from a pig and pigs are generally considered to be bad luck—so bad in fact that in Scotland a euphemism is invariably used for the name.

The vessel completed—at least to the stage where the exterior is complete and she will float—is decked out with flags and bunting or with flowers as in some European countries such as France. The clergy are then called upon to say a prayer and in Roman Catholic areas to sprinkle holy water on the vessel. At this point the ship is christened with a name that is usually as hard to change as a human one, and on the east coast of Scotland a godfather is named to stand sponsor. Meanwhile most of the blocking holding the vessel has been cleared away, and as soon as the bottle breaks, the last block is knocked out or the hawser that holds her cut or, in big ships, the arresting timber sawed through with a great crosscut saw. The vessel actually quivers and then slides slowly seaward, gaining momentum all the time. A rumble turns to a roar, the rails hiss and smoke as she runs for the sea. Lest she go too fast, a snubbing crew stands by with a hawser to slow her down, since it is impossible to stop her. She runs stern first into the water with a huge splash, the stern lifts, she comes free and floats out of the cradle and into the ready hands of tugs or wherries, which turn her clockwise and take her to a berth where she will be rigged.

Not until she has been safely berthed is she free from the watchful eyes of the critics ashore. They want to see if she "runs true" in the water, if she is successfully stopped by the attendant boats and gear. Most especially is she watched to see how she performs and floats—whether she rolls inordinately, pitches or "comes to her marks," i.e., whether she floats evenly and upright without a list.[26]

A typical launching ceremony in eastern Scotland—where the fishermen are, according to Niel Cameron of Crinan on the west coast, "vurra canny" —might be noted, for in almost every area the ceremonies differ slightly. Here the vessel was launched on a coming tide and she was not named until afloat, at which time whiskey was spilled over her bow and she was liberally sprinkled with more whiskey, with barley, flour and bread. The vessel was addressed at the ceremony with:

> Frae rocks or saands,
> An' barren lands
> An' ill men's hands
> Keep's free
> Well oot, weel in,
> Wi' a guid shot[27]

After this the master and his crew partook liberally of cheese and bread and ended up in a stag party at the local pub, where they had a meal of skate washed down with whiskey.

Once the launch had been completed the vessel was ready to be fitted for sea—mast stepped, rigging rove, engines aligned, etc. At this point money was invariably placed under the mast step—preferably silver, although gold coins appear to have been used on occasion. So deep-rooted was this custom that today a sixpence is often driven into the main beam of fishing vessels and a silver coin is used to shim (align) the engine or inserted under the engine bed. Niel Cameron recalled that when a vessel was broken up people used to gather around to pick up the "sovereigns" that invariably lay beneath the heel of the mast. The original purpose of these coins was to pay a tithe to the god of the winds but as the "eternal combustion engine" replaced sail it was only natural to think of the coins as propitiating the god of noise.

Finally, before going to sea a vessel invariably required a certain amount of inside ballast to improve her trim, improve her righting moment and generally contribute to her stability. Any heavy, inexpensive and reasonably stable objects could be used, but some care was taken in the selection of this material. I was informed recently by salvage divers that ancient wrecks could be identified as to nationality and age by the kind of ballast lying above their timbers. Some used broken rock, others gravel and so on. Today lead, scrap iron and poured cement are popular forms of ballast, but each type is shunned by users of another type for various, largely spurious, reasons. Lead is too expensive, but the folk using scrap iron in New England say that lead is too heavy and makes the vessel respond too fast and strains her. On the other hand, the users of lead say that iron fouls the compass and rusts and makes the bilge water dirty. Cement is believed by nonusers to be too bulky and to prevent the ship from "breathing," thus promoting dry rot or rust.

Years ago when stone was used, basalt and broken rock were invariably preferred. In Scotland, ballast was often brought to the east coast from the Island of Lewis—a distance of hundreds of miles. Round, water-washed gravel is not used, and no white stones or stones with holes in them are to this day allowed to go into the bilge according to Malcolm Macdonald of Stornoway.[28] Certainly broken rock is less likely to shift than smooth stones and dark stone is generally heavier than stones with holes in them or porous rock, but there is more to the ideas than this. One need only recall that David slew Goliath with a smooth white pebble and that faeries cannot harm a man with a water-washed white stone in his pocket, to be aware of the magic implications. When one notes a statement made by Ian MacClennan that "what comes frae the sea must return to the sea," one is not surprised that sea gravel is not used.

Although many of these customs and beliefs may have arisen from what Sir Thomas Browne called "Vulgar Errors" and have been handed down from beyond the shadow of prehistory, the fact remains that they are, many of them, directly functional. For frames, oak is tough and resists water, for planking cedar is light and strong. Beyond this, however, they have a further function—a psychological one that is as difficult to measure as the strain exerted by a vessel upon her anchor in a gale. Sailors believe these things and, because they have or have not been adhered to, the efficiency of the crew is psychologically enhanced or depleted. Indeed, the very fact that taboos have been broken or followed may well dictate the kind of crew a vessel will acquire. Why should a good seaman go in a ship reputed to have been unlucky in building or launch? And beyond this there is evidence to support the beliefs. The *Great Eastern* was first named *Titanic*.

Two riveters were supposedly walled up within her double hull. Several men were killed building her and another at her launch. She stuck on the ways. All her life long she was a heartbreak ship, ruining owners, drowning sailors, in gales, shipwreck and collision.[29] What more proof is needed? Even such an educated, sophisticated writer as Lieutenant F. M. Bassett asks if a certain vessel may not have been lost between New York and Norfolk because she was not christened on the launch with champagne.[30]

An old sailor said once, "Of course there may be nothing to it but on the other hand . . ." when you live within the shadow of death and it costs nothing to take precautions, it is a daring man indeed who breaks taboos and courts disaster.

A haven of rest, Roundstone, Ireland

CHAPTER II

NAMES ON THE SEA

Superstition is a quality that seems indigenous to the ocean.

—James Fenimore Cooper: *The Red Rover*

THE study of sea names is at once immensely fascinating and almost totally discouraging. They fascinate, first because behind each one there is some kind of story and, second because there is such a vast difference in the criteria for nomenclature not only in kind but in nationality. Sea names are discouraging because of their number and because they are so difficult to type. To realize the problem, one need only look at the more than a thousand charts covering the British Isles and North America, where every large headland, bay, harbor, cape, point, island, islet, rock, reef, bar and ledge, to say nothing of shoals, deeps, currents, rips, eddies and overfalls are named. And beyond these charted names there are a myriad of local names used solely by the people in one area to mark some marine object or condition that does not appear on even the most detailed harbor chart. As if this were not enough, the names appear to be in almost every known language and to cover a myriad of contingencies.

It is my purpose to try to bring some kind of order out of this chaotic jumble of proper nouns that dot the seas and coasts of North America and the British Isles. I should like to demonstrate that there is, first, a marked difference between names on the sea and names on the land in North America and second, a marked difference between Old and New World onomastics. Further, I should like to establish some general ideas as to why these differences exist, and to suggest that there appear to be perhaps ten reasons basic to the formation of marine place names. (These reasons in the British Isles result in one kind of name, in North America another).

Finally, I should like to show that sea names rarely change, but when they do, it is again in response to limited criteria.

When we glance at a map of the New World we are aware immediately that names like Boston, Oxford, New London, New Haven, Truro, Tiverton, Bristol and Cambridge dot the land and are derived from places in the British Isles. Another group of names like Halifax, Baltimore, Fort William and Queen Anne are derived from noble or royal personages. With this as a beginning, one would expect that marine names would come here in the same way. It is not so. As our eye runs down the chart of the British Isles, we notice Rhu, Mull, Hook, Ness, Foreland and Bill—all names denoting promontories. We see also Haven, Hole, Loch, Sound, Sands, Water and Bank. To this we could add Inish, Papa, Stack, Stag, and a number of suffixes like -head, -sheer, -ay, and -vore. Of the first six of these words, only one or two appear at all on American charts. In fact almost none of these words are used to identify places in North America, and when they are employed, their meaning is somewhat different. American promontories are usually capes, points or heads, as Cape Fear, Point-No-Point or Sankaty Head. Our ship refuges are usually harbors, ports, coves and, very rarely, holes or bights. If American towns are named for English ones, why not sea names as well?

Sea names in the Old World have grown up out of an antiquity dating back over a thousand years, and this antiquity has shaded their meaning. To the British seaman Portland Bill has a distinct and singular flavor, analogous to a child calling his parent "Dad." We see the same thing in America when a sailor on the Maine coast says, "We was four hours southeast the Rock." Everyone knows there is only one "Rock"—Mt. Desert. To the sailor, it would be ridiculous to transfer such a name.

In America the early seamen were confronted with a problem they had never had to face at home. Before them lay a vast, unnamed continent. In order to make navigation easier for their followers, these men were forced to embark on a crash program of naming. Whereas names at home had largely been derived from folk etymology, in the New World they were established by fairly sophisticated men—navigators such as Sir Francis Drake, Sieur de Champlain, Captain John Smith. These men sought mainly to identify the great sea marks. Like the sophisticated people who gave names to towns in an attempt to dignify them, in one case changing Skunk's Misery to Scrantonia, Pennsylvania,[1] these seafarers gave many of the more striking places they encountered noble names. For these reasons the place-names in North America are different from those in the British Isles.

When we consider that the original settlers came from England, Ireland, Scotland and Wales, it is indeed strange that they did not employ some of the old terms like Inish—Irish for island, Mull—Gaelic for point, or Bill—meaning literally a beak in Old English; or some of the Scandinavian words so popular in the British Isles like the suffix -ay for harbor. The full answer to this problem may never be known, but at least a partial one lies in the fact that sea names are landmarks to the shipman. New names were generally preferred to old ones to avoid confusion and help distinguish the particular aid or obstacle to navigation. Another reason might be found in the time of naming many of the places in the British Isles, which often dates back to the Celts and to the Norse invaders. English seamen coming upon unnamed objects and not conversant perhaps with the true meanings of home place-names would use current terms to describe the new areas.

Looking at British sea names, we find we have a kind of cumulative index of the people who were at one time on the coast. The Picts, the Celts, the Danes, the Norse have vanished, as have the French, Dutch and Spaniards. Yet no matter how fleeting or long their stay, we have monuments to their passing in such names as Spanish Point, Galley Head, Orford Ness, Skiport, Sule Skerry and the like.

American sea names seem to follow the same pattern. Our earliest names are Indian ones, and some of these are preserved in translation—as "Cocoharbuks," meaning "Head of an Owl"—now Owl's Head, Maine. These were followed by all manner of names, mainly Spanish, French and English but with a smattering of Dutch, Swedish, German and others thrown in. We need only recall Hispaniola, Cape St. Vincent, Oche Rios from the Caribbean, Baja California, or Cape Sable and Isle au Haut from Nova Scotia, or Maine, Staten Island and Block Island.

All of the above leads one to ask how these names came to be and causes one to wonder if any rules can be set down as guide lines for naming. The answer seems to be in the affirmative. Indeed, as far as the New World is concerned, we can come to some reasonably accurate determinants. The Spanish and southern European explorers seem to have taken delight in calling places after saints, as one can see by glancing at a map of the coast of California, Florida or the West Indies. The French showed a proclivity for native names or, if we take Champlain as an example, for people known to the explorers or for things that happened at the spot. The English, being Protestant at the time of their coming, shunned saints and leaned toward naming places for themselves or benefactors at home.

Beyond these generalizations we can move to more specific ideas. Since islands and rocks are often sea marks used for navigational purposes, one of the most important ways of naming them was to identify them by their salient features. "I saw," said Champlain, "an island of seven desert mountains"—Mt. Desert, Maine. Gay Head is so called for its variegated cliffs that gleam in the sun. We have High Island, Flat Island, Mud Island (in Nova Scotia). There is Spectacle Island, probably so called because it is subject to mirage or looks like glasses. In Scotland we have Mull (the island of points) and nearby Skye (the island with wings). We find Bald Head, One Bush and Two Bush Island. There are Pond Island, Iron Bound and the Porcupine Islands—looking for all the world like a mother hedgehog followed by her young. There are White, Black and Green Islands. And far in the north lies Rockall—a solid boulder in the middle of the sea.

Next in importance comes what goes on at the place. Thus we have Stage Island, for the fish-drying racks there; we have Deer Island, Cormorant Rock, Seal Ledge, Dry Tortuga, Duck Cove, Sheep Island, Clam Cove, Bass Rocks, Mackerel Cove, Hake Ground, Dogfish Ledge.

A further category would be names derived from characteristics of the place but not dealing with them in exactly the same terms as the others. In the Islands in the Sea off Scotland we find Compass Head, so called for the magnetic anomaly that exists there. Bloody Foreland may be so called for a pink light reflected off it, although there are other possibilities that will be mentioned later. Halfway Rock, Maine, lies midway between Cape Small and Cape Elizabeth. The Wild Bellow is a sunken ledge on the west coast of Ireland, and not far away is the Bull's Mouth where the tide runs hard. In Trinidad a similar spot is called the Serpent's Mouth. The Roaring Bull is a rock off Maine. Overfalls Lightship is located in a tide race off Cape May, New Jersey. The Horse Race is a tide-run spot off Cape Sable Island, Nova Scotia, where the current achieves considerable speed. One entrance to New York Harbor is via Hell Gate, where the tide runs with velocity sufficient to pose a threat even to large ships. Smutty Nose is an island wreathed in fog most of the time, and the Squeaker Guzzle off Maine has, some say, a very peculiar noise attendant with it. Big Kettle Pool, Outer Hebrides, has a small islet in its middle where the ebbing and flowing tides bubble and sing like a teakettle on a stove. One is not surprised, therefore, that the island is called Wizard Island, and the small pool adjacent, Little Kettle Pool.

Still another category of sea names would be names derived from people who lived on or owned or used the particular piece of real estate, submerged or otherwise. Goodwin Sands Lightship, off the Kentish coast, lies above what was once an island owned by Earl Godwine and used by him as a farm in the eleventh century. In early Christian times hermits from Ireland moved up to the Western Isles of Scotland and set up monasteries among the remoter and more inaccessible islands. Out of this movement came a number of names: Papa Westray, Papa Stour and Barra (St. Barr's Island) among others.

During the colonial period the Crown gave what is now the state of Maine to a gentleman named Sir Ferdinando Gorges. Not only did he acquire the territory of Maine but he acquired all the fishing rights as well. Several leagues east and south of Maine lies one of the most profitable fishing grounds in North America, a shoal called Georges (originally Gorges) Bank. In Plymouth Bay, Massachusetts, lies Clarke's Island, the onetime property of the pilot of the *Mayflower*. Lion Gardiner gave his name to an island in Long Island Sound, and Richmond Island, Maine, belonged to a man of that name who kept "a tolerable inn" there during the first half of the seventeenth century. Carver's Harbor, Crockett Cove, Maine, and Drake's Pool, Ireland (where the doughty Sir Francis is said to have hidden from the Spanish), all were named for such reasons, as was Coggeshall Ledge and Cox's, both elegant fishing grounds off the New England coast.

Occasionally, too, places are named for strictly navigational purposes. We have Land's End, Kintyre (Gaelic for Land's End), North Cape, East Port, West Port, Skiport (Ship Harbor), Northeast Harbor, Hurricane Hole, Snug Harbor, North Sea (called by the Germans Mord See—Murder Sea—because of its wild gales) and The Thread of Life in Maine. Halfway Rock, Cape Fear and Elbow of the Cross in Delaware Bay all fit this category. Such names, however, seem fewer in number than the others.

Now and then there is connected with these names a kind of wry humor which occasionally requires translation. Running down the New England coast we see Mistake Harbor, Bailey's Mistake, Daggart's Downfall and Moll's Misery (where an old drunk is supposed to have fallen while clamming and broken his nose while his wife lamented on the other rock).[2] There are the Boo Hoo Rocks and Barney's Joy—a bleak piece of coastline off Massachusetts. Near Mt. Desert Island lies a rock called Bunker's Whore. Captain Bunker was a famous privateer skipper during the American Revolution. He also had an eye for the women. He was inordinately fond of one island girl who visited him aboard ship when he was near Mt. Desert. One night she rowed home, struck the above-mentioned rock and was drowned. Her name is forgotten but the rock recalls, to the literal folk, her business.[3]

In the Outer Hebrides there is a tiny cove. An old man kept a boat there and the neighbors constantly "borrowed" the "wee boatie." Every time the owner wanted it, someone else was off in it. He named the little harbor Port na striopaich, The Whore's Cove, because the boat "was always out at night." And the name stuck. Because of this the harbor became Whore Boat Harbor.[4]

Off Rockland, Maine, lies an island where a stranded sailor spent a miserable, cold, wet night. Cold Arse Island was its original name.[5] And further east there are the Virgin's Teats, with a low black rock nearby called the Lecherous Priest.

Occasionally, too, there are little stories and rhymes that go with these names. In Narragansett Bay there are a considerable number of islands that were once owned by the Potter family. According to a local rhyme they are "Hope, Prudence and Despair, and little old Patience right over there." The saying is that Potter named these for his daughters, the fourth being Despair. A similar story concerns the two largest Elizabeth Islands, telling how a father gave them to his daughters. One became, therefore, Martha's Vineyard; and as for the faraway island, "Nan tuck it."[6]

All of these names taken together, however, do not begin to compare with the final set. These are usually, but not always, reefs and obstructions to navigation. They acquired their names the hard way—from marine tragedies. On these obstructions unlucky or imprudent masters have from time to time been driven ashore and lost both vessel and crew. The rock usually bears the name of the first person to come a cropper on it; later and perhaps more fearful tragedies are forgotten in favor of the earlier one. It is correct that nearly every maritime name has a story of sorts connected with it, but by far the most interesting, as well as the grimmest, are these tales of shipwreck and despair. It is not the gale in the open ocean that the mariner fears, nor fire, nor collision, starvation or disease, half as much as the rocks and ledges that dot the waters along the hundred-fathom curve. The plight of the mariner was a desperate one when the gale caught him on a lee shore, when the fog shut in obscuring sounds and blinding vision, or when it came thick of snow and he groped blindly for a harbor. All too often he missed, and it was not given to many to miss twice.

Sometimes it is easy to spot these names. Between the Blasket Islands and the mainland, where all the names are Irish, lies Stromboli Rock. The tide runs hard in Blasket Sound and navigation is difficult. In bad weather H.M.S. *Stromboli* came through the sound and hit a rock. She must have been moving because she knocked the rock down when she hit it, but she also took her bottom out. Where the rock stood the chart reads Stromboli Rock. Farther along the coast of Ireland we find Galley Head, where a Spanish galley went ashore while trying to regain Spain after the fiasco in the English Channel. In Scotland we find Jemimah Rock—a Yankee name—off the Isle of Canna where the names are mostly Gaelic, and off the coast of Nova Scotia, Brazil Rock where a steamer struck and was lost. Rose and Crown Shoal off the backside of Cape Cod marks the spot where two British warships were lost one wild and windy day, the H.M.S. *Rose* and the H.M.S. *Crown*. One pleasant day the world's largest ship, *The Great Eastern*, was plugging up Long Island Sound. Not far from the grave of H.M.S. *Cerebus* (Cerebus Shoal) she hit a pinnacle rock and ripped a great gash in her bottom, which revealed the skeletons of the riveters previously mentioned. The chart still shows Great Eastern Rock nearly thirty feet beneath the surface.

Not infrequently one name will beget another; and so we find that there are the Old Man and the Old Woman of Hoy, the Double Shots, Green Island and Little Green Island next door. Off Maine we find Horse Island and its attendant Colt. In Ireland, where they apparently like to name places for kine and swine, we have some interesting place names: the aforementioned Bull's Mouth in Blacksod Bay where the tide runs with ferocity, and further down the coast we come to the Wild Bellow. Nearby are the Sunk Bellow and the Bellow. Still further south we come to the Bull, the Cow, the Calf and the Heifer—spectacular but desperately danger-ous islets. (These islets are almost the westernmost land masses in Europe and were once called the Islands of the Dead, for it was here that all souls paused on their final journey to the Other World.)

A final name from Ireland might be noted from the haven of Glandor, where we find Adam and Eve islands. The sailors say that on entering the harbor, which has an encumbered entrance, "When Adam's on Eve you can take your ease"—meaning when the two are in line the passage into the port is clear.

Generally speaking, Americans employ these same tactics in naming, but their combinations are most prosaic. Although we have Brenton's Reef and Brenton's Key at the entrance to Narragansett Bay, and the Sow and Pigs and Hen and Chickens reefs barring clear entry into Buzzards Bay, a great number of our combinations are directional names like the East and West Hue and Cry, East and West Brown Cow. Nova Scotia does better with the Limb and the Limb's Limb (euphemisms for Devil and Imp.)

Not all of the names are quite so easy to understand, however. Two or three might be mentioned. Toward the mouth of Chesapeake Bay lies the Wolftrap. The name makes no sense until we learn that H.M.S. *Wolf* stranded there early in our history. Off the Rhode Island shore is Noble Biting, where the blackfish are abundant. On the Isle of Shoals is Money Rock. One wild night a vessel running blind in thick snow struck there with such terrible force that she burst open the strongbox, and next day the inhabitants are said to have found, along with frozen bodies in their very dooryards, coins atop the boulder.

Sometimes these names have what we might call peripheral tales attached to them that aid in their memory—or explain what to the folk has become unexplainable. Off the coast of Maine lies Monhegan Island (The Faraway Island, in the Penobscot dialect). A story goes that an Englishman vanished many years ago and there was reason to believe that he was on the island. Indians were hired to search, and when they had combed the island to no avail, one Indian said to a white man, "Man he gone." In nearby Meduncook Bay an Indian is said to have dropped his kettle overboard and repented ruefully, "Me done cook".[7] A number of years ago an old salt told me that an English ship with a Dutch mate was approaching New York in a fog. "Land ho!" cried the lookout. "'S tat an island?" asked the mate. "And," said my informant, "It's been Staten Island ever since."

Once long ago there was a huge giantess, sometimes called a hag or a caillish (witch). She is said to have stood astride the entrance to the north end of the Irish Sea between Kilmorey in Ireland and Carrick in Scotland. Whenever a ship tried to pass her she would drop a stone on it and sink it. She would then eat the crew. One day as she stood there she spied a French ship, but the captain adroitly luffed in such a way that his mizzenmast tickled her genitalia and she dropped her boulder in shallow water: the Frenchman escaped. The boulder so dropped is Ailsa Craig.[8]

As one looks at a chart one invariably sees names that make no sense by any rubric we have yet devised. The Wolftrap has already been mentioned. A shoal spot off the southern coast of New England is the Sheep Pen—where one can catch a good supply of sheepshead (kind of fish). At the opposite side of the continent we find three other names to illustrate our point—Cape Disappointment, Desolation Bay and Cape Venerable

Bede. The first two were named by Captain Meaves in order to vent his frustration at not being able to locate the fabled river of Martin de Aguilar and the latter by Captain Cook to show the world that the English could venerate the clergy as easily as the Spanish could immortalize their saints in lands away from home.[9]

Infrequently we run into place names that never were. Usually these are the figments of early explorers who either did not understand what natives told them or were hoodwinked by their informants. Cabeza de Vaca told the world of the seven cities of Cíbola, and either to counteract that tale with another or through genuine misunderstanding the explorers to the north gave up hunting Vineland and went after Nourembec, the fabulous city of ivory and fur which, according to the very best accounts, seems to have been located on the bank of a river that flowed into the head of a bay in which were many islands. The position of this bay was somewhere between latitude 38° north and 45° north on the east coast of America. In this modest 420 miles of crow-flying, one can pretty well take one's pick of a hundred "exact spots."

Recently in Scotland a fisherman told me an equally spurious tale but one that is quite modern. He had never been there, but he had it on good authority that off the harbor of Kinsale, Ireland, lay two rocks, a large one and a small one. On them was an inscription in Latin: "We be the rocks of misery/For Christ's sweet sake steer clear of we." "That's the spot where the *Titanic* went down and hundreds of people were lost," he said.

This is an interesting little story. Off Kinsale there are two rocks—one larger than the other—called the Great Sovereign and the Little Sovereign. Seamus O'Neill of that town said that the king of Kinsale in ancient times stood on the largest rock and hurled a dart seaward at designated times. The distance the dart fell from the rock marked the seaward boundary of his domain. A few miles from these rocks the *Lusitania* took a torpedo and sank with great loss of life, and helped precipitate the United States into World War I. Off these rocks, David Thomson tells us in *People of the Sea*, two Irishmen caught the king of all the mackerel—a fish weighing over five-hundred pounds and revered by its finny friends.[10] John Lorne Campbell informs me that this mackerel was in actuality a horse mackerel or tuna. The point is, however, that these rocks—which must have been known to the Phoenicians—seem sure to have some sort of magical tale-catching property. There is no inscription on them in any language.

Once a spot has been "christened" with a name, it is highly unlikely that that name will change no matter how prosaic it is nor how titanic an event takes place at that spot in later years. This is, perhaps, where nomenclature and names on the land differ most widely. Pigeon Roost may be changed to Wayne after a paranoidal American patriot, and local hucksters may change the names of harbors or headlands for commercial and/or patriotic reasons—as Holmes' Hole to Vineyard Haven; The Herring's Gut to Port Clyde; or Rogue's Point, Maryland, to Rhode's Point. Recently, in the West Indies, Prune Island was changed by developers to Palm Island in the belief that the name would attract more opulent guests. However, not all attempts to beautify or enhance names are successful, for according to John Lorne Campbell the name of the Island of Muck in the Hebrides—which in Gaelic means Pig or Whale (Sea Pig)—was to be changed to Monk's Island, but the change was resisted.

In 1693 young Anthony Collimore set out from Scituate, Massachusetts, for Marblehead. He had not gone far before he was caught in a squall, the boat capsized and went down near a clump of rocks henceforth to be called the Collimores. Since 1693 there have been hundreds of wrecks off Scituate. Indeed, so many vessels were lost in the area that Minot's Light was built in an attempt to warn shipping. Many vessels and many men have drowned singly and collectively on these Collimores since that day, but the name remains unchanged. As a matter of fact, Minot's Light has a story attached to it that is far more dynamic than the name of the early settler that embellished it—and will be treated elsewhere.

Off the coast of Maine lies an island christened by Champlain Isle au Haut, but referred to in early charts and by many natives as Isle O'Holt. Many years ago a tug was towing a raft or "boom" of logs down the coast when a breeze sprang up, the raft went astray and washed ashore on an, until then, unnamed shingle. After the event the beach was known as Boom Beach. Les Grant of Isle au Haut narrated the above tale and added a second story that took place a few years later:

> A schooner, the *Nellie E. Burns* out of Portland, was trawlin' late one fall. It was clear, and bright so's you could see clear to Matinicus but it come on to blow a gale o' wind from the northwest and she lost the dory. Well, the fella in the dory he starts to pull for the harbor but the breeze kept freshenin' an' he kept comin' an' so he pulled in past the headland an' he only had about a hundred yards to go to the beach an' it blowed so no livin' man could ha' made it an' he seen he wa'n't goin' to make it so he tried to get up on the Eastern Ear [of Head Harbor—Isle au Haut is flanked by two

islets known as the Eastern and Western Ear] an' it come thick o' snow an' he was gone. Next day they saw the schooner goin' by with her colors at half-mast and they knew she'd lost a man.

About a week later some of the people here went for a picnic on Boom Beach an' one feller decided to walk around by the Eastern Ear. He saw the bow of a dory stickin' up an' he looked an' he saw a man jammed head down in a gully just above high water. He was stark naked an' not a mark on him and W.C. tattooed on his arm. Well, they fetched him over to the church an' when they could they buried him an' put up a stone with W.C. on it, an' about a year later a young girl come askin' if anyone had seen the man she was goin' to marry but who had gone astray in a dory. His name was William Crowdy an' his initials were tattooed on his arm. They took her an' they showed her the little stone an' she went away an' the next year she sent a team an' wagon an' they dug him up and fetched him away somewheres.[11]

That is the end of Crowdy—no Crowdy's Ear, Crowdy's Gully or Crowdy's Beach instead of Boom Beach. Even though Crowdy's tale is past tragedy, it is insufficient to move the folk to change a name.

Names on the sea do change, infrequently it is true, but often enough to make one attempt to give some reasons why.

The names most frequently changed were those first given areas by explorers. Their locations were too vague to pinprick their position on a map, and often the names meant little or nothing to later voyagers. John Smith named one place Cape Tragabigzanda for a Turkish bene-factress. If it meant anything to anyone, it indicated that a heathen name had been given to a Puritan headland. The name was changed to Cape Ann. Another spot he called Smith's Isles, but because of the sea bed around them, they soon became the Isles of Shoals, and the little town there Appledore, for an English place-name. Smith had bad luck with names.

Another reason for changing early names was that frequently more than one explorer discovered the same spot at times not too distant from each other. Depending upon subsequent events the name may have been changed. Champlain named one area Bai des Isles and another Cape Malebarre. Later, John Smith named Champlain's cape Cape Cod, and the English, when they arrived, named the other spot Massachusetts Bay—apparently preferring the Indian name to the French. An interesting liter-ary explanation of the latter name comes from a nineteenth-century source in which we are told it was named by a Negro slave. When asked where he was going the slave replied, "I go where massa go. I go where massa choose it."[12]

Words frequently became confused in the oral transmission. Bare Island becomes Bear at a later date, Stage Island may change to Stave Island. Golden's Island, Rhode Island, became Gould Island and Talent's Harbor, Maine, eventually became Tenants. In Loch Swilly, northern Ireland, lies Scraggy Bay, so named not because it is a raggle-taggle place, but because the shore is full of "scraggs"—a word meaning brush or a thorny place. Often, too, language barriers help to confuse people in this regard. Champlain, who liked to named things for characteristics he observed about them, called one harbor Brune Côte, but it soon came to be changed, into Burnt Coat Harbor. Off Florida, islets called cayos by the Spaniards, often become *Keys.*

In Hillsboro Harbor in Carriacou, Grenada, lies Jack A Dan Island or Bar. No one seems to know why this peculiar name is applied to the little islet, but an early map lists the spot as Jack Adam. When one realizes the singular pronunciation of the natives, the name is easily understood. Usually they accentuate the first and last syllable of a word and slur the last letters. Hence when a boat sinks she *"go bottome,"* and when speaking of the island they say *"Jack A. Dan."*[13]

Vessels standing in to Gloucester from the Grand Banks against a prevailing southwesterly breeze frequently found themselves to leeward of Cape Ann, and when they reached a certain point it was time to tack. Hence the name of the headland became Haulabout Point. On the chart it is Halibut Point.

It is interesting to note, in speaking of Halibut Point, that a very similar name exists in Ireland. Inside Roaches' Point on the way to Cork we come to an island where square-rigged sailing vessels were forced to tack. This island is called Haulbowline Island. One can confuse the term "haul about" for tacking a schooner and come up with "halibut," but "haulbowline" fortuitously does not lend itself so easily to bastardization.

Of all the confused names, perhaps the best known is that of a rock in the West Indies. Just north of the island of Grenada there is a passage, once much used by sailing vessels, which is encumbered by a large jagged rock on which the sea beats fiercely. The French named it "Caye qu'en gêne," which roughly translated means "the ledge that constricts." After the French left, the natives slurred and anglicized the name into "Kick-em Jenny."[14]

Now and again names and locations can become confused and the name shifted to another site. While exploring Chesapeake Bay, Captain John Smith hopped out of a boat barefoot onto a stingray, which had the temerity to stick its dart into his leg. It was a foolish act on the part of the fish, for Smith was no common man. Instead of trying to get clear of it, Smith held it to the bottom with his foot, drew his hanger, hacked the fish to pieces and ate several collops raw. The site of this melodrama became Sting Ray Island, but the location, like Plymouth Rock, has been moved and the name applies now to Sting Ray Point.

A classic example of two of these mistakes has recently come to light in the name of the westernmost island of Europe—St. Kilda. For years it was thought that the island derived its name from a very holy person who lived there. Unfortunately, hagiography exhumes no St. Kilda. Further study revealed that a cartographer in the sixteenth century made a mistake. Later cartographers compounded the felony by moving the position of the initial error nearly fifty miles west and a little north. The islands of Skildar (Old Norse "shields") a few miles west of the Hebrides were set down on a chart as S. Kildar and S. Kildar was moved from the original rock pile to a somewhat larger one further seaward. A "t" replaced the period and the "r" was dropped, and St. Kilda was the result.[15]

At the Isles of Shoals a vessel named the *Londoner* was wrecked. At Gloucester, eighteen miles away, is a rock that appears to lunge into the sea. Lunging Island is the name at "The Shoals" and The Londoner is now off Gloucester.

So far we have contented ourselves with the rubric of naming. Better entertainment can be had by recounting a few stories taken from random spots to illustrate in some magnitude the ideas set forth here. However, when one sets down legends one must always bear in mind the fact that, when used by the folk, a legend or tale is not simply a witty way to entertain a witless audience. The story usually is devised to impress some fact on the mind of the listener. It may be that the story simply aids the listener in remembering a particular name, or it may be that its purpose is to impress upon the mind of the listener the characteristics of the place or the hazard to navigation that it mounts. This latter is usually true when you have two or three stories current about the same place. Let us take an anecdote about Lady Rock in the Sound of Mull, Scotland. Actually there are two versions about the origin of this name, gathered about seventy miles apart, and it is rather interesting, I think, to set them both down for comparison. For obvious reasons the names of both informants have not been included. The first is from Crinan, Scotland, the second from the island of Mull. Here is the first:

> Now years ago you see, there was a MacLean of Loch Buie and Mull and then there was MacLean of Duart and then MacLean of Ardgour. Now there are three definite MacLeans. The Duke of Argyll had seven daughters and the MacNeils are the chief clan in Barra. Well you see one of his daughters married MacNeil of Barra—they've Kisimul Castle—he goes to Canada and makes a lot of money and comes back and spends it so they say—and then another daughter married MacLean of Duart—and seemingly was very bad to her and to get rid of her, eventually he went and took her in a boat and put her on Lady Isle—and that's why Lady Isle is called Lady Isle—that's a rock that's off Duart Point, south between the Point of Lismore and Duart—you'll know it off the chart. Well, the tide would come in and drown her, but before the tide came on right, somebody came out and rescued her—and she went home to the Duke of Argyll and that's what started the enmity between MacLean of Duart and the Duke of Argyll.

And the second:

> One of the early Lords of Duart Castle married the daughter of the Laird Argyll. She was a Campbell. Now when the MacLean found out his wife would not produce an heir he marooned her on a half-tide rock in the Sound of Mull not far from the castle. When the tide had rose she would be drowned. After the tide had come and gone the MacLean wrote the Duke of Argyll and told him that his daughter had met with an unfortunate accident while fishing and been drowned. The Duke invited MacLean to come to dinner and MacLean came and gave the details of the accident. After that they went in to dinner and who should be sitting on the right hand of the Duke but the "drowned" girl. She had been rescued by some fisherman just before she drowned and returned to her father.
>
> Apparently the girl's father didn't care much for her for he didn't do anything about it at the time and the girl later returned to Duart Castle and things seemed to go on much as before. Ten years later the girl's brother murdered MacLean and avenged the insult to the name of Argyll.
>
> That is how Lady Rock was named—for Lady MacLean—but somehow the name was moved from the half-tide rock to a small rocky islet about half a mile away where Lady Rock Light now stands. Nobody could drown on that rock. It is always above high water.[16]

Very close to Lady Rock lies Lismore Point on the island of Lismore. The following tale does not explain the name, but anyone who hears it will remember that point for a long time by association.

And there was Lismore Island. Well, there was the Campbells and the Macdonalds, and who else was it? Anyway there was a race and the first fellow that landed there and went ashore on Lismore owned it. Of course the Duke of Argyll, tough old codger that he was, he was settin' in the bow of the boat—eggin' his men on, eggin' his men on and he was ready to jump from the bow of the boat and he seen he was goin' to get beat so he put his hand around and pulled his axe out of his belt and put his hand up on the thwart of the boat and cut it off. He caught his hand and threw it ashore— so he owned the island after all.[17]

West and north of Lady Rock in the Outer Hebrides lies Nicholson's Leap—a pinnacle rock a short distance offshore. The story behind its name is interesting to us because of the manner in which it was changed and because it is known—unwittingly—to many in North America who do not follow the sea.

According to early accounts, a man named Nicholson was accused of a crime and sentenced by the chief to be castrated in public. When he heard his fate, Nicholson suddenly burst his bonds, seized the chief's only son as a hostage and fled with the clan in hot pursuit. He had not gone far before he found himself on the edge of a precipice. Behind him came the clansmen. Two hundred feet below him lay the sea. His only route of escape was to jump across a yawning abyss to the aforementioned rock, which he did with the child in his arms. When the clan arrived they found Nicholson on the rock with his hostage, and a Scottish version of a "Mexican standoff" developed. No one cared to jump after the culprit, for even if they were lucky enough to reach the rock Nicholson could easily kick them off when they lit, and Nicholson refused to come back (if he could) until the chief had agreed to castrate himself publicly. Once this had been done, Nicholson gathered the child in his arms and said, "You have sentenced me to die without issue and you shall die the same way." With this remark he leapt from the pinnacle into the surf and rocks below, carrying the child with him.

In Sidney Lanier's poem written in the nineteenth century and called "The Revenge of Hamish," the deed was performed after Hamish had been unjustly whipped for letting a deer escape on the island of Rhum.

When the story was recovered in Loch Boisdale on South Uist in the Hebrides in 1968, the account was that Nicholson was sentenced to death for the crime of murder, of which he was innocent, and jumped with the child after its father killed himself.

A vessel bound for the Clyde from the Caledonian Canal or Oban must steer a course roughly south by west. To save two hundred miles around the Mull of Kintyre she probably will go through the Crinan Canal, about four leagues along the way. But to do this she must pass through some of the most rock-strewn, tide-wracked water to be found in the British Isles. Her skipper must be cognizant of the time for, to reach Loch Crinan, he must pass through the Dorus Mor (the Great Door, sometimes called the Turning Door) where the tide achieves speeds of eight knots and the sea, when the wind is against the tide, might be called nasty at the least. (I once missed the turning of the neap tide there by fifteen minutes and barely nipped through.) Should the vessel miss her chance, she stands in a fair way of being caught in eddies that flow between the island of Jura on the south and Scarba on the north. Here lies the Cailleach (the Hag), better known as the Coirebhreacain or Corryvreckan, the second greatest whirlpool in the world. It is about the Corryvreckan that we shall speak at length.

Dread of this place has spread from Norway to the west coast of Ireland, and well it might. The *Coast Pilot*, normally a most prosaic document, says of it, ". . . Navigation . . . is very dangerous and no vessel should . . . attempt this passage without local knowledge."[18] Never is the area quiet, and seas break there in the calmest weather. Locally it is stated that the roar of the whirlpool can be heard a distance of twenty miles and that the confused seas attain a height of twenty feet. Recently when Seaton Gordon told an old Scots sea captain how a yachtsman in a high-powered motorboat had managed to squeak through, the old man said drily, "That man should not be alive today."[19] Ronald Gilbert of Crinan recently stated that he was aboard a forty-foot fishing vessel with a hundred h.p. Gardner engine, and with the engine "flat out" he was dragged backward toward the maelstrom and only escaped by chance. If twentieth-century man fears the place, one can imagine what effect it had on primitive people.

How long this spot has been identified with a name would be hard to say, but stories about it move from historical fact to legend and beyond to myth. Probably the earliest name was The Hag, for the ancient people believed in underwater monsters, spirits and demons. They believed that the tide rips were the Hag's deer feeding and that this whirlpool was the spot where she scrubbed her clothes. It was said that when she tramped her washing, all the tartan in Scotland turned white.[20] (The explanation of this statement is found in the meaning of "vraickan," which means sometimes "speckled" and sometimes "tartan" or even "pocked." As the whirlpool spun around, according to Neal Cameron of Crinan, the bracken and heather were reflected in its sides. As it became more violent the vraickan soon became obscured by white foam.)

It is said that the Hag tramped her washing most fiercely before a coming gale. Although much of the Hag's story is now forgotten, she is still remembered in a weather epigram cited by John MacLeod of Crinan, "When the Hag wears her white cap [when the whirlpool foams] a gale will surely come."

Over the years and with the coming of Christianity the Hag tales gradually were superseded by another series of stories. By the time of St. Columba the place was referred to as Charybdis Brecani. The name is supposed to come from Prince Brecan (Vreckan), son of the King of Lochlann, who fled from Ireland to escape the wrath of his father. The prince arrived at this spot on his way to Norway—as he logically would in following the coast homeward. Not knowing of the maelstrom, he ventured into the passage and was drowned with his entire retinue in fifty currachs. Later his body was either washed ashore or was dragged ashore by his great black hound, and buried in the cave facing the whirlpool on Jura. Here Martin reported seeing his gravestone, now gone, at the end of the seventeenth century.[21]

According to Dr. John Lorne Campbell of Canna, J. W. Watson in *History of the Celtic Place Names of Scotland* notes that the drowned man was actually the son of Niall of the Nine Hostages, and when St. Columba passed that way the drowned man's rib rose to the surface of the maelstrom to greet him.

A somewhat different tale was told by a woman in Crinan. It seems that the son of the King of Lochlann, Prince Brecan, fell in love with a beautiful princess near Crinan. She had taken a vow never to marry anyone who could not ride out three nights in the whirlpool. The prince was upset by this news, but he met a witch nearby who told him how he could win the woman. The first night he must anchor his vessel with a rope of horsehair. He did so, and the warp held the night and he came ashore safe. The second night he was instructed to anchor on a hawser made of sealskin. Again he complied, and again his vessel rode out the night although the whirlpool was more violent. The third night was the crucial one, and to survive he must use a line made of virgin's hair. The prince promptly procured hair from his intended bride and fashioned a golden-haired anchor warp. Again he anchored in the dread spot and the hawser held 'til shortly after midnight, when it parted and he was drowned. His body came ashore and was duly buried in the cave on Jura.[22]

The Corryvreckan may also be associated with Balor of the Evil Eye on Tory Island, although it is possible that the tale refers to another whirlpool inside Rathlin Island in Ireland. At any rate, the story is worth telling, for Balor features in a number of ways in maritime folklore and is even remembered on Cape Breton, where the late MacEdward Leach collected a story about him.[23]

Balor was a giant who lived on Tory Island and preyed upon shipping. From the ships he captured, he amassed a treasure of nine tons of gold, and the captives from the ships he kept in a hole in the ground in the middle of the island called Balor's Prison. Among other pecularities he had a third eye, located according to some in his back and to others in his forehead. This eye was covered by a protective lid which was opened only in times of battle or dire stress, and anything it looked upon was destroyed.

Balor had a daughter, and it was prophesied that she would give birth to a child that would be the death of him. To prevent this, according to local legend, he built a round tower (which still stands) and mewed her up in it with serving women and instructions to keep all men away from her.

Now it so happened that two brothers named MacKineeley lived on the mainland nearby. One had a white cow, the other was a smith. Balor raided the mainland and stole the cow, whereupon her owner disguised himself as a woman and with supernatural help went to the island, spent the night in the tower, impregnated the girl, retrieved his cow and went home.

Balor became enraged, pursued the MacKineeley, killed him in a great battle on what is now known as Bloody Foreland, reclaimed his stolen property and went home. No sooner had he arrived and settled down to enjoy his booty than the girl gave birth to twin boys. Balor promptly ordered that they be put into a sheet, taken to Corryvreckan and tossed in. This was done, but one child was washed out of the whirlpool and dashed ashore, where he was found by a smith, who raised him and taught him the trade.

The years rolled by; the boy grew and Balor fell upon evil times. His island was attacked, his army destroyed, and Balor was forced to flee to the mainland to recruit more men. So intent was he on his errand that he left the hooded eye open and as he passed the smith's forge the boy saw him, attached a gland of white-hot iron to an arrow and let it fly at the giant. The iron struck him in the eye and Balor dropped dead. The cow meanwhile escaped, and another series of stories begins about her.

As stories of the Hag were augmented or replaced by tales of the dashing prince, so these stories were assailed by tales of the clergy, who wanted more Christian attitudes inspired by the place. To this end Adam-

nan, abbot of Iona, inferred that God had made the whirlpool to increase
St. Columba's already fervent enthusiasm for prayer still further as he
crossed it. But these stories have suffered more than those of the Hag and
Prince Brecan, and have been replaced by hundreds of stories of ship-
wreck and disaster. Of them all perhaps the best is one told by Neal
Cameron.

In the old days when transport was poor we used to run cattle from the
islands into the market like Islay, Jura, Colonsay into the market in Oban.
Now there was a small boat belonging to a Mr. Andrew Patterson who ran
passenger trips in the summer and cattle in the winter. I would say roughly
she was about 450 tons. He ran to Port Askeig to collect cattle for the sale
and he took about 103 head aboard to be carried on the top deck. Now just
as he was leaving the minister came running down to the pier to go with him
and the crew saw him and they said, "Quick, take in the gangplank and cast
off!" for they didn't want to take him but they weren't quick enough and the
minister came aboard. He then put out to come through and the weather
had deteriorated and he came through on the outside of Jura and the wind
being to the westward made it very uncomfortable with the result that the
people owning the cattle got alarmed and they wanted him to come inside
of Jura to escape the bad roll. So they sent a delegation to come in through
the Corryvreckan and he wouldn't agree to that as it was too risky but they
told him they would take all the responsibility if he would come through the
Corryvreckan. So he did come through with the tide slightly against him which
caused the whirlpool with the result that she took charge of them and they went
into the whirlpool. When she started to go down she started to list and the
cattle all slid to the one side and she must have been lying flat because it
took all the life belts off the one side. Now they had this minister aboard,
the one they didn't want to take and it was this minister that managed to
open the gangway and managed to get all of the cattle out and the minute
the cattle went out it choked the whirlpool and the vessel righted and
floated out. Those cattle bloated and they washed ashore for weeks after
that.[24]

I have gone into considerable detail about this particular spot—not
only because it approaches a world wonder but because it illustrates a
number of interesting points of marine onomastics. First its name, the Hag,
is very ancient, going back into prehistoric times, while the more modern
Corryvreckan is at least fourteen hundred years old. The original name and
tale was enough to warn mariners away from it, and the later name with
its attendant story is not conducive to making seamen venture near.
Further, we note that the original name has not wholly vanished, which

supports the theory that sea names are not conducive to change once they have been accepted.

Another point to note is that all the stories about Corryvreckan are stories of disaster or danger. As the years roll and vessels go down in its maw, the dread of the place is kept alive and enhanced by adding story upon story to impress upon the mariners the danger and the folly of attempting to pass through this area.

If the anecdotes so far seem to have been weighted in Scotland and in a particular area of the Hebrides, it is for a couple of reasons—first to give the reader an idea of the profusion of stories in any locality, and second because a folklorist, like a good folk narrator, should choose his material with an eye for content.

Passing down the coast of Scotland to the wild west coast of Ireland, one comes eventually to an island called Inishbofin. Although it has lost much of the importance it had during the Middle Ages when it was a center of culture, it still has one of the very few decent harbors on the whole coast. Its name means Island (Inish) of the White Cow (Bofin).

Years ago the island was said to be uninhabited and hidden in mist until two fishermen drifted onto it and lit a fire. Instantly the mists were dispersed and they saw a witch driving a cow, which she turned into a rock just as it reached a lake. The fishermen beat the old woman for her cruelty and were themselves transformed into rocks and so remain.[25]

Captain O'Halloran recalled a somewhat different story. Originally the island was under water until one day there was a great storm and slowly the island rose from the sea. The people living on the neighboring island of Shark (Inishshark) were startled to see this event and more startled to see a great white cow run down off the side of the island toward Inishshark and plunge into the sea. Since then it has been called Inishbofin.

Mr. Day of that island said that it was given its name because a great white cow came up out of the loch and then vanished back into its depths. His story was corroborated by another resident, who added that the cow reappeared every hundred years.[26]

Although a secure anchorage, the entrance to Inishbofin's harbor is encumbered by a rock called Bishop Rock and the passage between it and Fort Point (so named because it was once the site of a Cromwellian fort built on the spot where a Spanish pirate, Don Bosco, had a castle) is extremely narrow. (In conjunction with this story one cannot help but remark on the necessity of knowing something of the background of a place name. There is a Bishop Rock in San Diego Bay, so named because a clipper ship, the *Bishop*, struck there in the nineteenth century.)[27]

Captain O'Halloran said that when Cromwell's troops were on the island they were very cruel to the Roman Catholics there. These they hanged in the fort and slipped overboard through a hole in the wall and their bodies washed out to sea. The bishop was captured and chained to a rock in the harbor at low water. When the tide rose the bishop was drowned and the rock is now Bishop Rock.[28]

On the other side of Inishbofin is Royal Oak Cove. Years ago a vessel of that name, carrying a large cargo of money, ran headlong up the narrow inlet one wild night and was wrecked. She went so far up the cove, however, that the crew walked ashore over her bowsprit. Her treasure went to the bottom and divers were sent for to recover it. They went down, found the treasure and were about to haul it up when they saw something. What it was they would not say, but they were so terrified that they came to the surface and would not go down again. No one has since felt it worth his while to go for the treasure which still lies at the bottom.[29]

A similar tale is told of a little cove near Cutler, Maine. Here one stormy night a pirate ship laden with gold, running for Cutler Harbor, missed her bearings and piled up. No one recalls her name, but the place is known as Money Cove and the treasure still lies at the bottom.

Let us now move rapidly to Nova Scotia. On the eastern shore lies a little promontory called Saladin Point. This is the very spot where the 550-ton barque *Saladin*, Sandy MacKenzie, master, piled up on May 13, 1844, ninety-five days and one mutiny out of Valparaiso. Although much of her story is now forgotten, the saga of her demise merited the point being named after her.

In October of 1842 the barque *Vitula* left England under the command of Captain Fielding. He was accompanied by his fourteen-year-old son, George. Eventually they made Valparaiso, and the skipper—being short of cash—tried to steal a cargo of nitrates. He was caught, a battle ensued, Fielding was wounded, the ship impounded. Fielding attempted to cut and run but was caught and thrown in jail. He immediately broke out and tried to get passage out of the country, but no one seemed inclined to take him. Eventually help came in the form of a philanthropic Scot who offered the Fieldings free passage to Nova Scotia aboard the *Saladin*, which had 150 pounds of silver stored in her run.

No sooner had the vessel cleared the land than Fielding fell out with his benefactor and decided to seize the ship. To do this he enlisted the aid of a one-legged carpenter, an Irishman, a Pole and a handsome young blond Swede, Charles Gustavus Anderson. Next he stole the carpenter's tools. Although warned of danger, the captain stubbornly refused to believe it and did nothing.

Sunday, April 14, the mate was snoozing on the hen coop where he was killed with an axe and thrown overboard. The captain was called on deck and killed with a hammer. Next the crew were called up and all but two were murdered, with young George Fielding doing his bit with a butcher knife. After this the *Saladin's* bronze figurehead was painted white to disguise the vessel.

Things were working out very well and Fielding got two of his henchmen to poison the other two—whom he had persuaded, meanwhile, to murder the poisoners. Unfortunately for the Fieldings, the two factions compared notes, concluded that the Fieldings were rogues, seized them, bound them and threw them both overboard. From then on, the five remaining crewmen lived aft in great luxury in the captain's quarters.

Eventually the *Saladin* piled up under full sail near Country Harbor. Before the crew could abandon her they were seized, clapped in irons and taken to Halifax, where they were tried by two judges. Four culprits were found guilty, hanged in chains at Hospital Point and exhibited for a year and a day.[30]

If the crew of the *Saladin* received their just deserts, justice occasionally miscarried. Such was the case (perhaps) during colonial days in Boston Harbor.

The Puritans were zealous in following the dictates of the law and from time to time made short shrift of wrongdoers and confiscated their money. The captain of the brigantine *Charles*, before he was turned off, is said to have warned fellow seamen to beware coming into Boston Harbor with too much gold lest they be hanged for it.[31] At any rate, another man, the mate of the *Nixie*, was tried in Boston, found guilty of piracy and sentenced to hang on an island. Despite protestations of innocence, he was taken to the place of execution and asked if he had a farewell message to the assembled crowd. He did: He was innocent, and to prove it he said that God would wash away the island of execution within ten years. Innocent or guilty, the fact remains that from that day onward the island began to shrink. Ten years to the day after the hanging a great storm arose, and in the morning the island was gone. The shoal where it once stood is now Nix's Shoal.

While on the subject of pirates, we will turn to the Cape Hatteras region. It seems that Captain Teach, alias Blackbeard, lay there one night in his vessel *The Queen Anne's Revenge*. In a drunken stupor he blew out the light and pointed his pistol under the table in the direction of his companions and swore that after he had counted to a certain number he would fire at them. The mate didn't run and was crippled by a ball through the knee. Later Teach was surprised in the same place and beheaded. The spot is known as Teach's Hole, and his headless ghost is said to float upon the surface when the weather is propitious.[32]

The whole attitude toward piracy and the law has given rise to such names as Execution Rock in New York Harbor, Hangman Hill in Bermuda and Dead Man Cay at Kingston, Jamaica, where buccaneers convicted of their crimes were exposed, sometimes in an iron cage, "to dry" in the sun, a punishment that drove them mad in a few hours and killed them in about two days.

Closely allied with piracy is privateering. From Les Grant at Isle au Haut, Maine, comes the following story.

During the Revolutionary War there was a fellow named Morris had a brig an' he went privateerin' an' he was some successful. Twarn't long before he had a whole load o' prisoners aboard. One morning Old Morris woke up an' he had the whole British fleet after him an' he had to run for it. Well, sir, the wind was light and they was gainin' all the time, but Morris seen a fogbank an' slipped into it an' that hid him for a while an' then the breeze come on to freshen an' Morris, he began to crack on an' tried to lose 'em. He come down by the Isle O'Holt, carryin' everything he could and maybe a little bit more and he fetched up on a ledge. Didn't hurt her none, you understand, but it stopped him an' before he could get off the British were on him again an' he couldn't do nothin' but run for the Penobscot. He made it all right an' he blowed the brig up on Bowen's Ledge after he put the prisoners ashore in charge of a feller named Knowlton who was supposed to march 'em to Thomaston. Well on the way them prisoners revolted but Knowlton warn't long in aquietin' 'em down an' what was left he fetched to Thomaston all right. Knowlton was my great-great-grandfather an' the rock old Morris hit is Morris' Mistake to this day.[33]

Now I should like to turn to the Windward Islands in the Caribbean for a moment, for on the windward side of Tobago lies an exposed bight called Bloody Bay, and a small cove in one end is known as Dead Man Cove.

According to several informants on that island, long ago there was a terrible naval engagement in the bay and the havoc was so great that the water was turned red with blood. After the battle the survivors threw their dead shipmates overboard and they all drifted into the little cove, where they remained until they rotted or were eaten by sea creatures.

The stories, however, do not end there. The place is said to be evil, and should a vessel pass there in the night and ring her bell, or a crewman whistle, a terrible storm will rise and overpower the ship.

Sometimes, too, ghosts are seen there. One man related that he had been fishing one night with a goodly crew when suddenly they heard the sound of oars and saw a cutter full of armed men coming after them. The terrified fishermen bent to their oars, yet despite their best efforts they could not distance their pursuers or even gain on them. All night they rowed as if their backs would break and just managed to stay ahead of the spectral ship until they reached Fort James miles away. Then the sun came up and the pursuing boat and crew vanished.[34]

One final place from the West Indies must be mentioned here, not because of its story quality but because it is a truly singular case.

Off Martinique lies "H.M.S. Diamond Rock," the only bit of stone I know of to be commissioned as a sloop of war. This was done in 1804 by the British to blockade the island. Five guns and 120 men were placed atop the rock, where they played hob with passing shipping. Finally the French captured H.M.S. Diamond Rock but paid a dear price in killed and wounded before it fell. It is said that British warships passing there to this day fire a seven-gun salute to the only unsinkable, and nearly invincible sloop of war in the British Navy.[35]

This, then, has been a sampling of sea names and a suggestion as to how they are given. If one area has received more attention than another, it is simply because that area—thanks to the geography and the people— seemed to be more fruitful to the writer.

As we look over the names, it becomes obvious that those around the British Isles are older and, despite the fact that they were created in similar ways, they are different from the names in the New World. The Old World tales are more complex and detailed, and not infrequently one spot will have a cluster of stories around it, whereas "one tale per ledge" seems to be the normal situation in America. In the British Isles and Ireland the place-names seem to be predominantly Gaelic and English, with a strong overlay of Scandinavian nomenclature to the north and in the west, Dutch in the east and south, with here and there an odd Celtic name or two. In America the base names are Indian, English, French and

Spanish, with occasional names from other nationalities. Gaelic is practically unknown and Scandinavian names—save for the legendary Vinland—are few. Also, since many of the obstructions and aids to navigation were not named until the nineteenth century, it is not surprising that the name and even the story connected with it have more sentimental tones than those of the Old World, as we can see by opposing the Boo Hoo Rocks to the Longship Sands.

As the days go on, more and more places are identified—all too often through tragedy. Wire drags and sounding are constantly improving navigation and reducing the possibility of tragedy. Still, tragedy recurs—and names will still be formed along the lines set down here, with diminished frequency it is true, that will continue to mark the unhappy end of hope and life and substance—the site of horror and heroics. An old fisherman in Maine told an anecdote—one with analogues all over the ocean—which illustrates this point.

A foreign brig picked up a pilot to run up Penobscot Bay. The weather was thick and the captain nervous. He asked the pilot, "Do you know where you are?" "Oh eayh." "You sure you know?" "Eayh." "Do you know all the rocks in the bay?" "Oh eayh." Just then the brig fetched up all standing. "There's one or 'em naow, God dammit," said the pilot.

But sea names, entrancing as they may be, are only one part of a language—sea language. It is now high time to examine this rather large area in hope of finding some rationale behind its development.

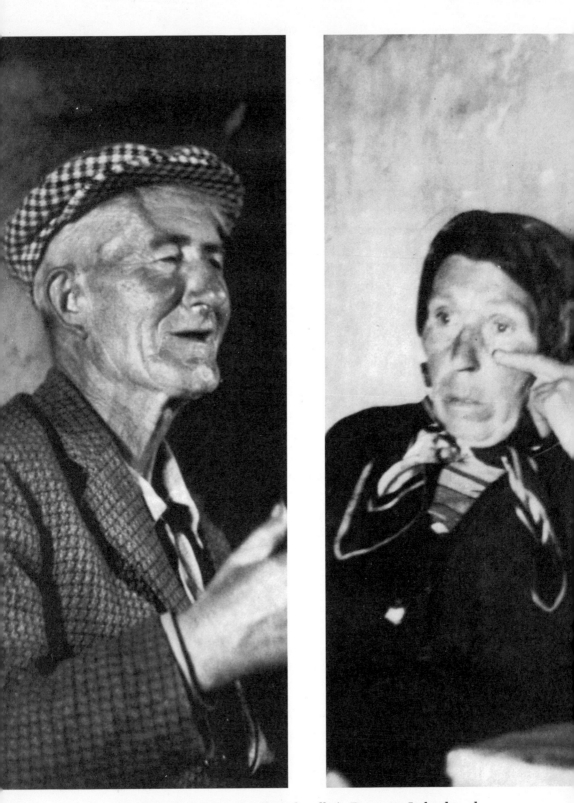

Michael Guheen, the *file* (tale-teller), Dunquin, Ireland, and
Mrs. Curran, the Listener, Rossaveal, Ireland

CHAPTER III

LANGUAGE

"Language ... is the dialect of common sense."
—Walt Whitman, *Complete Poetry and Selected Prose*
(Boston, 1959), p. 426

WHEN I was a teen-ager I once earned five dollars as a sound man for a morning radio program. The show was run by a woman, and each week she had a new experience to tell "the girls." For some reason this program was supposed to be "a cruise on a windjammer," but since the lady in question had an aversion to water she hired a schooner and took the cruise made fast to the wharf. She had a record that played wind sounds and at appropriate moments I was expected to rattle a block or slosh a bucket of water down the deck as "we crashed into foaming billows." Above the hubbub she shouted "salty language" to the recorder—such phrases as "She's yar, shiver me timbers, ahoy there, avast ye swabs." We ended our cruise with the command, "Throw out the anchor." (A term that particularly annoyed Joseph Conrad).[1]

Such is a rather conventional opinion of sea language among landsmen —it is strange, colorful and rather jolly. Nothing could be further from the fact. Moreover, nautical terms are not only misused, they are grossly misunderstood by the landsman.

Three excellent examples of nautical terms that are often misunderstood originate in directions, keeping the watch and tying a ship up. First, in a collection of poems by Philip Freneau the writer referred to Ocracoke Inlet, and the editor in his *explication de texte* said this place was twenty-six miles northeast by southwest of Cape Hatteras.

Second, perhaps the most misused or misunderstood phrase from nautical language after "throw out the anchor" is the term "dog watch," which writers constantly refer to as "that long watch in the middle of the night" or "that most tedious of long watches." The term "dog" is used in many senses at sea, often in an uncomplimentary one. A sailor is said to be "dogging it" if he does not do his full share or "pull his weight in the boat." A hatch is "dogged down," i.e., tightened to make it watertight with a "dog iron" to give added leverage against the dogs or clamps that hold it shut. However, the dog watch is the best watch on shipboard. The usual four-hour watch is split into two between four and eight in the evening every few days so that no man is forced to stand the same four-hour period continuously. Sailors are always envious of the "gangs" that "pull" the "dog watch." It is the midwatch, midnight to four in the morning, unrelieved as it is even by normal shipboard activity or by any change of light, that is hated, despised and thought to last forever. Man at this hour is at his lowest ebb, and since there is nothing to see and little to do it is almost impossible to measure the passage of time. Moreover, it cuts bitterly into the sailor's few precious hours of sleep.

The landsman often asks, "When will the ship dock?" The answer is, of course, "When she is in dry dock," for a ship "moors" to a buoy, "lays to" an anchor and is "tied up" to a dock or "moors alongside."

Every occupation has its own special words. The more venerable the occupation, the older the words; the more total the involvement required by the occupation, the greater the vocabulary; the more complex the tasks, the more particular the words. It would be difficult to find an occupation much older than seafaring, or one more complex or more totally absorbing. Men work in the mines all day but come home at night; the lumberman sometimes spends as much as three months in the woods before returning to town, but whalemen went to sea for seven years. Joseph Conrad records a passage of 130 days as an ordinary event in a merchantman's life.[2] And all that time the seaman's life hangs in jeopardy.

It is safe to speak, I think, of a nautical language. This language comes in several parts. The first is, of course, nomenclature—the identification of every plank, block, sail, fastening, line, rope, walking beam, spar and boiler. It includes not only the parts of the ship, her gear and cargo but also the crew, their clothes and the food they eat. It even extends to their dockside activities. Next comes speech attitudes—how a thing is said, what may be expressed and what must be kept in limbo, available only to the knowing mariner who can translate the unspoken ideas. Finally there is the speech rhythm itself—what kinds of inflections are used, whether the conversation is rapid or slow, cheerful or morose, sparse, or voluble.

Basically, nautical language is subject to a few simple controls. Once we recognize them, the lingo of the seas begins to take on a new and more important meaning. Above all else, sea language is functional. It does not much matter on land if you do not understand a word or phrase. But at sea, a misunderstood command can be embarrassing at the least, costly or fatal at the worst. Frequently there is no time to repeat a phrase. It must be heard and understood the first time. Further, sea lingo must be comprehensible under the most adverse conditions from considerable distances. With seas breaking across the vessel, with the wind roaring in the rigging and a broken line flogging a sail, with the ship groaning and grunting and emitting her thousand private, plaintive sounds and the night dark, foggy or thick with snow, the captain or his mate on the poop or bridge must be able to hear the lookouts forward or at the masthead. He must be able to understand what they say in the greatest stress of weather, and he must be able to call his men and give his commands in such a manner that they will carry above the chaos of storm and will sink into a half-frozen, exhausted or still sleepy mind.

In order to be effective, most nautical words are short, resonant and distinct from one another. Once it was steerboard and leeboard, which changed to starboard and larboard, but this soon changed again to starboard and port, two distinct entities that carry better on the gale than "right" and "left." Instead of telling the helmsman to "point the bow more toward the wind" or "away from the wind," the command is simply "Come up" or "Fall off." Here we have a redundancy that is effective. The "come" or the "fall" reinforces the meaning. Should it be necessary to come still closer to the wind, the command would be "Luff," an action that is often taken when the vessel is near to being overpowered and is therefore an urgent one. On the other hand, a decided change away from the wind follows "Bear away!"

The desire for accuracy takes many forms. In the United States Navy, course, speed and time are clearly distinguished. The former is always given in three digits as "Steer zero one five"; and the second in two "Maintain a speed of fifteen knots;" while the last is in four digits. Since vessels seldom achieve speeds of three figures and there are only 360 degrees on the compass, this is a useful kind of redundancy. Further, the command is given, "Come left fifteen degrees. Steady up on zero one five. Steer small. Nothing to the right." Thus there can be no margin for mistake.

This use of redundancy for purposes of certainty is carried out in other ways as well. In Maine and the Maritime Provinces, where people steer by the thirty-two points of the compass—as they do in many parts of the world—the seamen often change the value of the vowels. They talk, not about North and South but "Nothe" and "Sothe." In the eastern hemisphere of the compass the command would be "Steer nothe-east; steer sothe-east." In the compasses' western hemisphere we hear "nawthwest," "saouth by west."

Unlike the automobile and its attendant miseries, seafaring has been going on for centuries, and as seafaring and shipbuilding developed the language developed with them. The seaman is, strangely, a conservative person by nature and he is reluctant to change. Because literacy was not for a long time part of his knowledge, he tended to commit to memory all the terms of his profession, and rather than drop an obsolete term, he would adapt it to a new purpose and invent or acquire more terms to meet novel situations.

The phrases of seamen had become sufficiently complex and interest in them by landsmen sufficiently aroused by 1627, that that doughty marine captain, John Smith, brought out an 80-page booklet on the principal sea terms and ship nomenclature, entitled *A Sea Grammar*. By 1769 William Falconer had compiled his *Dictionary of the Marine*, the fourth edition of which appeared in 1815 with over 800 pages! The interesting point to be made is that Smith's terms are all there in Falconer and most of Falconer's (barring ordnance terms) are still known to seamen today, albeit the spelling and pronunciation have changed somewhat, as "lanners" (Smith) to lanyards (present day).

As a further indication of the conservative nature of the seaman and his dedication to tradition, one point could be made. Captain Smith pointed out that the worst pests a vessel could encounter were termites. To rid the vessel of them the best method was "to breame" the ship—haul her out of the water and build a quick, hot fire under her. This would burn some of the wretched creatures and boil the rest. After this, before the vessel was launched it was customary to grease the hull so it would sail faster. At the present time both of these practices are still in use by bargemen in Lisbon, Portugal, despite the fact that there are many cheap, easy and less dangerous ways to keep out teredos.

From the foregoing it becomes apparent that the development of sea language was a cumulative process. As ships changed the language tended to be adapted to the newer types of vessels rather than to become obsolete. A term dropped out only when there was a chance of confusion in terminology, or when the object referred to no longer existed in any form whatsoever—a rare occurrence.

From the Middle Ages until the time of the Spanish Armada, vessels were equipped with large boxlike edifices on the bow and on the stern. These had a double purpose—that of keeping large seas from breaking aboard and at the same time of serving as small blockhouses from which sailors could hurl rocks and spears and shoot arrows at hostile ships. They were called "fore castle" and "stern castle" and indeed they resembled little castles more than anything else. As time went on, these little turrets were gradually reduced in size and their function became purely that of keeping out the sea. The forward one was abbreviated and became the "fo'c'sle" or "foredeck" under which the crew lived and atop which stood the windlass or capstan. The after-turret was abandoned, but the area remained raised to prevent the waves breaking in over the stern and poop-ing the vessel, a serious hazard at sea. This area became known variously as the "poop" or the quarterdeck because it enclosed a quarter part of the deck, and was traditionally "officer country." From the "break in the poop" the captain could contemplate the "waist" where the crew worked and could look forward beyond the fo'c'sle.

Hundreds of years ago, in order to cleanse themselves of the dread disease, lepers would often take passage to the Holy Land in ships. In order to prevent contamination of the rest of the passengers and crew they were kept separate aft, where their stench would not permeate the vessel. The hold where the Lazars lived has been preserved to this day in the word lazaret, a malodorous little cubbyhole in the stern where little-used gear is kept.

Down below in the great sailing ships were located the blocks and tackles that helped to maneuver the rudder. The space was airless, dark, cramped, damp and noisy. Here in the steerage lived those passengers who paid the least passage money. The work is now done by hydraulic engines, but "to go steerage" is still a meaningful term aboard ship.

When a square-rigged vessel sailed to windward, the windward edges of her square sails were likely to curl and blow backward. Should this happen, the sail would collapse and the vessel would find herself "in irons," i.e., manacled by the wind and unable to maneuver. To prevent this a line was run from the windward edge of the sail to the bow and hauled tight. Should the vessel go too close to the wind, the weather edge of the sail would not buckle. The rope and the knot so used were called the bow-line. Often the command would be to "keep her on a tight bowline"—a term still used occasionally; but the phrase is best remembered by the name of the most useful of all nautical knots—the bowline.

In early fighting ships the guns were located on the main deck, primarily in the waist. For protection the sides were raised above the deck and the men crouched behind them. The guns fired through apertures in this planking, and to this day the raised side is the bulwark, the covering piece atop it the gunwale or "gunnel."

Many of the words preserved are very ancient, dating back at least as far as the Anglo-Saxons. The word "bos'n," for example, is really a corruption of boatswain—"swain" being an Anglo-Saxon word meaning, roughly, keeper or controller, hence "bos'n," a boat keeper. And, as in many cases, along with the word is preserved a certain amount of tradition. The badge of office of this worthy is the boatswain's "call" or "pipe." It is traditionally made of silver, shaped like a dog's penis and worn around the neck on a carefully plaited thong called a sinnet. All activity was once ordered by this small wind instrument (the only wind instrument allowed on early ships). Not only was the call used for purposes of command but for purposes of ceremony as well, at which time it was referred to as a "pipe." When a dignitary or the captain came on board he was always "piped over the side." When a boarding party was required or boats were to be sent, the command, in America at least, was "Call away the boats," "Call all hands," "Call the boarding party," each call being composed of different notes. Since he may pipe only with the right hand, the bos'n is the only man in the U.S. Navy allowed to salute with his left. To the present day these customs are preserved in the American navy. And although the order may come over the loud hailer, "Now hear this——" it is always preceded by the piercing but tremulous call of the boatswain.

It is interesting to note that by the seventeenth century a trumpet had also been introduced aboard ship and was used to supplement the bos'n's call. This has been continued with the use of a bugle which blows different tunes for different activities, which are remembered by the men through rhymes like the one for the "Liberty" call: "Who's going ashore? Who's going ashore? Who's got a dollar for a Newport whore?"

Not only are the words of the sea ancient, they are also adopted from many peoples, chief among them being the Dutch who, no matter what their ability as seafarers, have added largely to the language. Words like skiff, schooner, skipper, hooker, boat and yacht all appear to have their origins in the Netherlands. The French have contributed words like seine, jollyboat (*joli bateau*), frigate and captain. Many of these foreign words have gradually changed and melded until they have become accepted Anglo-American terms whose origins are known only to the patient etymologist.

As mentioned earlier, there is always a functional determinant in word selection. The necessity for exact terminology has been noted, as well as the necessity for clarity so that one knows exactly what is meant. Another function is that of brevity, for the longer the phrase the greater the chance of being misunderstood, and the greater the possibility of the wind blowing away a part of the phrase. For this reason things at sea are "to leeward" or "to windward" rather than "on the leeward side."

But there is another functional determinant that is as old as seafaring and sometimes as faint as a horizon in the fog. It is perhaps the most salient determinant of all—the seaman's outlook on life and his regard for the sea. The former is both pessimistic and fatalistic. The latter is a strong tendency toward animism and the belief that although the sea may indeed have human qualities, it (or "she" as the ocean is often called) is essentially a hostile force probably in league with the elements. The seaman, in league with his bark, survives only by outwitting both of them, who wait with inscrutable patience for man to give himself away—and because he is man their patience often is rewarded. This idea is dimly felt sometimes by poets who talk about "old Ocean," remark that "The Injun Ocean sets and smiles," or exclaim "Break, break, break on thy cold grey stones, O sea," but it is as ingrained in the seaman's nature as the wrinkles etched by sun and spray and wind around his eyes and buried as deep within his soul as the rheumatism that is brought on by the constant dampness embedded in his bones.

This fact was recognized very well by Ernest Hemingway, who says about one of his heroes:

> He always thought of the sea as "La Mar" which is what people call her in Spanish when they love her. Sometimes those who love say bad things about her but they are always said as though she were a woman. Some of the younger fishermen, those who used buoys as floats for their lines and had motorboats, bought when the shark livers had brought much money, spoke of her as "el mar" which is masculine. They spoke of her as a contestant or a place or even an enemy. But the old man always thought of her as feminine and as something which gave or withheld great favors, and if she did wild or wicked things it was because she could not help them. The moon affects her as it does a woman, he thought.[3]

In order to survive, the sailor knows he must either placate or dupe the elements—especially the sea. Ulysses offered libations to the sea and, to be on the safe side, had himself lashed to the mast. From time immemorial to the present, man has tried to propitiate the sea with gifts. It matters little whether it be a human sacrifice in pre-Christian days, or wreaths of flowers thrown on the ebbing tide in Gloucester, Massachusetts, or St. John's, Newfoundland, every summer in this century—the motivation is largely the same.

However, by far the most ingrained security action is to be found in language, in tone, in figure and in attitude. The Anglo-Saxon did not say he was going to sea; he said he was going "on the whale's way." He did not pull an oar but an "ash." Rather than go in a ship, he went in a "lone wanderer," a "far flyer." This use of metaphor or kenning was not for the purposes of poetic license but to prevent, if possible, the sea from finding out about the mariner's business. The practice is carried on to the present day. One need only listen to two fishing vessels conversing, and it matters little if it be on the Grand Banks off Newfoundland or the Bressa Bank off the Shetland Islands. A typical example would be as follows. A tired, hopeless voice breaks the air:

> "The *Girl Vivian* to the *Cigar Joe*, the *Girl Vivian* to the *Cigar Joe*, come in, Cap."
>
> "This is the *Cigar Joe*. Hello Fred. Where you at?"
>
> "Just about the same place as before. Where are you?"
>
> "About where I was the last time. How's the weather down there?"
>
> "Oh, so-so. Could be worse, could be worse. How's it with you?"
>
> "Not too bad, not too bad. Had a breeze a while ago but it's gone now. Probably layin' back to ketch a better holt. Anything your way?"
>
> "No, no, few boxes trash fish, that's all. Don't expect we'll ever get a trip this rate. You?"
>
> "No, nothing doing here at all. Poorest I've seen it. Suppose I'll go back empty. Hard way to make a dollar."
>
> "Yes, yes, that's the way it goes. Well, I'll see you at the market. Over and out."
>
> "O.K., Cap. See you then. The *Girl Vivian* over and out with the *Cigar Joe*."

Two days later both vessels turn up at the market with excellent catches. Of course it could be argued that the entire conversation is a ploy to keep other fishermen away, but since vessels usually fish in sight of others and one can easily get a radio bearing on the vessel in question, this won't work. What is much more apparent is the fact that inquisitive Nature will be put to it to discover the whereabouts of the two vessels, and from the despondent tones plus the poor catches related, it would hardly be worth Nature's while to seek after them.

The idea that God and/or the elements take a malevolent interest in man has often been expressed in story form. It is best illustrated by the story of the Flying Dutchman, a tale about a man who defied the elements and swore that no matter what the weather did he would round Cape Horn. As every sailor (and Samuel Taylor Coleridge) well knows, he is still trying to gain his westing to round Cape Horn. In more prosaic language but with equal force Jack London, in a short story, *Make Westing*, concludes: "Captain Dan Cullen read over his literary effort with admiration. . . . He felt the *Mary Rogers* lift and heel, and surge along, and knew she was making nine knots. A smile of satisfaction slowly dawned on his black and hairy face. Well, anyway, he had made his westing and fooled God."[4]

For those who would argue that such ideas are the idle fancy of yesterday, two modern stories from Chesapeake Bay lend added currency. A man was out on the bay and a violent storm blew up. It continued hour after hour and no matter what the captain did he could find no shelter, gain no port. Finally he jumped up in rage, shook his fist at the sky and shouted, "You sonofabitch, if you're really up there you'll stop this!" According to the narrator, "The wind then blew harder than ever."[5]

On another occasion the weather forced an oyster boat to seek shelter in a small creek where she anchored. The wind blew so furiously that no one could get ashore, and after a couple of days supplies began to run low. The mate said to the captain, "Captain, you got to do something." "What can I do? I've done all I can." "Well, you might try prayin'." The captain prayed for two hours and then went to bed. The next morning he awoke, threw back the scuttle and stuck his head out. "How is it, Captain?" "Just as I expected. A little mite worse."[6]

This suppression of emotion noted in the radio conversation seems to dominate seafaring speech. To the newspaper reporter ashore, a strong wind at sea is a terrible hurricane. At sea it is "a breeze of wind" or at most "a living gale of wind." "Titanic waves" to the landsman are "a lump of sea" to the sailor, not because he has seen larger or is more used to high seas, but because he intuitively fears upsetting Nature. Should wild weather scare him or jeopardize his life, then his talking about it will serve to stimulate Nature's activities.

Not only does the sailor suppress his opinion and remarks to the extent that he is reluctant to give a time of arrival, his course or speed, but in order to escape adversity he may also resort to humor in his remarks. Often this is accomplished by minimizing the extreme. In England, when a vessel runs aground inadvertently, the captain will note he "got on the putty," while in the United States the ship "hit the bricks." A man will remark to his mate that it is a "lovely night" when the seas are breaking aboard and the temperature is below freezing. Should he fall overboard into icy water, the sailor is apt to remark that it was his "first bath of the year," that "the water was just right." Once when a vessel was rolling so heavily that most of the crockery had been broken and it was impossible to keep one's feet, I heard an old fisherman remark, "You know, if she was to put her mind to it, I expect this vessel might roll considerable." In an old log the captain remarked on the difficulty he encountered in steering his vessel. He was very glad, he said, that Africa was so far from South America because it just gave him room to come about.[7]

This kind of dry humor, satire or irony, if you will, is long-lasting and often goes into nomenclature. For example, in America the galley chimney is called the "Charlie Noble." This, according to sailors' tales, dates back to the eighteenth century, when the British admiral Charles Noble is said to have insisted that his stack be kept polished. The sailors resented the task and gained their revenge by naming the piece after him. (It might be noted at this point that many terms aboard ship have personal names: the Plimsoll line, marking the depth to which a ship may be loaded; Matthew Walker, a knot; Jimmy Green, a type of sail; Prince Alberts, a kind of improved foul-weather clothing popular in Cape Horners during the reign of Queen Victoria.) The "lubber line" is the post in the binnacle which the inexperienced sailor steers by instead of watching the sails, stars or other objects as experienced seamen do. Field day is not a holiday but one on which the entire ship is cleared, and "rope yarn Sunday" is a day off. The "lucky bag," alias "slop chest," is a supply of worn-out or cast-off clothing which the unfortunate sailor may use at some expense to replenish his supplies.

Irony is not restricted to the ship alone but extends to people, things and nations. A Portygee man-o'-war is a kind of jellyfish with a toxic sting. Johnny Crapauds are Frenchmen. Herring chokers are men from Nova Scotia and bluenoses from Newfoundland. An Irish pennant is a trailing line, an Irish hurricane a flat calm, and a Philadelphia sea lawyer is one who professes to know the answers to all questions. "Piccadilly weepers," on the other hand, refer to a kind of beard worn by sailors long at sea. A pogue is both a fish and a homosexual, and pogey bait is candy—which is popularly believed to be the diet of homosexuals. Limejuicers are Englishmen because of their habit of serving lime juice periodically to prevent scurvy. Widow makers are bowsprits, so named because of the number of men lost from them when trying to shorten sail at sea. One who is generally ineffectual is said to be about as much good as a spare boiler or not to amount to anything "more than a hen fart in a gale."

Nowhere, of course, is this irony more apparent than in maritime cuisine. The galley was never a place of assembly like the scuttlebutt—the water barrel located beside the scuttle where the crew paused to swap rumors (hence "scuttlebutt has it that . . .") while slaking their thirst. The crews, especially in fishing vessels, did occasionally assemble there for coffee or tea, known as "mug-ups" or "'levenies," because it was served in mugs at eleven o'clock. (This was not of course exclusively a sea term but originally came from the land, like martingale, a stay under the bowsprit, which relates to a piece of harness.)

The cook was usually called the doctor, and he was either a Negro or a worn-out sailor who sometimes actually did serve as ship's doctor. (The doctor, in American parlance at least, was called a "croker" because he carried the tools of his trade in a "crocus bag." And because he was inept at the trade. The term came to mean "die" when used as a verb.) His position very often was a terminal one to a seafaring career, and he was assisted by an apprentice boy who was just starting his career. He was disliked by the crew not only for his bad cooking but because he was in charge of the stores. Opinion of the cook may be summed up from an account in a log of the seventeenth century. A vessel was cast away on Boone Island, Maine, and the crew was reduced to cannibalism. They ate the cook, and the captain explained the choice by saying, "He was a fat, loutish fellow."

Not only was the cook inept but the provender was also execrable to begin with. Salt fish, salt beef and salt pork served as the main staples along with hardtack (ship's biscuit). Each week a portion of meat would be stashed in barrels fastened to the poop with horseshoes, (earning for them the sobriquet "harness casks") and doled out periodically. The meat was known as "salt horse." Salt fish passed under several names—hairy Willie in Scotland, Block Island turkey in the United States. Lobscouse was a stew of meat, biscuits and potatoes; duff was a kind of bread, while "dandy funk" was a kind of hasty pudding made of broken biscuits, weevils and molasses. Coffee was called Java or Joe, and both tea and coffee were said to be good only when they would "float a marlinespike."

Incidentally, an interesting custom was followed for years in fishing vessels. When the voyage started, a huge kettle filled with water and a handful of tea or coffee was placed on the galley range and kept simmering. The crew would pour off the tea or coffee, which they drank with sugar and "tinned teat" (condensed milk). When all the liquid was gone, another handful of tea or coffee was thrown in, the kettle refilled and the process continued. When the kettle was full of tea leaves or coffee grounds, it was time to head for home.

One of the areas that has been heavily encrusted with sea language is the weather. The wind is said "to back" (go counterclockwise), "to haul," (go clockwise) and "to veer" or be "fluky" (shift suddenly). The term is also used in anchoring when one "veers," i.e., lets out more cable, and once referred to turning a ship around with the wind—now more commonly called "jibing" on fore-and-aft vessels and "wearing" on square-rigged ones. A cat's-paw is a small puff of wind that ruffles the water, a white squall is one where the water is turned white with the wind, while a black squall is one with a dark line in the water. A "smokey sou'wester"—sometimes called in extreme cases "a white-livered sou'wester"—is a strong wind that brings with it spray and reduced visibility. A so'easter is a gale from that quarter, and a nor'easter is automatically recognized as a three-day blow. The absence of wind is called a dead calm or flat-arsed calm. A severe gale is "a whole gale" or "a living gale of wind." Sometimes when these conditions arise and the question is asked, "How's the wind"? the reply is, "Up and down the mast." Light along the horizon is called "a glin" and a mirage "a loom." Fog, if it greatly reduces visibility, is "tick o' fog" or "a great dungeon of fog."

So intricate and involved is sea language that it is a source of great sport for the old "shellback" (seasoned sailor) to torment the apprentices to the trade. Many an innocent youth has been sent to the giddy crow's nest (lookout) to gather eggs for breakfast, to go find Matthew Walker, to ask the sextant to give a prayer. He has stood long hours scanning the empty sea for the mail buoy. Ashore one may answer a foolish question of "What's that?" with "Cat fur for kitten britches" or "Layovers to catch peddlers," but at sea the reply to "What are you doing?" is "Why, I'm making a scrudgeon." The word has a faint resemblance to gudgeon—which is a part of the rudder—but further inquiry reveals that "a scrudgeon, young man, is a rudder for a duck's arse." Sometimes it is a "blivitt" which is being constructed, and further inquiry reveals it is "ten pounds of shit in a five-pound paper bag."

When the old salts tired of this game and the watch retired below, the hazing kept on. Someone would ask, "Why has the flatfish got a crooked

Passing on tradition, Alexander Charles, Castries, Saint Lucia

mouth?" When the answer was "I don't know," the response would be "Because he called the herrin' 'a bony buggar'."[9] Or the green hand might be asked a riddle:

> "The wind was West and West steered we
> The wind was aft. How could that be?"

The answer, much to his chagrin, would be, "West had the hellum."[10]

These things fall into the category of the "tall tale"—a device very popular amongst the folk afloat and ashore. To be effective, the tall tale requires a certain situation. There must be an "in" group, in this case the shellbacks, and an "out" group—the neophyte. The story told is well known to the "ins," and the humor lies in the effect the story has on the outsider. Generally the story takes the form of an exaggerated fact which is either blown up to the point of absurdity or stops just short, whereupon the gullible listener asks the fateful question.

Captain Bart Robbins of Stonington, Maine, asked an admiring tourist, "Madam, did I ever tell you about the time I was ninety mile to sea and the vessel went down in a hurricane with all hands?"

"No, sir, what did you do?"

"I was drownded."

One of these stories very popular in the northeast concerns the great storm that blew away the rig, the paint and even the skipper's whiskers. When all seemed lost the vessel passed through the eye of the storm. The wind veered 180 degrees and blew everything back on board.[11]

In Chesapeake Bay there is a story about a house that was struck by lightning, and the lightning passed through the house and went into the ground, leaving a deep hole. When the gullible sailor asks how deep it was, the reply is, "I dunno, I dropped a soundin' pole into it and it went 'thurrtle' right out of hearing."[12]

From the same area comes a story about a man who meets a girl on a stormy night and they eventually wind up before a fake minister, who marries them with a very strange kind of ceremony. Again the dupe asks what took place, and he is told the minister married the pair with the following quatrain:

> Dark is the night, dismal is the weather
> I now join this whore and thief together.
> Run thief, catch this whore,
> Live together evermore.[13]

Fortunately—or unfortunately, depending upon how one looks at it—sea lingo has hardly been restrained by the manacles imposed by the dictionary on any language. It has therefore grown independently on both sides of the ocean. As a result, differences have arisen in nautical terms that are wont to lead to confusion—"Give us a growl at half past three" in Yankee ships is "Give us a shout" in British vessels. Americans "get some shut eye" but the British "get their kip." American fishermen "set their trawls" but the Scotch and Irish "shoot" their "nets." Americans keep a "gurry bucket" for garbage but the British put theirs in a "gash bucket." Americans have cables and hawsers but the English have warps and tiers. The American is told to "bear a hand," or "shake a leg" if he is expected to hurry, but the Britisher is told to "show a leg." Americans wear "foul weather gear" and "oil up," i.e., put on oilskins. The British wear "oilies." In the British navy the command is "Shoot, shoot, shoot" but in the American it is "Fire." To the American, "Chips" is the carpenter, but the English understand the term to mean fried potatoes.

Not only do we find general differences between the maritime speech of Americans and seamen from elsewhere in the English-speaking world, but we also find a number of localisms that are heard only in one area, sometimes only in one place. In Nova Scotia, "poor" before a man's name indicates he is dead, as "Poor Charlie, he used to say. . . ." From the same area comes "blue" meaning hard or desperate—"I've seen times, I tell you, when things looked mighty blue." "Civil" in Maine means pleasant, while "grand" is the cognate phrase in Ireland. From Labrador we hear of a "tickle" which elsewhere means an inlet. In Scotland the fisher folk talk about a "lum" instead of a "Charlie Noble." Elsewhere in marine lingo "lum" is a nickname applied to a clumsy sailor. Down in Chesapeake Bay "a tump" means a point. Nowhere of course are these localisms more common than for violent winds, and so we have "chinooks," "mistrals," "Portuguese trades," "Santa Anas," "Tehuantapeckers," "williwaws" and many more. While "ground" is the general term for a fishing area like "Hatteras ground" in New England and the Maritimes, the term "haul" is often used.

Such phrases as they roll from a sailor's tongue serve to place him, just as the use of words like "stream," "brook," "creek" and "run" identify the landsman as being from a particular region of the country.

These local names are prevalent in the identification of birds and fish. In one area a "bluebill" is a great scaup, while somewhere else it refers to a bufflehead or skunk. Codlings are caught in Scottish waters, but they are

tomcod off New England. In southern Massachusetts, a skilagalee is elsewhere called a swordfish. Sea trout, weakfish and squeteague all refer to
the same fish in different areas.

Usually these words have an interesting etymology, and none better
illustrates this than the phrase "smooring up" as used in the Elizabeth
Islands off southern Massachusetts. In Scotland until recent times it was
customary for an old woman in the family to cover the turf fire with ashes
before going to bed. After she had covered it, she made a circle in the
center and drew a number of lines like wagon spokes outward from
the center. For each of the pie-shaped pieces thus created she said a prayer,
and the ashes kept the turf smouldering all night and ready to be rekindled
in the morning. This art was known as "smooring the fire." The same practice was employed in Ireland, but here it was known as "raking" the fire.
In the United States the idea is preserved in a Southern saying, "Don't
try to teach your grandmother to lap ashes." But at Vineyard Haven this
phrase has a slightly different meaning. "It's smoorin' up," they say, meaning that visibility is diminishing and trouble lies ahead.

At the same time, there are surprising parallels between English and
American ways of saying things. Captain Bob Roberts of Pin Mill in England remarked that the only thing that kept a certain vessel afloat was "the
maggots holding hands," while in Maine a seaman said that "the only
thing that kept a vessel together was the maggots and the termites holding
hands." In Nova Scotia a man said he would have nothing to do with a
vessel because if he scraped off the gurry (fish slime) and the paint, she'd
fall apart.

While the dialectics of other occupations tend to remain solely within
the occupation, sea language is expanded by the seafarer to fit requirements
other than at sea. Quite unconsciously, he applies sea terms to things
ashore. There is a story that an old salt watched a woman trying to catch
her son. A strong breeze was blowing, the woman's skirts were ballooning in
front of her and she was gaining steadily on the child, who had aroused
the sailor's sympathy. "Come about, mate," he bawled, "and take her by
the wind."[14]

The sailor ashore "swabs" the floor of his house. When it rains he tells
his wife to "close the hatch" and invites his friends to come in the "fore-
door." His clothes "slat" on the line, and he persists in saying "port" and
"starboard." Someone moving fast is "carrying sail," and when the conversation gets out of hand the speaker is told to "take a round turn." An old

man who is not well is "all stove up," "weak in the waterways," "butt sprung" or "gone limber," and if he is senile he is "about gone in the top hamper." Should a sailor go on a trip he "takes a cruise" and "ties up" for the night. He goes to the post office to hear the "scuttlebutt" and "stands up" to help, not his friend, but his "mate." He doesn't wear new clothes but a "new rig," and before going to a party his wife puts on her "Sunday bunting." When his friend visits him, he "breaks out" the liquor and they have "a gam" and "splice the main brace." They sit, not out of the wind, but "in the lee of the house." When the friend leaves he says, "Fair winds," and if he is from Massachusetts he will add "Keep off the Middle Ground" (a reef in Vineyard Sound). Incidentally, in the West Indies he is careful not to shake hands and say "Goodbye." Rather he slaps his friend on the shoulder and says "Good luck!" In Ireland they say, "Go with God." Before "turning in" he will have a "mug up" and after a sound sleep "turn out" around "seven bells." He doesn't have breakfast in the kitchen. Instead he "chows down" in the "galley," gets his "gear" out of "the locker" and "shoves off for the town," where he argues with the tax collector and tells him something "that slacks him off." On his way home he is "rammed" by another car which "carries away" his bumper, and as a result the whole car is "badly stove" or may even be a "total wreck."

Eventually the old salt, his "voyage complete" (as distinct from "passage"), "slips his cable" and departs for "Fiddlers' Green."

In a still broader sense, the vocabulary of the ship, along with that of the horse, seems to pervade our language. We talk about "horsepower" and we "harness" rivers and streams, but we also have our "ship of state" with a leader at "the helm." Pioneers crossed "the sea of grass" in "prairie schooners" and cowboys still climb on "the hurricane deck" of their ponies. After being "in amongst the reefs and shoals" of economic adversity, the banker "weathers the storm" and "has all plain sailing" until business once again "falls into the doldrums," at which time the politician "keeps a weather eye out" to see "which way the wind blows" so he can "trim his sails" to the feeling of the time and get "a good haul" of votes. When said politician is caught "rigging" the voting machines, he is "taken aback" and is forced "to take another tack entirely" to recover the confidence necessary to restore himself and "his crew" to office. To do this he may "take soundings" of public opinion "to get his bearings" before "charting a new course." With public faith once more firmly "anchored" in his policy, he will "stand by" and calmly await the results of the campaign, knowing full well his hopes may go to "wrack and ruin" and the campaign be described as a "total wreck." Or he may take "a little cruise" amongst his constituents by train and wave to them from the "caboose"—a term formerly applied to the deckhouse on a ship.

After the results are in he may exclaim, " 'By the Lord Harry,' I knew we'd win even if there was 'the devil to pay' over that scandal. Now we can carry on with all sail set." He probably does not know that the Lord Harry refers to the loss of a great ship, nor that paying the devil refers to caulking a seam, any more than he realizes that most of the foregoing remarks ascribed to him are really mixed metaphors. Indeed these phrases, and hundreds like them, have become so completely landbound that they are almost like the farmer's trout that become so used to following his friend around the farm that when he accidently slipped back into the spring he was drowned.

Not only does sea terminology approach a language in itself; to the landsman, at least, it is highly romantic. Animism, restraint, alliteration and metaphor have long been recognized as worthy tools of the poet which he acquires with great effort. These are commonplace tools of the sea-faring man, and over the centuries he has honed them to a razor's edge. Singly or collectively his vocabulary catches the feel of wide waters, danger and excitement. Under his tongue his vessel ceases to be a composite of wood, iron, or plastic but becomes an animate cohort allied with him against the hostile forces of wave, weather and the hazard of the reefs and shoals. Having laid on his supplies and stowed his cargo, he clears for sea. He takes his departure, sets the watch and gains a good offing. In the horse latitudes where there is no wind and the horses were thrown over-board to conserve water, his sails slat in the calm. He crosses the line (equa-tor), works down through the trades and into the roaring forties, where the winds blow clear around the world uninterrupted and are sometimes called the brave west winds. Here he meets with head beat seas and is forced to bear away through the dark that's thick o' snow. Perhaps he's caught in the black fog—the dreaded mist that freezes to everything it touches. His sails blow out of the bunt. His vessel is knocked on her beam's end. He may be forced to seek port for stress of weather. Meanwhile he passes growlers (little icebergs), sees the corposants (St. Elmo's fire) in the rigging, Mother Carey's chickens flock around him and a great gray albatross hangs in his wake (believed to be the spirit of drowned sailors). Eventually, if he has stuck close to his rhumb line he will make a landfall, pick up the loom of land, and let go the best bower (anchor) from the cathead in ten fathoms. The mud hook will take hold and the vessel will tend nicely. He will write in his log not the usual "So ends this day" but "So ends this passage."

Should he be less successful, he may lose his rig and be forced to clear away the gear. He may be stranded, the vessel bilged on a ledge, and then he is forced to man the boats, for he is cast away. But still he has cheated Davy Jones. After an appropriate time in Lloyd's of London an entry is made, "Posted missing. The barque *Vitula*, five hundred tons. New York to Melbourne overdue and presumed lost."

"I can't keep my pipe lit!" Somewhere in the Gulf Stream

CHAPTER IV

WEATHER LORE

Wild geese, wild geese
Gangin' out to sea
All fine weather
It will be.
> —Horace P. Beck,
> *Folklore of Maine*
> (Philadelphia, 1957). p. 81

SINCE time immemorial, weather has been a prime concern of man. It has ordered his activities, ruled his way of life and may, perhaps, have had a profound influence on his personality. The ability to predict and control it has been an important aspiration of both primitive and civilized man. Even today this ability is an integral part of certain occupations and a concern of most people, and has been developed to a high degree amongst outdoorsmen, farmers and sailors.

Skilled though he be in weather lore, the farmer is primarily concerned with prognosticating rain and cold. Rarely is this knowledge essential to preserving his life. Rather its value is economic, and because the farmer is by his very occupation sedentary, his understanding of the elements, no matter how deep, is local in nature. The sailor, on the other hand, needs accurate meteorological information to save his gear from damage and to make a quick passage, both economic in nature; but most important to him is the knowledge that the ability to foretell the weather correctly may mean the difference between life and death. To this end, his understanding of the subject must be all-inclusive. He must be able to predict storm, rain, calm, fog, ice, snow, sea conditions, as well as accurately gauge wind shifts and velocity. If he directs his knowledge toward any particular weather aspects, these would include storm, fog, snow, wind shift and calm in about that order. Last, unlike the farmer, his understanding because of his calling must be much less local and may include information pertinent to areas halfway round the world.

Like so many elements of marine life, weather lore at sea is only an adaptation and ramification of land lore, to which has been added a further dimension—the action of the ocean and its inhabitants. Furthermore, the sailor's criteria by which he interprets coming events are far more inclusive than the farmer's.

For the sailor, weather lore comes in two parts. To be able to predict coming events accurately is the first and most important. To be caught unaware by a fog, wind shift, or gale can be both costly and fatal. The second part is the ability to control or order the weather to his particular designs. Many years ago a fisherman was bound home from the Grand Banks with a great haul of fish. He was racing for the market against another schooner when the wind fell flat calm. In desperation the skipper jumped up into the main shrouds and produced a half-dollar. "O God," he said, "just give us a half-dollar's worth of wind," and he threw the coin into the sea. Half an hour later the schooner was laboring under a close-reefed fores'l alone. The old man again jumped into the shrouds and shouted to the heavens. "Christ, ifen I'd knowed ye was sellin' it so cheap I'd only asked for a penny's worth!"[1]

Forecasting may be broken down into the overall forecast, signs that pertain to wide areas and those that are accurate only in a particular locality; and it may also be classified as long-range (varying from a week to a season) and short-range (seventy-two hours or less) predictions. By and large, the more local the forecast and the shorter the duration of the period forecast, the more accurate the prognostication. Most weather-wise sailors can predict an impending wind shift or three-day blow with uncanny accuracy.

Of course the great problem that confronts the mariner in a divination of the future is that the weather patterns in one part of the world often differ from those of another—the signs that point to changes may differ, and signs that indicate one thing in one season may indicate quite different conditions in another. A west wind is a good wind in the United States: it seldom brings rain or gale. But an old song bids the mariner beware "of them cold nor'westers on the Banks of Newfoundland"[2] and some of the wildest weather on the European coast comes from the west. In North America, or at least in New England, a nor'wester may bring heavy snow in the winter, but in summer it usually is a sign of clear bright conditions with mild winds. Finally, we must not forget that storms move clockwise in the northern hemisphere and counterclockwise in the other, and one must take different tactics to elude them.

At this point it is important to remember that most weather changes are brought about by a change in barometric pressure. This is especially true of short-term weather patterns. As a result, an accurate and sensitive barometer is one of the meteorologist's most important instruments. Seamen have long been aware of the importance of a barometer and have used the "glass" to forecast coming events for a long time. It was not necessary for the folk to have a column of mercury or an aneroid barometer to achieve results. They made a satisfactory glass out of two bottles, a cork, some putty and a little water. A wide-necked bottle was partially filled with water, and a cork, through which the "scrig" (neck) of the smaller bottle had been forced, was fitted tightly into the neck. The neck of the smaller bottle protruded an inch or two beneath the surface of the water in the larger one. The whole was then tightly sealed with putty or some other material and the crude instrument gimbaled, if it was going to sea. When the water rose or fell in the smaller bottle, the mariner knew that a weather change was imminent, and when dew formed inside the little bottle he knew rain was expected. Lest he forget the importance of the barometer in predicting weather, the old-timer had a number of simple rhymes attached to the action of the glass.

When the glass falls low,
Prepare for a blow;
When it rises high,
Let your kites fly.[3]

Long foretold, long last,
Short notice, soon past,
Quick rise after low
Sure sign of stronger blow.[4]

It is highly probable that a great many of the signs on which the sailor depended for his predictions were caused by barometric changes, yet it is doubtful if even the most knowledgeable of these weather prophets ever connected them more than superficially in their minds. At best, they would note dew in the glass, rain clouds on the horizon—and be doubly sure it would rain. But then, the highly sophisticated Greeks long believed that mice were generated spontaneously in old rags.

Very often the sailor depends upon his galley to tell him what the weather will do. If the teakettle boils very quickly or "sings" on the stove, he knows he is in for a weather change; if he sees a blue flame on the galley coal fire, he may be sure of impending weather; if the fire sputters, it is "treading snow"; if the smoke falls to the sea or if it rises straight up, the sailor takes due notice for it augurs weather change. One can even predict coming weather by the rate of rise and volume of expansion of bread dough. There can be little doubt that all of the above phenomena are the result of barometric pressure, although even the best sailor will not make the connection.

One area of forecasting that has very little dependence on the barometer is the long-range forecast, and of that we must speak. Long-range forecasts are most often achieved by observing conditions at the time of seasonal change, as on the twenty-first of March, June, September and December. Two of these dates are close to the time of the vernal and autumnal equinoxes, and the other two fall approximately at the solstices.

In New England, the sailor notes intently the direction of the wind on these days, for whatever way the wind blows "when the sun crosses the line, that wind will rule the weather" either for forty days or for the season. Since he knows easterlies bring rain and fog and westerlies clear weather, he invariably prays for a westerly breeze on those days.

Long-range forecasts are also predicated on certain saints' days, on the moon, and quite frequently on the actions of flora and fauna. We have, for example, Groundhog Day, and hard winters are often predicted by the size of muskrat houses, the thickness of the corn husks, the activity of squirrels, the bands on a caterpillar. The migration of birds—especially waterfowl—early or late is also used for a prediction of coming events, as an early winter or a late spring. There is a saying in New England that "a green Christmas means a fat cemetery," and in the West Indies the hurricane season is gauged by the following rhyme:

> June too soon,
> July stand by,
> August look out,
> September remember,
> October all over.[5]

A further word must be said about these forecasts. They tend to have an accuracy that beats the law of averages and makes one wonder about them, until one examines them more carefully. It is normal for weather to have a general seasonal consistency. Along the Atlantic seaboard we expect that winds in the summer will blow from the southwest. Usually the weather develops slightly ahead of the seasonal change, and so when the sailor notes the wind was southwest "when the sun crossed the line" in June, and predicts that it will continue from that quarter for most of the summer, he really is using loaded dice. One also notes that the same thing holds true for saints' days, a considerable number of which fall on ancient pagan holidays. Three such days are Martinmas (November 11), Candlemas Day (February 3), and St. Swithin's Day (July 15). By midsummer and midwinter the weather pattern has been established fairly clearly and we should not be surprised that the adages for Candlemas Day—

> Just so far as the sun shines in,
> Just so far will the snow blow in.

or

> If Candlemas be fair and clear
> There'll be two winters in the year.[6]

—prove correct rather frequently. Neither are we surprised at the efficacy of the rhymes for St. Swithin:

> All the tears St. Swithin can cry
> St. Bartelmy's mantle wipes them dry.[7]
>
> St. Swithin's Day if it dost rain
> For forty days it will remain.
> St. Swithin's Day if it be fair,
> For forty days 'twill rain nae mair.

When we realize this last is a Scottish adage, where it rains so constantly that they have a sardonic proverb,

> The day ye see nae gull,
> There'll be nae rain on Mull

we can understand that the first part of the quatrain above is very likely to be correct.

The moon is one weather prophet that seems to operate differently. Usually it is used (and with some accuracy) to forecast short-term weather, but it is popularly believed to control precipitation for the coming month. There is a popular saying that "the moon and the weather oft change together."[8] To this end the weatherman observes the new moon carefully to note the condition of the horns. If the horns point up or in such a way that water can't run out, some prophets say it is a "dry moon" because it "holds the water"; and when the horns tilt downward, the water will run out, and it is a "wet moon." Other prophets, however, interpret these signs exactly in reverse, thus supporting Josh Billings' famous weather prediction of "perhaps rain, perhaps not." It might be added that this is one of the rare cases of an ambivalent prediction in weather.

If long-range predictors are somewhat sketchy and relatively few in number, short-range forecasters are quite the opposite. Just about everything that flies the air, creeps the ground or swims the sea, dead or alive, animate or inanimate, plays a part in this most highly developed skill, which borders on a science and is indeed, as Alexander Haggerty Krappe once said, "the science of prescientific people."

When reading the weather, the first and most important tools at the sailors' disposal are the elements, and of them all, cloud formations are paramount, as they are to the meteorologist. The folk refer to them as "thunderheads," "mares' tails" and "mackerel skies," while the scientists call them cumulus, cirrus, altocirrus and so on, but to both folk and scientist they mean thunderstorms, wind and rains, and weather. Lest they forget, the folk set up some of their beliefs in various mnemonic devices as:

> Mackerel skies and mares' tails
> Make tall ships carry low sails."[9]

or

> If clouds look as if scratched by a hen
> Get ready to reef your topsails then.[10]

or

> If clouds are gathering thick and fast
> Keep sharp look out for sail and mast.
> But if they slowly onward crawl
> Shoot your lines, nets, and trawl.[11]

There are literally hundreds of weather signs derived from clouds, only a few of which need be mentioned to appreciate the dimension of this aspect of prognosticating. When there are clouds in the east at dawn, wind may be expected and

> When clouds of the morn to the west fly away
> At sunset with a cloud so black
> A westerly wind you shall not lack.[12]

Small puffy clouds, called "oilskin jackets," portend rain,[13] and "mist upon the high hills" is a sign of rain—while clouds evaporating mean no rain will fall.

A second and almost as important method of predicting coming events is by noting changes in atmospheric conditions, particularly when observed in conjunction with celestial bodies. The seaman puts great store on rings around the moon or sun, on the clarity of the stars, on northern lights, mirages, rainbows, double suns and moons, moondogs and sundogs, most of which are thought to presage storms. He is careful to note how the sun and moon rise and set.

> If the sun sets clear as a bell,
> It's going to blow sure as hell.

He places greatest emphasis upon the moon, about which there are literally dozens of rhymes and sayings. A sailor, according to the old ballad, cautioned Sir Patrick Spens:

> I saw the new moon with the auld moon in her arm,
> And if you're going to sea, Captain, I fear we'll come to harm.

—and the skipper of Longfellow's ill-fated "Hesperus" ignored the fact that signs pointed to a hurricane:

> Last night, the moon had a golden ring,
> And to-night no moon we see!

Generally a red moon is said to betoken wind, a pale watery one, rain—and a ring around the moon indicates a storm or snow. The density of the ring foretells the degree of violence, and the number of stars within the ring indicates how many days before the arrival of the storm. The moon in a bank of clouds is said to foretell a tempest, but a full moon will scoff off any kind of weather. That this is not always the case may be seen in a little anecdote from New England.

During the days of the Triangle Trade, a small brig from Maine was bound for the West Indies. On a fine night the captain left the deck in charge of the mate and went below to do some bookkeeping. His final charge to the mate was, "It's a fine night so keep her a-goin'. There won't be no weather on a night like this—the moon will scoff it off."

He had not been below very long before the vessel took a little list and the mate stuck his head in the skylight "Breeze freshenin', Captain. Do you want to shorten?" "Oh no, there's nothin' comin'. Let her go. The moon will scoff it off."

A little while later the vessel laid over sharply, and the mate again approached and remarked it was blowing very hard, and shouldn't he shorten sail? "No, no"; and again he was told, "the moon will scoff it off." The mate said no more but went back to his watch, and the brig drove on.

Shortly before midnight, the old man was rudely interrupted by a terrific crash. The skipper rushed wildly up on deck. "What in hell was that? What's happened?" "Oh, that was just the foremast goin' over the side, Captain. No weather around, though. Guess it must have been the moon that just 'scoffed it off'."[14]

The same general feeling prevails about the sun as about the moon. The larger the ring around the sun, the longer the gale will hold off, and the more distinct the ring, the heavier the gale. Whereas considerable attention is paid to the phases of the moon in predicting weather, great emphasis is placed on the rising and setting of the sun. Perhaps no weather sign is more widely known than the little rhyme:

> Red sky at morning, sailors take warning.
> Red sky at night, sailor's delight.

However, the writer would caution from personal experience that a bloody sunset is not likely to augur well for the mariner.

Sundogs (small rainbowlike patches in the sky), moondogs and double suns and moons are all signs that portend bad weather. These "double" suns and moons are most frequent in high latitudes and most likely to occur when the celestial body is near the horizon.

In most places in the world rainbows are considered to be a sure sign of clearing weather and to augur prosperous times. I was, therefore, somewhat startled to observe a fishing sloop leave Scarborough, Tobago, one pleasant morning and return twenty minutes later. They had seen a rainbow, and in that area the position of the rainbow is important; to weather it is a good omen, to leeward a bad one.

Also in the West Indies is an unusual omen dealing with the sunset. When a green flash is seen as the sun vanishes, local sailors predict rain

Opposite: "What lies over yonder?" H.P.B. and Tommy, Kim Bay, Ireland

for the following day. Moreover, if it is calm at sunset a change is usually predicted.

Before leaving these two objects—sun and moon—we must also note that their size and color are important. A large bright moon usually indicates cold, a large red sun in the morning (especially in a cloudless sky) is said to presage a hot day, while the same thing in the evening augurs either heat or cold on the following day, depending on the season. A dull moon indicates heat.

The moon and the sun are not the only celestial bodies watched by the mariner. He watches his stars with care, and in Ireland if "the stars are too near" we can expect a storm. On the Atlantic coast of North America, sailors expect cold weather when the stars seem near, and foul weather when they are pale and dim. And we must not overlook the northern lights. These are considered both to be weather breeders and to forecast cold. The writer read a journal of two cruises taken by a folklorist in Scotland. In the course of both trips he noted northern lights followed by a gale. The writer also notes in his own log on the coast of Ireland under the date of August 3, 1969, the following: 2300 hours, Wind S.S.W., force 4. Strong display of Northern Lights . . . August 4, 0700, Wind S.W. Gale 8."

The sailor is also very conscious of the side effects of the sun and moon, and he pays attention to moonbeams, sunbeams, and the light upon the water. In the morning "an easterly glin is a sure sign of a wet skin." When the rays of the sun dart through the clouds, the sun is said to be "drawing water" (as is also said of the moon)—and during a storm, if one can find a patch of blue sky variously described as "big enough to make a pair of Dutchman's (kitten, sailor's, or Frenchman's) britches" or "a napkin," the storm is over.

Finally, in the area of atmospheric conditions, we must point out the importance given to the mirage and visibility. When the mariner can see objects at a great distance or when distant objects appear very close, he is invariably suspicious that a storm is pending. These mirages are studied with some care and when he sees a ship, island, or some other object, he generally makes more preparations for a wild night, especially when the island or ship alters shape—i.e., enlarges, grows taller or smaller—or when parts of it vanish.

After observing all these things, the sailor turns to the sea itself and studies it with care. He notes the color: a gray sea with a gray sky bodes ill, while a bright sea indicates fair weather. Perhaps one of the most important indications he has, however, is the ocean swells. These he examines with great care, noting their height, fetch (distance between swells), width and especially the direction in which they move, for these things tell him how far away a storm is and the quarter from which it is likely to come. Of all swells he likes least an oily sea, for that is a weather breeder.

Still another omen of things to come is "fire" in the water (phosphorescence). Sometimes at night in the summer a vessel will have a green wave at her bow and her wake will be visible as a greenish line for a mile or more astern. Sometimes when the phosphorescence is thick even the top of a cockling sea will be full of this luminous fire, and when the sailor sees it he prepares for a blow.

A final sign of bad weather is found in "the singing of the sea." When the night is calm, very often the sailor ashore or near the beach will hear the surf upon a bar, the heavy rumble of stones being drawn down the shingle or the heavy boom of breakers upon cliffs. There may be no other portents of trouble, but when such things occur the man in port is not very keen on going to sea, and those upon the deep either seek haven or make efforts to haul off and get sea room while they can.

If "All signs fail in the time of drought" is a farmer's proverb, the mariner's parallel would be "Anything can happen in 'onsettled' weather." At such times he is extremely careful to examine the wind and rain for immediate results. Just before the hurricane of September 1938 the late Captain Charles Ross, from Halifax, said to the writer, "If the wind backs east one more point we will have a hurricane." This was at eleven o'clock in the morning, and by one P.M. both parts of his statement had come to pass.

The seaman is careful to note whether the wind hauls, backs or veers. When it hauls he is fairly certain of good weather, but when it backs or "goes against the sun" he is leery of a blow. On the other hand, when it veers or "can't make up its mind and blows every whichaway," he anxiously watches to see what will happen, for this bodes a change—usually an unpleasant one.

Once the weather has "settled in," a good weather prophet has a better than fair idea of what to expect. In New England, if the wind comes northeast and it is clear, he is reasonably sure that it will stay there in that condition for three days—called a dry nor'easter; but if it comes in with rain and squalls he knows he is in for a "three-day nor'easter." When it comes from the southeast he expects rain, and from the northwest clear weather or possibly snow in winter.

At this point it is imperative to note the precipitation. According to the old statement, "Open and shet, sure sign of wet." The seaman is particularly anxious about squalls, for these can dismast, capsize or, at the very least, cause damage to spars and rigging. To this end:

> When the rain's before the wind,
> Strike your tops'ls, reef your main.
> When the wind's before the rain,
> Shake 'em out and go again.[15]

To these omens may be added another that, although not as important as the others, still has apparently been successful enough to remain in the seaman's bag of meteorological tricks. This is the element of time.

> Rain before seven,
> Clear before eleven.

> or

> Between the hours of one and two
> Will tell you what the weather'll do.

A final time belief, and perhaps the most tenuous one, is that the days of the week control the weather, at least for the following day, sometimes longer. To most sailors a "civil" Wednesday is a good sign, but whatever the weather on Friday—a notorious day on almost any seafaring man's calendar—Saturday will find it reversed.

> Friday dawns clear as a bell,
> Rain on Saturday sure as hell.

As the moon is thought to control the weather and the tide, the mariner puts considerable store on the tide as a helpful indicator. Not only are extremely high tides thought to precede gales, but the wind's force and duration are closely linked to the state of the tide when the gale strikes. Gales that arrive on a coming tide are usually considered to be more severe than those that come on the ebb. Further, the turning of the tide is watched with great care, for should the breeze continue past slack water, either flood or ebb, it is generally thought that it will continue until the next change or for another six hours. Moreover, the state of the tide is important, for great gales are thought to strike on the "spring tides" (sometimes called "high coast," "full drene" [drain] or "moon" tides). Likewise tides are thought to control rain, but in this respect the reverse seems to be true, for the old adage runs:

> Rain on the flood,
> Only a scud.
> Rain on the ebb,
> Sailors to bed.

This rhyme is typical of how the folk often reason—namely by opposites. If the flood brings in water, then it won't fall from the sky; whereas if the ebb draws the water away, the sky will compensate for the lack.

Whether or not these statements about the tide can be proven correct by "the scientific method" is of little moment. The fact is that a gale that comes with the tide invariably does more damage than one of equal force on the ebb, for the water is deeper along shore and flooding may occur. Tops of breakwaters are closer to sea level and vessels receive less lee from them, and a larger sea can get up along the shore. Moreover, these extreme tides cause rips and tidal eddies not experienced normally and require vessels to pay out more cable—which they may not have—when at anchor.

Here we must expand on the role played by the moon and the tide in the sailor's life, for no two phenomena are more important to him. Said Athneal Ollivierre, head harpooner of the whale fishery in Bequia in the West Indies, "The moon governs everything, the fish, the whale, the crops, the tide—even women. Everything!" The tide, on the other hand, is not only important in weather and ship handling but in fishing, and it is popularly believed by most old salts that it rules birth and death. Thus if an ill man survives the turn of the tide, he'll make it to the next one, and when he eventually comes to die his life will go out with the ebb. In Scotland it is said that boys are born on the flood and girls upon the ebb.[16]

So important is the state of the tide that the sailor employs all his senses to determine what it is; sometimes when far from the sea or when other means fail, he adopts bizarre methods to determine the state of the water. Sometimes the sound on the shore tells him it is high tide, or the burying or exposing of a hundred Half Tide Rock(s) around the Anglo-American world tell him this is part of the tide's progress, while the smell of the clam flats announce low water at distances where neither eyes nor ears avail much. Far from the shore on Newfoundland the mariner can tell the state of the tide by the pupils of a cat's eyes—if vertical and narrow, tide's in; if round or slitted horizontally, tide's out.[17]

We have already spoken fleetingly of sounds, and before leaving this area a further word would be worthwhile. Very often a sailor judges the weight of the wind by the sound it makes.

In sailing ships, for example, a slight breeze sets the reef points to rattling and the halyards set up a chatter against the mast, and the wavelets make little lapping sounds against the hull. To the coaster lying in port waiting for a breeze, this is an alarm clock, and he is up and away. As the breeze freshens it goes from a whine to a shrill whistle and mounts steadily to the terrifying heavy roar of a great gale. The pitch of these sounds as much as the action of the vessel tells the skipper when to put in "for stress of weather," to heave to or to scud before it.

The nose, too, can help in weather detection, and an old salt is said to be able to smell fog, rain, wind and snow. In calm, fluky weather, especially near shore, the knowledgeable shellback can often sniff out a breeze to keep his vessel going. He does this in large measure by sorting out what he smells—dampness from off the sea tells of a sea breeze or a fog, while the aroma of new-mown hay, clam flats, or a pigsty warns him before the first ripple is seen that the breeze will be off the land. This phenomenon was noted by John Winthrop, who wrote after six weeks at sea that at last he "smelled the sweet smell of a garden" as he worked in on the Massachusetts coast; and the author several years ago was saved running past Bermuda on a thick night by the smell of flowers in the murk.

Of all the predictions, those that are by far the best are strictly local in nature. These usually belong to an extremely small area—perhaps only one harbor—and are the result of long years of protracted observations which seemed to witnesses to be accurate. Although they often are the butt of considerable derision by scientific meteorologists, they frequently prove more correct for the area in question than the forecast prepared miles away by scientists mewed up in an office complete with computers and a battery of instruments.

In back of the harbor at Cohassett, Massachusetts, is a salt marsh that empties with considerable force through a reversing fall. Usually the stream coming out is clear, but every so often it empties as a stream of brown suds. These suds sometimes are a couple of feet deep, and they annoy boatmen because they stain whatever they touch. Local knowledge will inform you that these suds usually precede a blow and the depth of the suds is proportionate to the intensity of the storm.

Three thousand miles away another strange phenomenon takes place. At certain times the Moray Firth is visited by the world's largest fish, the great basking shark. These creatures, from time to time, can be seen leaping into the air and falling back into the Firth with a truly alarming splash. They do this apparently to stun herring, which they guzzle voraciously. The peculiar thing about this acrobatic visitation is that, according to the fishermen in the local ports, the sharks do it only before a storm. We observed this phenomenon in 1967 and were blown ashore two days later in the Caledonian Canal.

Sailors in Newfoundland will tell you that lights appear at the entrances to certain harbors before the approach of an easterly gale.[18] On the island of Tobago fishermen are careful to observe the flight of birds at dawn along a certain beach. By the height they are above ground and the distance they are from the water, the men claim they can predict the weather for the rest of the day.[19]

Throughout the British Isles and in many other places in the world, the association of cloud with certain objects is considered a weather-breeder—but not necessarily at that very spot. It is said that clouds over Bell Rock Light (England) bring rain at Arbroath; that clouds on the Orkney Isles presage rain at Cape Wrath, Scotland; and even in far-off Cape Town the seamen say that it is a sign of bad weather when "the tablecloth is spread on Table Mountain."[20] As early as 1638, John Josselyn, the celebrated traveler, noted that when the White Mountains could not be seen from Black Point (now Scarborough, Maine) a storm was in the offing.[21]

I was told by Captain James Buchan, of Frazerburgh, that over on the west coast of Scotland the fishermen believed that when the Coolin Hills on the Isle of Skye or the mountains on the mainland of Scotland could be seen clearly from the Outer Hebrides, or vice versa (a distance of thirty miles) one could expect a storm, and the clearer they loomed the worse the storm. Sometimes they stand out so clearly, he said, that "they seem scarcely a mile away." When we recall the adage about gulls and Mull quoted earlier, we realize that this view would be all the more remarkable (and as a general rule the folk distrust the unusual). I might add that the same thing is said along the Connecticut shore—that "when Long Island comes to Connecticut, expect bad weather."

Off the coast of Ireland lies the island of Inishshark. Here there is a cliff that has an odd-shaped chalk deposit on it. Local fishermen say it looks like a full-rigged ship under sail and that the ship changes with the weather. Sometimes she appears to be standing out to sea, and the natives know the weather will be fair. At other times she heads toward port, and the local people batten down for a gale.

Very often before a storm a peculiar red glow is seen, the natives say, in Mahone Bay off Chester, Nova Scotia. This is popularly believed to be a re-enactment of the burning of the privateer *Teaser* during the war of 1812, and local weather prophets say it is infallible. Usually it appears as a rosy glow in the fog, and old-time fishermen will not go to sea when it burns. Nor is the *Teaser* the only vessel that predicts a storm when it is seen in a special place, but these apparitions will be discussed elsewhere.[22]

Exactly why these strange events come to pass is of little moment to the folk. The result of the action is what interests them, and the writer can only state that he has observed all of the local signs mentioned here, barring one (the Table Mountain saying), and in each case the prophecy has proved accurate.

Next to be mentioned are portents at least partially derivative of man's handiwork. Such small things as smoke attract the mariner's eye both afloat and ashore. Smoke on shore or smoke from a vessel hull down in the offing is observed with care, for it tells both the wind velocity and the direction which might be quite different from the wind in the observer's immediate vicinity. Ashore, smoke rising straight up indicates rain or snow, and smoke lying in the valley without rising or diffusing denotes rain.

At least as early as 1627 mariners observed the effect of atmospheric conditions on their rigging, for John Smith mentions it in *A Sea Grammar* and says it indicates rain when the rigging goes slack. Somewhat more recently mariners have noted that when the telephone wires begin to "talk"—i.e., hum—it is a sign of impending storm.

Far older than telephone wires is the belief in underwater bells in certain places in the sea. Three such places are off the coast of Brittany, off the coast of Cornwall, and in Kingston Harbor, Jamaica. In each case the story concerning these bells is quite similar. The inhabitants of Porto Bello (in Kingston Harbor) were a miserable lot, being composed mostly of buccaneers, whores and slaves. They spent most of their time drinking, wenching or gambling until God gave them a taste of what he gave Sodom and Gomorrah. One day an earthquake and a tidal wave struck the place and it sank into the sea—and along with the town went the church. For many years the place was visible beneath the waves, and to this day mariners say that they can hear the church bell ring before a hurricane.

None of these omens is so much feared or so old as is St. Elmo's fire, which puts sailors into such dismay that they refuse to call it by any of its numerous names, Castor and Pollux or the corposants, but refer to it instead as "the Fire." In all it has over fifty names, including Corbie's Aunt, Davy Jones, and Jack Harry (Sailor Devil). This peculiar object is actually static electricity, engendered at least in part by the laboring of the vessel, and one, two, three and sometimes more of these lights appear in the rigging. (Columbus on his second voyage saw eight, Magellan three, Dampier two.)[23]

These ethereal lights were noticed by mariners at least as long ago as when Orpheus prayed for relief in a storm aboard the *Argo* and two lights hovered over the heads of two oarsmen—Castor and Pollux. Since that time they have appeared constantly in marine literature, and there is scarcely a person who has kept the sea for any length of time who has not seen them. Furthermore, they are a startling sight which is in no wise abated by the conditions under which they occur. It is scarcely surprising that they prognosticate all sorts of things both good and bad, and that countless stories are told about their origin and the happenings following their appearance. These will be considered later.

Despite the fact that there is some disagreement as to how to interpret their appearance, it is generally agreed that one light is a warning of a storm, two lights are a sign that the storm center has passed, and three lights are a sign of a gale of overwhelming proportions. As Longfellow puts it:

> Last night I saw St. Elmo's stars
> With their glimmering lanterns all at play
> On the tops of the masts and the tips of the spars
> And I knew we should have foul weather today."[24]

William Falconer, the seaman poet, who saw the lights, experienced a blow and escaped for a time, only to vanish later in the Madagascar Straits:

> High on the masts, with pale and lurid rays
> Amidst the gloom portentous meteors blaze.[25]

What the lights do is important. If they go up, usually good weather is expected, but if they come down, things are likely to get worse.

> . . . for sailors have a notion that if the corposant rises in the rigging, it is a sign of fair weather, but if it comes lower down there will surely be a storm. It is held a fatal sign to have the pale light thrown in one's face.[26]

Strangely enough, this belief in the Fire seems to be both short- and long-range. According to an old whaleman interviewed in New Bedford, Massachusetts, in 1950:

> I am the only man that was presarved in the barque *Viola*. My father went mate in her and on the way home we had a bad gale. We saw the Fire in the rigging and my father came to me. He said, "If we get out of this I don't want you to go in this vessel again." So when we got to New Bedford I took my pay and I never signed on for the next voyage. My father did because he

was the mate, and she went down that time with all hands except me. I am the only man that was presarved from the barque *Viola*.[27]

So far we have concerned ourselves chiefly with inanimate objects as signs. There is another area—the living things—and the weather-wise consider both flora and fauna to be determinants for future conditions. Just about every kind of animal, insect, and fish is featured somewhere in weather lore, and many of the remarks about them may be pertinent although if one took as his only warning the saying that if a kingfisher drops dead on the ship a storm will come soon after, he might miss forecasting a number of gales.

Operating more or less on the premise that "Nature looks after her own," the mariner puts great store on the actions of animals. By far the largest number of predictions are based on the activities of domestic animals. The sailor predicts rain if a cat washes its face or lies back to the fire; a storm if sparks come out of its coat. If dogs sleep back to the fire, if they turn around many times before lying down, it is thought to be a sign of weather; and if they eat quantities of grass one is reasonably sure of rain at least and perhaps a storm. If a pig carries straw in its mouth, a storm is imminent. The direction cattle and horses move when feeding indicates the direction of the wind. Cattle and sheep lying down is a sign of weather, and sheep feeding on a hill presage fine times. If a rooster crows in the night, it means weather is coming.

> If the cock crows on the fence,
> Rain will go hence.
> If he crows on the ground,
> The rain will come down.

If cattle or chickens eat in the rain, it will be a long storm, but if they seek shelter it will soon pass. According to an old Scots quatrain,

> When you hear the burlie cry
> Let you the boatie lie.
> Two ebbs and a flude
> Be the weather ere so quele.[28]

The actions of wild birds are very important to the weather prophet. The flight of swallows over water predict rain; gulls and seafowl flying inland, or curlews calling, are an indication of severe gales; and the absence of birds around a ship is a sign of trouble in the offing. When sea birds are seen sitting on the shore, it is said to be a sure sign of storm. On the other hand, shore birds lighting on a ship are thought to bode no good.

Going down the list a little way, we come to amphibians and reptiles. We know that tree toads are "singing for rain," that bullfrogs "croak for water," and that salamanders and lizards predict weather.

If one meets a snail in Scotland he says:

> Snailie, snailie, shoot out your horn,
> Tell us the weather tomorrow morn.

To most Anglo-Americans the spider, alive or dead, is a strong weather prognosticator. If the spider "runs extra lines to his web" a gale is at hand. If his web is covered with dew, fine weather—if dry, look out. If you kill an ordinary spider, it will rain, but if you mash a daddy longlegs and observe him carefully, he will point his leg in the direction of the coming storm with his final spasm. Moths around a lamp, swarms of insects, an abundance of flies are all barometers of things to come. Even the chirruping of crickets, grasshoppers, locusts and katydids foretells weather and temperature.

Plant life is observed with care. When the poplar trees' leaves turn upwards it is a sign of rain, and when leaves droop, it indicates warm weather. Dew on the grass indicates fair weather, the action of dandelion seeds indicates wind, and the pimpernel is thought to be so accurate a prognosticator of wet that it is called Poor Man's Weathervane.[29]

So far most of the signs that predict change have been available to the mariner in profusion only when ashore. At sea he employs all of these he can and replaces much land material by closely observing the sea and its denizens. To this end he is careful to watch the actions of fish, porpoises, seals and whales, weeds in the water and anything else he can find.

One weather-breeder already alluded to is the actions of fish and, in conjunction with fish, the actions of gulls. Great shoals of bait offshore, birds working and schools of fish leaping about are generally taken as a sign of good weather. On the other hand, when smaller fish like the herring appear inshore, the sailor mistrusts the elements. In general, fish feeding on the surface is a good sign, while feeding deep or not at all is a bad one.

Nothing so pleases the sailor as the sight of porpoises playing in the sea. When they are close inshore it is a sign of storm; when they are offshore, good weather. When they play around a ship it is thought to be a sign of good weather, especially when they play around the bow. But if they are seen flocking toward the vessel from all directions, a storm is presumed to be in the vicinity. At such times they are observed with great care, for it is believed that they always go off in the direction from which the wind will come. What is true of the porpoises is equally true of the dolphins, and knowledge about these deep-water creatures is especially comforting for, contrary to popular belief, there are very few fish in the sea beyond the limits of the continental shelves.

To this long list must be added people and their use as barometers. This takes several forms, the first of which could best be described as diagnosis by infirmities. The expression "I feel a storm in my bones" is fairly accurate. Old sailors say that their rheumatism or arthritis is painful before bad weather, that their joints are stiff or that an old injury pains them. For some reason, old wounds seem to be particularly sensitive to this kind of thing. Many years ago an old fisherman told me he could never sit down before a storm. Further questioning revealed that he was a Civil War veteran and he had been shot by a sniper "right next to the tech hole." Whether or not this was a blessing or a curse could be open to discussion, but at least he was consulted by his neighbors as if he were an aneroid barometer.

Closely allied to these symptoms is the intuitive feeling for weather often experienced by seamen. This is probably based on real but subliminal responses to ingrained weather knowledge. Such intuitive diagnosis is usually expressed by the prophet with "I don't like the feel of the weather," "I've got a hunch we're in for something." It is rare for a sailor to go against a hunch, and disregard for the old salt with a reputation for this kind of prophesying is not necessarily an indication of intellectual acumen.

Sometimes these intuitive feelings are given a kind of rational framework, which the person to whom the experience occurred does not recognize himself. Such a story was told me by a man from St. Margaret's Bay, Nova Scotia—Captain Seymour Harnish, who fished in a little vessel called the *Caroline*.

Captain Harnish always went alone—except for a little dog—and he followed the seasons from Nova Scotia to Virginia and back, fishing the various banks and ledges as he went. One night he was lying on Georges Bank off the Massachusetts coast. The water on Georges is shallow, and he was at anchor one pleasant evening in company with a number of other vessels both great and small. About two o'clock in the morning he awoke and went on deck. Nothing seemed unusual in any way, but something made him glance toward the bow. As he did so, a dripping sailor clad in boots and oilskins climbed aboard and came aft. The man said nothing, but when he reached Captain Harnish he looked at him earnestly, shook him by the hand, walked aft and vanished over the stern. The fact that he was better than ninety miles from land, coupled with the fact that the visitor seemed to have a greenish cast to his skin, gave the skipper a fright. He grabbed an axe, rushed forward, cut his cable, started his engines and headed for Gloucester Harbor. Just as he rounded Eastern Point, the gale struck him with a vengeance. Had he been on Georges when it hit instead of well into Gloucester Harbor, he would undoubtedly have been lost—as were several of his companion vessels that he left anchored there.[30]

The story sounds fantastic, but it can be explained as an intuitive reaction. Harnish had followed the sea all his life. He knew the signs and portents. He also knew and believed in the idea that the drowned sometimes befriended the living at sea. While he slept the weather had changed imperceptibly. Perhaps the wind hauled, the motion of the vessel changed, the humidity increased. No one thing was sufficiently pronounced to be noted in itself, but the cumulative effect gave Seymour a dream so vivid that when he awoke he found himself on deck. The rest of the tale needs no explanation.

In every community, aboard every ship, there is usually someone who is known as a weather prophet. To him the rest of the people defer in all meteorological matters. At the same time there are people who can raise a storm. Finns are believed to have this ability, and they share it with witches, who also raise gales, sink ships and generally make life unpleasant for seafaring folk. This is still a common belief in the remoter sections of Scotland, Ireland and the New World. Today such people are generally ostracized by their neighbors, but as late as the eighteenth century they were tried in courts of law. Many methods were employed by hags and warlocks, but one that seemed to have been most successful as well as gruesome was used in Scotland, where a witch raised a fatal tempest by tying bits of flesh from a corpse onto a black cat and throwing it into the sea, muttering incantations the while. Fortunately we have a description of this event preserved from the trial records of the day.

While James I of England (VI of Scotland) was crossing the North Sea, a coven of witches at Leith led by one Agnes Sampson responded to a letter that they should raise a storm "universal through the sea." They

> . . . baptized a cat in the Websters house. . . . First two of them held a finger in the one side of the chimney crook, and another held another finger in the other side, the two webs of the fingers meeting together; then they put the cat thrice through the links of the crook and passed it thrice under the chimney. Thereafter at Beige's Todd's house, they knit to the four

feet of the cat four joints of men; which being done Jonet Campbell fetched it to Leith; and about midnight, she and the two Linkops and the two wives called Stobbeis, came to the pier-head, and saying these words, "See that there be no decict among us"; and they cast the cat into the sea as far as they might, which swam over and came again; and they that were in the Pans cast in another cat at XI hours. After when by their sorcery and enchantment, the boat perished between Leith and Kinghorn.[31]

Sometimes these witches could be persuaded to do well instead of ill. In this regard it was popularly believed in Scotland that the Spanish Armada met defeat through the efforts of witches on the island of Mull, who brought about the storms that scuttled and drove so many of Philip's ships to wrack and ruin along the coasts from Norway to Spain. It was accomplished in the following manner, according to the tale still believed today:

In former times there were many witches in Scotland, but the ones on Mull were the strongest. The greatest of all was Cailleach Bheu in the Ross of Mull. After living thousands of years, she died on the banks of Loch Bu when she heard a dog bark. It seems that in order to keep alive she had to wash every hundred years in the Loch before the sound of a living creature was heard. This she did until she reached the fatal day when she heard the dog.

The second most powerful witch was the Doiteag Mhuileach, who lived on Ben More toward the end of the sixteenth century. Now the daughter of the king of Spain dreamed of a handsome prince in Scotland, and she sailed to Mull to find him, and dropped anchor in Tobermory Harbor. Here she saw the man in her dream, Lachlan Mor Maclean, who was so big he measured ten inches from ear to chin. The princess fell in love with him, but Lachlan's wife became jealous and called on a man named Pennygown to blow up the ship. He did so, and the explosion was so great it blew the cook through a rock at Strongarbh which is still known as the Cook's Cave. The girl fell into the loch and was eventually buried at Kiel (across the sound).

When the news reached Spain, another vessel was sent out to cut the right breast off every woman in Mull. When the Lady of Duart (Lady Maclean) heard this, she sent for the Doiteag Mhuileach, who destroyed the vessel by sending cats on board. The captain had the Black Art himself and could fight against eight or nine cats, but the Doiteag sent eighteen cats and the ship went down.

At the same time she destroyed the Armada by calling together all the witches in the islands for help. They arrived and spent the entire night raising and lowering a great quern to the rooftree. As a result, a terrible gale, accompanied by gulls, hoodie crows and black cats fell upon the entire Armada in the narrow seas and drove it to ruin. So great was the gale that it blew down the Doiteag's house, but she was happy because the vessels had gone down.[32]

Of course these three witches were not the only ones capable of kicking up a fuss. From Scotland to New England to the West Indies, witches have ever been the nemesis of sailors. They have been known to stop ships, turn the wind and raise general havoc. This very often was done, as we have seen, by using cats as familiars. I have already mentioned how it was popularly believed that cats carried fire in their tails, and we have seen what happened to the Armada. To raise a storm or to divert the winds, witches and warlocks often were believed to achieve their end by inflicting great physical discomfort upon cats, crows and other animals. One device was to take a live cat and shove a gland of iron through it, being careful not to strike a vital organ. The creature was then placed over a bed of coals and slowly revolved on the spit until quite cooked. While this was going on the witch continued to utter the directions she wished followed. Meanwhile the impaled cat would roar and howl, and it was believed that other cats hearing the commotion would come to see what the trouble was. When they saw what was happening to their comrade, they would fly to do the witch's bidding lest the same thing happen to themselves, thereby bringing on a storm or altering the wind or whatever.

At the present time there is on the island of Mull a ruined church with an attendant graveyard, in which lie two graves with effigies of the dead man and woman carved on the gravestone. It is said that a man named Maclean and his wife were torturing cats there and such a storm came up that the roof blew off the church. Moreover, every time a new roof was put on it was immediately blown off until the church was abandoned.[33]

Very often in order to achieve their ends witches were believed capable of turning themselves into animals—hares, whales, gulls, cormorants, cats, rats or sheep—and performing their offices while in these disguises.[34]

Although the following belief—which was popular until recent times— could not be called witchcraft exactly, it certainly borders on it. When a vessel had been overlong at sea or the neighbors had special reason for communicating with it, a very strong young girl was induced to fall into a deep sleep. While sleeping, her spirit would away to the vessel and return with the desired information. However, it was thought a dangerous practice, for should the wind change before the job had been completed the girl would go mad.

Today the belief in witchcraft is still alive in Scotland. I was told about a woman in a seaport town who was thought to be so powerful that fishermen would not go near her lest she do them mischief while at sea. However, the popularity has waned somewhat, probably in part because a tailor over a century ago sorely depleted their ranks. He was on the island of Lewis (a great haven for hags), where he discovered a group of them flying off to sea to fish, leaving one member ashore holding a red thread to haul them back. The tailor tactfully persuaded them to let him hold the line so all could go afishing. He also persuaded his wife to go with them, and when they were well out to sea he snipped the thread, thereby ridding the world of eighteen witches and one scold.[35]

While witchcraft was also popularly believed in the United States to be a reasonable way whereby vessels could be stopped, sailors discomfited, storms raised, and in some instances pleasant breezes encountered, the happenings documented here never held a candle to the antics performed abroad.

In New Hampshire in the eighteenth century lived Aunt Patty, whose fame George Lyman Kittredge had heard about orally. Three "big boys" had been teasing her, and she became irate and waited until they got into a boat to cross the Squamscot River. She filled a pail with water and slopped some out three times and then capsized it, saying, "There you go, you dogs." Before the lads could reach the other side, a squall struck and all hands drowned. "Tain't safe to hector a witch no way."[36]

This belief in witches being able to raise storms—and a good deal of attendant weather lore—has a rather reasonable explanation. For centuries it was popularly believed—and is still believed to a considerable measure by the folk, along with other more "sophisticated" people—that the world was ruled by two powers, God and Satan. Most of the good was ordered by God and most of the bad by Satan, although for various reasons each occasionally trespassed in the other's vinyard. This belief was given clear expression by one Reginald Scot, who said ". . . neither haile nor snowe, thunder nor lightning, raine nor tempestous winds come from the heavens at the commandment of God: but are raised by the cunning and power of witches and conjurers; insomuch as a clap of thunder or a gale of wind is no sooner heard, but either they run to ring bels, or crie out lo burne witches."[37]

In a sense the belief is a rational one. Kittredge, in *Witchcraft in Old and New England,* notes occasions when a church was struck by lightning and damaged or destroyed. Sometimes the necks of the faithful would be wrung or those at prayer burned up. Invariably the sky was dark and the wind was howling, and after the catastrophe there was the strange stink of sulphur and ozone in the air. Who but Lucifer smells like this, and would devastate God's house?

Before closing off these people, one must add an interesting belief most prevalent in Scotland but extending into Ireland as well. This is "the first fitte." There seem to be several meanings attached to this phrase, but, according to one informant, the first person a seaman met in the morning on his way to the ship would, by this circumstance, be given the gift of prophecy and could forecast the weather. Another belief was that the person himself predicted the weather. An "ill fitte man" was a dark-haired man, and upon seeing him one knew that he was in for trouble; while a fair man, if he was first seen in the morning, would augur fine weather. A third definition was that one knew the shape of the whole year by the first fitte of the New Year. If the person was fair, a good year—if he was dark, a bad one.[38]

Not only was weather predictable, but the folk believed that it could be controlled and that the breeze could be induced to blow, the storm made to abate, and the billows reduced by a number of methods. In this regard I have already mentioned buying the wind with a coin, as well as the power of Finns and witches. There were other methods, one or two of which are worth mentioning.

Most sailors carry knives. In Ireland and Scotland they have black handles, and formerly they were usually sheath knives. They contained cold iron and made, with the guard, the shape of the crucifix. Since the cross and cold iron were thought to be controlling forces over the other world, we can readily see they were not kept merely for gutting fish and cutting lines but for controlling the other world as well.

Should the weather fall calm, two ways of many to raise a breeze were either to "scratch the mast and whistle" or to "stick the knife into the mast and whistle." So great was the power of whistling believed to be that it was forbidden on board ship except in times of flat calm. In fact, there is a saying in Newfoundland about whistling—"Whistle to your plough boys, sing to your ship."[39]

When the weather became too severe or the sea too high, it was long thought beneficial to make the sign of the cross with a knife, say a prayer and throw the knife overboard. Such activity would reduce the wind and calm the sea. If one were beset by a waterspout he would shoot at it to frighten it away, but if he had no gun he would throw his black-handled knife at it.

In the West Indies there is another way to dispel a storm—or at least divert it. According to Captain Paul Mitchell, of Harvey Vale, Carriacou, if you are caught in a severe gale you (if you are the skipper) should face the wind, tear off the smelliest portion of your clothing (usually an undershirt), make it into a ball and heave it far to leeward as you face the elements. When this is done the storm will abate. The idea behind this of course is that storm is brought about by a soul-hungry demon who traces his victim by smell. By throwing the shirt to leeward, the fiend smells it and rushes away after it, leaving the mariner to make the rest of his trip in peace and quiet.

It must also be pointed out that the weather prophet seldom bases his predictions on one sign. He notices that the sea is dirty and full of weed, a sign of a storm; then he finds that the gulls have flown inland; he sees ducks and geese oiling themselves (a sign of rain). He sees the red sunset and a watery moon with the scud flying past, and he puts them all together and concludes he is in for a bad blow.

If the barometer is a prognosticator of change, it may be possible that nature as well as man takes note of it. If the day is hot and sultry and a dog is thirsty, he may eat grass to quench his thirst. The writer has noticed that it is almost impossible for him to stay awake before a thunderstorm, and there is no reason why barometric pressure plus humidity may not affect plants and animals. That crickets chirp at different rates at different temperatures has been known long enough to entomologists for them to amaze their students by counting the chirps, applying a formula, and coming up with the degrees centigrade for the day.

It remains only to attempt some evaluation of this material, almost all of which the scientist has been at some pains to disprove. The first point to be made is that the folk seldom stick with things that do not "work." Of course, the idea of "working" may to them include personal solace, whereas to the sophisticated person it requires pragmatic results. Nevertheless, if the weather omen does not produce at least half of the time, in all likelihood they would discard it.

Furthermore, many of these beliefs are ancient. Not only are they to be found in treatises written as early as the Middle Ages and before, but the folk have found many of them sufficiently efficacious to couch them in rhyme form that they may be more easily committed to memory; and it might be pointed out that the folk seldom do anything simply for amusement. One could argue, of course, that a rhyme like "Snailie, snailie shoot out your horn" serves as a charm as well as mnemonic device, but this is more an exception than a rule.

In a science-oriented age the mariner has gradually been taught to disregard and then forget weather signs and to ignore the local weather prophet and rely more and more heavily upon meteorological material prepared for him at a distant spot and covering a wide geographical area, by a scientist who is often indifferent to the results of his findings so long as he is right half the time. If he supplements this material at all, it is by glancing at a barometer that is infrequently set. If any part of the forecast proves correct in the area under consideration, the meteorologist considers that he has given a good prediction. Local disturbances, though they may endanger or overwhelm a small vessel, are of little moment. Even if the prediction is wrong for the whole area, it is of little import, for in the long run the forecasts are probably more accurate than not. Yet one gale, one fog, even one squall is sufficient to undo a ship and all her crew.

Most important is the fact, as Captain Buchan pointed out, that the mariner becomes dependent upon the radio. If the wireless breaks down, in all probability he cannot fix it and he no longer has any knowledge to fall back on. He has lost an instrument as important to his well-being as his compass. I speak with some feeling on this subject, for I can recall on more than one occasion that, were it not for "local knowledge" as opposed to "meteorological science," this chapter might never have been written.

Where the seals sang, Fidra Island, Firth of Forth

CHAPTER V

NAVIGATION

Nothe-nothe-east and South Sou'west
From Round Hill Island to Cape Bonavist
And if the course is still steered true
Twill take you South to Baccalieu.

— Folklore and Language Archives,
Memorial University of Newfoundland
(collected by Marcus Hopkins)

NAVIGATION is defined as the science or art of conducting ships from one place to another. More generally, it is the ability of the master to complete a voyage successfully bringing home ship, crew and cargo as nearly intact as possible. It is this broader aspect of navigation that I will discuss.

To be able to position himself accurately at sea, the mariner requires certain tools. He must have a compass, a chart, a means for measuring distance, a device for plumbing the depth of water, an instrument for taking the altitude of heavenly bodies and some means of determining time. Finally, it is helpful if he knows where he is going.

Until well into the Middle Ages almost all of these things were denied the sailor, and even today there is a great deal to be desired in chart making. Yet without any of these devices early mariners made remarkable voyages. The Phoenicians circumnavigated Africa, and seamen from ancient Carthage reached the shores of the British Isles, where they loaded tin for the people in the Mediterranean. The Norse in their long ships penetrated to the Black Sea, certainly sailed as far west as Newfoundland and Hudson Bay and possibly reached Central America, while St. Brendan may indeed have rowed his skin curragh to the Azores, Madeira, the Canary and Cape Verde islands and back. Prince Henry's men talked of the frozen seas to the south.

The problems confronting these early navigators are difficult for us to comprehend. How does one prepare for a voyage of unknown duration to an unknown place? How much water, how much food do you take? What kind? How do you cook? Where do you sleep? What does the seaman wear? What do you take for repairs? When do you terminate your passage? How do you get home? It was one thing for Columbus to trundle before the trades for three thousand miles, but how could he ever hope to fight his way back against them?

Even more important are some questions that are seldom asked. How does the master control the crew, prevent mutiny, arrest personal quarrels, maintain discipline and at least the semblance of a happy ship? Also, what are his personal feelings as he wallows across an ocean infested with monsters, floating islands and demons, with the fear of tumbling over the edge of the world in the middle of the night or being consumed by the sun as it returns to its nightly home in the sea? What is his reaction to a landfall, an unusual bird, a bit of strange weed or flotsam? We know, for example, that the Spanish feared the island of Madeira because it was covered with cloud, that the English thought Bermuda was an enchanted and foul land inhabited by witches.[1] Last but not least, the ancient mariner lived in an age when life was valued differently and time had little meaning. When he went to sea no one noticed very much, and if he failed to return it was doubtful that a search would be instituted; or, if it were, it might prove to be two years too late.

One cannot help but wonder, too, how vessels navigated at night in the early days. A compass is of little use if you cannot see it, and if a vessel came suddenly on land or on a reef with no warning during the hours of darkness, she would have little chance of escaping wreck. The answer is that vessels did not travel much by night until they were able to fashion a binnacle light out of a cow's horn and a candle. Instead, they "lay ahull" (simply took in their sails and drifted) until first light.

Today the modern liner, tanker or yacht has few of these problems, but there are areas where some of them still exist. In Nigeria the native must learn "to read and hear the water" before he can go to sea. In the Canary Islands I was told that boats regularly passed between those islands and Africa—a distance of several hundred miles—without even a compass. The same is true in the West Indies, where small vessels sail great distances in any direction without benefit of compass, chart, log or sometimes even lead, relying strictly on the shape of the sea, clouds, trade winds and stars to guide them for days at a time.

But the West Indian is not the only sailor who ignores compass and chart. Many of the old-time fishermen, bargemen and traders along the American and British coasts use a compass sparingly if at all and never look at a chart or have the faintest idea of navigation. Captain Bob Roberts explained a popular view of charts to me one night in Pin Mill, England. "If you are looking at a chart you are not looking at what you should be doing. You don't need a chart unless you don't know where you are. If you don't know where you are you have no business being out there."

Actually, although the modern navigator depends heavily on the chart, one wonders at its necessity when one realizes that Captain Cook had twelve charts (seamen never use maps) to circumnavigate the world in an old coal carrier, and hundreds of explorers before him had no charts at all —or charts so inaccurate as to be a hazard rather than a help. A mild disdain is expressed among the "longshore fraternity," on both sides of the Atlantic for the man who uses a chart, and similar stories spring up about their use.

Captain Pat Ohrin was known years ago as a hard-driving skipper and a terrible fish-killer, and many stories are still told about him. Once when he had returned to Gloucester with a tremendous cargo of fish from the Grand Banks a reporter asked him, "Did you have a hard trip, Captain Ohrin?" "No, no, grand trip, no trouble. Only lost one dory and two Portygees. No trouble at all." At any rate, the captain was so successful that the city of Gloucester gave him a testimonial dinner and presented him with a large-scale chart of Georges Bank, one of his favorite fishing grounds. The skipper was duly grateful; he rolled the chart up and stuck it into a convenient place in the overhead of his cabin where it sat for several years, its chief use being as a home for countless flies. After a particularly difficult trip when the wind had been fluky and the fog persistent, Captain Ohrin began to doubt his position and one of his crew recalled the testimonial chart. Pat went below and unrolled it. The entire chart was covered with fly specks. "My, my" said the old man, "I never knowed they was so many rocks on Georges."[2]

A similar tale is told about the Pentland Firth in Scotland. It is said that a British admiral took aboard a local pilot to run through that tide-tortured bit of water and insisted the pilot use a chart. The pilot took one look and shook his head. "My, my," he said, "If I had known there were so many wrecks in here I'd never have come."[3]

Without the exact time it was impossible to determine accurately either distance or longitude, but latitude could be found with ease. Hence the typical route of a vessel bound across the Atlantic was to sail along shore until the desired latitude was reached and then head for the other shore. When opportunity presented, the captain observed his latitude and altered course either north or south. "Take her south 'till the butter melts and head east," was a popular expression among transatlantic mariners in those days.[4]

When the navigator reckoned he was approaching land he would stop during the night and either heave to or lie ahull. Every day he would take soundings, sometimes using as much as a thousand fathoms of line. Eventually he would find bottom and know he was on the continental shelf. Cautiously he would sail ahead until the hundred fathom curve was reached, and then he would proceed only during daylight, often with a boat ahead taking soundings as the water shoaled.

Since it is difficult to measure a long line, the lead line is marked in such a way that it can be read in the day or at night. Attached to the line at the two-fathom mark is a piece of leather with two tails, at three fathoms a piece of leather with three tails, at five a white linen rag, at seven a red woolen rag, at ten a leather with a hole in it and at twenty a piece of cord with two knots.[5] (In the West Indies, where the lead is still essential to navigation, this practice is altered somewhat. At a fathom and a half is a piece of white cloth, at three a leather with three tails, at five one strip of leather and at ten a bit of red cloth.)

As he came in over "the edge" (the hundred-fathom curve) the skipper would be careful to "arm" the lead, i.e., put tallow or butter in the hole in the end. In this way he could pick up bottom samples—bits of shell, mud, sand, weed or whatever lay on the bottom. As time went on the skillful navigator learned to read the bottom with phenomenal accuracy, not only by sight but by smell and taste as well. In time, the bottom became so well known that merely by sampling the lead a man would know, not simply that he was north or south of Cape Cod, but about ten miles east of Boston harbor.

A typical coasting passage in a modern schooner was described by Captain Louis Ollivierre of Bequia, West Indies.

> When we take soundin', suppose we leave here in the *Earl Tate* on dead reckoning on the course we steer from Mustique on Balliceaux. We generally steers southeast by east from Balliceaux for Guyana on dead reckoning. After forty-eight hours we cross the latitude of Tobago. We generally heave to [there] and take the sounding of the bottom to get the depth of water that we are in and then they get under the lead whether it's dark shell, sand and shell, black sand, or sand and mud and then they goes to the chart

to find the position in the chart and then you take your bearings from there. The course, shape the course from that back to the compass on the chart. And then you get your bearings from there. Change your course then from there to the beacon. Then we pull off. All dead reckoning. Now if you are on the westward of the beacon you get always soft mud, dark soft mud. Direct on the beacon you get sand and shell, dark sand and shell and you generally get ten fathoms, ten fathoms. You go in and you get five fathoms. After you get in five fathoms you are direct on the line of the river. If you don't see the beacon at that time, well you will still be in trace of it and every half-hour you check on your depth until the beacon is in sight. The beacon is forty miles out from Georgetown in Guyana."[6]

In large craft the lead is rarely if ever used nowadays, but it is still very popular among coasters and fishermen, especially among the latter, who know by the bottom exactly what kind of fish to expect. Again, this skill has incurred some awe and a good deal of humor amongst the seafaring fraternity. Typical is a series of stories from Chesapeake Bay that are repeated in both Canada and the British Isles. One tale takes the following form.

There once was an old man who had been an oyster fisherman on the Bay all his life. It was said that he could tell exactly where he was at any time, day or night, fog, rain or snow by tasting (or smelling) the lead. In the middle of the night he would order the lead out and after it came aboard he would taste it. "Two miles off Corn River." "Coming up to the Choptank." "Coming in to Gibson Island." And so on. One foggy day the crew decided to fool him. When he wasn't looking, they took some hen manure out of a crate of chickens sent to market by Mrs. Murphy of Smith's Island and stuck it in the tallow. After a time the captain ordered a sounding and then demanded the lead. First he looked at it, then he smelled and finally tasted it. He became very excited and shouted, "Luff up, boys, luff up! Something's terrible wrong! Accordin' to the lead, we're in the middle of Mrs. Murphy's hen yard on Smith Island!"[7]

Most captains in the coasting and fishing trades were their own navigators. Their trips were short and their need to take sights infrequent. As a result, their estimates of where they were were usually very rough, and the taking of a sight was an unusual and entertaining diversion for the crew. One story from Lunenburg, Nova Scotia, that is told in both the United States and the Old World, with appropriate adjustments to fit the particular locality, is as follows:

An old-time skipper had been on the Grand Banks for over a month, and the entire time it was thick o' fog and the wind blew every which way.

When it came time to head for home, the old man was in considerable doubt as to his position and the crew, as a result, were somewhat nervous. To calm things down, the skipper got out the sextant and with a great flourish took a sight when the reluctant sun finally appeared through the fog. The crew watched in awe and stood around the break in the poop waiting anxiously for the result. After about two hours the skipper reappeared and grimly told his crew, "Keep a good watch, byes. According to my calculations we're about 120 miles into the woods already."[8]

Another person who is often the subject of humorous anecdotes is the man called pilot. This individual usually has acquired a certain familiarity with a small area of the coast, and his presence is required by most large vessels entering a port in that area. The position is, or was, jealously guarded and the office of pilot was handed down from father to son.

The method employed to obtain a pilot was as follows. A vessel would appear in the offing flying code flag "P," and a small vessel with a pilot aboard, usually a schooner, waiting hove to for such a contingency, would come close, lower a small boat and transfer the pilot, who would clamber up a rope ladder called "monkey" or "Jacob's ladder" and board the ship. An alternative method was to signal a lookout station ashore and the pilot would be brought out aboard a surfboat.

Once aboard, the pilot took complete command of the vessel, but interestingly enough, if he ran the ship aground it was the captain and not the pilot who bore the burden of responsibility. The worst that could happen to the pilot would be a dent in his reputation.

For his service the pilot usually charged either by the tonnage or the length of the vessel, and the business in a busy harbor was extremely lucrative.

According to Marion Brewington, the first pilot in America was a man named Clark and he was connected with the Jamestown colony in Virginia. One day a Spanish vessel appeared in Chesapeake Bay and the colonists ordered her to leave or they would fire on her. The Spanish captain replied that he was unable to go out without a pilot, for he had blundered into the bay and was afraid he'd be wrecked on the shoals. Pilot Clark was set aboard with the promise that he would be sent back as soon as the vessel cleared the bay, but once out of danger the Spaniard made all haste back to Spain, where the pilot was closely questioned for the next few years. When at last his brains had been picked clean he was released and made the best of his way back to England, where he inquired for a ship bound for North America. The one he found was called the *Mayflower*, and he signed on as mate. The services he rendered the Pilgrims were so greatly appreciated that they gave him an island in Plymouth Bay off Duxbury which bears his name to this day. Clark, however, preferred Virginia and made his way back there and continued his profession.[9]

As one probably has noticed, most navigation depends on pilotage rather than celestial navigation. This is to be expected, since even today far more vessels operate along the coasts or at most a few hundred miles offshore than go transoceanic. Further, the man who navigates by the sun and stars must have some knowledge of trigonometry and general mathematics, excelling what one would expect in a member of the folk.

Although the coastwide navigator does not ordinarily use charts, he has a number of interesting and useful devices to help him. We have already mentioned the weather glass in the previous chapter. A couple of further examples will suffice to give an idea of some of the popular methods. Rather than use parallel rules to establish their course by "walking" the rulers to the compass rose, New England and maritime fishermen sawed the handle off a broom or swab. They would then lay the round bit of wood on the chart, position it on two points and roll it over to the compass rose. In order to tell speed more accurately (seamen can usually judge within a knot the speed of the vessel by her wake and the sound she makes) both English and American seaman had recourse to a "dutch log." One man would throw a chip or small block of wood over the bow and a man at the stern would either time it with a watch or count until it passed the stern. If, for example, the chip took ten seconds to pass the length of a hundred-foot vessel, it was an easy chore to figure out how many knots the ship was making.

Of course, to be able to tell how fast the vessel is going depends upon some knowledge of time. Clocks and the sea have never been very good bedfellows, and the search for a way to develop really accurate time readings—good enough to obtain longitude—has gone on for a long time. One crude method was using an hourglass, which someone turned over every time it ran out, if he remembered it. The untutored seaman, however, has an uncanny ability to tell time and many interesting ways to figure it out.

In Tobago an informant told me that at sea one could tell time by stars. He said that at home there were four stars that rose after midnight. Depending on how far offshore he wished to go, he sailed with "the rising of the first star," or the second and so on.

While fishing with whalers in Bequia, I noticed that the whalemen arrived at the boats every morning at 6:15; they started for home every afternoon between 2:15 and 2:20 without a watch amongst them. When they "went on a whale" and the whale sounded, they knew she should come up in eighteen minutes. Every so often someone would say, "She comin' now" or "Time she breach." If she didn't "come" it was the whale's fault. The time had been kept to within seconds without a watch.

To tell short spaces of time the seaman had clever little devices. For example, it was important that a naval salute be spaced at five-second intervals. The gunner's mate would march up and down the deck saying, "If I wasn't a gunner, I wouldn't be here! Number One, fire!" Another crude device for second-counting was "One alligator, two alligator" and so on.[10]

Many times fishing vessels offshore would want to stay on the ground all night over a spot where the fishing was good. If they couldn't anchor, they would jog back and forth between bearings. Sometimes when they couldn't see the shore and the weather was thick and they had no compass, they would tow a block of wood behind to make sure they steered a straight course, and often devised clever ways of estimating the proper length of time. In Labrador a fisherman had a slow leak in the vessel. He placed a tin can under it, and every time the can filled up he tacked the vessel and emptied the can.[11]

Before the advent of radar, a vessel navigating in restricted waters had great recourse to its whistle in fog or snow. This was particularly true in areas where there were cliffs. It was said that a good navigator in Puget Sound could tell exactly where he was in thick weather by blowing his whistle and waiting for the echo. The time it took for the echo to come back told him how far offshore he was, and the timbre of the echo told him which particular bluff or cliff he was passing.

Even today the mariner in the remoter parts of the Anglo-Saxon world depends to a very large extent upon local knowledge to find his way. In Ireland the braying of a donkey serves the Irish fisherman as well as a foghorn. The condition of the tide and the sea tells an experienced seaman in a certain area exactly where he is. He knows that certain birds roost on certain rocks and he is careful to note their passage. In the tropics, a sailor watches the clouds, and by reading their formations carefully he can detect islands by the shape of the clouds. The folk navigator also uses his nose and often "smells out" the land.

Another aid to the navigator, especially in the tropics, is the color of the water. In the West Indies the skillful seaman can tell within a very small margin the depth of water by its color. Basically, the bluer the water becomes the deeper it is, and the lighter green it becomes the shallower. Brown or black spots, still known to the folk as "niggerheads," denote shoal spots of coral. Usually this is live coral, and a vessel sailing in tortuous waters tries to stay in the white or sandy areas, knowing that if he runs aground he will be in less jeopardy then if he hits the coral.

Despite all his local knowledge and ways and means to locate himself, the folk navigator is not particularly accurate and on long trips is likely to get into great difficulty. Typical of what can happen on a long coasting voyage is the saga of a smuggling expedition to St. Barts (St. Bartholemew's in the West Indies). A twenty-five-foot sloop, without engine, chart or compass, departed from the island of Carriacou and eventually landed at St. Barts, where it took on a cargo. Lest they be taken by the coast guard of Martinique or Guadaloupe, the men kept out of sight of land on their return and eventually picked up an island which they thought was St. Lucia. They altered course for port. Unfortunately, it was not St. Lucia but, according to the skipper, Grenada which they had seen, and so five hours later they arrived on the coast of South America.

Acting on the premise that one should never discourage a dreamer, I said nothing to the person who told the story, but it is well over a hundred miles from Grenada to South America. No smuggling sloop of that size could make the run in five hours. The captain had not mistaken Grenada for St. Lucia but Tobago for Grenada—which he thought was St. Lucia. Tobago is only about thirty miles from South America and the distance could be traversed in five hours. All in all, local knowledge and piloting had missed port by approximately two hundred miles!

With modern aids to navigation and the "eternal combusting engine," piloting along the coast is no longer so difficult. Vessels move faster, hence the tide and currents do not affect them so rigorously. They no longer have to beat to windward. They are never becalmed. In North America, local fishermen usually know the course from buoy to buoy and how fast their vessel goes at a given number of engine revolutions. They simply "run their time and shut down and listen." Usually they will hear or see the buoy and proceed to the next course. Occasionally they will miss it and will have to cruise about a bit before picking it up.

Closely allied with navigation is seamanship, and the good skipper takes care that he has an experienced crew. An able-bodied seaman had to know how to "hand, reef and steer," and in order to speed his learning all kinds of devices were employed. Especially effective were rhymes devised to fit the occasion. When two vessels approached each other in the dark, the helmsman knew from the approaching lights whether there was danger of collision by the rhyme that begins:

> Red to red or green to green
> No danger can be seen
> Red to green and green to red
> There's a vessel dead ahead.

When the weather was rough and the command was to "steer small," the helmsman could remember how to hold the course by "Ease her when she pitches and catch her when she rolls," and to console himself about the motion he had a little rhyme that went:

> Pitch, pitch, Goddam your soul
> The more you pitch the less you'll roll
> Or roll, roll, you sonofabitch
> The more you roll the less you'll pitch.

To teach the neophyte the various parts of the vessel, there was a little poem that alphabetized various parts of the ship: "A is for anchor as you very well know. B is the bobstay that goes down below...."[12]

In order to apply compass variation, the novice, instead of learning to "add westerly variation to the true course and subtract easterly," learned that "east is least and west is best."

Some of these little rhymes served both the green hand and the professional, for captains—especially of coasters—used them both in North America and in the Old World to remember how to make the various harbors, what could be expected there and how to shape his course from one point of departure to another. I have been told that old skippers like Stutterin' Hall had mnemonic rhymes giving courses, distances apart and names of the various light vessels and lighthouses from New York to Maine. Unfortunately, in the hunt for the folklore of big ships these poems have been overlooked, and today it is very difficult to find anyone who remembers more than a smidgeon of them. Captain Buchan said there was a poem that named all the major lights and light vessels from Land's End to the Moray Firth. But, like many others, he could recall only a few lines:

> First the Dudgeon, then the Spurn
> Next comes Flamborough Head in turn
> Scarborough Castle standing high
> Whitby Rocks lie northerly

Sunderland lay all in a bight.
Kenny Old Shields [a tavern] before dark of night.

Thanks to the recording of Ewan MacColl, we have preserved two
more of these rhymes used by Lowestoft fishermen. One from the south is:

As I to the mizzen backstay clung
I saw three lights and loud I sung.
"West three points nothe and Agnes bore
The Longships bearin' nor-west-by-nor
The Lizard Lights I do design [make out]
I wait your pleasure to resign?"

The second poem quoted here deals, as so many English sea stories
and seafaring beliefs do, with the fifty-odd miles of coast north and south
of Lowestoft. Like a number of these rhymes, this one marches south to
north. Rather than directions, it points out the charms of various harbors:

Pakefield for Poverty
Lowestoft for Poor
Gourleston for Pretty Girls
Yarmouth for Whores
Caister for Water Dogs
California for Pluck
Then back in old Winterton
How black she does look.[13]

These same kinds of rhymes are also used in Newfoundland, where
they are still a very real part of navigation:

When Joe Bett's P'int you is abreast
Dave's Rock bears due west
West-nor'west you must steer
Till Brimstone Head do appear

The Tickle's narrer, not very wide
The deepest water's on the starboard side
When in the harbor you is shot
Four fathoms you is got.[14]

A final one, more complicated than the others, was collected by
Marcus Hopkins in Newfoundland:

Hair on your Head and not on your Souls
There's wood on the point and none on the Poles.[15]

In addition to such rhymes, there were other means used to train the green hand and initiate him into the fellowship of the sea. We have mentioned the often crude hazing he had to endure—being sent to the bilges to "polish the golden rivet," to the crow's nest to gather eggs, to ask the sextant for a prayer and so on. But there were also certain rough ceremonies, on special occasions, that welcomed him into the ranks of shellbacks. Chief among these ceremonies were those pertaining to "crossing the line" or the equator, and on longitude 180 degrees. The former made one a son of Neptune, the latter a member of the order of the Golden Dragon.

A considerable amount of writing has been expended on these celebrations, especially the one crossing the equator, and some of the questions raised and conclusions drawn are as entertaining as the ceremonies. One author is surprised to discover that there are no accounts of Father Neptune prior to the sixteenth century, and remarks that anyone would know he was on the equator simply by observing that the sun was directly overhead.[16] Another feels that all ceremonies of this type were inspired by German trade unions.

The fact is that no one could celebrate crossing either the equator or the international date line until they could be found by sophisticated navigational devices, for there is no line in the sea at longitude 180 degrees, nor does the sun shine "overhead" at the equator except on two days of the year. Yet these ceremonies are but extensions of earlier, more savage rites performed along shore. As early as the days of Ulysses we learn that from time to time he tossed members of his crew overboard to appease monsters in the deep, and if we read the Odyssey aright, these monsters dwelt in places that marked boundaries between bodies of water.

Off every large cape, headland, point or bluff, at the entrance to any body of water like the Baltic Sea, the Mediterranean or the Black Sea, one is likely to encounter strong tidal currents and confused seas. To the unsophisticated mind that knew nothing of tidal streams, ocean currents and the rest, these disturbed waters were the result of the action of subaqueous monsters. In order to propitiate them, some kind of ritual varying from human sacrifice to prayer had to be performed. A successful crossing led to festive activity. As time went on and man thought he was more knowing, awe of the monster gave way and was replaced by terror of the tide, and sacrifices were abandoned. Still, in many places in the world the memory of yesterday lingers on. Those vessels that venture north of Ardnamurchan Point in Scotland may wear a sprig of heather at the stem head, those that pass east of Petit Manan in Maine may fix a bit of spruce to the bow, and passengers flying down the coast of Europe are given a certificate saying they have passed Point Roca, the westernmost continental land mass in Europe. All in all, there are literally dozens of these spots where people formerly made sacrifices, then paid "host," and today still commemorate the passage with some kind of certificate.[17]

Of all the ceremonies, the one connected with crossing the equator is the best known, best documented, most rigorous, most involved and most popular. Even today there is scarcely a sailor who does not covet the distinction of being "a son of Neptune" or a shellback, and there is not a neophyte or "pollywog" who approaches this aquatic Mason-Dixon Line without distinctly mixed emotions about it. As the ship draws nearer and nearer to this line, excitement mounts—partly in anticipation of the event and partially because no one is immune to initiation, and this is a moment when the crew can be revenged upon the officers who have not already been initiated for all the real and imagined wrongs they have received at their hands.

The earliest known account of this maritime puberty rite dates back to 1529; the next, to 1557.[18] At that time it was referred to in terms that indicated it had been in existence for a goodly number of years. This early rite was primarily a religious one: prayers were said, a fish was eaten and some silver coins were tossed overboard.[19] Before the century was over, however, the ceremony had acquired most of its present characteristics. First .there is a visit from a person crudely disguised as Father Neptune, who demands a tithe in silver from everyone who is not already initiated. Should the "host," as it is often called, not be forthcoming, the neophyte is shaved and drenched in water either by being dunked into the sea from the yardarm, dowsed in a barrel of sea water, or soused from cans or buckets. The whole is accompanied by a feast.

About six in the evening—a sail was discovered to windward on the larboard bow. Shortly afterward the man on the fore top-gallant yard saw she was making for us on the other tack. There seemed to be something mysterious in the appearance of this sail and the course she was keeping. . . . The captain eyed her with his glass; she was under courses and topsails with her jibs and a broad pennant [flag flown by an admiral] at the masthead. . . . On a sudden a tremendous conch roar issuing from under the bows of the ship startled me. . . . It was eight o'clock, and a hoarse piratical Atlantic voice hailed us and demanded who we were; the captain answered with his hat off . . . [and] having told our name and other logbook particulars requested his Majesty to come aboard. Neptune . . . replied that he could not leave his car that night but he would visit us the next morning . . . The conch's tritonian sounded again, the God rushed by in a flaming chariot which the sailor heaves from the forecastle. . . .

At nine next morning the King came in through one of the brided ports. He was seated on . . . a gun carriage drawn by four marine monsters. Amphitritty was by his side and their only child . . . was in her arms. The King was crowned with Atlantic water flowers and he bore in his hand the trident. . . . He was proceeded by six Tritons . . . and Mercury came with wings caduceus and a scroll under his arm. A white bear . . . acted as body guard and another troop of Tritons closed the cavalcade. We all took off our hats, civil things passed between Neptune and the captain . . . and . . . he desired all his children who had not entered his kingdom's capital . . . before, to listen to his public crier and do accordingly. . . . Mercury read an oration . . . he urged us to admire Amphitritty . . . he finished by repeating those three invaluable maxims which will carry a man safe through the world. 1. Never heave anything to windward except hot water and ashes. 2. Never drink small beer when you can get strong. 3. Never kiss the maid when you can kiss the mistress.

The pagent passed off but two water boys came and . . . said, 'You're wanted'. They wished to blindfold me . . . As I walked to the forecastle I was . . . washed by a dozen buckets of water—from the maintop and yard . . . I mounted a ladder. At the top stood the doctor on one side and the barber on the other. The doctor felt my pulse . . . gave me a saline draught from an eau de cologne bottle and gently pushed me into a deep purse bag half full of water. Thrice I assayed to get out and thrice the . . . sail tripped me up and Bear . . . who was rolling about at the bottom caught me in . . . hug and dallied me with his tarry palms. At last I doubled him up with a smashing hit in the wind, . . . clambored out, knocked down the Knave—and ran through a Niagara of water to my cabin.

After this ducking began in all forms under every possible modification . . . . A fine water piece.[20]

The following is a summary of a boarding during World War II:

As the ship approaches the equator a sharp lookout is kept forward for Neptune's boat. Eventually it is sighted and the ship heaves to (if a steam vessel the engines are stopped). A Jacob's ladder or gangway is lowered and sideboys are summoned. Neptune (most often the bo's'n although other venerable persons who have "crossed the line" may take the position), festooned with bits of spun yarn and tar, comes aboard with his triton and retinue who hail the captain. They ask where the ship is bound and if there are any "pollywogs" on board. The unfortunate pollywogs are then lined up, marched before Neptune, questioned and passed on to the barber, who anoints them with a paint brush which he dips in a bucket of tarry substance and shaves them with a rough razor (sometimes a saw). They are then made to run the gauntlet between shellbacks who souse them with sea water and give them a whack with a paddle as they go by. Similar treatment is afforded the passengers. When all have been initiated, Neptune departs and the ship gets under way, all hands having promised faithfully, should the occasion arise, to do unto others as was done unto them.

At one time ceremonies almost identical to these were performed at Cape Horn, and the Cape of Good Hope, by whalers going to the Arctic and by sailors entering the Baltic Sea.[21]

If the present-day ceremony represents little more than horseplay, it still suffices to ease tensions and to afford a vent for frustrations that build up on a long voyage. The unusual aspect of the ceremony is its lack of variety over the years. Aside from two facts—first, that one can no longer buy out of initiation with silver, and second, that the more violent aspects of the ceremony have been reduced—there is no discernible difference between the rites now and a century ago.

Years ago, when voyages were longer, there were many more ceremonies, some religious and others merely horseplay, but as voyages have become shorter, men more sophisticated and devices for entertainment, especially on big ships, more elaborate, most of them have been forgotten—with, perhaps, the dubious exception of the dead horse ceremony, which is still remembered in name at least in the United States Navy.

For some reason, horses have been prominent in the minds of seamen for a long time. All along the coasts of the British Isles, Ireland and North America we find White Horse, Horse, Black Horse and Colt Islands as well as many bluffs or headlands incorporating the word. Moreover, a number of items aboard ship bore names that included "horse" or had something to do with horses: a frame to rest a boom on; "harness casks"—barrels in which the week's supply of meat was kept, and deriving their name by the fact that they were usually secured to the break in the poop or fo'c'sle by horseshoes. A "martingale," sometimes called a "dolphin striker," referred to a chain that went from the end of the bowsprit to the stem. Salt horse was the name invariably given to the wretched meat the sailor ate, and "horse pieces" referred to chunks of part-meat, part-blubber from a whale that were allowed to putrify in a barrel. There is even a bit of doggerel, sometimes called the sailor's litany or sailor's grace, which goes:

> Old, horse, old horse, what do you here?
> You've carried my bags for many a year

And now worn out with sore abuse
They salt you down for sailors use
They gaze on you with sad surprise
They roll you over and buggar your eyes
They eat your meat and pick your bones
And send the rest to Davey Jones.[22]

In the old sailing ships there was a tradition that sailors could draw on their advance wages—usually up to a month's salary. During World War II it was still done in the United States Navy, and a man receiving such money was "drawing a dead horse." When he paid it back, he was "paying off a dead horse."

There used to be a ceremony to commemorate this event aboard ship after a month at sea. A mock horse would be constructed out of "a donkey's breakfast" (straw) and canvas, and it would be drawn around the deck while sailors kicked and struck it. After everyone had had a chance to abuse the effigy, it was thrown overboard, symbolizing the freeing of the sailor from his debt and in a strange way his freedom from the land.[23]

Another ceremony was "drawing the watch," when all the hands were mustered aft at the onset of a voyage, given a speech by the mate, who then picked the men he would have in his charge for the voyage. Still another took place when the crew were mustered and surrendered their knives (as much a part of a sailor as his arm or leg) to the blacksmith, who broke off the points to make them less effective should mutiny occur or individual "courage rise."

Still another had to do with a punishment known as "captain's mast," because it was held traditionally at the butt of the main mast. This usually occurred on Saturday, for Sunday—in spite of the poem mentioned later—was not a day when the crew did more than was necessary to keep the ship moving. Therefore, the culprits had a chance to recover for a day from their punishment.

The crew would be mustered, the offender brought forward, the charge made and punishment passed. For major crimes like mutiny the offender would be hanged at the yardarm or keelhauled. In the latter case a line was tied around his hands and feet with one end passed under the vessel. The offender would then be drawn under the ship and up the other side. If he didn't drown, the beating he took from barnacles and bits of copper on the bottom usually proved fatal, but if they didn't the culprit usually thought better of his ways. For lesser crimes he would be triced in the rigging, spread-eagled over a gun or flogged up to one hundred lashes on the bare back, an act carried out by the bos'n at the gangway. Or he might be clapped in irons and confined to the brig—a dark and dismal hole —for a few days on a ration of "piss and punk" (bread and water). All of this was done before the entire ship's company, and had a strong deterrent effect on all hands.[24]

Although crimes consisted of many things, the chief ones were mutiny, assaulting an officer, sleeping on watch, theft—especially of food—refusal to obey an order, malingering, gambling and "silent insubordination." If the punishments seem severe, it must be remembered that the times were different and the situation quite foreign to modern living. With the crew confined in close, damp quarters, eating poor food and drinking poorer water, the ship's officers were sitting on a powder keg, and unless the crew was continuously "brightened up" it could and often did blow up. A man who had a successful run of luck at cards might well turn up dead, a man asleep on watch might send the entire ship's company to the bottom and any allowed objection to authority simply opened a Pandora's box. Contrary to some landsmen's belief, there is not time between an order and its execution to permit either explanation or argument. Nor is a good officer inclined to divulge his reasons for an order, lest the aura of mystery so important to obedience be shattered. A ship's captain commands by a tenuous thread that links him to the divine. To maintain it, his life and his officers' lives must be lonely ones.

Of course some of the captains abused their station to a tremendous degree. There are many records of sea captains who starved and flogged their crews beyond belief. In one instance a captain beat a man to death for not eating two mouthfuls of meat, and in another, a skipper did not even luff when a crew member went overboard but spent a week later on dragging for a lost anchor. However, despite the avidity with which these instances of brutality were cried up, the average sea captain was and is a man of temperance in all things.

To the landsman the greatest hazard a vessel experiences is a storm offshore. This is not true. With plenty of room a mariner can take his choice. He can heave to, lie ahull or scud under bare poles, depending upon his preference and his ship's capabilities, and usually the vessel will survive. She may lose her rig, she may strain and start to sink, but the chances are good she will stay afloat even if it means pumping at least until the storm has blown itself out. The thing the sailor most fears is the land —especially the lee shore. More vessels have been lost going aground than ever sank at sea, for a stranded ship has little chance. In calm weather she can jettison her cargo, run out her kedge perhaps, but all this takes time and a vessel will often bilge before she can be lightened or winched off. In heavy weather she may not even be able to do these things.

Despite the old seaman's adage, "When in doubt, stay out," the harbor in an approaching fog, toward night, in snow or in a gale is always inviting. The skipper, tired of the sea, yearns for a night's rest, and all too often he gambles he can make it—and loses.

For the ship caught on a lee shore, the situation is desperate. The skipper must show enough sail or have enough power to work out against the sea. When it blows too hard his canvas either won't stand the strain or must be reduced to the point where it will not force the ship through the seas. His screw, more out of water than in, will not give him enough bite to drive ahead. Slowly, surge by surge he is driven back and back to death and destruction. He has only three alternatives left: to anchor, and anchors seldom hold in these conditions; to hang on, and hope that the wind will let up, and it never seems to until he is ashore; or to square away and run ashore; hoping to reach high enough ground so that the crew can jump to safety. But this, too, is seldom successful, and usually the vessel will strike, broach, and all hands go overside.

A ship at sea can throw out cargo, cut away the masts, use oil or do a number of other things that, if they would not save her, will at least keep her afloat till the storm slacks and the crew can get off. A ship run ashore allows no such delay. In a few minutes or a few hours she will be torn apart and the crew gone.

When one recognizes these hazards, one begins to understand that perhaps the greatest aid to navigation was the invention of the lighthouse with its light and its attendant gun, horn, siren or bell. Coming in off soundings a light would give a mariner warning miles at sea of ledges ahead, help position him on his chart and guide him to some harbor, or allow him to bear away while he still had room. These lights were not long in coming in the Mediterranean, for the one at Alexandria was reckoned as one of the seven wonders of the world. They came later in the rest of Europe, and in America the first lighthouse was either off Boston on a point called The Graves, or off Newport on a peninsula known as Beavertail, depending on what tourist manual one reads. Whenever and however their beginning, the great age of the lighthouse and the lightship appears to have been the nineteenth century. Prior to that they were few, and during this century, when there are more vessels at sea than at any time in history if we include yachts, the tendency has been to remove them or abandon them or replace them with fixed beacons that are unmanned.

The light today does not need to be lit and therefore no keeper is necessary, but a light without a keeper is but half a light. The keeper did what the light cannot. The keeper could sight and report and sometimes even save vessels in trouble. But it costs money to keep a crew in a light or a light vessel at sea, and it has become politically expedient to do away with them. No doubt the few thousand dollars saved will better augment the billions spent on space travel.

The saga of lighthouses could fill a volume, beginning with the problems of building them, the struggles to maintain the lights and the hazards involved in tending them. Elsewhere I have told how wreckers would extinguish the light, but here I should like to mention two or three stories that are illustrative of other aspects of lighthouses.

Almost everyone has heard of Grace Darling, daughter of the light keeper on the Farne Islands, how she tended the light when her father was ill, and how she and her father together rescued nine men from the wrecked *Forfarshire* who would probably have drowned had the light been unattended. On the other hand, unless they know the history of a yacht club's flag, almost no one today has heard of Ida Lewis, "The Grace Darling of America," who made a name for herself on more than one score.

Ida Lewis was, as far as I have been able to find out, the only female lighthouse keeper in the United States. She came by the job quite naturally, her father having kept the light before her. It was a miserable little light on Lime Rock inside Newport harbor, where nothing catastrophic ever seemed to happen. Still, the young woman kept it, and in order to get ashore she had a heavy lapstrake pulling boat hauled up on the beach— the kind of boat a husky fisherman would row. During her lifetime she yanked from Neptune's grasp no less than eighteen people, some of whom she had rowed nearly four miles to get, under near-gale conditions. For her efforts she received a congratulatory letter from the president of the United States, and was the first woman to receive a medal for bravery. Shortly afterward she was forced to retire, an act that local people say caused her death. Her monument today is the Ida Lewis Yacht Club, whose flag shows a lighthouse on a red field with eighteen stars.

A story of a different nature is connected with another light further east. Although not spectacular as lighthouses go, Minot's Light is one of the more photogenic lights in the United States, for in a gale the spray sometimes goes over its top eighty feet above sea level. (Those who think this remarkable should recall that, before it was abandoned, a sea put out the light, washed the keeper down the stairs and ripped a three-ton rock out of the top of the light on the Calf, off Ireland. This light was 175 feet above the sea.)[25]

According to one story, there had been a good many wrecks around Cohasset, Massachusetts, brought on by vessels seeking Boston in thick weather, and an effort had unsuccessfully been launched to build a lighthouse there. One day a vessel groping for Boston in fog came on soundings and anchored. The captain, not knowing where he was, had himself rowed ashore to find out, leaving the ship in charge of the mate. While he was gone the wind hauled into the east and a gale sprang up; the vessel dragged, struck on one of the rocks and went to pieces. From Cohasset to Provincetown the shore was littered with wreckage and bodies of drowned Irish immigrants. For days the people picked up these bodies, many of which they found by watching for the birds feeding on them.

Although no lighthouse in the world could have in any way averted the wreck, the government decided to construct one as a result of it. The structure was made of metal and resembled a birdcage on stilts, with the keepers and the light housed in the cage high above the water. There the structure remained for many years, but eventually it began to feel the effects of the continuous jabbing of the sea. The keepers and local citizenry felt it was unsafe and asked to have it repaired, but the government was indifferent. In order to strengthen the structure the keepers attached a hawser from the cage to a great rock that lay below the light to serve as an anchor. This was an excellent move, for it absolved officialdom of any blame in the ensuing events.

One day the head keeper went ashore, leaving the light in charge of his two assistants. While he was ashore it began to breeze up and he couldn't get back. The breeze increased until it became one of the worst storms in memory. Gradually the lighthouse began to shift and the storm continued to gain force. People on the shore could see the beam of the light gradually pointed more and more skyward. Finally, just after midnight, faintly over the roaring of the sea came the terrible tolling of the great lighthouse bell. It ceased, the light went out and the storm began to ease. In the morning people looked across an empty expanse of sea.

Before the accident one of the keepers swore that if the light ever went he would swim ashore. One man's body was found, but not the assistant keeper's.

Inside Cohasset harbor is a small island a few yards from shore. Several days after the disaster a fisherman happened to go onto the islet. There, nestled in a crack high above the tide line and bare yards from sanctuary, he found the body of the assistant keeper, dead from exposure. Apparently he had made it to the isle, crawled out and given up.[26]

Sometimes lights could prove more of a hazard than a help. Should something happen to the light, a vessel running for it might be in serious trouble before she realized it. Typical of what can happen is a story about Baker's Island off Salem, Massachusetts.

A vessel from Salem was bound home with a handsome cargo one December in the early part of the nineteenth century after two years in China. One day the captain discovered that his reckoning put them close enough to Salem so that if he drove hard he could make port Christmas Eve. Christmas at home was tempting, and he began to push his vessel. The day before Christmas was a lowering one and by midday it began to snow. Visibility was lowered and the lookout was doubled. As evening approached a gale sprang up and the ship raced for home. All they needed was to find Baker's Island Light and they could "be home and dry."

Not long after dark the light was sighted and the course shifted to leave it a good berth to port. The vessel was going like a freight train and everyone was looking forward to the next day. Suddenly there were breakers under the bow; before anything could be done, the vessel was ashore and within a very short time she was a total loss. The captain managed to reach shore with a few of the crew, but many were drowned.

Unknown to the captain, the light had been moved from one end of the island to the other while he was in foreign parts, and when he hauled off to give it a berth he lined up with the center of Baker's Island.[27]

Another lighthouse further up the coast has a different story attached to it. This is the light on Matinicus Rock, where many years ago it is said that a keeper committed suicide. As with most suicides, the ghost of the dead man is not easy, and it is probably his ghost which haunted the lighthouse until at least ten years ago.

At that time part of the original dwelling was unoccupied and used as a kind of a storehouse. When the older keepers were relieved by new ones, they neglected to tell them about the building. Consequently the relief crew opened the door to this part of the structure and were immediately plagued by unexplained occurrences: cups fell off the table, doors banged, cupboards wouldn't stay closed. Most annoying of all, light bulbs burned out almost daily and even the light itself was extinguished. Someone finally closed the door and all returned to normal. Someone opened the door and the trouble started again.

Since the ghost did no physical harm and since there was nothing of importance in the old wing, it seemed a simple thing to keep the door shut. That way there was room enough on the island for both the quick and the dead. Things went peacefully for a time until an officer came out to inspect the station. He ordered the door opened, and over the expostulations of the crew it was opened, for the officer was not one who believed in ghosts or had much time for those who did. "I want that door open and I want that door left open," he said.

Before he left the island the shade put on a real show. Lights went out, the generator quit, cups fell off the table and hell broke loose in general. The officer's last command as he left the rock was, "Shut that damned door and keep it shut!" Needless to say the crew were happy to obey, and tranquility has reigned on Matinicus Rock ever since.

An event of a far more serious nature took place in the Flannan Islands in the Outer Hebrides. These rocks (they are little more) had been a hazard to navigation and a source of grim stories in the surrounding islands for hundreds of years, when around the turn of the century a light was finally established there. It took a long time building and according to local informants was not made operative until Christmas Eve, 1905. And a grand Christmas present its beam must have been to the shipman anxiously checking his course, for tide, current and poor visibility do nothing to abate the hazard the islands present.

A year to the day passed and nothing untoward happened. Then a passing vessel noticed something wrong with the light. A signal was made and no reply came back. The ship reported the incident. A few days later another ship noticed something wrong and also reported it, and an inspection party went out to check up. The vessel arrived off the light and made a signal but received no answer. A boat was lowered and went ashore. No one greeted it. The crew went to the dwelling and found it empty. Coats and caps were hung on their pegs, the table was laid for a meal, and the meal was sitting in pots and pans apparently ready to eat on a cold stove. The last entry in a journal found in the dwelling was dated December 24 and showed no indication of trouble. Further search of the island revealed the little lifeboat nestled on her cradle, but nowhere could they find track or trace of the keepers. Nowhere on the islands, either, could they find any sign of violence or foul play. Moreover, from a time several days previous to the first report of trouble till they arrived there, there had been no violent storms in the neighborhood. To this day no bodies have washed ashore.

Islanders seem to cling to the belief that the crew was swallowed up by a monster. Other people feel that one of the crew may have fallen overboard and the others drowned trying to get him back. If this was the case, why hadn't they tried to launch the boat? Why hadn't somebody pulled off his pants, thrown off his shirt, tossed aside his hat before jumping overboard? Why wasn't the door of the dwelling open or some signs of hurrying or urgency evident? I would suggest that one solution to the mystery is as likely as the other, and since half a century has drifted by without an answer, it seems apparent that it will not be solved immediately.[28]

Closely allied to the lighthouse is the lightship. The latter is more hazardous duty than the former, for the light vessels run not only the hazard of being knocked down but of dragging and more particularly of being run down, since ships often home on them and if their navigation is too perfect, they cut them in two. A story told on both sides of the ocean, that is almost identical save for the names, is probably more an exact relating of fact than an amusing folk story. One told about southern New England should suffice.

Years ago there was a fleet of lightships in the Cape Cod area. There were the Hen and Chickens, the Vineyard, Handkerchief Shoals, Pollock Rip, Stone Horse and, well off Nantucket Island, Nantucket Shoals light vessel, to mention some. Each had the name of the station painted on her side. A coaster had been coming up from New York with a load of coal and she had had heavy fog most of the way. The skipper was anxiously looking for the Hen and Chickens light vessel. On one hand lay the Sow and Pigs and on the other Hen and Chickens, both of them dangerous reefs. To get through, he must run close to the light vessel. The time had already passed when he should hear her, and all hands were straining to see or hear any sound that might come over the light breeze.

Eventually a bell was heard ringing, but no horn. The skipper decided that the horn was out of order and kept on until suddenly out of the murk loomed a red hull—the lightship! On her side was written "Nantucket." "My God, stop her! Stop her and let go the hook!" The coaster was duly anchored, and there she sat for twenty-four hours while the captain puzzled over how he had got so far off course as to nearly miss the continent. When the fog cleared he found the answer. The Nantucket light vessel had been in port for refit. She was on her way back to her station when the fog caught her and she decided to anchor, her conservative skipper meantime dutifully having the bell rung periodically, as is required of an anchored vessel.

Down in Maine the story is still told of another important part bells played in navigation.

Until about thirty years ago a steamer used to come up to Maine from Boston, calling at all the little harbors on the way. One day she was bound for Boothbay Harbor in terribly thick fog. Ashore at that time was a church. The people who attended it gradually removed themselves to the other side of the bay, and when they wanted to go to church they were faced with a passage across the bay or a long ride around it. To remedy matters, it was decided to move the church.

A barge was obtained, a couple of lobster boats were donated, and the parishioners banded together, jacked up the church and rolled it aboard the barge at low tide. The tide rose, the barge floated and away went the church. At the same time the fog rolled in. On board with the church was one man, and it occurred to him that it might be fun to ring the bell—and he did.

The skipper of the steamer knew nothing of this and was smelling his way in when the lookout reported the church bell. The captain recognized the bell and knew exactly where he was. The next thing he knew the sound had changed remarkably. He was puzzled, but he put it down as the effects of a stronger tide than he had expected and kept on forging ahead. Next the lookout shouted, "Church dead ahead!" and out of the fog loomed a church roof and a belfry. "Jesus Christ! Stop her! Full astern!" roared the old man. The church and its tolling bell receded in the fog. "Let go the mud hook," was the next command, and the steamer came to anchor. The fog was three days scaling up and the steamer lay at anchor three days while passengers fumed and fretted.

Along with lights and light vessels a great assist to navigation came in buoys and beacons, sometimes called perches (English), spindles or day markers (American). The buoys come in various sizes and shapes. Some have bells and some have gongs. Others have whistles (called by sailors hooters or groaners), others are lighted and still others have no lights, bells or whistles, but can be identified by their shape and color. Unfortunately their use is a little confusing, for in the United States sailors have a rhyme "Red, right, returning," which means all red buoys should be left to starboard entering a port, but in the rest of the world the case is reversed.

For a vessel coming from offshore it was and still is customary to run for the light, pick up the hooter or bell and come in. Sailing ships in thick weather would sail and then lie to and listen and go again until they heard the buoy. Modern fishing vessels and coasters in thick weather still "run their time," shut down and listen, then start up. If they hear nothing, they circle, and if they still hear nothing, they anchor and wait if possible. Marine lore is full of stories of people who missed their buoys, and the bottom of the sea is littered with their ships.

Probably the oldest of these aids to navigation after the beacon was the bell. At the entrance to the Firth of Tay lies what was once called Inchcape Rock but is better known to seamen today as Bell Rock. The tide ran heavily there, and in thick calm weather an unsuspecting vessel could be swept upon it; in a gale it was an even worse hazard. The good monks of Arboath, who were particularly interested in shipping, constructed a bell to warn mariners of the danger. A reaver (as pirates are called in Scotland) discovered that the bell could be a great asset to his business: all he had to do was tie the clapper, lie over the edge of the horizon and wait to pick the bones of the unwary.

Eventually he fell prey to his own scheme. He stopped the bell and waited, the fog rolled in, the tide turned and the sea was calm. Rolfe, the reaver, began to drift. There is nothing worse than a calm sea and a fog, for then one is deprived of his only other aid to navigation—his ears. There was a dull shock, a heavy crash and the reaver was ashore. When the fog cleared, the North Sea was free of one more pirate.[29]

Perhaps the most difficult task a shipmaster had to face was the training of the crew, and the two things hardest to teach a young seaman were to go aloft and to steer. It was one thing to haul lines on deck or even go aloft in port, but it was quite another to scamper up ratlines sheathed in ice in the face of a squall, with too much sail. It was not easy to get a man to lie out on a hundred foot yard in a gale of wind and put gaskets on a flogging sail eighty feet above the deck. Nor was a neophyte enamoured of going out on the bowsprit—often called the "widow-maker"—and fist a jib with the vessel diving her catheads under. When the greenhorn refused to go, the mates or the bos'n would force him aloft with a rope's end, and when he froze coming down, a sea boot in the face did more than a psychiatrist's couch to allay his fears, or rather replace them with a greater fear of having his head kicked off.

Under this kind of treatment the young sailor became proficient at running aloft and coming to deck again by sliding down the backstay like a fireman coming down his pole. Now and then, of course, one of these ordinary seamen would get in trouble. There is a story of the U.S.S. *Constitution* that is still popular in fo'c'sles to this day. Although it is undoubtedly apocryphal, it is worth telling and could have happened with officers like Decator or Preble in command.

On a bet, the captain's son, who was but ten years old, climbed to the main truck. He had no trouble getting there, and he stood balanced on the cap before he realized his problem, which was how to get down, for all the lines were beneath his grasp and the place was too small to allow anyone to climb up and rescue him. There was only one chance to be saved and that was to jump clear of the vessel. The captain grabbed his speaking trumpet and roared, "Jump!" The boy remained frozen. His father tried again with no result. He then put down the speaking trumpet and grabbed a musket. Standing where the boy could see him plainly, the captain deliberately cocked the gun and then roared again, "Damn ye, jump! Jump or by God, I'll fire!" He slowly brought the rifle to his shoulder and sighted it. The boy jumped, landed in the sea and was picked up.[30]

While the mates and the bos'n were overcoming acrophobia in the young, the skipper was aft tearing out his hair and trying to teach greenhorns something about steering. (I know of no stories telling of a successful attempt on the part of a captain to teach anyone anything, but there are numerous ones telling of his dismal failures.)

On one occasion a master tried to tell a new hand about the compass but soon perceived that that would be too difficult. It was a clear night with a good breeze, and he showed the boy a bright star and told him how to follow it as sailors have done beyond memory. Pleased with himself, the captain turned in for a quiet nap.

No sooner had he put his head down than the vessel went about. The old man grabbed his pants and burst onto the deck. "What's wrong? What happened? Didn't you follow that star I showed you?"

"Nothing's wrong, sir. I'm doing just like you said, only I lost that star. But don't you mind, Captain, I found a couple others just as good!"[31]

On another occasion the captain of an American coaster was "blown off," and before he could make sail for home he had gone a long way out to sea. The captain called the cabin boy and showed him how to steer and told the boy he had nothing to worry about for they were a long way offshore. Down below went the skipper and turned in.

The boy steered happily on, looking at the compass intently. After a couple of hours he looked up, and there close aboard were the masthead and two running lights of a big vessel dead ahead on a collision course.

Down below the captain was suddenly rudely awakened. "You're a hell of a navigator! You'd better come up quick. There's a drugstore ahead, and if you don't stop her in about five minutes we'll be in the front door!"[32] (In those days all drugstores had a red and a green light on each side of their door.)

As one looks at shipmasters, he soon realizes there were two sorts, the lions and the lambs. The first were hard-driving, dangerous men like Joshua Barney, Bully Waterman and Samuel Samuels, who drove his passengers below, spiked down the hatches and went hunting hurricanes to blow the *Dreadnaught* hurriedly across the sea; or Bucky Walters of the *Bluenose* and Jimmy Buchan of the *Girl Vivian*. In war they fought like tigers, and in peace they drove their vessels without mercy. Some even padlocked the halyards or put stoppers on them aloft to prevent anyone shortening sail. The only way that sail would be reduced was via the old adage that "what comes down blows down."

The lambs were more numerous. They loved their vessels and went by the adage "You must treat your vessel kindly and it'll treat you well." These men were good seamen, made good passages and year after year carried the major business of the ocean traffic on their backs.

Crews liked to ship with the lambs. It was easier and safer, and there was an excellent chance that one might survive to have a social glass in The Dog and Duck or some other pub. But when the sailor remembers, these are not the men he recalls. Lovely days at sea are no more plentiful than gales, and more ships go under the wrecker's hammer or rot up the creek than go down at sea. But the seafaring folk even more than other folk are tensed for danger. They think danger and they remember danger. It is only the violence that they recall—the great gale, the wreck, the fast passage. Even their humor is violent, and they derive more pleasure from feeding a spike to a seagull than they do from a pun or a bit of satire. Even in their memory of shipbuilding and navigation, this fiber of their makeup shines through.

Hauling up the seine boat, Friendship, Bequia

CHAPTER VI

SONGS

"If you'll listen awhile I'll sing you a song of the
bold, the noble and true."
—Captain Archie Spurling, in recording session, 1946,
Great Cranberry Island, Maine

SCHOLARSHIP in maritime lore has been, to say the least, uneven. Some areas
have been closely examined while others have been largely neglected, with
folk-song scholarship greatly exceeding work in any other field. To give the
reader some idea of the vastness of the material on this subject: Professor
MacEdward Leach compiled a bibliography of Child ballads (305 in
number) for *Wells Manual* and discovered he had 85,000 items! When one
considers that Child comprises but a tiny part of the folk-song canon, one
begins to realize the enormous amount of time and effort spent in this area.

While it has been the intent of the present work to examine those
areas of marine folklore least widely studied, no book dealing with sea
lore would be complete without some mention of this, perhaps the most
popular of all art forms. Therefore, I have included a brief summary of
songs and chanteys for the reader's perusal—and since most of the work
done in this field has been in the particular examination of individual
songs, my remarks here are of a more general nature.

Sea songs divide themselves nicely into two major categories, chanteys
and fo'c'sle songs. The former are work songs; the latter, songs sung in
idle times for entertainment. These in turn may be subdivided into "long-"
and "short-haul" chanteys on the one hand, and on the other, songs that
either originated at sea or were born ashore and adapted themselves to a
marine environment. It is primarily with chanteys and sea-born songs that
I will deal.

Exactly how or when the chantey came into being is in doubt.[1] Some writers hold that its origin is French and suscribe to the "chantey" spelling. Others spell the word "shanty" and feel that it came from singing by American Negroes along the Mississippi who loaded cotton on the wharves at New Orleans. The word, they think, derived from the shacks in which these people lived. Still others believe that the songs originated among Negroes in the West Indies, and were picked up by white sailors and spread throughout the maritime world.[2]

No matter what the spelling, certain facts are irrefutable. The mid-nineteenth century, with its great number of square-rigged vessels requiring immense gang effort, was the heyday of chanteying. American chanteys, probably because there were more American ships, outnumber English songs of similar nature. These songs were so popular that they were sung in almost every known language; I have heard "Rio" sung in French, German, Danish and English. Unlike the fo'c'sle songs, these work songs seldom came ashore (except as popular choral renditions), but declined along with the wind ships. Finally, it seems a dangerous hypothesis to ascribe their origin to one particular time or place, for the songs are too varied and widespread to be relegated to a small segment of the world's shipping going in and out of a limited number of harbors.

Working in unison to a given rhythm is very ancient; and to suggest, because more chanteys were being sung in the nineteenth century around cotton ports, that the songs originated among southern or West Indian blacks is not altogether a viable position to adopt. We know that people sang to their oars in the Middle Ages, and Martin Martin mentions the Scots singing as they rowed afishing in the seventeenth century. Further, to suggest that chanteying was a nineteenth-century diversion because it was so popular then and we have so many songs that originated during that period is to put the emphasis in the wrong place. It was to be expected that chanteying would boom along with the wind ships; and when steam finally overrode sail at the turn of the century, vitiating the need for chanteying, it was only natural that scholars would find old sailors still alive who could sing chanteys recalled from their days in the big ships.

What has been said of chanteying could also be said about the Negro origins of the chantey. Not only was chanteying done abroad long before the advent of blacks upon the Anglo-American scene, but Negroes were never numerous aboard sailing craft. They shipped as cooks and stewards' mates but were infrequently members of the working crew. (Until World

War II black people worked in the United States Navy almost exclusively as stewards' mates.) They did not, therefore, have an opportunity to disperse chanteys. However, while one cannot deny the similarity between the chantey and the African digging songs, it can be attributed to polygenesis rather than to a single origin. But to return to the chantey.

These work songs have a number of singular characteristics. First, they are what might be called "open-versed." That is, the narrative content is at a minimum. The song can be continued by adding new verses and the verse sequence is of minimal importance. Each verse can stand more or less alone, as:

> Whiskey is the life of man.
> Whiskey Johnny.
> Whiskey is the life of man,
> And it's whiskey for me, Johnny-O.

Most chanteys had a single part sung by, and indeed often invented by, one person. This part was attached to the next by a simple chorus which, unlike many folk songs, was not doggerel. Take, for example, two verses, one from "South Australia" and the other from "Highland Laddie":

> In South Austraylia I was born,
> *Heave away, haul away,*
> In South Austraylia I was born,
> *Heave away your rolling chain*
> *We're bound for South Austraylia.*
>
> Were you ever in Quebec,
> *Bonnie laddie, Highland laddie,*
> Stowing timber on the deck,
> *My bonnie Highland laddie-O.*[3]

In all chanteys the words are of less importance than the rhythm and the rhythm is set to the tempo of the work, with the effort made by the men on the stressed syllables of words. When at last the effort is complete, the last line is often spoken rather than sung, and often a redundance is employed by adding a term at the end of the song—as " 'Vast heavin' " or "Secure" and not infrequently the entire song is interspersed with instructions to the gang.

Generally speaking, the tempo of the short-haul chantey is quicker than that of the long-haul and the line itself is shorter, as one can see by comparing:

Up aloft this yard must go
You say so, I say so

with

Oh Shenandoah, I love thy daughter,
Heave away, I'm bound to go
Across the wide Missouri.

The short-haul was used to do quick short work like sweating up a halyard, raising a barrel of rum over the side or bracing round a yard. Often it was work done so quickly that the hands would "tail" onto a line and then run away with it to a rhythm that would prevent one man from tramping on another's feet. In the vernacular, these were often called "run away" chanties.

Work that required longer and more sustained effort usually had not only a slower tempo, but the song was more detailed and its maritime characteristics better formed. Perhaps the two most notoriously tedious tasks aboard ship were getting in the anchor and manning the pumps. In the former situation the vessel might be lying in twenty fathoms of water with a hundred fathoms of chain out to an anchor weighing nearly a ton. The sea and the wind would maintain a considerable strain on the ground tackle, and the anchor might be bedded deep in the mud. Human heart and muscle straining at the capstan bars would bring the chain in link by grudging link. Eventually the man in the bow would sing out, "Anchor's at short stay," "Anchor's up and down." By a titanic effort the crew would break the "hook" out of the mud and the cry would be, "Anchor's aweigh." Then the tempo of effort would increase, for the anchor presented a hazard to ship-handling at this point, as it might at worst foul another ship's cable or swing back under the ship, or at least impede her steering ability to a dangerous degree. The next call would be, "Anchor's in sight," and the tempo would lift again, for the swinging hook could damage the vessel if it struck her a substantial blow as she pitched in the sea. The final cry of "Anchor's home" would put an end to labor and " 'Vast heavin' " would be the cry of the bos'n.

The majority of sailing ships were made of wood, and as they moved through the sea they were wracked by the thrust of the rigging and twisted by the swells. As a result, most leaked and had to be pumped continuously, with the water gaining on the pumps in the gales and the pumps gaining in the calms. Sometimes two men would be employed at the great pitcher pump at the main mast. Sometimes four men would be used to man the brakes on each side and the monotonous clank of the pump would continue day and night. It was work the men hated, and the chanteys they sang at the pumps were long, slow in tempo and not infrequently splenetic in content.

Jack Tar's life was never a very pleasant one. His wages were low, his food bad, his hours long, his bunk damp. If he didn't sink or fall overboard, he would eventually return to port, where he would be inveighed against by the clergy, cheated by the merchants, robbed by the whores, drugged and sent back to sea by the landlords or "crimps" whom he encountered during his brief stay ashore. Generally speaking, he bore all these vicissitudes with a Joblike stoicism, but from time to time he would express himself and commemorate the names of his tormentors. This he usually did in his chanteys. When he mentioned Paradise Street or Tiger's Bay he was referring to red-light districts. When he spoke of "Madame Gashee," "Sally," "Newport Tony" he was naming whores. Shanghai Brown was a famous crimp who flourished in San Francisco during the mid-nineteenth century, and Bully Hayes was a violent skipper who became a pirate and finally retired to live a venal life in the South Pacific. Reuben Ranzo was a tailor —a breed despised because they sold inferior clothes to seamen at exorbitant prices, and because when they occasionally wound up at sea as sailmakers, it was their duty, along with sewing canvas, to sew up the dead in a canvas shroud and run the last stitch through the dead man's nose (a way, along with the use of a mirror, to determine that there was no life in the body). On the other hand, Jack occasionally ran across a benefactor, and he too was given a bit or a whole song like "Paddy West."[4]

Chanteys were often used as rallying calls, and generally speaking, particular chanteys were sung for particular purposes. When a watch was turned out on a wild night with the ship laboring heavily, the waist full of water, no lights, and nearly a hundred lines to tend, a sailor hearing a song over the roar of the wind would know where to go and what to do. Among the long-haul chanteys this specialization had a further refinement. Aboard American ships "Rio" was the song used to get the anchor when outward bound from America to a foreign country. When the vessel was ready to put away for home she invariably flew the "nighthawk," a long black streamer pennant, from the masthead and the crew sang "Shenandoah" as they "walked the capstan 'round." Vessels lying in the harbor, seeing the bunting or hearing the song, could deliver mail and messages bound across the water. English vessels bound home sang "Homeward Bound" in place of "Shenandoah."

Because chanteying was most popular aboard big ships and because of the polyglot nature of big-ship crews, the chantey soon became a multi-lingual song. Probably because sailing ships in their heyday were commanded and owned principally by Englishmen and Americans, the songs had an Anglo-American beginning, but they were quickly translated into German, French, Norwegian and even Chinese. Strangely enough, the proper nouns and more important phrases were preserved in English when sung in a foreign tongue and it was a little startling to hear "heave away," "Ranzo" or "wide Missouri" in the middle of a German song.[5]

As the years passed, steam took over sail and sailing ships changed. The clumsy, dangerous square-riggers requiring big crews were gradually superseded by the more weatherly, more easily handled fore-and-aft rigs, and the clippers and packets and brigs were replaced by schooners both great and small. These required smaller crews and less work, for they lacked yards and braces and the complex rigging necessitated by the square rigs. Hence there was less emphasis on singing. Later still, sailing vessels were equipped with a "yawl boat" (a small launch with an engine) to push them around and a "donkey engine" with a winch to which lines could be led, and the necessity of gang hauling was no longer very important. To be sure, the ships still leaked like baskets, but even the chore of pumping was taken over by the "eternal combustion engine." Finally, the engine (sometimes called an "iron jib") replaced sail almost entirely, and chanteying aboard ship stopped in most parts of the world, for these chanteys were considered only "work songs" and were not sung except when actually pertaining to an occupation.

Today, the chantey in the British Isles, Erin and America is dead for all practical purposes. Now and then a folklorist turns up an old hulk somewhere, "weak in the waterways" and "gone in the top hamper" who can quaver a chantey into a recording machine. Folk singers who have no connection whatever with the folk and know nothing about salt water sometimes make records of what they think chanteys ought to be like. To these may be added a few singers and salts who have preserved them through memory of days gone by—such as Captain Bob Roberts and A. A. Lloyd—but this is not chanteying.

There yet remains, however, one area of the English-speaking world where chanteying is still very much alive—the West Indies. It has survived there for a number of reasons. Because the wind nearly always blows and almost always from the same quarter—a quarter which makes sailing from island to island feasible to wind ships—chanteying is still greatly in evidence.

Although the "engine boat" is becoming more and more popular, it is not essential in the area and still remains more of a status symbol than a necessity.

The people in the West Indies are very tradition-minded and not quick to accept change. Many still believe, as one man told me, that the only sure engine is man's heart and muscle. "Slower," he said, "but surer." Moreover, these people are black, and have in their background a heritage of digging songs that makes the use of chanteys easy for them—since both chanteys and digging songs are short, rhythmical and do not stress narrative. Last, in the West Indies there is a good deal of labor that still requires gang effort, as loading and unloading "kyargo," getting vessels on the careen, launching ships, hoisting sail, rowing and hauling the great fish seines ashore. They still use "shantee" for most of these tasks—with the exception of careening, which for some reason is done to a melodious "one-two" chant.

At the time of this writing, these West Indian songs have been largely unstudied. They are different from chanteying as it was done elsewhere— at least the versions I collected are, for they do not have close analogies among the multitudinous printed collections on the subject. At the same time, they follow the patterns established in the Old World and in North America.

There can be little question that these songs have derived from the corpus of chantey-songs used elsewhere, but they have been radically altered. Many of them have been composed around phrases found in traditional chanteys and set to traditional chantey tunes. Phrases like "across the wide Missouri," "whiskey Johnny," "Hilo," "bound away in Mobile Bay," "I'm bound right over the mountain," "It's time for us to leave her" are scattered throughout the songs.

These songs appear to differ markedly from chanteys that were sung in other parts of the English-speaking world. For one thing, apart from the occasional traditional phrase their words have a strong flavor of local attitudes and environment. Moreover, they seem to lack any stanzaic form, but adjust themselves to normal work pauses when the tackle comes "two block," when the crew take a round turn and prepare to heave again and so on. Next, they are often sung in what used to be called "first and second part." The chanteyman sings a line and all hands come down on the chorus. He sings a second line and someone else—perhaps all hands—sings the first line but in a lower tone, then all come together on the chorus.

Most of the songs are short haul chanteys used to shift cargo, to haul nets, in "heaving down" (a term applied to shoving a boat or schooner afloat in the West Indies), in ship launching, and sometimes for cadence count in rowing.

As the song is sung, it is customary for the chanteyman to admonish the crew in various ways—to keep the lines clear, to heave harder, to stop or any number of things. These remarks are always kept in the rhythm of the song if not on the tune. This suggests that the chanteyman is not just anyone, but a person of authority in the crew.

Certain songs are used for special purposes. "Yado" is a song always sung at a launching, according to Captain Dean MacFarlane of Carriacou. "Where has Boney Gone" is sung "most generally when heavin' down vessel" according to Captain Arlington Richardson of Paget Farm, Bequia, while "Do Old Moses" was used to pull for a whale.

Since these songs are little known to the rest of the world, have remarkable rhythms and are still a real part of a viable tradition, it seems well to present a number of them as illustrative material. At the same time, there is no urgent reason to include any of the well-known traditional chanteys, for while they have been widely preserved in printed sources they are seldom sung today by seafaring people.

Variant

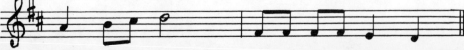

Yado

Yado yado Bellirena yado,
Hay yea Bellirena yado.

Yado yado Bellirena yado,
Hay hay hay yea Bellirena yado.

If you want to see the monkey dance
Break a pepper in his tail.
Yado yado Bellirena yado.
Hay hay yea Bellirena Yado.

Massa dead he leave no money,
He left no cent to wash he clothes.
Yado yado Bellirena yado,
Hay hay yea Bellirena yado.

Massa dead he no left no money,
He left he son for catch de cow whale.
Hay hay yea Bellirena Yado,
Yado yado Bellirena yado.

Massa dead he no left no money,
Mistress have to beg a penny.
Hay hay yea Bellirena yado,
Yado yado, Bellirena yado.

This is one of the most popular songs found in the West Indies. The tune is consistent but the verses—except for the chorus, "Massa dead he left no penny," and "If you want to see the monkey dance/Break a pepper in his tail"—are almost infinite in variety and are often made up on the spur of the moment.

Although the lines "Massa dead he left no money,/Mistress have to beg a penny" will undoubtedly please the scholar looking for signs of social protest, the fact remains that the thought of someone losing his money and dying a pauper is as amusing to the singers as the antics of a monkey with a pepper in his tail.

Sam Gone Away

Well done, well done for Sam.
Sam gone away on bully man-o'-war.
Hoorow, hoorow, hoorow for Sam.
Sam gone away on bully man-o'-war.

I wish I was a bos'n aboard the man-o'-war.
Sam gone away on bully man-o'-war.
Hoorow, hoorow, hoorow for Sam.
Sam gone away on bully man-o'-war.

Well done, well done, well done, brave boy.
Sam gone away on bully man-o'-war.
I wish I was the chief mate aboard the man-o'-war.
Sam gone away on bully man-o'-war.

Well done, well done, well done, brave Sam.
Sam gone away on bully man-o'-war.
I wish I was a cook aboard the man-o'-war.
Sam gone away on bully man-o'-war.

Hoorow, hoorow, hoorow for Sam.
Sam gone away on bully man-o'-war.
I wish I was the chief mate aboard the man-o'-war.
Sam gone away on bully man-o'-war.

"Walk back de tackle you pass. Take up de slack." (spoken)
Start again! Sam gone away on bully man-o'-war.

"Walk back the tackle you pass" (spoken)
Hoorow, hoorow, hoorow for Sam.
Sam gone away on bully man-o'-war.

"Steady jocking, steady jocking [Don't let it swing]" (spoken)
Sam gone away on bully man-o'war.

Hoorow, hoorow, hoorow for Sam.
Sam gone away on bully man-o'-war.
Well done, well done, brave boy.
Sam gone away on bully man-o'-war.

"Whatch out for that roller there! Keep that roller clear." (spoken)
Sam gone away on bully man-o'-war.
"Block on block." (spoken)

RING DOWN BELOW

Ring down below. Ring down. Ring down everybody.
Ring down below. Ring down. I tell you
Ring down below. Ring down. Yes, I meet up de debbil
Ring down below. Yes, I meet de debbil. Beat hell out
of the Bible.

Chorus: *Ring down below.*
Yes de debbil he tell me he prayin' for sinners.

Chorus
Ring down, ring down everybody.

Chorus
Going down yonder meet up de debbil.

Chorus
Yes, de debbil he tell me he prayin' for sinner.

Chorus
Yes, I meet de debbil and he beat hell out of de Bible.

Chorus
Yes, de debbil he tell me he prayin' for sinner.

Chorus
Going down and meet de debbil.

Chorus
Oh ring down, ring down everybody.

Chorus

Ding Well

Ding well, ding well. Oh where Boney gone O?
Oh ding well, Oh ding well. Oh where Boney gone?

Heave Away (spoken)
Boney gone to de river. Go wash baby clothes
Ding well, Ding well, Oh where Boney gone?

Heave Away (spoken)
Ding well gone to the river. Wash Boney cloth
Ding well, Ding well, O where Boney gone?

" 'Vast heav'n'." (spoken)

Mountains so High

Oh de mountings so high and de valleys so low
Hurrah, hurrah Oceania
Oh Oceania Mother I'm sorry has to say
We are bound right over the mounting.

When the mounting so high an' the valley so low
Hurray, hurray Soussana, Oh Oceania Moder
We're sorry to say we are bound right over the
    mounting.

Yes we are bound right over the mounting
Where the green grass does grow
Row, row, Oceania Moder
I'm sorry have to say/We are bound right over
    the mounting.

When the mounting so high and the valley so low
Oh row, row, Oceania Moder,
I am so sorry to say
I'm going over the mounting.

Drive Her Captain[6]

Oh drive her, Capting, drive her
And away Hay Yaah!
Oh yes I'm for Alebama
And away Hay Yaah!

Well the steamboat is due in tomorrow
And Away Hay Yaah
So drive her, Capting, drive her
And Away Hay Yaah!

Oh drive her, Capting, drive her
And Away Hay Yaah
We are bound for Alebama
And Away Hay Yaah!

Oh yes, come leave all, you all
And Away Hay Yaah
When the steamer is due in tomorrow
And Away Hay Yaah!

Well, you call yourself a Capting
And Away Hay Yaah!
Oh you're bound now to Alebama
And Away Hay Yaah!

Well drive her, Capting, try her
And Away Hay Yaah
We are bound for Canada
And Away Hay Yaah!

STORMALONG

Storm along, stormalong my boys, stormalong,
Yankee Johnny would you stormalong.
Brave bad Johnny, would you stormalong.
Yankee John, stormalong, brave bad Johnny
  stormalong.
Yankee John stormalong. Oh brave bad Johnny
  would you stormalong.
Oh what you holler?
Stormalong, Yankee Johnny, would you stormalong.

Long time was a very good time,
Bully blow, blow, blow, boys,
Long time in Mobile Bay,
Bully long time ago.

Long time was a very good time,
Bully weigh, weigh, weigh, boys,
Dogglin' line in Old Mauby Bay,
Bully long time ago.

Long time was a very good time,
Bully blow, blow, blow,
Khaki drilling was four pence a yard,
Bully long time ago.

Long time in Mobile Bay,
Bully aye, aye, aye, yah.
Long time was a very good time,
Bully long time ago.

Litty, Letti look, Ah catch him at last,
Bully blow, blow, blow, boys.
Litty, Lettie look I'll catch him at last,
Bully long time ago.

Long time in Mobile Bay
Bully blow, blow, boys,

Long time in Mobile Bay,
Bully long time ago.

"Blow, Boys, Blow"

A Yankee ship bound down the river
Blow, boys, blow
A Yankee ship bound down the river
Blow, my bully boys, blow, well done.
Let it blow today but not tomorrow
Blow, boys, blow
Blow, my bully boys blow, well done.

A Yankee ship bound down the river
Blow, boys, blow
A Yankee ship bound down the river
Blow, my bully boys, blow well done.

Let me tell you what the white men eat for
   they dinner
Blow, boys, blow
Mosquito leg and sand fly liver
Blow, my bully boys, blow well done.

Tell you what the white man use to their
   dinner
Mosquito leg and sand fly liver
Blow, my bully boys, blow.

Oh the Yankee says, "Goddam these niggers,"
Blow, boys, blow

Oh the Yankee says, "Goddam these niggers,"
Blow, boys, blow
Let it blow today and not tomorrow
Blow, my bully boys, blow well done."
"Now remember to walk back the tackle you pass." (spoken)

Bulldog

Massa, where you get this dog?
Bulldog, don't bite me.
Massa, where you get this dog from?
Bulldog, don't bite me.

Beau, Beau, Beau is a big bulldog.
Bulldog don't bite me.
Bull, bull, bull is a big bulldog.
Bulldog don't bite me.

Massa, where you get this dog from?
Bulldog, don't bite me.
Massa, where you get this dog from?
Bulldog, don't bite me.

Massa, where you get this dog from?
Bulldog, don't bite me
Bo Bo is a big bull dog
Bulldog, don't bite me.

Man-o'-war Sailor

You better leave me 'lone, you better leave me 'lone,
Man-o'-war sailor, you better leave me 'lone.
You 'member the night when you jump through me
     winder?
Man-o'-war sailor, you better leave me 'lone.
You jump through me winder—you mash up all me
     china
Man-o'-war sailor, you better leave me 'lone.
You better leave me 'lone. You better leave me 'lone,
Man-o'-war sailor, you better leave me 'lone.

Oh man-o'-war sailor, dey is damn bad sailor,
Man-o'-war sailor, you better leave me 'lone.
Oh man-o'-war sailor, dey is damn bad sailor.
Man-o'-war sailor, you better leave me 'lone.

You better leave me 'lone, you better leave me 'lone
You better leave me in me long nightgown.
Man-o'-war sailor, dey is damn bad sailor.
Man-o'-war sailor, you better leave me 'lone.
"Walk back de tackle you pass." (spoken)

also:

Hilo

Hilo boy Hilo.
Hilo bully from Baltimore
Hilo boys Hilo.

Oh Monday morning in the month of May
Hilo boys Hilo.
Hilo bully and away we go
Hilo boys Hilo.

This Monday morning in the month of May
Hilo boys Hilo.
I meet up a woman and I knock her aground
Hilo boys Hilo.

Oh she fall upon the ground
And we see all she [have?] tongue
Hilo boy Hilo.

Monday morning in the month of May
Hilo boys Hilo.
Oh I meet Mister Devil with a big old Bible
Hilo boys Hilo.

He reading the sermon of a dead jackass
Hilo boys Hilo
Oh he meet up with two men and he knock them aground
Hilo boys Hilo.

He jump on the back and he ride them around
Hilo boys Hilo
Oh he meet up the women and he knock them aground
Hilo boys Hilo.

Oh they fall upon the ground and we see all they
    tongue.
Hilo boys Hilo
Oh an old mammy pass and we laugh it off
Hilo boys Hilo.
Hilo bully and a ha ha ha
Hilo boys Hilo
Oh two old men they pass and they laugh it off
Hilo boys Hilo.

Monday Morning in the month of May
Hilo boys Hilo
Oh I meet Miss Fifi in Anse la Pin
    "Walk back the tackle!" (spoken)

Rosabella

Come let me join Rosabella. "Heave away"—(spoken)
Come let me join Rosabella. "Heave away." (spoken)
Come let us join. Come let us join,
The saucy Rosabella. "Heave away." (spoken)

Contractor beat the *Orinaca*, "Heave away" (spoken)
The *Orinaca* beat the *Contractor*, "Heave away." (spoken)
He beat her once, he beat her twice
He beat her right down the Orinoco. "Heave away." (spoken)

Come let us join (Come let us join) Rosabella. "Heave away." (spoken)
Come let us join Rosabella. "Heave away." (spoken)
Come let us join. Come let us join
The saucy Rosabella.
"Watch for that block, haul back that thing tight." (spoken)

Come let us join (repeat stanza three)
"Take in the slack)" (spoken)

Come let us join Rosabella, "She make a start!" (spoken)
Come let us join Rosabella, "Here she going now." (spoken)
Come let us join, Come let us join
The saucy Rosabella.

The *Orinaca* beat the *Contractor*. "Heave away" (spoken)
The *Orinaca* beat the *Contractor*. "Heave away" (spoken)
He beat her once, He beat her twice,
He beat her right down the Orinoco. "Heave away." (spoken)

Come let us join Rosabella. "Walk back that tackle." (spoken)
Come let us join Rosabella. "Heave away." (spoken)
Come let us join. Come let us join the saucy Rosabella.

"She make a start." (spoken) Come let us join Rosabella
"Here she going now." (spoken) Come let us join Rosabella
"More and more." (spoken) Come let us join. Come let us join
The saucy Rosabella. "Make fast and slack back that tackle." (spoken)

Old Moses[7]

Do old Moses try your best
Do old Moses try your best
Do old Moses try your best
St. Hillary gone ahead of you.

If'en they know they strike you there

If'en they know so long ago
If'en they know they hold you there
St. Hillary gone ahead of us.

Do old Moses try your best
Do old Moses try your best
Do old Moses try your best
St. Hillary gone ahead of we.

If'en they know they can hold you there
If'en they know where to wear you out
If'en they know where to hold you down
St. Hillary ahead of us.

Chorus.

If'en they saw the big cow whale
If'en they know it ahead of me
If'en they saw the big cow whale
St. Hillary ahead of us.

Chorus.

If'en they strike that big bull whale
If'en they strike by one, by two
If'en they strike that big bull whale
St. Hillary gone ahead of me.

Chorus.

If'en they see a big cow whale
If'en they see it's bulls and cow
If'en they see that big bull whale
St. Hillary ahead of us.

Chorus.

Do old man Moses—"walk boys!" (spoken)
Do old Moses try your best—"spring ahead!" (spoken)
Do old Moses, "Row boys" (spoken)
Do old Moses. "Go for him now!" (spoken)

"Pappy You Done Dead"[8]

Blow, boys, blow
Bully Pappee you no bully for me
Bully blow, boys, blow
You climb up the riggin' you can't
    get aloft
Bully beau, beau, beau.
Pappee you try and you don't make a foot
Pappee you don' go
You take a piece of fire rope, make de knee rope
Bully blow, blow, blow
Oh Pappee you try, but you can't make it
    last
Bully blow, blow, blow.
Oh you try an' make land but you can't
    get on dock
Bully blow, blow, blow
Oh you head with liquor, your foot with marra
Bully blow, boys, blow.

A drunken man can't make up aloft, Pappy
    don't you know.
If you pass up the jack and drop the
    mainsail

You've got a long time to live.
If you get a hand on the top of that mast
Pappy you don't know
If you fall right down and drop on de
  deck
Pappy you're dead, you're dead like a fish

So Pappy me boy don't drink any rum
Any more 'fore to climb
You must climb with your head very clear,
  Pappy boy.
You forgot the liquor inside your pocket
Pappy don't you know
  When you get aloft and you get the (——)
Pappy down comes you.

Now you gives the sailors a lot of trouble
  Just to get you ashore
And report your death to your daughter dear
Pappy you done dead.
We goin' get down the waist and sew you up good
Pappy we will leave you
We will carry you off in the deep of the sea
And will bury you there.

We will send the note to your children and
  wife
That you died under rum
For the rum was sweet and you was most sweet
And you fell from aloft.

And the captain was into the cabin himself
When he first saw you
Your hand is broke and your leg is broke
Pappy a hard day's work
Then they try to make a bonny sail boat
For to take you ashore
But there is no use for no doctor's ashore
Pappy you don't know.

So we try to hustle right out to sea
Pappy you done dead
But you given the sailors so much hard work
For to sew wet sails
But they patch you up somehow when death come
  to you
And we do it the best. And two big chunks of iron

We put on your head. And we sank you down.
And we notice you going to the bottom at least
In the deep, deep sea
And you gone out of sight.

But the smallest sailor he stop by the taffrail
And he was asleep and when he saw some bubbles
He think you come back but you was done gone
And the family news they remember it but they
    say in the heart
But the mostest thing that the captain done,
    "Look," he cry, "Wait there."

For Pappy was good and a good drunk sailor. Pappy
    he is gone.
And they send the cable home to his wife. 'Pappy he
    is dead.'
And they wonder to know he don't speak how he dead
They do not know at all. But the ship reaching port
And they tell their family.
"That's the time cry start."

A far more artistic kind of singing took place in the fo'c'sle. There the songs were more sustained, their narrative quality more fully developed and their variety greater.

On a long voyage the sailor had scant time to himself. According to the little verse set down by Dana, life was rather drab:

> For six days thou shalt labor
> As hard as thou art able
> And on the seventh holystone the deck
> And overhaul the cable.

Yet when he did have leisure, he seems to have amused himself in a limited number of ways—with knot work, carving on wood and bone (called scrimshaw), painting, yarning and singing. Many of the songs he sang were hits of the day that he picked up in places of amusement ashore. Some were bawdy, some sentimental, and they may or may not have borne references to the sea. He might sing songs written by hacks ashore about sailors—like "The Ocean Burial," "The Jacket of Blue," or "The Cottage by the Sea," which begins:

> Just one year ago tonight Love
> I became your blushing bride

> You promised I'd be happy
> But no happiness I find
> For tonight I am a widow
> In the cottage by the sea.

As a group, sailors have a tendency, as do most folk groups, to be sentimental, romantic and obscene, and these songs fitted into their needs very well. A third type of song was really a sea song and not, like the others, an adjustment or an adaptation. Very often they were made by the sailors themselves, and these are the songs that need the closer scrutiny.

To the critic, it becomes immediately apparent that the folk composer had very definite criteria to which he adhered closely when making up a song. First he must select a topic. Usually it was a dramatic one and stressed action over philosophy. Sometimes he sang of his vessel, her beauty, speed or seakeeping qualities. More often he sang of tragedies—shipwrecks, storms, battles, mutinies, spectres or sudden and awful death.

Once he had hit upon a topic he needed a tune, and although he sometimes made one up, he usually selected one from another song—either a sea song or a popular ditty heard on shore in the rum shop, in church or at the dance hall. To this tune he fashioned his verse, sometimes driving the words to fit the music—and in order that others might recognize the tune, he frequently incorporated the original song's title in the text, a device known as "signature." Hence, somewhere in the text one might find the line "He played 'The Braes of Ireland' for nine hours long," or "She would fly 'the stars and stripes forever.'"

Quite frequently the song would have a set opening. Particularly popular among Irish composers was a "come-all-ye" beginning, as "Come all ye seamen bold and harken to my song." Otherwise it would open with a line that would fix the song in time and geography, as "It was the fourth of July when we set sail," or "All the skippers o' Scarsburgh/Sat drinking at the wine,/There fell a rousing them amang,/On an unsealley time." Sometimes, too, the opening line would supposedly identify the original singer or event—"Charles Gustabus Anderson, it is my Christian name," or "She's the schooner 'Lucy Foster,' she's a seiner out of Gloucester."

Often between each stanza there would be a chorus which could be sung by all hands but often was rendered solely by the singer, and it was frequently the practice among American sailors to conclude with a moral which urged men to shun liquor, women, bad company or some other pestiferous force in the life of the ordinary sailor. Frequently, too, the last line would be spoken rather than sung to let the audience know it was truly over.

It has been popularly believed that a singer was hired in each crew to sing songs and lead chanteys. If true, no record of such transactions has ever been found. Moreover, no skipper would willingly hire such a person for entertainment purposes. Singers and chanteymen were always in demand on shipboard to give work harmony and to brighten leisure hours, but they were hired to work first and to play after.

With the shape of the song before him, the composer now had to fill in the details and develop the language of the poem. In the latter category, certain lines and phrases were very popular among the seafarers, and these lines and phrases, even stanzas, would occur in different songs until they reached the status of clichés. (I once noticed that the phrase "the girl I left behind me" turned up in over a dozen songs and "root hog or die" in almost as many.)

We now have before us most of the tools of the singer's trade; it remains only to see how these things were used. Of primary importance was accuracy of detail and adherence to events—not as they ought to be but as they "really happened." (This writer, on a passage from England to Ireland, followed the track of Paul Jones given in "The Stately Southerner"— a song of the American Revolution—and the landmarks popped up one after another in position and on time.) Beyond this, the composer always tried to identify the vessel by her characteristics; thus we are told that you could know the brig *John* by "the ringtail on her driver." And whenever possible the crew, from captain to cabin boy, would be included and each one of them would be identified in some special way:

> Our mate he was a Dartmouth man, his name was Mr. Wood,
> And when it came to boat steering, he was really very good.[9]

Not only did the composer identify his vessel and his crew, but the seaman always seemed to develop an affection for his ship, although it may at times have been grudging. At any rate, songs about ships seem invariably to perceive them as "She's the Liverpool packet, O Lord let her go," or "Now, the Flying Cloud was as fine a ship as ever sailed the seas/Or ever spread a main tops'l before a pleasant breeze." Further, he always accepted the ship's best qualities, generally her speed: "She could easily outsail any ship coming out from Baltimore."

When the singer was not extolling the virtues of his ship and her crew, he usually recounted a story of tragedy. Often he incorporated customs, beliefs and superstitions in these stories. In a song like "William Glen,"[10] for example, the entire story hinges on the fact that a murderer is aboard. As soon as this is discovered, the crew throws the guilty party overboard, the storm subsides and the vessel goes on her way. The idea behind the story is, of course, that the sea will allow no person with blood or debts on his hands to survive on its surface. Closely read, sea songs become a microcosmic expression of both marine lore and life.

There now remains one point to clear up—the singer and his instruments. Usually the songs were sung without accompaniment, although sometimes a concertina (called a seagoing piano) was employed, and very often the audience would keep the rhythm by stamping on the deck or rapping the table. The popular concept of banjos, violins and guitars as accompanying instruments is simply ridiculous. There was no room in the fo'c'sle for such dunnage, and anyway the sea is hostile to glue, catgut and all that is used to make up those instruments.

Contrary to popular belief, seafaring men are a bit clannish and there is a strong inclination to stick to one kind of ship or occupation at sea. Charles Nordhoff points this out in his book *Whaling and Fishing*, where he shows how hard it was for a merchant seaman to find a berth on a whaleship. He says in part, "It is a singular fact that the seaman can tell . . . at a single glance what special department . . . he has most generally followed. . . . A Man-of-Warsman is known by a certain jaunty neatness of attire . . . the Merchant seaman is rough . . . the whale man . . . is round shouldered . . . He has a singular air of shabbiness about him."[11]

As a result of this, there was a strong tendency to make up songs that pertain to the specializations of seafaring. Since the kinds of seafaring are very different, the songs differ markedly although they cling to the same patterns of design. For instance, whale ships were notoriously dull sailors and the dirtiest vessels afloat. (It has been said that when the *Charles W. Morgan* returned to New Bedford from her final voyage, the stench nearly drove the population of the city away, and the Board of Health had her towed out to Buzzards Bay until she was cleaned up.) As a result of this, the songs composed about whale ships said little about spotless sails, great turns of speed or facility of ship handling. Rather they talked about whales taken and lost, pulling contests, the hazards of killing whales, and the danger of ice or the tedium of a long voyage. Of considerable interest to most sailors, but particularly to whalemen, were low wages, poor food and such alongshore parasites as crimps, saloonkeepers, and boardinghouse managers who depended on stealing their wages for a livelihood.

Fishermen, too, have their own songs which extol various things about their occupation. Sailing in smallish vessels "of a hundred tons or more" with a fore-and-aft rig, they sing of the special characteristics of their own hazards—going astray in the dories, being run down by larger ships in the fog and the ability of their skippers to drive the vessels to market.

Coasters also have their songs extolling or making light of their vessels, discussing their characteristics, and mentioning local ports, humorous experiences and hazards of the immediate coast. Since coasting, at least in the United States, was not really considered seafaring and was often a part-time business run on either a family or a local basis, the attitudes of the crews were somewhat different from those of the deepwater men. (Captain Spurling of Islesford, Maine, observed in this connection, "My father wa'ant a seafaring man.. He went in coasters but never went foreign, don'tcha know." He also stated that his brother was "a fisherman" because he had been on the Grand Banks in schooners.) Each and every type of coasting craft had songs and stories made up about them, from the song about *Eliza Jane*, which "would have been a fine old craft with her bow on aft," to the songs of the Thames barges once popular on the English coast.

The big ships, the privateers, packets and clippers, tended toward other types of songs. The privateer sang of the chase, the close battles, the heroics of war, and the great ability of the skipper and the toughness and speed of the vessel, the prowess of the crew. A few of the songs like the one about Captain Death, a famous privateer of the seventeenth century, have come down to us today.

The merchantmen talked about fire, shipwreck, Cape Horn, Australia, "flash girls" and the hazards of life ashore, but particularly they stressed the speed of the vessel—as in "The Liverpool Packet," "The Flying Cloud" and other songs. Not infrequently they sang of hardships aboard ship, the various ethnic groups in the crew or what happened on a voyage. Strangely enough, these songs did not have to have a connection with famous ships to survive. One, "The Josie Walker," is about a packet ship that belonged to the Walker family of New York. She burned at dockside after the completion of her first trip and in so doing seriously damaged a vessel belonging to Cornelius Vanderbilt. The litigation incurred in this mishap long outlasted the life of the vessel.

Many of the songs of the deepwatermen told stories embodying not only the perils of the sea but beliefs and superstitions of sailors as well. "Twas on a Friday Morning" shows what happens when a vessel leaves port on that day and then meets a mermaid. "The Flying Dutchman" tells what occurs when one meets with that dread vessel off Cape Horn, and "The Ghostly Fishermen" recounts the "living proof" that drowned men will board the vessel from which they were lost when next she visits that fatal spot.

This is not, of course, to say that particular kinds of songs were sung only in particular ships or that there was no changeover from ship to ship. There was, and whalemen went in a man-o'-war and man-o'-warsmen went in merchant ships from time to time. These migrant souls took their songs with them. Hence "The Monitor and the Merrimac" might be used to regale a watch below while rounding Cape Horn, or a whaleman might sing "The Banks of Newfoundland" aboard a packet bound for Ireland. Eventually these songs, if they struck the fancy, would become part of the repertoire of all deepwater sailors; but, by and large, the majority of songs sung in any given class or type of ship would pertain predominantly to it. Finally, the longer the voyage the more songs one could expect to find. It is not that collectors have been more avid in their search for whaling songs, but simply that whalemen had more time to compose songs and longer to sing them.

As opposed to the chantey, the fo'c'sle song has had a better life. When gang work was replaced by mechanical devices, the chantey died, and it has only been revived to be played by orchestras or as popular entertainment. Its relation in this form to the real thing is analagous to an animal in the zoo compared to one in the wild. The longer, more organized fo'c'sle song has survived great change. It came ashore, was sung in homes and adapted itself to other occupations. Some have remained popular as cowboy songs, as mining songs and as songs sung in the lumber woods. In fact, we are told that when times were hard and jobs few in Michigan, no man would be hired to work in a lumber camp without being able to sing all of "The Flying Cloud."

The songs in the following group have been selected from hundreds to illustrate the ideas mentioned here, and do not represent even a miniscule corpus. Let us look at the songs themselves and see how well they jibe with the foregoing facts.

YOUNG ALLAN[12]

All the skippers o' Scarsburgh
   Sat drinking at the wine;
There fell a rousing them amang,
   On an unseally time.

Some there rous'd their hawk, their hawk,
    And some there rous'd their hound,
But Young Allan rous'd his comely cog,
    As she stood on dry ground.

"There's nae a ship in Scarsburgh
    Will sail the seas wi' mine,
Except it be the Burgess Black,
    Or than the smack call'd Twine.

"There's nae a ship amang you a'
    Will sail alang wi' me,
But the comely cog o' Hecklandhawk,
    And Flower o' Yermanie,
And the Black Snake o' Leve London;
    They are a' gane frae me."

Out it speaks a little wee boy
    Stood by Young Allan's knee;
"My master has a coal-carrier
    Will take the wind frae thee.

"She will gae out under the leaf,
    Come in under the lee,
And nine times in a winter night
    She'll turn the wind wi' thee."

When they had wagered them amang
    Full fifty tuns o' wine,
Besides as mickle gude black silk
    As clathe their lemans fine,

When all the rest went to the tows,
    All the whole night to stay,
Young Allan he went to his bower,
    There with his God to pray.

"There shall nae man gang to my ship
    Till I say mass and dine,
And take my leave o' my lady;
    Gae to my bonny ship syne."

Then they sailed east on Saturday,
    On Sunday sailed west;
Likewise they sailed on Mononday
    Till twelve, when they did rest.

At midnight dark the wind up stark,
    And seas began to rout,

Till Allan and his bonny new ship
   Gaed three times witherlands about.

"O," sighing says the Young Allan,
   "I fear a deadly storm;
For mony a heaving sinking sea
   Strikes sair on my ship's stern.

"Where will I get a little wee boy
   Will take my helm in hand
Till I gang up to my tapmast
   And see for some dry land?"

"O waken, waken your drunken men,
   As they lye drunk wi' wine;
For when ye came thro Edinbro town
   Ye bought them sheen o' ben.

"There was nae shoe made for my foot,
   Nor gluve made for my hand;
But nevertheless, my dear master,
   I'll take your helm in hand
Till ye gang to the tall tapmast
   And look for some dry land.

"And here am I, a little wee boy
   Will take your helm in han'
Till ye gang up to your tapmast,
   But, master, stay not lang."

"I cannot see nae day, nae day,
   Nor nae meathe can I ken;
But money a bonny feather-bed
   Lyes floating on the faem,
And the comely cog o' Normanshore,
   She never will gang hame."

The comely cog o' Nicklingame
   Came sailing by his hand;
Says, Gae down, gae down, ye gude skipper,
   Your ship sails on the sand.

"Come down, come down, my gude master,
   Ye see not what I see;
For thro and thro our comely cog
   I see the green haw sea."

"Take fifty ells o' gude canvas
   And wrap the ship a' round;

And pick her weell, and spare her not,
   And make her hale and sound.

"If ye will sail, my bonny ship,
   Till we come to dry land,
For ilka iron nail in you,
   Of gowd there shall be ten."

The ship she listnd all the while,
   And, hearing of her hire,
She flew as swift threw the saut sea
   As sparks do frae the fire.

The first an shore that they came till,
   They ca'd it Howdoloot;
Wi' drums beating and cannons shouting,
   They held our gude ship out.

The next an shore that they came till,
   They ca'd it Howdilee
Wi' drums beating and fifes playing,
   They bare her to the sea.

The third an shore that they came till,
   They ca'd it Howdilin
Wi' drums beating and pipes playing,
   They tow'd our gude ship in.

The sailors walkd upon the shore,
   Wi' their auld baucheld sheen,
And thanked God and their Lady,
   That brought them safe again.

"For we went out o' Scarsburgh
   Wi' fifty ships and three;
But nane o' them came back again
   But Young Allan, ye see."

"Come down, come down, my little wee boy,
   Till I pay you your fee;
I hae but only ae daughter,
   And wedded to her ye'se be."

"Bold Princess Royal"[13]

'Twas the fourth of July when we set sail
Oh the man from our masthead said, "Sail ho!" He cry
With a loud speaking trumpets said, "Where are you
  bound?"

"We are bound down northwestwards Cairo to
  go view
We are down, down to northwestward, Cairo to go view.
Will you back up your topsails and heave your ship to?
For we have a few letter to send on by you."

Up comes our chief mate and says, "That cannot be."
Up springs our captain says, "What will he do?"
Up springs our captain says, "What will you do?"
We'll rock our nice ship and likewise our crew.

Then step forth our chief mate says, "That will not be."
Then step forth our chief mate says, "That can not be."
Then step forth our chief mate says, "That will not be.
For we'll shake out our courses and home she must go.

"Then get down below, boys, and shake down those wedge,
Get down below, boys, and back out those wedge
Get down below, boys, and back out those wedge
For The Princess in danger, the colors she'll fly."

They fired their shot, man, but it cannot prevail
For all of their shot, boys, it cannot prevail.
For all of their shot, boys, it cannot prevail.
Get down below, boys, and sing merrily
And the buckets of liquor like salt water will flow.

"Tell him the reason now why that song."
"You see, they was pirating and every ship that pass they
used to go and sink the ship and take all that they have;
take all the money and everything, see, and sometimes all the
men drown. And every other time they sunk them—they can't get
them, but this one was going and when she see it, she going at
it, but the mate will save them. It was the mate was wise."
"Was she a rum-runner?"
"Yes."
"It was the mate. They [would] take all them and they
kill 'em. But the captain got frightened and he didn't know
what to do and he run up on the deck and he tell the mate. He
say they lost their nice ship 'and likewise the crew.' And
the mate says, 'That cannot be.' He rather would drown, die,
before he should burn; so 'Get down below, boys, and shake out

those wedges.' That mean shake out the wedge from the mast
that every time the mast do like that [bending the hands]*
she going another mile and the mast can't break because how
he forcing her and going ahead, and they fired a shot but
they couldn't break in. So after she get out of gun reach
he say, 'Get down below, boys, and sing merrily, and the
buckets of liquor like salt water shall flow.' And he ran
her on shore and she open in two. And she was the finest,
and she was lost. They sunk her down."

"Yes it was the mate that have that. That's why, you
see, you have to look for a good mate and bold enough that
will stand behind . . . "

*In order to force the most out of a vessel in former days, when the masts
were made of solid wood, the captain would knock the wedges out of the mast
and thus allow it to stand free from truck to heel. As the vessel moved in the sea,
the mast would whip, and under the tremendous weight of the timber, the ship
must go ahead or be ripped apart. It was as dangerous a venture as tying down
the safety valve on the later steam vessels to increase speed.

THE BOLD PRINCE ROYAL[14]

'Twas the eighteenth of February we sailed from our land
On the *Bold Prince of Royal* bound for Newfoundland.
With fifty brave seamen for our ship's company,
We sailed from the eastward to the westward sailed we.

We had not been sailing more than days two or three,
When a man at the mast-head a sailor did see;
She came bearing down upon us to see what we were
And under her main-mast black colors did wear.

"O God!" cried the captain, "What shall we do now?
Here comes a bold pirate, to rob us I know."
"Fear not,"· cried ship-mate, "that cannot be so,
For we'll hoist up our sails, boys, and from them we'll go."

And when this bold pirate ran up alongside
With a loud speaking trumpet "Whence you?" he cried
Our captain being exhausted caused him to say so,
"We came from fair England and we're bound to Ka-ro."* [Cairo]

"Then haul down your sails, boys, and lay your ship to
For I have a letter sent from England to you."
"We will haul down the sails, boys, and will lay our ship to
But 'twill be in some harbour, not along side of you."

We hoisted our main sails and top sails also,
Top-gallant sails and royals and from them did go.

They fired shots after us but they did not prevail
For the *Bold Prince of Royal* soon showed them her sail.

It's now we're at sea, boys, and free from all harm,
"Go down to your grog, boys, go down every one!
Go down to your grog, boys, and be of good cheer,
For there's plenty of searoom, brave boys, never fear!"

THE STATELY SOUTHERNER[15]

'Tis of the *Stately Southerner*, that carries the Stripes and Stars,
With a whistling breeze from the west-north-west blowing through
   her pitch pine spars;
Our starboard tacks we had on board, hung heavy on the gale,
One autumn night as we rose the light on the Old Head of Kinsale.

It was a clear and cloudless night, the wind blew steady and strong,
And gaily o'er the bounding deep our good ship speeds along.
The dashing billows around doth roar, as fiery seas she spreads,
While bending low her waist in snow, she buries her lee cathead.

There was no sign of short'ning sail by him who walked the poop,
And by the weight of her ponderous jib her boom bent like a hoop;
The groaning of those chess-trees that held the strong maintack.
He only laughed as he glanced beaft at the bright and sparkling
   track.

What rises on our weather bow, what hangs upon the breeze
It's time the good ship hauled her wind abreast of the Saltees.
And by her wondrous spread of sail, her long and tapering spars,
We found our morning visitor was an English man-of-war.

"Out booms, on board the *Southerner!* Out booms! and give her
   sheet
The fastest keel that cuts the deep and the pride of the British
   fleet
Comes bearing down upon us, with a high foam at her bow.
Out boom, on board the *Southerner!* Spread out your canvas
   now!"

The nightly robe our frigate wore was her three topsails large;
Her flying jib and spanker and her courses had been furled.
"Come lay aloft, my gallant tars!" The words had scarce been
   passed,
When royals and topgallant yards were crossed upon each mast.

Away! away! a shower of shot come through our rigging and mast;
The fastest keel that cuts the deep was heading our frigate fast.
Those British tars they gave three cheers from the deck of their
   corvette,

The singer, Audrey Ford, Paget Farm, Bequia

We answered back with a scornful laugh from the deck of our
   patriot bark.

Up spoke their noble Captain, as we shot in the Hadian Pass,
"Haul up your flowing courses! Lay your topsails to the mast!"
There was not a cheer from our privateer, nor did our seamen
   dread,
As the starry banner o'er our head from the mizzen peak was
   spread.

Up spoke our noble Captain, a cloud was on his brow;
He says: "My gallant heroes, our great distress is now;
We carry aloft the Stars and Stripes against that royal host;
Paul Jones the terror of the sea, shall flog them on the coast."

The night fog had not cleared away, that scarce obscured the
   shore,
A heavy mist hung o'er the land from Erin to Kingshore;
With light sails set, and booms rigged out, and stud sails hoisted
   away,
Paul Jones down in the North Channel did steer before the break
   of day.

THE GREENLAND WHALE FISHERY[16]

It was in the year eighteen hundred and one,
March the twentieth day,
We hoisted up all our topsails
And for Greenland bore away, brave boys,
And for Greenland bore away.

Greenland is a barren land,
There's nothing there grows green,
But the ice and snow,
And the whale-fish he blows,
And the daylight seldom seen, brave boys,
The daylight seldom seen.

The boatswain on the crosstrees stands,
With a spyglass in his hand,
"Here's a whale! here's a whale!
And whale-fish," he cries,
"And she blows at every span, brave boys,
And she blows at every span."

Our Captain he's walking the quarter deck,
And a clever old man was he,
"Overhaul, overhaul, in the day we take a fall,

And launch your boats to sea, brave boys,
Launch your boats all three."

Our boats being launched, and the men got in,
Took all five of our jolly boat's crew,
To steer where the whale-fish blow, brave boys,
To steer where the whale-fish blow.

The whale being struck, our lines played out,
He gave us a fluke with his tail,   '
Which caused us to lose our five jolly tars,
And we did not take that whale, brave boys,
And we did not take that whale.

When the sad news to our captain came,
Grieved his heart full sore,
For the losing of his five jolly tars.

   .   .   .   .
    .   .   .   .

"Haul down with our colors low,
Haul down with our colors low, brave boys,
And for Liverpool we'll sail, brave boys,
And for Liverpool we'll steer, brave boys,
For Liverpool we'll steer."

THE BANKS OF NEWFOUNDLAND[17]

Ye rambling boys of pleasure, I have you to beware,
If ever you sail in a Yankee ship, no dungaree jumpers wear,
But have your monkey jacket always at your command,
For beware of the cold nor'westers on the Banks of Newfoundland.

We had one Lynch from Ballana Hinch, Jim Doyle and Michael
   Moore,
In the year of '56, when our sailors suffered sore;
They pawned their clothes in Liverpool and sold them out of hand,
Not thinking of the cold nor'westers on the Banks of Newfoundland.

Our captain bein' a Yankee, our first mate was the same,
Our second mate an Irishman, from Limerick town he came,
And all the rest were Irish boys, they came from Paddy's land,
Only four or five of our seamen belonged to Newfoundland.

We had one female kind on board, Bridget Walsh it was her name;
To her I promised marriage, on me she had a claim;
She tore her flannel petticoat to make mittens for my hands,
Saying, "I can't see my true love freeze on the Banks of
   Newfoundland."

One night as I lay on my bed, I had a pleasant dream;
I dreamt I was in Liverpool way down in city field,
With a comely maid beside me, and a jug of beer in hand,
But I woke quite broken-hearted on the Banks of Newfoundland.

But now, my boys, we have fair winds, and our ship she's bound to go;
So see boys scattered around the decks, shovelling off the snow;
We'll wash her down and scrub her round with holystone and sand,
And we'll bid adieu to the Virgin Rocks on the Banks of
    Newfoundland.

The steamboat she's ahead of us; for New York we are bound,
Where the boarding masters and runners, they all come flocking
    round;
Some they go to sprees and balls, and more drive out so grand,
But little they know of the nor'west wind on the Banks of
    Newfoundland.

Refrain: So boys, fill your glasses, and merrily they'll go round,
And we'll drink a health to the captain and the girls of Liverpool
    town.

THE GHOSTLY FISHERMEN[18]

Smile if you've got a mind to, or perhaps you'll lend and ear
For boy and man together, nigh on to forty year
I have sailed across the waters, from Western Banks to Grand.
I was in some herring vessels that went from Newfoundland.

And I've seen storms I tell you, where things looked kinda blue
And in somehow or other, I was lucky and got through.
But I'll not brag, however, I'm not so much but then
I'm not much easier frightened than most of other men.

But one dark night I speak of, we were off lee shores a way,
I never will forget it in all my mortal days,
When in my dim dark watch I felt a chilling dread
That bore me down as if I heard one calling from the dead.

When on deck that September came sailors one by one,
A dozen dripping sailors, just wait till I am done.
On the decks they 'sembled, but not a voice was heard
They moved about together but neither spoke a word.

Their faces pale and sea-wet, shone ghostly through the night.
Each took his place as freely as if he had a right,
And eastward steered the vessel until land was just in sight,
Or rather I should say, saw the lighthouse towers alight.

And then those ghostly sailors, moved through the rail again
And vanished through the mist, where sun can shine on them.
I know not any reason in truth why these should come
To navigate our vessel till land was just in sight.

They are the simple sailors, I hope God rest their souls,
When their ship went under that time on Georges Shoal,
And now you've got my story, it's just the way I said,
For I believe in spirits, since that time anywhere. (spoken)

Bonny Shoals of Herrin'[19]

I left my home on a pleasant day
And to Yarmouth harbor I was farin'
For a cabin boy on a sailing
Just to hunt the bonny shoals of herrin'.

When they make you a fisherman
And you've learned all about the sailin'
Let your education start with navigation
As you hunt the bonny shoals of herrin'.

Oh the work was hard and the hours were long,
And the great men shouted up from bailin'
And I used to sleep standing on my feet
As I dreamed about the shoals of herrin'.

On a stormy sea and a livin' gale
I an' the gear that I was farin'
Sailed ten thousand miles, caught ten thousand
    fishes
As we hunt the bonny shoals of herrin'.

Night and day you're sailin'
Come winter weather weather, winter gales
Sweating a course, growing old, growing old
As you hunt the bonny shoals of herrin'.

Stormy Weather Boys[20]

We were lying in the Surrey Dock one day
The mate knew it was time to git underway.

Chorus: *Stormy weather boys, stormy weather boys*
        When the wind blows our barge will go.

He's homeward bound, but he's out of luck
For the skipper's half drunk in the Dog and Duck.
Chorus:
Then the skipper came aboard with a girl on his arm
He's going to give up bargin's and take a farm.
Chorus:
So the mate ran for'ard and the cook fell in
    the dock
And the skipper got his fingers in the main
    sheet block
Chorus:
At last we're off down Lymus Reach
But her leeboards knocked on Grimsby's Beach.
Chorus:
Cause the mate's at the wheel and he jibed her twice
Cause the skipper's got his fingers in a bowl of ice.
Chorus:
We shoved her off and away we go
But the skipper's got a bottle of beer below.
Chorus:
She fills away and she sails like heck
But there ain't no bargemen up on deck.
Chorus:
There's a crash and a bump and she's ashore
The mate says, "God, we're on The Nore!"
Chorus:
Then up jumped a mermaid covered with slime,
We took her down the fo'c'sle and had a good time.
Chorus:
On the top of the tide the barge did fleet
When the mate seen a ghost on the tops'l sheet.
Chorus:
So away we go and the ghost did steer
And the cook drank the dregs of the Old Man's beer.
Chorus:
We laid close-hauled 'round Orford Ness
When the wind backed round to the south-sou-west.
Chorus:
We reached 'ome port all safe and sound
And tied her up in Yarmouth town.
Chorus:

So after all our fears and alarms
We ended up in The Druid's Arms.
Chorus:

THE SAILOR'S GRAVE[21]

My bark is far, far from the land
When the bravest of our gallyant band
Grew deathly pale and pined away
Like the twilight of an autumn day.

We watched him through long hours of pain.
Our cares were grave but our hopes in vain.
Death's stroke—he gave no coward's alarms
But smiled and died in his messmate's arms.

We proudly decked his funeral bed
With the British flag upon his breast.
We gave him this as a badge of the brave.
Then he was fit for a sailor's grave.

We had no costly winding sheet,
We placed two round shots at his feet.
As he laid in his hammock, as snug and sound,
As a king in his long shroud—marble bound.

Cheeks they grew pale, each heart grew weak.
Oh the tears that was seen on the brownest cheek.
A quiver displayed on lips of pride
As we lowered him down by the ship's dark side.

A splash and a plunge and the task was o'er
And the billows rolled as they rolled before
As it's a loud prayer hallowed the wave
As he sank beneath, to a sailor's grave.

CHAPTER VII

ART

And the Devil bubbled below the keel:
"It's human, but is it Art?
—Rudyard Kipling, "The Conundrum
of the Workshops"

BESIDES song, there were several other art forms very popular among seafaring men, namely painting, model-making, carving on bone and wood, plain and fancy knot work and, strangely enough, tattooing.

When discussing folk art, a few principles must always be kept in mind. It is representative, it is functional and it may be decorative. These are the characteristics that separate folk art from primitive art—which is highly stylized—and from sophisticated art.

Recently a folk artist, James Dixon of Tory Island, Ireland, was referred to by an art gallery as a "folk impressionist." Such a term is a conflict in ideals. The folk artist is distressed if his creation is subject to interpretation. He does not simply draw a boat. He draws an actual vessel. When he is finished he has captured, to the best of his ability, the image of the schooner *Montanna*. If the viewer thinks the schooner is a barque or even just a type of vessel, the artist feels he has failed. In order that there be no mistake, he may accentuate some peculiar characteristic of the vessel that he has noticed—an overlong topmast, an unusual stern. In this regard Captain John Osborne of Milford, County Donegal, Ireland recalled looking carefully and noticing something unusual in a picture. "Sea gulls?" he asked the painter. The artist looked at the painting, turned it the other way up. "No, buttercups. We'll speak no more of painting," said he, rolling and stowing his canvas.

The folk artist is generally somewhat restricted by his materials, by his

Opposite: "The Winning of the Silver Cup," Jimmy Dixon, Tory Island, Ireland

tools, by his personal ability and by his culture. An artist can probably carve a piece of soft pine with expensive carvers' tools far more easily and accurately than he can shape a narwhal's tusk with a sharpened nail. A camel's hair brush and a palette in a well-lit studio will permit better work than can be accomplished in a jumping, dark fo'c'sle with a bit of marlin for a brush and a meager supply of ship's paints "borrowed" from the paint locker. The man who has been taught perspective has a great advantage over the one who learns it by trial and error.

In speaking of culture in painting, one must realize that the use of colors is definitely connected with local tastes. The Scots are likely to use a predominance of dark hues, mauve, brown and black, whereas Americans tend toward a brighter palette. In the field of painting, many of the larger "folk" canvases were done, not by seafaring men nor folk artists, but by professional craftsmen exercising "primitive" techniques. Men like Porter and Chalmers, who bulk large in books on folk art,[1] were really commercial artists with little or no maritime experience. Of course known painters are not responsible for all of maritime art, but it is safe to say, I think, that the majority of anonymous paintings of maritime scenes and ships, if done by seafaring men, were done after they had "swallowed the anchor" and retired to a life ashore. A heaving deck and crowded fo'c'sle were not conducive to painting and it would be a rare sea captain who would condone an easel on deck, a rarer crew that would tolerate it. There was simply no time or place for such work in ships.

Generally speaking, the folk artist tends toward a limited number of scenes. On the one hand, he likes to depict violence—pictures of vessels hove to in gales, wrecked, on fire; or rescues at sea and the like. On the other, he paints vessels under the most pleasant conditions, sailing with a gentle breeze abeam across a tranquil sea. The former paintings are designed to catch the stress and hazard of the moment and preserve it for history. "That's the way it was" is almost a motto with the artist; and such a picture is admirably described by Melville:

> A boggy, soggy, squitchy picture truly; enough to drive a nervous man to distraction. . . . It's the Black Sea in a midnight gale—it's the unnatural combat of the four primal elements—it's a blasted heath—it's a hyperborean winter scene—it's the breaking-up of the icebound stream of Time . . . Something in the picture's midst . . .

And then after studying the picture carefully Melville concludes:

The picture represents a Cape Horner in a great hurricane, the half foundered ship weltering there with its three dismantled masts alone visible; and an exasperated whale purposing to spring clear over the craft, is in the enormous act of impaling himself upon the three mastheads."[2]

That Melville did not recognize this scene immediately was due to the artist's ineptitude, not his intent.

The pictures in pleasant weather are ship portraits. They are rendered in serene conditions so that one can see and recognize the vessel under normal canvas. To this end, her house flag and a pennant with her name on it are often appended to the masts, while every line, shroud and sail is carefully drawn in.

Much less frequent are scenes of shipboard or shipping activity, but when these occur they almost invariably are scenes of considerable agitation. Pictures of harpooning whales, clubbing seals, spearing walrus or breaking ice floes far exceed paintings of cargo loading, watering and similar mundane activities. In short, action, violent action, is a very important ingredient in maritime folk art.

If large canvases were not readily available aboard ship, there was one area that was open to a good deal of art—the log books; and in these day-to-day accounts of the wanderings, pleasures and vicissitudes of the ship and her crew, one finds much artistry preserved, and almost all of it functional.

From time to time the skipper or master would include in the log sketches of harbors, drawings of unusual landmarks, sketches of islands, pictures of vessels sighted or spoken, and sometimes unusual scenes encountered on the trip. For the most part these were simple pen- and-ink sketches, but some of them would be embellished. Charts would include sketches of dolphins, clouds would surround the volcanic islands, birds would hover over the becalmed ship, and her shadow would be traced in the water. Sometimes several different colors of ink would be used and minor scenes sketched from life ashore—like native huts or people in canoes. Always, however, the artistry was kept subservient to the function. One drew the picture not to depict nature wild and grand, but so that it would be possible to make a landfall at a future date, enter a harbor or recognize a friend by the cut of the other vessel's jib. Anything that enhanced the possibilities was included. Anything that materially detracted from these things was excluded.

These drawings occurred in the logs of many ships, and sometimes in journals kept by crew members, but probably more were in the logs of whale ships and vessels bound to the East than in other vessels. The plodding coasters and the rapid packets bound to well-charted ports in familiar seas had little need to make pictures for future reference, and the friend sighted at sea would in all likelihood turn up at the next port.

Another functional bit of art found in whaleship logs were neat little black whales—very accurate little silhouettes of the various species, humpback, sperm or right whale. These were neatly colored black with a small blank rectangle in the middle in which would be entered a number, say "24" or "68." Actually these silhouettes were made from careful little carvings of the various species which the captain kept locked in his desk. When he killed a sperm whale, he stamped it into the log of the appropriate day and wrote the number of barrels of oil it rendered in the little box. When the chase had been a failure, the skipper simply traced in a whale's tail in a vertical position to indicate it had sounded and escaped. Now and then a more esthetic skipper would add a spout to his silhouette, embellish the margin with a harpoon or two, or possibly a stove boat, should disaster have struck during the chase.

The carving of the little whale stamps leads us quite naturally into the two art forms best known among the Anglo-American seafarers, model making and scrimshorning or scrimshaw.

Model making is a very old craft. In the chapter on shipbuilding it was noted that most vessels were formerly lofted from carefully carved wooden half-models, but the art of model making was by no means restricted to the designer. From the number of ship models extant it would seem that every sailor who survived a life at sea left behind a model when he departed for "fiddler's green." The seaman loves his ship, and it is his desire, if possible, to recapture the charm of that vessel—no matter how ugly she may seem to a stranger—for his later days. I can remember as a child time and time again being shown the model of some old hooker that the owner had carved. Almost always it was a model of a vessel "that I went in as a young man" or "the first ship that I ever made a passage in" or both. This was almost invariably followed by a description of her career, if not from initial launch, certainly from the time the model maker went in her until she vanished into oblivion, "burnt," "broke up," "cast away" or "sold foreign."

The typical model, as opposed to the builder's half-model, was usually a complete vessel with masts, sails, rigging and all her gear. Although they varied in size, most wooden models were between eighteen inches and three feet long. While some were whittled from small billets of timber, a large number were constructed like a ship. The keel was laid, the frames sawed, the planks attached with rivets or treenails and the copper sheathing tacked on. The vessels often were complete inside as well as out and crewed by mannikins. During the 1930s I recall watching the late Captain George Wright construct a model of the schooner *America*. Her hold was full of basalt ballast, her spare gear was stowed, the hammocks slung and the galley fitted out with cook, utensils and mess gear. As the vessel progressed, her decks were laid and all the interior vanished from human eyes forever.

As one might suspect, the object was to create an exact replica of a particular vessel reduced to Lilliputian size, and every effort was made not only to be accurate in all details but to have everything in proportion. It is one thing to scale down a 150–foot vessel to 36 inches, and it is quite another to reduce the fastenings, the planking, the lines, blocks and sheaves to be in proportion; yet it was done meticulously. The sheaves still spin in the blocks, the rudder turns, the ports fly open and the cannon trundle out. Only the mannikins are a travesty. They are not alive.

The artistry in these models is found not in their creation (for the best of them are no better or no worse than the ships they copied) but in the skill of construction, the faithfulness to detail and as a symbol of man's love for and patience in constructing something which at one time or another was a part of himself.

Such models are not constructed in a short time, nor can they be fashioned with crude tools, or withstand rough handling. In short, they are the products of the sailor turned out to pasture. During the long hours of retirement, he once again recalls some of the joys of his youth and re-captures them in a diminished thing.

So far we have talked of wooden vessels. There were others. I have in my possession a fine steel barque about two feet long equipped with metal sails and wire sheets; and I have seen straw models, glass models and models in bark; but in many ways the finest models of all, judged by the foregoing criteria, are those that were made of bone. Like the wooden models, the vast majority of these were made by sailors in retirement, and the best were made during the decades immediately preceding and follow-ing the close of the eighteenth century, by prisoners of war incarcerated in British and French prison ships. Some were done in whale, walrus or elephant ivory, but many more were made from fish bones or from the bones of dead animals, carved with the most rudimentary tools—a sharpened nail, a screw, a knife made out of a spoon.

In former days one of the dreaded scourges of man was the malady of "nothing to do." In the prison hulks of the Napoleonic Wars this disease, more than fever, bad food, rats or a cell in which the tide rose and fell, often caused men to go mad. At other times it reduced them to shadows that resembled the man who once served a gun less than the prison hulks resembled the lofty ships they once had been. For these men model making was the thing that gave them hope and kept their sanity intact.

Many of these models are preserved in museums around the world. I have seen them in Norfolk, Virginia; Mystic, Connecticut; Greenwich, England; and Lisbon, Portugal: but there are two in the Peabody Museum of Salem that are remarkable. The first is a small bone frigate (most of these are eighteen inches or less in length) complete in every minute detail. Trailing astern on a bone painter is a tiny wherry, and in the wherry is a bearded bone man smoking a pipe!

The second is also a small model. This one, too, is amazingly accurate as to scale and detail, but unlike any other model I have seen, it is made entirely—hull, sails, masts and rigging—of matching pink fish bones gleaned from the mess kits of a prison hulk after the chowder had been consumed. Should anyone need testimony to life aboard a prison hulk or to the tenacity of man's spirit in adversity, this should suffice.

This leaves us with but one more type of model to discuss—one that emphasizes the technique as much as the model, if not more. In Aeroskobing, Denmark, there is a small museum that houses several thousand tobacco pipes and nearly fifteen hundred ships in bottles. It is of the latter I would speak. These are by no means all of the ships in bottles in the world, but they do afford a rather compact sampling.

I have heard that during the Middle Ages, when it was considered clever to create small things, the scene of the Last Supper was preserved inside a walnut and the Lord's Prayer was inscribed on the head of a pin. During the present century we lean more toward skyscrapers and giant billboards, but apparently the old urge holds on in this particular type of model building.

Because of the problem involved in shoving a full-rigged ship into a largish bottle with as small a scrig as possible, the accuracy of detail and proportion achieved in other models is somewhat lacking, and although these little ships may present a pleasing spectacle at a distance, they all too frequently will not bear close scrutiny. Indeed, accuracy of detail is not always the bottle worker's chief purpose. Rather it is either to fill the bottle with the largest ship its height and girth will hold or to create a marine diorama within the glass. To this end, sometimes several vessels, cliffs, reefs, lighthouses and even birds soaring on the gale are added, and one is taken aback by the amount and variety of material found in one small bottle. Further, in the best bottle models there is no evidence as to how all this material gained access.

To achieve his desired end, the model maker constructs his whole ship outside the bottle. The masts are hinged, the yards are cockbilled (laid parallel to the mast) and the whole made fast to strings. Then the entire rigging is laid on deck and the whole slipped skillfully down the neck of the bottle. Now at rest on a previously prepared ocean, a string is given a tug, the masts spring erect, the yards square away, and the vessel is afloat, shipshape and Bristol fashion in her little sphere. Once everything is securely in place, the string is removed or hidden, a cork is shoved in the bottle, and the job is complete.

Another art form highly developed during the nineteenth century was a type of carving and etching known variously as scrimshorn or scrimshaw. Generally the term was, and is, applied to carving on bone and sometimes on wood, but more properly I think it should be restricted to carving on sea ivory—whale, walrus and narwhal bones. On such materials it would be largely restricted to the whaling industry, where indeed it flourished and seemed to reach its highest development among American whalemen.

Very little seems to be known about the origins of the term or the art. It has been suggested that it may be derived from exposure to the Eskimo carvers of the far north or to Portuguese wood-carvers who went to sea in whaleships. In 1791 John Haskins in his *Narrative of the Second Voyage of the Columbia* mentions that the crew carved objects from time to time, and one of the earliest known pieces of scrimshaw, dating from the last decade of the eighteenth century, is in Mystic Seaport's collection.

The first known appearance of the term "scrimshaw" appears in the log of the whaleship *By Chance* (1825–26), and thereafter appears with regularity, but is spelled variously as scrimshaw, scrimshander, scrimsha, scrimshorting, scrimshowning and so on. Interestingly enough, most of the entries refer to the practice of the art when vessels were becalmed, without whales, or otherwise inactive.[3]

One possible explanation of the term is that it is a combination of "scrim," a kind of tracery, and "horn," bone. Hence "bone etchings." A second explanation may come from "scrimsharker," which Wells lists as an old term used in the British Navy to designate anyone who was adroit at avoiding work.[4] When we note that it was most often done in idle times and when we learn that owners did not always like having the crews so employed,[5] perhaps this is a logical explanation.

Whatever the origin, whatever the meaning of the term, we may be sure of two things. As seafaring art or as a form of folk art, scrimshaw is a young expression belonging to the heyday of the American whaler, and is one of the very few truly American additions to folk material.

Aboard whaleships there was generally a good supply of whale teeth, whales' bones, baleen (the black throat bones of the whale), and occasionally even walrus and narwhal tusks. Bits of these materials were generally available and were even parceled out to the crew from time to time.[6] The pieces made from them, unlike ship models, were very durable and generally small—which helped in their preservation.

Sea ivory seems to have lent itself surprisingly well to carving with only the crudest tools. A great deal of the earliest scrimshaw was done with a sailmaker's needle, a hacksaw, a jackknife or a file, plus variously colored inks. Bits that appear turned made use of the internal structure of the bone (like a narwhal tusk cane in my possession) or were turned at the cooper's bench on the same lathe used to make equipment for the whaleship.

Basically, scrimshaw seems to divide itself into two, possibly three categories. In one we have the art of sketching scenes on whales' teeth and bones, usually in black but often with overlays of red and green. Although these sketches have many themes, women are most prominent, followed by marine scenes—ships laid to for "a gam," whale hunts, towing a dead whale, pictures of an island or a volcano. Often, too, we find a naval engagement traced on the teeth, but these were by no means as popular. Although undoubtedly done to preserve a memory, these scenes were primarily artistic.

The second type of material consists of artifacts that had a real purpose in their creation—carved objects of some utilitarian worth. Although ranging from fids, marlinspikes and small blocks on the one hand to crochet hooks and snuffboxes on the other, there are a number of recurring themes and motifs among them.

A final type of scrimshaw would be a composite object of sea ivory and wood, metal, leather and/or rope. There are dozens of different objects in this category, but again, we see a definite preference for certain items, decorations and motifs.

Mystic Seaport has a very adequate collection of scrimshaw, and a description or discussion of it is germane. In all, the collection comprises nearly twelve hundred objects. Among these there are some that are similar but no duplicates. There are two hundred fifty decorated teeth and tusks, the majority bearing pictures of women and children, closely followed by whaling scenes. Among artifacts there are sixty-one jagging

wheels, forty-two busks, thirty-six canes, twenty-two swifts, twenty-four knives, thirty-three bodkins, eighteen cribbage boards (mainly of Eskimo origin), eighteen fids, fifteen sets of clothespins, nine boxes, six tattoo needles and a number of blocks. To these could be added sixteen other artifacts reproduced more than twice—as, of all things, three cornhuskers. In compiling this list, scant notice was taken of the myriad tools—scribers, serving mallets, gimlets, awls, pod augers, planes, yardsticks, net needles and other items—for their function was primarily utilitarian and not artistic.

Of all the scrimshaw items produced, three should be discussed because of their frequent occurrence, their high degree of perfection and stylization. These are jagging wheels, canes and busks. The jagging wheel or pie crimper required a considerable amount of dexterity on the part of the carver, for the wheel was movable and fluted, and it frequently occurred in conjunction with a pricking fork. The whole was attached to an intricately carved handle, very often representing a buxom girl's leg with the wheel attached to the foot. Variations on this motif were frequently an entire female figure or an arm, and occasionally a horse, a bird or a tree. Sometimes, too, a serpent twined around the lot.

Although walking sticks varied considerably in design—from intricate carvings the entire length of the cane which was fashioned to represent a rope or which had a snake twined around it—to unadorned shafts with a single knob or a Turk's head on top, a number of designs predominated. Most frequently encountered were a girl's leg, a dog's head, a clenched fist with the thumb tucked under (a sign of health and strength to the seaman), a fist holding a ball, and a horse's leg and hoof.

Somewhat different was the busk or "stomacher," a thin, flat piece of sea ivory or baleen approximately ten to thirteen inches long, and one and a half to two inches wide. This was the most intimate item a sailor could carve, for it was made to be inserted into a corset to hold a woman's belly flat. Because the object afforded a considerable flat surface and its use was an intimate one much cherished by the sailors, the designs were often more personal and sentimental than those found on other objects. A typical piece in my possession is thirteen inches long and one inch and a half wide. The top is carved with two hemispheres. A border of roses (the flower of passion) is worked along the edge, and the center portion is divided into scenes by drawing straight lines across the piece, which bears designs on only one side. Starting at the top is a diamond shape flanked by two stars, with two beneath. This is followed by an eagle with shield bearing the motto "E Pluribus Unum," lightning in one claw, laurel leaves in the other, and the whole flanked by two stars. Next are two coconut palms and below are two hearts entwined with long curling lines in red on each side. Next comes a brig under full sail flying the "nighthawk," indicating she is homeward bound, followed by a basket of flowers and the inscription, "Roses never can exceed the beauty of a pretty maid." Finally there are two trees of life entwined.

Other scenes often depicted a languishing damsel, joined hands and sometimes a child, while a number of inscriptions are used. Several favorite ones were: "Greasy Luck," "Death to the Living, Long Live the Killers, Success to Sailors' Wives and Greasy Luck to the Whalers," "Remember me," "To Our Wives and Sweethearts, May They Never Meet,"[7] "Help, help is there nowan to save the faire damsels from the freebooters embrace." Sometimes there were verses like these:

> This bone once in a sperm whale's jaw did rest
> Now 'tis intended for a woman's breast.
> This my love I do intend
> For thee to use and not to lend.[8]

> Accept dear girl this busk from me
> Carved by my humble hand
> I took it from a sperm whale's jaw
> One thousand miles from land.

> In many a gale has been the whale,
> In which this bone did nest
> His time is past, his bone at last
> Must now support thy breast.[9]

It is to be borne in mind that we have been talking here of the more popular motifs and themes of scrimshaw. No attempt has been made to describe the larger, rarer and often more ornate objects such as may be seen in profusion at Mystic Seaport, the New Bedford Whaling Museum, Kendall Whaling Museum or the Nantucket Museum. These objects are of great variety and are very complex in design. To discuss all scrimshaw and adequately describe it would require a volume. Suffice it to say that the common thread that holds all this art together is attention to detail, proportion, accuracy of design and masterful technique. It is the rare piece of scrimshaw that is subject to interpretation in either form or function.

Today this art form still exists. Artists like Charles Sayles and Miss Macey, both of Nantucket, still work with sea ivory and continue many of the old forms, albeit for new purposes like ladies' pocketbooks or lamp stands. Equipped with better tools, better lights, a stationary platform, and seeing scrimshaw as a vocation rather than a hobby, they have developed the old art form to new heights of technical precision.

Perhaps nowhere in the maritime world do function, art and prestige meld more completely than in what one must call, for want of a better word, knot art. Traditionally a sailor was a man who could hand (take in sail), reef (shorten sail) and steer. A bos'n's mate or any petty officer was required to have, among other things, a proficiency in "marlinspike seamanship," i.e., knowing how to tie certain knots and make various splices in hemp and wire. A rigger and a sailmaker, on the other hand, had to be proficient in a myriad of knots, splices, hitches and stitches. A rigger carried a knife, marlinspike and grease horn attached to his belt almost as a badge of office, while a sailmaker was invariably equipped with a bench. Further, each of these individuals had his own special duties. For example, the rigger concerned himself primarily with reeving, maintaining and renewing the permanent rigging aboard ship. Much of his time was spent in splicing lines and in serving them, for which he had a special rhyme, "Worm and parcel with the lay/ turn and serve the other way." The sailmaker manufactured and repaired sails, hatch covers and awnings.

Like so much of maritime lore, knot making has been a cumulative development over millennia, and almost every use to which a piece of rope can conceivably be put has its attendant knot, splice or stitch that centuries of use have indicated is most efficient for the task. It is possible, no doubt, to invent new knots, but when amateurs assay it they are attempting to improve on literally millions of man-hours already devoted to the problem. *The Ashley Book of Knots*, the most encyclopedic work on the subject available, subdivides its material into forty-one chapters and lists over 3500 separate knots, splices, hitches and stitches. However, before going further, a few definitions are essential.

Just as a ship is "docked" only when in drydock, so things are "tied" only when the vessel is "tied up" or "fast" alongside the pier. Knots are "made" or "worked"; and, strictly speaking, a knot is worked into the end of a line to provide a handhold or prevent it from fraying. More practically, a "knot" is a figure worked into a line from the line itself, like a bowline or a square knot. A "hitch" attaches a line to some other object like a cleat or bollard, as a clove hitch. A "bend" unites two rope ends to make a single line, as a fisherman's bend or carrick bend. A "splice" marries two lines together, or a line back to itself in such a way that the two strands become an integral whole—a process done by braiding the line or lines together, as a short splice or an eye splice.

Each knot and splice has its own name, its own use, its peculiar method of construction and sometimes its own little story. A thief knot, which looks almost exactly like a reef knot, was so called because sailors used it to tie up their bags. A careless thief might pilfer the bag and retie it with a reef knot, thereby giving himself away.

Once detected, the thief might come in contact with the thieves' cat (cat-o'-nine-tails) and the blood knot. The former was a whip of nine strands of whale line about eighteen inches long, attached to either a bit of scrimshaw or a handsomely wrought piece of thick rope. At the end of each strand was worked a blood knot, or sometimes a bit of lead, to insure that blood would flow from its victim. The term "cat" was applied to the instrument because of the belief aboard ship that a cat carried fire in its tail. The thieves' cat was made of even tougher fiber than the ordinary one, for aboard ship theft was a truly reprehensible crime.[10]

Another knot that bears mentioning is the hangman's noose. The purpose of the contraption, which must run smoothly, is to break the neck as well as to strangle the victim. To this end, it was designed as a bulky knot. According to popular belief in the United States Navy, it is a court-martial offense to display such a knot—but should one wish to make one, it must have thirteen turns for the thirteen disciples and it should be wound widdershins about in order that the devil may more easily obtain his victim.

Lest this discussion be thought too gruesome, there is often a lighter side to the art of marlinspike seamanship. When salts get together they enjoy swapping yarns and watching skills. They also enjoy gulling the "pollywog." A great source of amusement is to ask the young fellow what he knows about knots. Depending upon his sagacity, he may then be sent to find Matthew Walker, a stopper knot, or feed the camel, a kind of fender; or someone may inquire if he has been on China station. He is then asked if he can make the most useful of all knots, the dragon bowline. When the answer is in the negative, some old salt will sigh, get up, tie a bowline and hand it to the neophyte. "There it is." "Why, that's only a bowline." "That's right. Now drag it."

A final example in the lighter vein concerns the monkey fist. This is a lumpy knot worked into the end of a long light line, like a sash cord, the purpose being to add weight to the end of this cord, called the heaving line. This is a line which is attached to a larger line, called a messenger, which in turn is affixed to a hawser. The bos'n throws the light line ashore, where it is picked up and hauled in and followed by the messenger, and then the hawser itself is dropped onto the pier. Heaving lines are made by and are the special property of the bos'n's mates. No one else is allowed to use them, and considerable care is taken in their preservation. To perfect his aim and his distance, the bos'n would spend a good deal of his time throwing the line and suppling it up, for stature was to be gained by the man who could throw longest and straightest. The heavier the monkey fist the further it would go, and it was always a temptation to "arm" the fist by inserting a heavy object inside. Navy regulations forbade such actions, as the monkey fist then developed characteristics akin to the blackjack.

During World War II, I was on a ship that tried to get alongside a dock in the Canal Zone. A second-class bos'n's mate threw two heaving lines to a longshoreman. The distance was great and the lines barely reached their destination and, since the longshoreman was not zealous in catching them, they fell overboard. At this point the first-class bos'n stepped up with his heaving line, in which was secreted a six-ounce ball bearing. The monkey fist sped like David's stone and smote the indifferent longshoreman squarely between the eyes. Down he went like a poled ox. With a twitch of the wrist the heaving line was off the dock, freed of the messenger and stowed in Davy Jones' locker. When the Port Authority came aboard to find who had knocked out the man on the dock and prefer charges, the bos'n admitted the heave with great pride, and showed the officer another un-armed heaving line. Not exactly folklore, perhaps, but certainly a by-product.

So far, we have spoken only of the functional uses of marlinspike seamanship. Yet in the execution of knots and splices there is a good deal of esthetic pleasure to be found. The stitches in the canvas have a geometric design, the long splice is so carefully laid up that it is difficult to see where it begins and ends, the lines are coiled with the sun and with a precision and neatness that astounds one, or the spare ends are "flemished down" in tidy symmetrical little mats.

From this functional aspect, one moves both quickly and easily into areas where the esthetic begins to have a share equal to the function. A mat is carefully woven and affixed to the deck at the entrance to a com-panionway. Were the purpose merely to clean one's boots, why not just tack down some line? The sailor could easily hold up his pants with a bit of old spun yarn, yet he spends perhaps twenty hours fashioning a sixteen-strand square-knot belt with a dozen different patterns and six different colors in it. The entire interior of the admiral's barge and the captain's gig are even today completely covered with a kind of seagoing lace—fancy knotwork that took months to complete and is kept spotlessly white by constant application of pipe clay. The bos'n hangs his call around his neck not by a string or a piece of cord but by a sinnet, colored either black or white. It is encased in the whistle knot.[11] It could be argued that this is functional, but the fact that this knot and this sinnet are invariably associated with this peculiar instrument would indicate a strong sense of ritualism—one of the earliest aspects of art.

Of the artistry of knots Ashley says, "There are two arts that belong to the sailor: scrimshaw ... which was peculiar to the whaling fleets, and knotting, which belonged to all deep-water ships, including whalers."[12] He further suggests that fancy knot work reached its peak prior to the clipper ship era during the nineteenth century, and suggests that contentment, long periods of isolation and illiteracy all contributed to its development—conditions that began to disappear with the advent of the clipper, the steam engine and the more modern improvements aboard ship. He also points out that the various trades sported various styles, naval people working in small stuff, merchant seamen in larger rope, and whalers—whom he considers the best artisans of all—in several media.

His points could be disputed. Life aboard ship was seldom very happy; the advent of the tall ship and the opening of trade with the Orient gave the sailor new knot problems and opened his eyes to the possibilities of knots popular in the Orient. What he says, however, in the main is correct, and of the two, knot making exceeded scrimshaw in quantity and variety and equaled it in technical finesse.

What did the knot makers manufacture? The list would be legion, but most of it was derivative of knots worked into rope, of splices and of weaving various forms of the sinnet. The knot maker created handles for implements, life preservers (blackjacks), billy clubs, handcuffs, needle cases, rope ladders, bellpulls and decorative chains, pucker strings for bags, lanyards, bracelets, quirts, table mats, rugs, handbags, magnificent handles for chests, necklaces, sashes, baskets, bottle and jar covers, shoes and an almost limitless number and variety of buttons and toggles.

These items were constructed out of different sizes of line; many were in plain colors, white, black or brown, but the artist could and did work with different colored strands to give an infinite variety to his work. As the composer works with notes and scales, the knot maker worked almost always with known forms of knots, but the artistry in him dictated that he experiment with different combinations, forms, fibers and colors. He was not content to make a simple square-knot belt. He insisted on working into his creation twisted strands, carrick bends, sinnets, different colors, and on expanding and reducing the number of strands. To him the art of his creation lay in the marriage of different knots and shapes into an harmonious whole. The more difficult the feat, the greater the art. He prided himself on finesse—his bottle cover must fit the bottle as closely as the bark clings to the tree, his knots must be uniform. His ability as a craftsman lay in the variety of his knots and the uniformity of his finished product. I have seen a seaman unlay an entire square-knot belt because one knot lacked the tension of the others, redo a tapered splice because one tuck was out of place.

Generally speaking, simplicity is one of the principles of art. We often complain that certain art forms are ornate, overdone. Only two things seem to defy this principle—the Christmas tree which never has too many decorations, and the art of marlinspike seamanship.

Like the scrimshaw, fancy knot work is still done—although on a greatly reduced scale. Unfortunately, modern line (nylon, Dacron and the rest) does not lend itself so well to the knot maker's purposes, and fancy-work has not progressed as has scrimshaw. But as long as man continues to go to sea, he will make double carrick bends, Turk's heads, round and flat sinnets and "fishermans' eyes"—not just to marry lines or stopper a water bottle or contain a thimble, but for the joy in making them, the pleasure in seeing fine work well done.

There is one final, fading art form that may not be overlooked—tattooing, which belongs almost exclusively to the seafaring profession. In the past a man could be identified as a seafarer by his tarry pigtail, by his rolling gait and by his tattoos. The pigtail has long since vanished and the rolling walk can be disguised, but the man of the sea still is likely to have a tattoo somewhere on his body, usually on his hand or arm or chest; and not infrequently the tattoo distinguishes the particular branch of the seafaring profession in which he was engaged—as, for example, crossed cannon are often worn by a gunner's mate, a fouled anchor by a boatswain.

The art of tattooing is both ancient and widespread. Along with scarification and mutilation, it was practiced by most of the American Indian tribes,[13] by the Eskimo, by Africans, by Europeans, and especially by the peoples of Oceania and the East.[14] It is from this area that in all probability much of the maritime tattooing came, and indeed where much of the best work was done. Here, on long voyages after whales or on trips to China and Australia, Jack became acquainted with Polynesians, Melanesians, Australian Bushmen and Chinese and Japanese for the first time. In many instances he found numbers of "Kanakers" sailing with him as shipmates. It was only natural that he should acquire some of their customs along with their women.

To suggest that this was a purely decorative practice is ridiculous. The process was entirely too painful, not to say hazardous, the results too permanent, and the motifs themselves all combined to make such an assumption untenable. Recently I made a voyage in a Scottish fishing vessel with a crew of eleven. Ten were tattooed in varying degrees. The only person aboard without a tattoo was a fourteen-year-old boy with but a short experience as a sailor. During his apprenticeship he had twice fallen overboard and had stoutly refused to allow his hide to be the receptacle for pictures. Because he would not allow himself to be tattooed, his shipmates to a man made his life a torment and told him that until he had been jabbed with the tattoo needle he could never become a sailor; and they further inferred that his two experiences of falling overboard were connected with his refusal to be marked by the tattooist's needle. In short, aboard Scottish fishing vessels at the present time tattooing seems to constitute a kind of initiation ceremony.

That this form of body decoration was something other than a lark is further strengthened when we look at some of the tattoos still in use today. One popular design, especially among Portuguese-American fishermen, is Christ on the Cross, which is customarily worn on the right arm. On the left arm a dripping dagger is often depicted—a symbol of strength and courage. Popular in Scotland is "TRUE LOVE" on the backs of the fingers. In America corresponding symbols are "HOLD FAST" or "GOOD LUCK" or "HARD LUCK." On old-time sailors it was fashionable to tattoo a pig on one foot and a rooster on the other. An old-time bos'n claimed that anyone so marked could not drown, for these creatures despised the water. Another old salt told me that anyone so marked would never starve aboard ship, for he carried with him two sources of food—ham and eggs. Anyone conversant with folklore will immediately recognize far older and deeper-seated significance in these symbols.

It would seem that the concept of tattooing as an initiation rite can be supported by the nature of the symbols used, many of them sexually oriented. Women, usually naked or half-naked, were often inscribed on the biceps, where they would dance or wiggle when the muscle was worked. While writing this chapter I had the opportunity to observe on a man's arm a tattoo of a girl wearing a hat; when he raised his arm, she became a naked woman with legs apart; when he flexed his muscles, her buttocks twitched. There were also extremely painful tattoos worked into the genitals, which were decorated with bees, flies, and even a barber pole.

Until fairly recent times it was not uncommon for sailors to carry numerous tattoos, and the older shellbacks were literally walking art galleries. While serpents twined round their legs and ropes and chains adorned their wrists, dancing girls, eagles, fouled anchors and square-rigged ships struggled for position on the rest of the body. In fact, the long comic song about the tatooed lady was in actuality more of a catalogue than a comedy.

Among the larger tattoos of an erotic nature were two very popular ones, the fox hunt and the rabbit chase. In the former, the dashing horseman on the back pursued the hounds yammering on the belly, while the fox was in the act of taking the ground with only his tail protruding from the posterior. The same motif was true of the rabbit scene, where the tracks led up to the navel and only the coney's tail was visible, the rest having vanished into the bellybutton. This motif was more popular than the fox scene because, according to one tattooer, "More people can see it. About the only time you'd see the other one is in the shower and who the hell cares about that?"

These larger pictures are not easily done and take literally days to make, and the days may stretch out over years. "Buddy" Mott, one of two remaining tattooers in Newport, Rhode Island, recalled that it took three and a half years to complete one large picture of an eagle and an anchor (symbols of strength and fidelity) on a sailor's back. "He'd come in and sit for awhile and then he'd ship out and it might be six months before he'd turn up. I figure I worked on that figure about thirteen hours." It might be added that the informant was working under modern conditions with an electric needle, which speeded up the work many times over.

At this point one might ask how the pictures are applied. In modern times the "tattoo parlor" is a small room down near the waterfront in a sailor town. The customer walks in and selects the design he wants from hundreds of samples on the wall, all of which have been made and many designed or adapted from older designs by the tattooer. If the customer is not satisfied with the available pictures or colors, he will consult with the artist, who will quickly sketch out the desired effect, color it to the buyer's satisfaction and begin the task. The customer removes his shirt, he is swabbed with alcohol, and the artist applies his pictures with an electric needle, which pricks the skin deeply and deposits a dye beneath the epidermis—black, green and red being the favorite shades. Each time the color is changed in the cartridge holder, a new sterile needle is employed. The task is not made easier for the artist by the fact that the process causes considerable bleeding, which must be mopped away if he is to continue his work. Should the design take more than an hour and a half, the customer is usually asked to return for another sitting.

In one parlor, which could be considered typical of most, there were 233 subjects to choose from. Many of the pictures were repeated in different colors, positions or combinations. Of these, 59 showed women (usually stripped to the waist); 44 depicted birds, including numerous eagles, 6 peacocks and several bluebirds; 8 were of panthers; 17 were of snakes, cobras mostly and usually in conjunction with something else—struggling with an eagle or twined around a panther; and 5 were of Christ. Popeye, a baby, and a host of other items appeared once, but the most popular one of them all today was what the proprietor called "the grim reaper"—the shrouded figure of death, which is very popular amongst the hippies, but which has widespread antecedants in seventeenth- and eighteenth-century gravestone carvings.

This parlor was quite different from earlier parlors in that the designs were smaller, fewer in number, and quite different. For example, there was only one scroll with "MOTHER" and, although he had "thousands of them," no anchor was displayed. A favorite amongst old-time salts was a picture tattooed on the chest: This was an eagle with a scroll bearing the sign "E Pluribus Unum" in its beak, lightning in one foot, arrows in the other. On each side was a draped American flag; beneath the eagle were crossed cannon and behind all a great fouled anchor—the illogical symbol of steadfastness and hope.

Scenes and objects that once were popular, such as the phoenix rising from her ashes, rattlesnakes, crossed harpoons, St. Anne, St. Elmo, large full-rigged ships (strangely enough, the fore- and-aft rig and sea gulls were very seldom portrayed) were not displayed; and the panther rampant with blood dripping from each claw, so popular as a back ornament during World War II, was reduced in size. Further, there was a certain amount of the comic, i.e., the frivolous—the "saucy" female sailor stripped to the waist, Bugs Bunny and Popeye, and a baby boxer—which had replaced earlier material. Finally, one tattooer pointed out that one, two or three tattoos was now the normal number, while years ago a dozen were not infrequent.

One tattooer admitted he had only twenty on his body—"For a tattoo artist that ain't many."

Formerly the work was done with a jackknife, sail needles (Mystic Seaport has a set of sea-ivory scrimshaw tattoo needles) or a sharp pin. Even today, the Japanese—who are renowned for their tattooing skill—employ thin slivers of bamboo dipped in dye. In earlier days the only attempt at sterilization taken against massive infection from the dyes—charcoal mixed with spittle, lampblack, shoe polish, paint, berry stain and the like—was the copious use of whiskey or rum taken internally as well as externally. Beyond this, the method of inserting the dyes beneath the skin was both very painful and highly septic. The triangular sailmaker's needle was dipped in dye and driven beneath the skin repeatedly, or a thread soaked in dye was stitched between skin and flesh and drawn through, or shoe polish was worked into a knife slit with the thumb. As a result of this, profuse bleeding, bruising, and toxic material beneath the skin were the plight awaiting the would-be tattooed man. The least he could expect was considerable swelling and a fever; the worst, death by septicemia.

When asked why he undergoes such discomfort, especially when it is well-nigh impossible to rid oneself of the result, the sailor's reply is generally both predictable and uninformative. Most say, "I dunno", but if pressed they say either, "I was with a guy and we all got it done" or "I was smashed." One man said he had a first tattoo done on his right arm when he was "smashed" and another one on his left arm when he was sober "to even them off."

Drunk he may be when he has it done, but Jack Tar talks about it a lot first in the fo'c'sle, as any man knows who has been to sea, and long before he goes to the parlor he may well have the design firmly fixed in his mind. The alcohol within him is for Dutch courage and the "guys" with him are a prearranged audience—if guys there be, for many a sailor goes to the parlor alone. Finally, the kind of tattoo offered and the fact that Jack may return again and again to his tattooer would belie the idea that getting tattooed is a drunken whim. That it is a love of art on the sailor's part is made doubtful to a large extent by the number of tattoos on the back, where they can be admired only as Perseus admired Medusa—with a mirror.

Perhaps this is not a high art, but if it fails as art, that is not the fault of the aspirations of the artist or of his skill, but rather that of the materials. The human hide does not lend itself well to bright colors, nor does it hold them. The fact that the painting is beneath the skin gives it an opaque quality, and over the years the colors tend to dull and diffuse.

After all, a full-rigged ship—no matter how skillfully done—is not improved by having to be seen through the epidermis, which is further befogged by a hirsute chest.

Certainly tattooing is an art, and perhaps more of an art than the other forms mentioned. Consummate skill is required by the artist to create his picture, which very often he has designed himself as a variation on an earlier traditional motif. Further, this art, although both functional and representative, often carries a symbolic meaning as well. The fouled anchor, the phoenix rising from her ashes, the eagle, the dolphin, mermaid, rattlesnake, pig and rooster—even "HOLD FAST" across the knuckles—all have a symbolic significance. While some may think "MOTHER" across the arm or a bare-breasted dancing girl named Joan on the biceps are sentimental and in poor taste, they do give the more charitable observer some insight into the sailor's hopes and thoughts, just as surely as the initials "W.C." served to identify poor, naked, drowned William Crowdy on the wintry shores of Isle au Haut. And to the observant critic the tattoos often tell the story of the sailor's life. "Joan" is replaced by "Lucy"; one tattoo from its color, design and technique bears the mark of Davy Jones of Seventh Avenue in San Francisco; a panther of a certain size and shape could have come only from a parlor in Hawaii; another smacks of Yokohama and so on.

There can be little doubt that tattooing, more than any of the other arts mentioned here, is dying out. To the sophisticated it is déclassé. In some areas it has been outlawed, and it no longer seems to serve some of the functions it formerly did. Yet when it goes there will be in its wake a vacuum that cannot be altogether filled by the modern adornments of modern antiseptic times.

CHAPTER VIII

SEALS AND MUCKLE MEN

Blessins be wi' de,
Baid de an da bairns;
Bit du kens da first love
Is aye da best."

—John Nicholson, *Restin' Chair Yarns*

SAILING along the coast of Maine one bright warm summer day, I noticed what appeared to be a dirty flour sack wallowing in the lee of a bell buoy. Closer scrutiny revealed that the object was not a flour sack but the bloated body of a dead baby harbor seal. The fish had eaten out its eyes and its nose was gone. A piece of frayed pot warp tied round it rear flippers attached it to the tolling red bell buoy. Its small rotting body rose sluggishly to the ground swell and it hung there in the clear blue-green water, a testimony to a peculiar satanic kink in the psychology of man. That incident took place many years ago, but somehow I have never forgotten it, and the impression it made has been with me many thousands of miles— from Maine to Fidra Island, to the Skaggerak, to the harbor of Schull in Ireland and back again to Cannouan in the Lesser Antilles. It prompted questions I might never have asked had I not seen that dirty white body, and the results have been fascinating.

Immediate inquiry revealed that the little seal had been shot and its nose cut off to collect the small bounty for killing seals, which have a poor reputation among Maine fisherman. "Why, them things will eat a hundred-weight o' herrin' in a day," I have been told. And logic does little good. The fishermen admit that the "herrin'" not turned into sardines are often turned into canned cat food, and they admit readily enough that one beam trawler in one day will probably destroy more fish than all the seals on the coast of Maine could eat in a year. Still, somehow, "that's different." For

Opposite: "All hands stand by to ram!", Tommy Beck, Dingle, Ireland

better or for worse, there is something about the seal that kindles fire under the imagination of man.

Not so long ago seals were plentiful along the coasts of North America. If we use place names as an indication of their appearance in numbers, we discover that they commonly ranged as far south as San Diego on the Pacific Coast and Rhode Island on the Atlantic side, occasionally farther. The same was true in the British Isles and Ireland, and although their numbers have been greatly reduced, they are still to be seen occasionally basking on a tidal rock or swimming, doglike, in the sea.

Actually, the seal is one of nature's more remarkable creatures. Biologists list twenty-one different kinds and they have a widespread habitat. They are found at both poles, in fresh-water lakes in Labrador, along the coasts in temperate zones. There is even one variety, the ring seal, that lives in the West Indies. Although scarce today, these must once have been numerous, for there is a Seal Island recorded on the charts of the Leeward Islands. It may have been one of these that Columbus mistook for a mermaid when he was there, and when one was seen on the island of Cannouan about fifteen years ago, it attracted the same kind of attention that Columbus accorded it.

If he is ubiquitous in his range the seal is not catholic in his choice of resting places. He seldom picks any old rock to haul out on, but prefers certain ones and repairs there even though the place is packed with his peers. Today we know these places by their names: Seal Bay, Seal Cove, Seal Harbor, Seal Ledge, Seal Rock, the Cow Yard; Wolf Rock, Wolf Point, the Wolves. All these are in North America. Abroad we find these names and others as well. There are Sule Skerry (Seal Island or Rock), Rona and even Mermaid Rock, which may have arisen from mistaking seals for mermaids long ago.

Abroad even today the seal, selchie, swile or ronne, as it is variously called, retains a strong aura of magic about itself—a kind of magic more in keeping with the Middle Ages than the present. In North America this magic is largely nonexistent and the stories about seals are most often about the seal fishery—at best a brutal business still conducted in Arctic and near-Arctic waters.[1] Yet there is evidence that even in the New World the seal once bulked larger in marine folklore and life than it now does. Seal flippers, for example, are still esteemed delicacies in Newfoundland and Cape Breton Island—regions not ordinarily noted for their gastronomic acumen—and seal oil is still thought to have great therapeutic value. And even now in the United States an occasional story turns up—or a shadow of one—that smacks of ancient things.

Dell Raines of Matinicus Island was a man who had spent a lifetime at sea. He had been nearly drowned by a shark, swept overboard in a gale, cast away by his neighbors, had had a vessel go down under him and had been maimed in an accident at sea. He told me, "The greatest thing I ever done was to pat a seal on the head." He went on to tell how one day out fishing he saw a young seal in the water near the boat. With infinite patience and care he maneuvered his dory until when the seal surfaced after a dive it was looking the other way. He reached out and patted it on the head, which "was just like a baby's," before the startled animal dove. Why should a man with such a wide and varied number of experiences select this one for special recall from his past?

Stanley Hadlock of Seal Harbor told another story:

There used to be great schools of herring that came into the harbor every summer. The people hereabout would take barrels of them by torching [attracting them with a lighted flambeau] and by catching them in the weirs. Some they sold for sardines, some was saved for bait and the rest went into grits [bait for lobster pots].

One summer the herrin' came early and day after day the harbor was full of them. The fishermen couldn't remember when they had taken so many. Now that summer a mother seal and her baby came into the harbor and fed on the herrin'. Now usually when the seals or the pollock or the mackerel get after the herrin' they run out of the harbor and nobody gets anything. This time it was different. The seals stayed there and the little one would play around the mother and they would chase herrin' but they never left the harbor and the mackerel and the pollock didn't come. Other summers there was a good-size crowd of seals in the harbor and the herrin' were usually driven out but this summer there was only the old seal and the young seal and the herrin' stayed. Still and all, the people was worried that those seals would drive out the money and so they tried to chase them out but they didn't make much headway. The seals stayed and sometimes at night they would bark. It would have been fun to watch them play if everybody hadn't been worried over the danger to the sardines.

Anyway one of the men told the others he would get rid of the seals and one moonlight night he loaded his shotgun with double-aught buck and rowed off into the harbor until he saw the old seal and the pup sittin' on a rock. He rowed as nigh as he dared and laid down the oars and took up the gun. He gave it to the mother with the first barrel and she just rolled off the rock and never came up again. He was goin' to shoot the pup too, but somehow he couldn't quite bring himself to fire and the chance was lost. The baby seal dove overboard after its mother and the man rowed home and told them he'd shot the seal.

For three weeks after that the little seal swam around the harbor all day long looking for its mother. Back and forth, back and forth, and at night it would haul itself out on the rock where its mother was shot and cry and whimper just like a baby all night long. It seemed to get thinner and weaker every day and it didn't make so much noise nights toward the end of it and then one mornin' it was gone. And the herrin' was gone.

From that time to this no seal has ever come back to the harbor and after that pup seal left it or disappeared there hasn't been a herrin' ever come into the harbor again. That was a long time ago now and there still aren't any herrin' in the harbor. The fellow that shot that seal felt pretty bad about it and he tried to catch the little one but he never did, you know. It sounded just like a baby and he made up his mind never to shoot another seal and he never did. I was that man.

Then he made a curious remark; "I always felt killin' the seal had somethin' to do with the herrin'."

One could argue that seals follow herring, their food. The seals never came into the harbor again and neither did the herring. Without the herring to eat, there was no reason for the seals to return. Still, there is an unanswered question. What happened? After all, the herring had come in there for years. As one listened to the story, one intuitively understood that the seal was inexorably linked with the herring and the killing of one drove away the other. Surely there is an element of magic in it.

As I suggested earlier, when one examines the body of folklore about the Pinnipedia (as biologists call the seal folk), one quickly learns that there are two distinct corpora of material relating to them. The one deals with seals in otherworld or supernatural terms, the other deals with them materialistically. The former is most decidedly the older of the two and is popular with the folk who live among seals but do not hunt them as a major source of their income. The latter is more modern; it stems from people who hunt seals commercially as a major source of economic gain. These latter people do not, generally, live in close proximity with seals but go to the sealing grounds to hunt them. The Hebrideans would be an example of the first group, the Newfoundlanders the second. It is the first group that concerns me most as a folklorist.

In North America, seals were common when the first white men came, and they remained so for some time. The Indians ate them regularly. With such numbers about, Americans began to hunt them, and by the end of the eighteenth century sealing in North America was a growing and prosperous business. When the China trade opened in the following century, sealskins, flippers and oil became such desirable commodities that the quest for these creatures expanded worldwide. Nathaniel Palmer, looking for seals in the little *Hero*, discovered a continent—Antarctica, and Captain Grey found the Columbia River and opened up the vast resources of the northwest while on the same business.

To men engaged in killing thousands of seals each year, there was little time or profit to be gained by telling stories about their quasi-human aspects or their otherworld affinities. In fact it might be bad for the business. Instead, they told stories about hunting seals, storms, wrecks, mutinies and the hardships of the sealer's life. There are stories of men left on the ice and how they survived. There are stories of the terrible cold, and how a hunter was found frozen solid with his gun at his shoulder and the hammer back in the act of shooting a seal more impervious to the cold than he. About as humane as these stories ever became were a number dealing with the greenhorn who was so distracted by the killing of the seal herd that he refused to take part and had to be brought home in disgrace, or of how a man refused to kill a mother seal until its baby grew up enough to have commercial value.[2] The Newfoundlanders who still hunt seals have developed a vocabulary with over twenty words applying to specific ages and kinds and conditions of seals, and over a hundred words pertaining to the seal industry, but they appear woefully short on the kind of stories that abound in the Old World.[3] Thus does Mammon destroy fantasy.

One of the stories told concerns a vessel named the *North Star*. It is representative of a number of sealing stories, and the reader will note that it is not dissimilar from stories told about the fisheries.

It was usually the practice to go north to the ice and moor alongside a floe. The men would then be put ashore to kill the seals on the ice by hitting them on the nose with a club or kicking them to death. While the crew was there it was customary to sound the horn, so that should it snow or turn thick the men could get back to base, for it was a hard lot to be left astray on an ice floe. If there was another vessel in the vicinity, she too would blow her horn if people were hunting even though they might not be her people.

Once the *North Star* was at the ice and the best part of her crew were ashore killing seals when the weather turned bad. The vessel was forced to put to sea, leaving seventy-five men on the floe. The weather remained bad and it was nearly three days before the ship could return; and when she did, she found seventy frozen men, but five others she could not find. She loaded her dead and sailed back to St. John's, Newfoundland.

The next year the vessel went again to the ice, and this time there was another vessel there. The *North Star* moored late in the day, and the other ship began to blow her horn, so the newcomer blew hers. After a time the other vessel stopped blowing and so did the *North Star*.

On the following day the captain of the *Star* went aboard the other vessel and met the skipper, who looked at him queerly and then remarked that his guest must be very hungry for pelts.

"How so?"

"Well, you had scarcely tied up when you had men on the ice and it was already near dark. And they didn't come back till almost night."

"I had no men on the ice last night. I only blew my horn because you were blowing yours."

"Oh, yes, you did. You had five men out. We saw them come aboard."

The word was out. There were five shades aboard the *North Star*. She returned to port but no hands could be found to sail her. She changed her rig, she changed her paint, she changed her name and her port of registry. Still no one would go in her, and at last she was sold to the south to become a fisherman. But she had no luck there either.[4]

In Newfoundland seals are a catalyst for other sorts of stories—especially stories of shipwreck, for apparently in that land the sealing disasters are comparable to the disasters suffered by Gloucestermen on Georges Bank. Men will tell of the Disaster of '98, when a terrible storm drove the *Greenland* from the ice, leaving forty-eight men to freeze to death. Some of those rescued had gone mad and others spent the rest of their lives as cripples. They will tell the tale of the *Newfoundland*, which lost nearly eighty men in a dense white fog. Some froze erect, others wandered into open crevasses and drowned. Or they will tell of the *Southern Cross*, which went to the bottom with all 127 hands and a fortune in sealskins.[5]

Not only are these stories told, but there are men who have seen the ghosts of these ships. The *Newfoundland* was seen hundreds of miles away from her trouble spot the very day and hour of her disaster. The *Southern Cross* "all white and shiny," was seen by sealers for years steaming across wide waters, and always when she was seen disaster came hard in her wake.[6]

It is to the Old World that one must go to find the lore of the seal as it used to be—to the Shetlands, the Orkneys, the Hebrides and the wild west coast of Ireland. And even here, where things change slowly, the beliefs and stories about seals are fading very fast. In his magnificent book, *People of the Sea*, David Thomson talked about rivlens (shoes made of green sealskin). I searched from the Shetland Islands south to Mizzen Head in Ireland for four seasons without finding a single pair. In Aran I found pampooties (shoes of green cowhide) but never the real article. Yet twenty-five years ago they were commonplace!

Probably behind all seal lore is the fact that they are believed to be children of the mythical King of Lochlann.[7] This accounts for a good deal of their supernatural ability and particularly for their association with humans. They make wonderful pets, and their physical properties and their personality are most engaging. Of all creatures in the northern islands, where there were never any monkeys and where bears have long since disappeared, the seal most closely resembles the human. They suckle their young at the breast; they are extremely social and lie around on warm rocks in the sun like bathers at a beach. The young must be taught to swim. They have an insatiable curiosity. They have wonderful eyes and not inhuman faces. They whimper and cry—the little ones—like human babies, shed tears, bark like dogs and sometimes sing. In the water, with their round heads, they could be mistaken for human swimmers.

There is another singular aspect of seals that is well known to hunters. Among the Scots and Irish it is popularly thought that they are ferocious and will bite. Once their teeth are locked on a person, they will not let go until they hear or feel the bone crack.[8] To neutralize this characteristic, hunters usually go equipped with a stocking full of coals or clinkers. This they toss to the seal, who thinks it has an arm or leg of its tormentor and crunches the bag instead of a shinbone. As soon as he hears the crunching noise, he lets go. Meanwhile the hunter either bashes him on the nose with a club or kicks him to death in the same place. Unfortunately seals are not always killed by this treatment, and regain consciousness after they have been skinned. Uttering terrible cries, the ghastly creatures drag themselves across the rocks and plunge all bloody into the cold and cruel sea to die.[9] What manner of sense do the folk make of these things?

It is believed that the seals can transform themselves into human beings ashore and revert to their old selves in the sea. It is believed that in human form they were the progenitors of two families, the McCodrums in Scotland and the Keneellys in Ireland. They are said to weep, talk, prophesy, exact tribute, extend help and sympathy. They are capable of terrible revenge. Their ability in magic is not dissimilar to that of faeries and mermaids. The credibility of faeries and mermaids has begun to diminish, and the beliefs and characteristics once attached to them now cling to seals.

Perhaps one of the most popular beliefs about seals is the one which folklorists call the "cast skin." It is thought that at certain times the seal can remove its skin and go amongst mortals as a human being. Like mermaids, they are discomfited by bell, book and candle and the church is anathema to them for, being seals, of course they have no souls—that commodity being restricted solely to humans. As with the mermaid's mantle, it is thought that if one can obtain the cast skin of a seal, that seal must remain in human form until it can get its pelt back, when it will return to the sea. In the meantime it will be in thrall to the finder.

Why this belief in the magic garment or cast skin should be so popular in northern folklore is hard to say, but in the case of seals we may hazard a guess. The answer lies in two points. The first deals with the practical aspect seen by the hunter. If a seal can come to life and crawl back to sea after being kicked in the face and skinned, why shouldn't it do that of its own accord on more auspicious occasions? Further, if it is descended from the King of Lochlann and really does have otherworld associations, why shouldn't it transform itself?

There is another possible answer to this question—one that lies very deep in the minds of the folk, so deep perhaps as not to be recognized by them. It may be that the idea of the seal casting its skin has at least part of its origin as a folk explanation of certain events in history. If so, it is very old.

Seals like to haul out on warm sunny rocks and snooze and rest themselves from the sea. Since man is a threat to them, they tend to choose inaccessible places where they can see danger coming. Among these are the offshore rocks and islets uninhabited by man. Even today in clear weather little groups of seals can be seen basking on the outer skerries or stags, reasonably safe from attack from humans.

From the eighth century through the tenth, most of civilized Europe trembled before the wrath of the Northmen, who raided as far south as the Mediterranean and Black seas and probably ventured as far as the shores of North America.[10] It was the misfortune of the British Isles and Ireland that they lay so close to the homeland of the Vikings. These people swept down like tourists swarming over a clam flat, and so destructive and sudden were their raids that the people prayed, "Oh, Lord, protect us from the fury of the Northmen."

The tactic most frequently used was an amphibious dawn attack on the villages and hamlets along the coast. The raiders would seize prisoners, cattle and whatever else they found of value and be off. Their raids took

Mending nets on Sunday, Dingle, Ireland

place in the summer, for the North Sea is no place for an open boat in the winter. If their tactics were like those used by any other warring group, they would first reconnoiter, then attack after learning where the strength and weakness of the hamlet lay. To obtain this information they would set men ashore on the outer skerries where they could watch the town, while the raiders came in to pick them up after dark. The important thing was not to be detected. Once the information had been digested, the attack would take place.

It is a well-known fact that primitive people in warfare and in hunting wore animal disguises. Both the American Indians and the Eskimo disguised themselves. Indians wore wolf and deerskins while hunting and reconnoitering, and Eskimos often wore sealskins as camouflage when stalking seals and polar bears. What would be more natural, therefore, than for the Vikings to disguise themselves as seals while they watched the enemy from the rocks. And what more natural for the victims than to make an association between seals and men? One day they see seals on the skerries, the next day they are attacked by people who have no regard for the Church. After the raid a survivor finds a sealskin on a rock, but no seal. The connection seems obvious.[11]

This idea is given added support by the fact that many seal stories in one way or another are connected with Scandinavia, as may be seen in the following account.

A Shetland Islander was on his way to his fishing boat one morning when he suddenly came upon a large bull seal sleeping on a rock. The fisherman crept up to it, drew his knife and stabbed it. But his aim was poor; instead of killing the creature he only wounded it, and it flopped and floundered away with the knife still in its body and regained the sea.

Long after this the fisherman took ship and went to Norway to buy some wood. When he landed, he went into a house where he was made welcome and sat down. Glancing up, he saw his own knife—the one he had left in the seal—sticking in a rafter. For a moment he thought he was done for, but the Norwegian arose, pulled down the knife and returned it to him. The only thing the Norseman did was ask him not to go around sticking sleeping seals in the future.[12]

By "cast skin," of course, I do not mean skinning, but rather the ability to take off one's skin at will. The following tales are excellent examples of the type I have in mind, and furthermore, they incorporate several items of seal lore in each tale and at the same time show the affinity of seal stories to those concerning mermaids.

In North Uist there once lived a man named Red Roderick of the Seals. One night he was fishing on a rock when he heard the sweetest music to ever reach his ears. It was so unearthly sweet that he followed the sound until he came upon a musician playing and a company of people dressed in magnificent clothes dancing to his tune. Nearby in the moonlight he saw a number of black and black-and-white bundles, which he took for cowskins. One of these skins he tucked under his jacket.

Eventually the music stopped and the dancers went to their cache of skins, put off their clothes and donned the hides. As they did so they all turned into great gray seals, flopped over the rocks and out to sea. All, that is, except one beautiful girl, who rushed around frantically looking for her skin, sobbing piteously all the while.

So great was the girl's beauty and so pitiful her cries that Red Roderick was smitten by her and asked her what was wrong. She said she had lost her garment, and Roderick said that if she would go with him he would get her a much better one in town, which they did.

The girl told him she was the daughter of the King of the Waves and was under a spell. Her stepmother had had her left on the shore, after having struck her with a magic wand, she said, and she was befriended by the seals.

The man's feelings for the girl increased. A priest was found to baptise her, and they were married and lived happily for some years, rearing a husky family of children. At last, however, the girl became lonely for the old life, her friends and the dancing and singing in the moonlight. She asked for her sealskin back. The seals, she said, would not touch her and could not help her because of "the blessed water on my face and fore- head." Then she asked that her husband never kill another seal for fear it might be she or her "mother" or "brother." The man agreed sorrowfully, and that night she danced in the moonlight with her old friends, although none would touch her, "for the blessed water was on her forehead."[13]

Another quite similar story tells how three fishermen captured three seal-women by stealing their skins whilst they were in human form. Despite offers of marriage, the women were disconsolate. The youngest brother gave his woman back her skin after one night. The woman immediately changed into a seal and returned to sea, but came back every ninth night to comfort the man and bring him presents. The other two brothers kept their skins hidden and their wives became drudges. The children of one eventually found their mother's pelt. She put it on and, forsaking children, husband and hearth, vanished forever into the sea. To prevent such an occurrence the other brother decided to burn his woman's sealskin. When he threw it on the fire it exploded and burned up his house and his wife as well.[14]

A third tale comes from the ballad "The Great Silkie of Sule Skerry,"[15] collected in Shetland and having an analogous story in Scandinavia. In this version a woman has a child but doesn't know who the father is, until one night a great gray selchie (seal) comes to her bed and tells her he is the father and wants the child. "I am a man upon the land; I am a selchie in the sea"; he then predicts the future, for seals sometimes have the power of deviation. The girl will marry a gunner who will shoot both him and their child:

> And thou shall marry a proud gunner
> An' a proud gunner I'm sure he'll be
> And the very first schot that ere he schoots,
> He'll schoot baith my young son and me.

And so it came to pass.

Another idea popular in Scotland amongst the seafaring folk was that after the cruel wife had transformed her stepchildren into seals, in order to make her cruel act yet more cruel, she added one further touch. Three times each year, at the fulling of the moon, the unfortunate children would automatically acquire human form and walk among men. By doing this they would be better able to realize what a wonderful life had been denied them—obviously this is an archaic sentiment.

Such bespelled humans are believed capable of befriending humans in many ways. Ashore, fishermen could tell a storm was coming "by the moaning and the crying of the seals."[16] At sea, by noting their antics and watching which way they went, one could not only forecast the weather but could divine where to go to make a profitable voyage. On a higher level, they were thought to nurse infants and, when the need arose, to help the distressed and even to carry people ashore who had been wrecked or stranded.[17] David Thomson tells a story that illustrates one of these points admirably.

A family named Cregan were supposed to have special gifts because one of them "did some great good to the faeries." Five of them put out in a small boat to fish and were caught in a violent blow. It blew so hard all they could do was hold the head of the curragh to the sea and hope.

When the gale was over they were afloat but out of sight of land, and didn't know which way to go until a seal appeared. They gave it fish, and it headed off in a particular direction and they decided to follow it, which they did until they became so exhausted they could go no further but lay down in the boat.

The seal, meanwhile, swam ashore and made such a racket that the keeper of the lighthouse was aroused. He searched the sea until he spotted the drifting curragh and rescued the men, who arrived home the night their own wake was being held.[18]

As the tale is unfolded, one notices a strong tendency to associate the seal and the faerie, if not as one and the same being, certainly as beings that are closely related in the minds of the folk.

Not only did the seals bring fish to people as the mermaids sometimes did, but they were associated with sea cattle in much the same manner as the merfolk, who had large herds which gave rich milk on the one hand and on the other tore up the countryside when the sea people were abused. Moreover, the seals had a love of milk akin to that of the faeries.[19]

On the island of Papa Stour in the Shetlands a Norwegian freighter came ashore and was a total loss. An islander paid her skipper a ridiculous price for the wreck, and the captain cursed him. After that a seal began coming to the island, and every time it came one of the farmer's cattle died. The farmer tried to kill the seal but he never could and at last, nearly ruined, he left the island.[20]

So far, we have been talking about live seals. The dead ones also have power, and the majority of the men of the islands used to hunt them sparingly and then usually either for food when times were hard, or for various portions of their bodies which were believed to contain magical properties. Today they seldom hunt them at all.

Ashore, the seal is relatively helpless and easy to kill. The killing is, according to those who have seen it, a horrible sight and one well calculated to make good legends and folktales. One would think that the tales springing from such a source would at least be stories of revenge, but this is by no means true, for the seal apparently is believed to be a forgiving creature, and although it sometimes takes revenge, it more often endures human outrages passively or with hopes for a better future.

A man once went on a seal hunt and killed several, skinning them on the spot. One of the seals he killed he thought to take home, so he fastened its flippers together with a withe and went after another. While he was gone the seal somehow revived and got back into the water. The hunter returned, found no trace of the animal and concluded it had somehow got overboard and died. Some time later the fisherman was caught in a storm and blown off course. He saw land, went ashore and was given an excellent meal by a man he met there. After the meal his host informed him that he had once put a withe through his hands.[21]

One of the things a sailor liked to obtain from seals was their flippers. Sometimes he ate them, but the right flipper had special virtues. With this worked into a wallet, it was popularly believed the owner could not drown, and it was further believed that the color of the wallet indicated the state of the tide.

Another item for which the seal was killed was his oil. For some strange reason, grease and oils in general appear to be esteemed valuable by the folk. In more primitive areas and times, human fat had special virtues. Bear, goose, skunk, snake and hog oil are all believed by rural people to have medicinal virtues, while among seafarers whale and fish oil—especially cod-liver oil—were thought to have great therapeutic value. This was especially true of seal oil, but here the selection of the creature and the preparation of the oil seem essential to its virtue.

Usually a young seal was considered the best kind to take for its oil and for its white skin, which was frequently worn as a jacket. Once caught, the seal was skinned and the fat stripped off. When this was done, the oil was prepared in one of two different ways. Thomson mentions pressing out the oil with special stones.[22] I was told in the Hebrides that it was prepared either by trying out the fat in a kettle over a slow fire or by drying it out by sunlight. The flayed seal is hung up head down and turned or allowed to spin in the wind. Through the working of the sun the fat is rendered into oil, which drips down and is caught in a pan. This, the slower way, is believed by many to produce the best oil. Unlike the boiled product, it is clear and amber-colored.

The oil so gathered is considered very potent and must be administered with great care. In Benbecula a woman told me that her brother had become very ill and the doctors despaired. In this crisis they caught a seal, dried out its oil (the sun method), and gave it to the sick man. At first he could tolerate only a drop, then two and so on, until eventually he could take a tablespoon at a time. As the doses increased so did his health, until at the end he was totally well again.

Apparently the oil is equally as effective when used externally. An Irish informant told us how he had cured a very badly strained and swollen knee by rubbing it with seal oil. The swelling went down in a few hours and he could walk as spryly as ever. The only drawback was the oil's terrible smell, which necessitated changing all his clothes and even the bed linen.

Not so many years ago a man in the outer Hebrides killed a baby seal and brought it home and skinned it. He cut off its tiny paws. He tacked its small bloody white skin to a board to dry and threw the mangled body on the midden. That night the man was wakened by a terrible noise—a crying and a moaning. It was the mother seal outside the house by the skin crying for her dead offspring. Again and again she would cry out, "All I want is Flora of the Wee Paws. Give me back Wee Paws." ("Spog fine-ghael, spog fifi fineghael.") Night after night it continued until at last the grief-stricken mother hauled back to sea and vanished. The man killed no more.[23]

At Dingle my wife and I were told another story about a seal killing, by a man who said it happened to him. He preceded the story by saying he believed that seals were humans under enchantment, that they had human babies under the sea and that they left their homes as seals and came ashore. He also told us that their very name, "rona," was similar to the word "rune," meaning secret. He said that it was generally believed that if you killed a seal you would go mad. Our informant and his friends did not believe this, but they did believe that seals were enchanted people with great supernatural power. One day he and his friends went out fishing and they caught nothing, but they had noticed thousands of seals on some rocks and they made up their minds to kill one. As they approached, the seals all took to the water except one great bull who remained on the rocks, and this one they hit "a terrible whack" with an oar and killed it. The seal was too big to go into the curragh. He was very old and covered with barnacles and limpets, and they had to tow him to a nearby beach to load him aboard.

Eventually they cut off his head and tail and draped the middle part over the boat, with both ends trailing in the water; and the blood ran out of the seal and dyed the sea red.

As they pulled for home, all the seals that had been on the rocks reappeared and followed the curragh like humans following a coffin. They moaned and cried and nudged the great dead body as they made their way home. But the men held onto the seal despite the protests of the seal people and pulled for the Great Blasket (with the killing thirty-six-strokes-a-minute pace used by curragh men), when suddenly astern there appeared a great sea monster. The men were terrified and swore that if they reached shore they would never kill another seal. The crying host followed them all the way to shore, and when the men landed they dumped out what apparently was the dead king of the seals. They took a little of his fat for oil and went home and kept their vow.

Whether or not the event actually happened is aside from the point.

The important thing is that these are the ideas that the seal still conjures in the heads of the people.

Earlier in this chapter I mentioned seals in relation to music. It is believed that they are charmed to hear music and will follow the sound of a pipe or a flute, much as a ghost can be summoned by music. One man tells how he saw a seal and played the pipes to her and she turned and followed the boat. He rowed with all his might and the seal increased her speed. He then lay by his oars and the creature, so bemused was she by the music, swam up to a "half pistol shot" from the boat before she discovered her mistake and he fired at her. The seal went down and he assumed he had killed her for he "never saw her more."[24]

It is also said that seals can sing, and their "song" has been recorded and an article written about it in the *Journal of the English Folk Dance and Song Society*.[25]

I have had the hair rise on the nape of my neck three times in my life: once when a wolf howled across a snowy lake in the Arctic one moonlit night many years ago, and once in the Moray Firth when I heard the cry or song of the great selchie. (The third occasion was when I unexpectedly came face to face with a stuffed bear in a dark hall one night.)

There was no wind, and rather than expend petrol futilely flogging into a head tide, we anchored to leeward of Fidra Island. It was so still one could hear the ripples pop against the rocks half a mile away. Suddenly about ten o'clock, a terrible sound arose and came across the water. It was answered by another and another. So like it was to how I have always imagined a banshee sounded, that when I recovered from the initial shock I thought it must be some wag on the shore, but shore (except for the island) was distant several miles and some of the noise came from seaward. It was a wild and lonely call not unlike that of a loon combined with the cry of a great horned owl. Despite its weird quality it was definitely musical, and I was later informed it was the "song" of the seals.

Although the noise was confused by the sounds of gulls and the ordinary noises attendant on shipboard life, it continued long enough, and had sufficient timbre, to allow us to record it. Had we not done so, I would not have had the audacity to remark on it here.

I mentioned earlier that the seal stories I have related were largely restricted to the Old World, and stories of seal hunting took their place in the new. There are, however, a few tales in the more remote parts of the New World that are similar to the Old-World stories. As one might expect, they are more fragmentary and less well known than those told across the ocean. Two that bear repeating come from Newfoundland.

Once there were two young boys who worked on the south coast who were known as the Jersey Youngsters, for apparently they were not native to the island. They were great workers, but every weekend they disappeared and no one knew where they went. Every Monday they turned up fresh and eager for work—which, incidentally, they preferred to do by themselves.

One day they were set to pit sawing. (This is an old-fashioned way of making boards, wherein one man stands in a pit and the other atop the log; between them they cut the log into boards with a two-man ripsaw.) After a time a man went to see how they were making out, and as he neared the pit he heard singing and the sound of a saw. When he came closer he observed the Jersey Youngsters lying under a tree singing a strange song and the saw going up and down in the log unaided.

After this they were watched more closely, and it was discovered that on weekends they turned into seals and swam home to the Isle of Jersey and returned on Monday. This was too much for the people in the community, and they dismissed them.[26]

On another occasion a man and his son went seal hunting. The two split up and the boy suddenly came upon three seals. He raised his gun to shoot, and one of the seals cried out, "Don't shoot yet." Startled, the boy lowered his gun but quickly brought it up again and again was told to wait. The third time the seal said this he fired anyway. Two seals dropped dead, but the third turned into a headless man and fell overboard.[27]

These are, then, the general ingredients that are to be found in the lore of seals. Occasionally one is fortunate to find a vast quantity of this material buried in one story. Thomson was such a man and in his inimitable way tells the story paraphrased here.

A man and his three sons were going fishing, apparently for salmon, when a strange man appeared on a white horse and told them to take with them an axe, a hook and a knife. This they did, and they had not been long at sea when a storm broke and they tried to make for the beach.

Suddenly a tremendous wave humped up and roared down on them. They hurled the hook at it and it broke and passed under them. Then came a larger one and they hurled out the axe, and again the sea broke and they lifted over it. Then came the great third wave, always the biggest of all. It towered over the curragh and it seemed as if nothing could withstand it. They threw the knife at it and it, too, split and lifted the boat and drove it high on the shingle, and as they stood there congratulating themselves on their escape they saw wreckage coming ashore from some not so lucky as they.

The men went home and had hardly had supper when the man on the white horse appeared and ordered them to mount up. Away they went until they came to a city, where the horse stopped before a house and they went in. Inside were three women. In the head of each was buried one of the instruments hurled into the waves and the men removed them. They remounted the white horse and went home. On the way the horseman warned them never again to go to sea and told them that thirty-odd men had gone down that night to become husbands to these women. Had it not been for his intercession, they would have joined the thirty.[28]

As one goes over these stories, he becomes increasingly conscious of the tremendous antiquity of some of the motifs. It comes therefore as no shock at all to discover that one of the oldest known *objets d'art* is a carved antler with a hole in it, which indicates it was probably a bull-roarer used in religious ceremonies. It is over twenty thousand years old, and carved on it are a salmon, something that might be a berry and two seals. In these stories, then, we may be looking at still more shards of a great fractured northern mythology.[28]

There remains one more denizen of the deep to be considered. In his original form he hangs on the very edge of memory, and it is almost impossible to get anything more than a dim assent to having heard about him. Yet in another form he is viable, and stories still circulate about him among the folk. I think the modern stories survive through a case of mistaken identities. This creature was known as a Fin, Finn, or Fion, and sometimes as a Muckle Man.

For hundreds of years there was a tradition in the Western Isles, the Shetlands and Orkneys, of a strange appearance. From time to time people at sea would encounter a lone voyager paddling along in a skin boat. The boat appears to have been double-ended, and the occupant clad in skin clothing. He was armed, or had aboard a spear. When approached too closely the voyager would flee, and no exertions of his pursuers were sufficient to close the gap between them. These lone wanderers seemed to like heavy weather, and they were frequently seen serenely paddling along in gales so wild that the people of the Isles could not imagine that a vessel could live in them. According to Wallace, writing in 1700:

Sometimes about this country are to be seen these men they call Finn-men. In the year 1682 one was seen in his little boat at the south end of the Isle of Eda, most of the people of the Isle flocked to see him, and when they adventured to put out a boat with men to see if they could apprehend him, he presently fled away most swiftly. And in the year 1864 another was seen from Westra; I must acknowledge it seems a little unaccountable, how these Finn-Men should come on this coast, but they must probably be driven by storm from home, and cannot tell where they are anyway at sea, how to make their way home again; they have this advantage, that be the seas never so boistrous, their boat being made of fish-skins is so contrived he can never sink, but is like a sea-gull swimming on the top of the water. His shirt is so fastened to the boat, that no water can come into his boat to do him damage, except when he pleases to unty it, which he never does except to ease nature, or when he comes ashore.[29]

Many interpretations of these strange appearances have been given, and folklorists attempting to make the stories credible to modern sophisticated man—who seems best able to swallow "magic" when it is spelled "science"—have suggested that they were Eskimos "blown off" who had reached the outposts of the European continent. Another idea is that they were the remnants of the Pictish people, whose last stand seems to have been in the islands. A third view is that these were really Northmen, and the lone paddler served the long ship in much the same manner as the frigate served the ship-of-the-line, as a fast-moving scout to spy out enemy strength and weakness.

All these views could be feasible. It is scarcely more than a thousand miles from Cape Farewell to Scandinavia, with favorable winds and currents, and at least two stops possible, one in Iceland and one in the Faeroes. Men less attuned to primitive living than the Eskimo have made longer voyages. In point of fact, a man with an apparently inordinate love of rowing is at the time of this writing making his way around the world. Moreover, the description just given of the boats and their occupants fits well with the kayak and the Eskimo. The fact that these sightings have been in regions where there are recent remains of Pictish forts and dwellings, plus the fact that these people are supposed to have been remarkable boatmen, could support the idea that they were in fact Picts and not Eskimos. And, finally, the idea about Viking scouts is by no means untenable.

For those who would discredit the whole business, there seems to be one scrap of evidence that gives authenticity to these sightings. One of their little boats was sent to Edinburgh, where it was on display at Physicians' Hall but was then removed to the University Museum.[30]

There is a story about the Finns that seems to incorporate much of the lore about them and bears retelling. A man went fishing one stormy day and hooked a fine fish. Just as he was about to boat it, a great seal chomped off the better half and he was left with the head. This happened several times, and the man's rage kindled with each loss. Finally the greedy beast swallowed the whole fish and then started to climb aboard. The enraged fisherman picked up a billet of wood and gave the seal a tremendous clout in the mouth, the line snapped and the seal went away, but a terrible storm sprang up immediately and nearly swamped the boat before it reached land.

The following year on a trip to Finland the fisherman met an old man and they fell into conversation. The old man invited the sailor to his house the following night and there revealed himself as the seal the fisherman had clubbed the previous year, and to prove it showed where he had had two teeth knocked out. Moreover, he told the sailor that his father-in-law was sick at home, and he gave him a knife the sailor had lost overboard and a spoon from his own table.

When the sailor reached home he found things just as the stranger had reported, and he also learned about the spoon. A strange big dog had walked into the house one day while the fisherman was away and carried it off in his teeth.[31]

This tale illustrates an interesting point. Originally the word Fin, Finn or Fion meant "small," but over the years it came to have different associations. On the one hand it connected itself with a great Irish hero of small stature, Fion the Fair, himself a great voyager, a titan in strength and something of a magician in his own right, and tales about Finns began to take on a coloring from the Fion saga.[32] In the other direction it went across the Baltic and attached itself to a group of people not particularly famous as sailors but who had a reputation as dealers in the black arts (possibly acquired from their neighbors the Lapps). These men were tall, dark and powerful.

As the years passed, the beliefs connected to the little boat people gradually moved over and attached themselves with more and more vigor to the Finlanders, until they were generally considered to be bad luck aboard ship. (Knowing this, it becomes increasingly apparent why Melville chose to have one aboard the ill-fated *Pequot* in his novel *Moby-Dick*.)

The Finns were generally thought to have a direct connection with the other world, and could do much good by directing shipmasters to places where a rich cargo could be found or by telling them how to avoid hazards to navigation. But if they had these good qualities they also had bad ones, like black cats, which were believed to carry storms in their tails. The Finns' magical powers were mostly believed to be connected with winds, which they could and often did raise at will.

For the purposes of conjuring up the wind, these warlocks used either a leather bag, stoppered and tied with thongs, or a black string in which was worked a series of knots. Whenever wind was wanted they would make incantations and unstopper the bag or undo a knot in the string and the breeze would spring up.[33]

One would think such a man would be in great demand aboard a sailing ship, but this was not the case for two reasons. In the first place, the Finn frequently let out too much wind and the ship would be overcome by the gale. In the second place, a man with this ability would be able, if he so chose, to keep the ship in thrall. Should anyone displease him, all he had to do was unstopper his bag or shake out his knots and send all hands to Davy Jones. There can be but one master aboard ship, and no captain would willingly ship a Finn.

Richard Henry Dana, in *Two Years Before The Mast*, recalls a conversation he had with the cook, who asked:

"I say, you know what countryman'e carpenter be?"
   "Yes," I said; "He's a German" . . . .
   "Are you sure o' dat?" said he . . . .
   "I'm plaguy glad o' dat" said the cook. "I was mighty fraid he was a Fin. I tell you what, I been plaguy civil to that man all the voyage."
   I asked him the reason of this, and found that he was fully possessed with the notion that Fins are wizards and especially have power over winds and storms. . . . He had been to the Sandwich Islands in a vessel in which the sailmaker was a Finn and could do anything he had a mind to. This sailmaker kept a junk bottle in his berth, which was always just full of rum, though he got drunk upon it nearly every day. He had seen him sit for hours together, talking to this bottle which stood before him on the table. The same man cut his throat in his berth and everybody said he was possessed.
   He had heard of ships, too, beating up the Gulf of Finland . . . and having a ship in sight astern, overhaul, and pass them with as fair a wind as could blow . . . and find she was from Finland. "Oh no!" said he; "I've seen too much o' dem men to want to see dem 'board a ship. If dey can't have dare own way they'll play the d—l with you."

To support his argument the cook called a man named John who agreed with him, and added that he had been in a ship where they had had a head wind for a fortnight, and the captain found out at last that one of the men, with whom he had had some hard words a short time before, was a Finn, and immediately told him if he didn't stop the headwind he would shut him down in the forepeak. The Fin would not give in and the captain shut him down in the forepeak, and would not give him anything to eat. The Finn held out for a day and a half, when he could not stand it any longer, and did something or other which brought the wind round again—and they let him up.[34]

C. S. Forrester in *Commodore Hornblower* gives an added twist to the Finn legend. Although Forrester is not exactly in the same category as the other writers listed, he has been praised for his accuracy in detail. Hornblower regrets having to have his secretary Bramm around but his orders are to listen to him because his "acquaintance with the Baltic countries is both extensive and intimate." Captain Bush asks Hornblower:

> "How do you find your Swedish clerk, sir?"
> "He's a Finn, not a Swede."
> "A Finn? You don't say, Sir! It'd be better not to let the men know that."
> In a sailor's mind every Finn was a warlock who could conjure up storms by lifting a finger, but Hornblower had quite failed to think of Mr. Bramn as that kind of Finn, despite those unwholesome pale green eyes.[35]

Although these people, or beings, have acquired an international reputation, it would seem that their origin was somewhere in the far north. The area round Shetland would perhaps be a good place to locate them because of its proximity to Norway, and the facts that Shetlanders often call them "Norway Finns" and that many stories have the Finns going to Norway and back in a day tend to support the theory of Norse antecedents. Finally, it is in the Shetlands where they gain their fullest stature as warlocks.

Among other things, the Muckle Men kept crows as familiars and through them acquired knowledge of what was going on around the countryside. Through them also they were able to acquire various objects at a great distance. The Shetlanders also believed that through magic they could cut chips off oars, throw them overboard and make ships out of them. It was said also that they had a magic sealskin which they put on to enable them to make long passages over the sea. Should you seize this skin you would have the owner in thrall till he got it back. Meanwhile his skill in magic would be greatly curtailed. Last but not least, in Shetland it was the Finns and only the Finns who could ride the water horse.[36]

Once a dog is known as a sheep killer it is hard for him to change his status, and so it has proved with Finns. Very few seamen today believe the winds are tucked into a bag. In fact, with the advent of steam and the internal combustion engine, dependence on wind has been largely abandoned and fear of gales and lee shores greatly reduced. Yet the fear of the Finn remains deep-seated and many sailors do not like going to sea with them. They are narrow-minded, they will tell you, ill-tempered and given to moods that erupt in violent action, and moreover "it's bad luck to have them aboard."

During the decade following World War II, in Rockland, Maine, there was a shipyard where the best lobster boats on the coast were thought to be built. Anyone "goin' lobsterin'" who could acquire one of these boats was considered most fortunate. The builder was a man whose family were from Finland and he was known generally not by his name but his heritage —The Finn. "If yew want a good bo'ot, go see The Finn. He's the best they is." And so perhaps even the magic of the Finn still remains.

"Aye, 'twas a long and weary night," Crinan, Scotland

MERMAIDS

Lorntie, Lorntie
Were it na for your man
Your hearts bluid
Would skurl in ma pan.

Quoted from Sabine Baring-Gould,
Curious Myths of the Middle Ages

FEW items of marine folklore are more widespread, go back further in history, are more fascinating, or pose more problems for the scholar attempting to arrive at workable conclusions than the belief in merfolk. This population is composed of mermaids, mermen, kelpies or water horses, water bulls, Finns, Blue Men and seals. No area of marine folklore, save perhaps sea monsters, has suffered more from the incursions of science. Yet so deep-seated are these traditions that in the remoter, more isolated regions of the English-speaking world they are still believed in, sometimes as a viable tradition and other times as a way of explaining the otherwise inexplicable.

Biological science has demonstrated beyond dispute that there are no such creatures—barring seals, and these creatures are quite incapable of the antics ascribed to the others. Nevertheless, scholars are still curious as to how such a group of beliefs gained so firm a hold on the minds of the folk, and many suggestions have been thrown out as the possible source of these traditions. Those who like to attach the fancy of folklore to the reality of fact have offered a number of theories that would connect these merfolk with creatures acceptable to the biologist.

There seem to be four explanations among scholars, and I hope to introduce a fifth, suggesting concrete origins for merfolk. The first concludes that there are no such creatures and those who attest to having

seen them are either mad or liars. This is a convenient attitude but hardly
jibes with the facts, for many people of considerable stature, including
Henry Hudson and several bishops, have reported seeing merfolk. What do
we do, for example, with the provincial governor who kept a "sea-wyfe"
fifty-nine inches long in a tub of water four days and seven hours, and
reported it cried like a mouse, refused shellfish and had excrement like
a cat?[1]

Second, some suggest that the mermaid is in reality the manatee, a
warm-water creature that floats upright and suckles its young at the breast.
Since these are uncommon and only rarely seen, it has been intimated that
the sailor long at sea could mistake them for the beautiful and alluring
creatures of storybook fame. Now there is a widespread folktale about (in
one instance) an Arctic explorer who always took the ugliest female cook
he could find to sea with him. When she "began to look good to him," he
knew that he had been at sea overlong. Taking this tale as a starter, it
would still be difficult to imagine a vessel keeping the sea for a sufficient
length of time to make a manatee look delectable. Moreover, many reports
of mermaids come from the high latitudes where the water is too cold
for manatees.

A third and very popular theory is that the mermaid is a poorly identified seal. This is credible when we consider that seals do have breasts
and reasonably human faces, live in both warm and cold water and in many
ways resemble the picture-book mermaid. Furthermore, in relatively recent times mermaid stories were told almost interchangeably about seals,
and they have now become an accepted part of the merfolk. This theory
satisfies the requirements for casual observations at a distance, but it does
not satisfy accounts of close scrutiny or actual contact. Neither does it
satisfy the requirement for those creatures that people have reported as
having an appearance "very similar to that of a seal."[2] Finally, since
northern fishermen, among whom stories of mermaids are most common,
live out their lives in close proximity to thousands of seals, it would be
ridiculous to think that atmospheric conditions or even strong drink could
prompt them to mistake seals for mermaids.

A fourth hypothesis is that the mermaid, or more properly merman, is
a walrus. While scholars do not endorse this, considerable credence can
be given it. In the first place, the name for walrus in the seventeenth century was "morse," possibly from the Russian *morskoi*, which means "sea
man."[3] These creatures are primarily Arctic dwellers but do on occasion
appear further to the south. John Josselyn recorded one on Cape Ann in

the seventeenth century, and they still are infrequently seen on the coasts of Scotland. I was told by Wallace Clark of Belfast that quite recently "a dead elephant" washed ashore at Tory Island. The people knew it was an elephant—it weighed well over a ton and had two teeth about eighteen inches long that grew down from its upper jaw. This meager description more closely fits a walrus than an elephant. The thing was too big to move and gave off a frightful smell. Fortunately, at the time the islanders were building a cement pier, and a slight deflection of direction carried the pier over the carcass; it is now entombed within tons of cement.

The walrus becomes even more plausible when we look at accounts of mermen by people who allegedly saw one. Unlike mermaids, mermen are scarcely ever noted for their beauty. Although the descriptions are not all in accord, a number of them state that the creature floated upright and had webbed fingers, a beard, a short neck, a double chin with a deep cleft, deep-set dark eyes, a broad flat forehead and heavy brows. It was covered with brown or reddish hair, and sometimes it was said to have two sharp protruding teeth.[4] In size the merman was described as being from "the bigness of a monkey" to a length of eighteen feet.[5] The latter size would not be out of keeping with the bulk of a mature walrus, while the smaller one would meet, perhaps, the proportions of a young one. These descriptions could indeed fit a walrus—especially an immature one, which would be relatively easy to capture and sufficiently rare in British or American waters to make it unrecognizable to the seaman's eye.

Most scholars have tended to identify the mermaid with a single biological entity. This has been, I think, a mistake. Rather, it could be identified with a number of sea creatures—the seal, the walrus, perhaps even the manatee. In rare instances one is led to believe that octopi, or even a madman, have qualified for this sobriquet. John Josselyn, for example, tells us that a Mr. Mitter encountered a merman while fowling in Casco Bay during the seventeenth century. The creature tried to board his boat until Mitter cut off one of its arms and it sank, "dying the waters purple with its blood."[6] Another merman was captured swimming off Spain. His captors learned that he came from Lierjanes, to which spot he was returned, and it was there revealed that his name was Francisco de la Vega. He had short red hair, vacant eyes, colorless, flabby flesh and some scales (eczema?), and showed a pronounced aversion to clothes. He was left with his family, but refused to speak, eventually escaped and vanished in the sea.[7] Finally there was a mermaid (or merman) that was a deliberate hoax. One Robert Hawkes, before he donned the holy robes of the ministry, used to disguise himself as a mermaid, sit on a rock and sing in the moonlight—much to the awe of the villagers round about.[8]

In my own opinion, when talking about mermaids and mermen, we are dealing with man's encounter with the rare, unique or abnormal. When he identifies what he sees, it is in terms of his own knowledge and belief. (I was once told that when they observed their first automobile the Indians of Maniwaki, Quebec, called it "the-frog-that-comes-hopping.") But more of this later.

So much for the agents that keep the beliefs in merpeople alive. What specifically are the characteristics of these underwater creatures? How old are the stories about them, where are their origins, how widespread are they and what can we learn from them—if anything?

First, they are believed to be near-mortal. They are thought to live under water and to come to the surface from time to time. On rare occasions they are said to come ashore in the guise of mortals. They are said to have breasts, long hair and a scaly tail which resembles the tail of a cod more than a mackerel, porpoise or shark. (Indeed they are often called "the maid with the scaly tail.") Often, but not always, they are said to have blue eyes and golden hair and to be beautiful. Usually they are seen sitting on tidal rocks, ledges and reefs, although not infrequently they are encountered swimming offshore. They are said to have a comb, a mirror and sometimes a cap, a shawl or a veil. When they are ashore on a tidal rock, they usually busy themselves combing their hair while looking in a mirror and singing a song. For the most part they are thought harmful to man, either luring him to destruction on the ledges with their beauty and their voices, or portending his unhappy demise by merely being seen.

This idea of disaster was so popular that an old ballad begins:

> Last Friday morn when we set sail,
> We hadn't sailed far from land,
> Till we spied, till we spied a pretty fair maid
> With a comb and glass in her hand, her hand, her hand,
> With a comb and a glass in her hand.

This vision prepares all hands for the tragedy that is to come, and no one is surprised when:

> The moon shines bright, the stars give light,
> And my mother is looking for me;
> She may look, she may look with a watery eye
> She may look to the bottom of the sea, the sea, the sea
> She may look to the bottom of the sea.[9]

On the other hand, for no accountable reason mermaids have sometimes been known to take a fancy to a person—even a town—and perform
rare feats in his behalf. Occasionally they are captured when the tide leaves
them stranded on a rock or when they are ashore for a party. At such times
a clever man is able to steal their veil, cap or scarf or to exact tribute from
them before returning them to the sea. Should a man capture one and hide
her magic garment, she becomes a woman, makes a useful, docile wife, a
great bearer of children, and almost always brings some benefit to the
husband—sometimes gold and silver, sometimes cattle, good fishing, the
gift of healing or some special power, as we have already seen in the case
of boatbuilding. However, no matter how happy the mermaid ashore may
appear, she spends her spare time looking for her hidden garment. When
it is found, as it invariably is, she reverts to her mermaid self and plunges
into the sea, leaving a grieving family behind, for the mer qualities are
usually recessive traits in her offspring, and they seldom can follow her.

At this point one must pause to discuss the magic garment without
which the mermaid cannot function properly. Although she is known the
world over and most of her properties are everywhere somewhat similar,
as can be seen by comparing Ulysses' sirens with the Lorelei, the idea of
the magic garment seems to be peculiar to the northern areas, specifically
those inhabited by the German, Scandinavian, English and, most im-
portantly, Celtic peoples. Moreover, the concept of gaining power over her
by possessing her garment does not seem to be well known outside the area
under discussion. Usually this garment is a shawl, a cap (often red, said
caps many times being associated with fairies) or a cloak; less frequently it
is a comb, mirror, vial of ointment or some miscellaneous object.

Mermaids are thought to live in an underwater paradise not unlike
fairyland. Indeed, in France the creatures are sometimes called Marie
Morgane, an appellation wherein the fairy queen's name is preserved. Apparently their magic garments, which so often cover their heads, are the
scuba apparatus that allows them to reach the land underneath the waves,
if not to dwell in it as well. It is still a firm belief among seafaring people
that persons born with the caul—that is, with the embryonic sack still
attached over their heads—cannot drown. Many fishermen in Scotland possess such cauls which they carry, dried, as a fetish to prevent disaster at
sea—and until recently they could be purchased for a small fee in England.[10] The idea behind this belief, obviously, is that the human fetus lives
in liquid. If it can obtain air from the liquid while in the embryonic sack,
then the sack must have the properties of a diving bell. I think it is possible
that this Germanic belief in the magic of the caul may be the ancient root

from which is derived the belief in the mermaid's magic cap or shawl. Other objects that are believed to have supernatural power over the mer-folk would simply represent a further diffusion of this older belief.

When one gains power over a mermaid by stealing her magic object, she usually remains in thrall for a long period. On the other hand, when a mermaid is rescued, or captured and promptly returned to the sea, the reward is of a different nature. The most common compensation is to grant wishes, as in the case of the boatbuilder mentioned previously, who asked for special shipbuilding skills. Usually, however, the wishes granted are of an impermanent nature, and once a wish has been used it is gone forever.

Yet if the mermaid is in any way harmed or rejected, she has terrible methods of revenge. In one case a mermaid killed a man who had offended her by blowing the roof off his house. In another, a mermaid is said to have driven a duke mad when he refused to marry her. When a mermaid saved a sailor from drowning, she asked him to visit her. He did not, and he and his whole village were washed away. After an Irish fisherman killed a mermaid, both he and his entire family were drowned by a peculiar wave.[11] In another case a person who seized a mermaid, wishing her bodily harm, was drawn irresistibly into the water and drowned.[12] Finally, the people of Norstrand stole the belt and the cattle of a friendly mermaid. This so enraged the creature that she returned to the sea, leaving behind her girdle, which she transformed into rushes, and a great savage bull which hooked and pawed the soil until the whole area became a desert.[13] With punishments such as these in store for anyone who tormented them, it is not surprising that mermaids were seldom abused.

There are a number of stories about a sailor who saw some mermaids sitting on the beach. He crept closer and discovered that they were primping for a party. They had a little vial of ointment which they passed around and rubbed in their eyes. This ointment changed them from mermaids into women, and after their metamorphosis they hid ointment, garments and tails and went to town. The sailor, after they left, rubbed some ointment into his left eye. From that time on he could penetrate any disguise. In this manner he exposed many people as mermaids and even revealed fish as being mermaids in disguise. Finally, he discovered some elves stealing various items at a country fair. He accosted them, and they asked him how he knew they were stealing. He said he could see them. They asked which eye he saw them with. When the simple soul replied that it was the left eye, one of the little people struck him with a stick and he remained, from that day forth, blind in the left eye.[14]

In 1969 I was introduced to Sarah Bennett of Brant Lake in New York. She told a story about some little people "with red hats" who were "gypsies." A boy spied them in the woods and watched them as they went into town. When they reached the village, they went to a fair and began stealing "cabbages and carrots and vegetables and putting them in a bag," but only the boy noticed them. After this had continued for some time, he went up and asked what they were doing "stealing that way." "Which eye do you see us with?" asked one of the little men. "The right one." Quick as a flash he struck him blind in that eye. "You know," said Sarah Bennett, "I never understood that story too well. Why do you suppose they knocked out the poor fellow's eye?"

From what we have learned so far, it is apparent that the ancestry of Anglo-American mermaids is both ancient and diverse. They seem to be related to the Celtic faeries through their coloring, their name—Marie Morgane—and their underwater cities, love of music and ability to grant gifts. Yet their enmity toward man and the violent retribution they exact from people seem to link them with the sterner otherworld figures of more northern folklore. We have mentioned the magic garment as a linking attribute among Germanic mermaids, as opposed to those in other parts of the world.

It is my belief that what we are dealing with when discussing Anglo-American mermaids is really a fractured mythology—beliefs so old as possibly to reach back to Neolithic times, beliefs long since vanished into limbo, with only fragments remaining. Onto these fragments have been grafted other lore from other lands, but at the core we are confronted with a mythology northern oriented.

Until now there has been a widely held concept that the mermaid was near-eastern oriented. First it has been held that these creatures are derived from a belief in water sprites lurking about springs—a belief most popular among early Greeks—and that these creatures gradually were transferred to the sea, where they carried on an existence comparable with their sisters on a bosky bank. Second, scholars have pointed out, and rightly so, that the ancient Babylonians had pictures of a fish god, Onans and/or Dagon, said deity being a hominoid from head to waist and piscine thereafter. Third, they point to the mirror in the hand of the mermaid and link it to the disk held in the hands of these ancient deities of the Mediterranean basin. Finally, through dexterous philological peregrination, they have linked various words from diverse parts of the globe to come to the same conclusion.

If we examine the stories from Babylonia, Greece, Egypt and other nations in that part of the world, we discover that they depict beings quite different from the mermaids and their friends in the north. It is true that the Lorelei are said to drown sailors, but the creatures Ulysses encountered guzzled them. The kelpie, it is true, is sometimes said to drown people and throw their livers back ashore, and a mermaid did express a desire to fry Lorntie's blood; but there is a difference between a wish and an act, and man-eating does not seem to be part of our mermaid custom. Neither are merfolk in the north possessed of all knowledge, and with what they have they are chary. The merfolk do make gifts to individuals, but not to mankind, and the gift is always limited in scope. It is correct that the fish god, Onans, looks like a mermaid, but it can be pointed out that there are only a limited number of ways to draw or carve a half-human, half-fish creature.

There is one peculiar thing about what I choose to call the Germanic mermaid that may have its origin in the Near East, and that is her strange relationship to the church. This can, I think, be best clarified by the story of Melusina, so popular in the Middle Ages, and its analysis.

A poor but nobly born young man named Raymond was befriended by a wealthy kinsman and they became fast friends. One day while hunting the two were separated from their party and lost their way. When they stopped to rest they were set upon by a boar, which Raymond killed. In the fracas he also inadvertently killed his benefactor. The young man fled the scene in great dismay and blundered onto a marvelous spring by which sat three beautiful women with golden hair and white dresses. To one of these, named Melusina, he told his tale, and she, in turn, advised him how he could fabricate a story that would divert suspicion from himself. She also told him to ask his benefactor's heirs for the amount of land that could be encompassed in a bull hide around the spring. After this, she promised to marry him providing he would promise never to look at her on Saturdays. He agreed and went off to ask for the land, which request was readily granted, although his relative was somewhat startled when he subsequently discovered the bull hide had been sliced into a thread and encompassed considerable acreage.

On this site Melusina built a castle and married Raymond. Each year she brought forth a child, and each one was a monster. One had a scarlet face, another a red and green eye, one was a Cyclops, and another had a great tusk instead of teeth. All were successful in their chosen fields, one becoming a famous monk, another a warrior, and so on. For each the mother built a magnificent home—for Gyot, her third monster, she built La Rochelle.

For many years all went well, until one Saturday Raymond was persuaded to peek through the keyhole. He saw his wife taking a bath and was distressed to find that from the waist down she was shaped like a fish. When she discovered he had spied on her, the lady uttered a great shriek and abandoned both her house and children, returning only to prophesy the death of a member of the family. This she did for years, flapping around the castle on bat's wings and uttering doleful shrieks not unlike those of the banshee.[15]

This story from a south-central European spring was used by Baring-Gould to open the mermaid trail to Babylon, for in his discussion he connects this rather atypical story to our tradition, and to the ancient Sumerian deities. He also suggests that the banshee who wails and flaps about before a death comes from this source. Actually, Melusina more closely resembles Lilith than any of the deities mentioned by Baring-Gould, and the banshee has a source closer to home than he realized, for she appears to have come from an ancient Celtic goddess named Matrona who possessed all the banshee characteristics plus a few more.[16] But to return to Lilith, about whom St. Augustine wrote a treatise. (He was curious about the offspring of the sons of Adam, who lay with this infamous woman. The fruits of these unions were said to have been monsters—one of whom, at least, was born with only one eye.)

The first mention of Lilith comes about 2500 B.C. She was related to Gilgamesh, a culture hero closely associated with water, and both were thought of as storm demons who visited humans at night. Further, Lilith was depicted holding a ring in combination with a rod. Since she was thought to sap the vitality of men by inducing nocturnal emissions, it was desirable to drive her away, and to do this one used verse charms.

By 1000 B.C. she had become the bride of Adam, whose unfortunate choice of mates was truly epic. When he discovered she "refused to lie beneath him," Adam ordered her to begone. Lilith refused, but after a considerable struggle she left and took up her abode in the Red Sea, where she supplied enough milk to suckle a hundred demons a day. Shortly after this we have pictures of Lilith as a beautiful nude woman with shapely breasts, long flowing hair, large genitalia and her legs chained together. By this time she had been cursed by God and could be driven off by the use of rhymes and amulets. She did not seem susceptible to superstition and continued to enrage the Deity until He cast her forever into the depths of the sea—after which, in one case at least, she was spoken of as a "female leviathan." Men realized what trouble they were in as soon as they saw her.[17]

Summing up, Lilith was a female. She preyed upon men—usually in a celibate condition—who found her charms difficult to resist. She dwelt in the water, had long hair, breasts, and legs fast together; was sometimes referred to in terms of a fish; and held in her hand an object not unlike a mirror. She liked the night and was connected with storms, and after coupling with men, went away. Finally, she could be rendered harmless with charms and amulets. All of these things are true of the mermaid except that, in her case, the charm has become a device employed by herself to curse men. Which is not to suggest that she is an outgrowth of this Semitic creature, but rather that the tradition about Lilith may have contributed to both the mermaid's present form and possibly her ultimate survival.

If Lilith aided in shaping the personality of the mermaid, there is still another, more important creature to be dealt with if we would seek ultimate origins for this maid-with-a-tail. This is the kelpie, variously known as nix, nuggle, *each usige* or water horse, and water bull. It may be that this peculiar animal is the most ancient and primitive type of all the mermaid's northern ancestors.

What could be the most primitive idea about these creatures was still believed in less than a century ago in the Shetland Islands. Here there dwelt a handsome little gray stallion. Aside from the fact that he was more beautiful than most horses, he differed in one other respect. Instead of a regular tail he had a wheel hanked onto his rump. When people were about, the nuggle (or nuzzle) was careful to roll his wheel between his legs so it wouldn't show. Strangers were so taken by his great beauty that they couldn't resist a ride. The beast would stand docile and allow the rider to mount, and away they would go until they came to water—a large puddle, a stream or a lake. At this point the docile beast became raving wild, hurled his rider into the water, then plunged into the depths and vanished away as a tiny blue flame.

The nuggle had one other annoying habit. When there were no riders to dunk, he spent his time standing on waterwheels and stopping the progress of the mills. There was only one way he could be dislodged, and that was by throwing a firebrand into the millrace. To facilitate this, a special trap door was constructed in many of the mills. No sooner had the brand hit the water than the trickster had to get off. Not only that, but the fire would turn his hooves backward (or reveal that nature had already placed them so and he had been able to disguise the fact).[18]

There can be little doubt that this creature is related in some way to ancient sun worship. To the Celts, the wheel was representative of the sun. Today, as mentioned earlier, in the remoter parts of the Hebrides, they still "smoor the fire" when it is banked for the night. That is, the old person who covers it draws a picture of a wheel in the ashes and says a prayer for each piece between the spokes. Back of this tradition stands the wheel on the Celtic cross, and behind the cross looms the wheel itself scratched on ancient stones.

Should there be any doubt that the kelpie is a sun symbol, the clincher comes with the departure of the little gray stallion, who vanishes into deep water with a tiny blue flame. It has long been known to a few observant mariners that a very peculiar phenomenon occurs when the sun sets in the sea. I was first made aware of this by the late Captain Halsey Powell many years ago and have subsequently observed it on a number of occasions through binoculars. On a calm, cloudless evening, when the sun sets clear of the land, just seconds after its upper limb dips beneath the horizon, a tiny brilliant blue-green flare, in shape like a candle flame, flickers for an instant on the horizon. If I am right, the color of the horse would be symbolic of the edge of night.[19]

Should the hypothesis prove correct, we may well be looking upon one of the most ancient of Old World folktales. Unlike Phoebus with his car or the supernatural beings in other ancient myths of the sun, the nuggle drags the sun attached to himself. Further, if the bit about blue light is as ancient as the rest of the story, then the origin of the water horse and even the mermaid herself may be in the sea, instead of in fresh-water ponds and streams as previously thought.[20]

But the story of the water horse does not end here. Further south, it takes a more sophisticated turn. In Scotland the kelpies, or water horses, are depicted as beautiful stallions. On the west coast they are dark-colored but on the east coast light-colored, and we must remember that the east coast is closer to the Shetland Islands than the west coast.[21] They feed along the edges of deep-water lochs or the sea itself. They can breed with earthly horses; the get are handsome and strong but lack the amphibious characteristics of their sires. Generally kelpies are seen richly attired with saddle, saddle cloth and bridle. Like the nuggle, they too have a distinguishing characteristic which is often overlooked by the unwary. They have sand in their manes.

They stand quietly at the approach of a stranger, and the luckless victim jumps on the back of one and takes hold of the bridle. The rider then finds himself glued to the beast, which promptly plunges into deep water with his luckless victim. In Scotland there is a story about a beautiful stray horse that stopped before a schoolhouse during recess. All the children save one mounted the horse, which stood placidly. However, one boy was slow in mounting. His mates taunted him but still he held back and, instead of mounting, touched the kelpie's hide with his finger. Instantly he was stuck to the horse and the whole lot started for the loch. Realizing his plight, wee Douglas managed to cut off his finger in time to save himself, but his little friends were all drowned.[22]

A very similar tale comes from Maryland. There we are told that the kelpie is a red horse that comes out of the sea and is very friendly. If you mount him he will take you down under the sea, where you can live but may never return. A boy saw one and, not knowing what it was, stroked its muzzle. Instantly he was glued to the beast and found himself being carried headlong toward the sea. Quick as a flash, he drew his knife and slashed off his hand. He was none too quick, for the water horse plunged into the sea, leaving him on the very edge.[23]

Another story from Scotland tells of a kelpie who came to a girl's house, disguised as a man, to watch her spin. Her father learned of her nocturnal visitor and disguised himself as his daughter. When the kelpie arrived the father scalded the supposed suitor's foot with boiling water, and the foot instantly turned into a hoof. The kelpie demanded to know who had seared him. "It was I," said the farmer. The kelpie rushed out of the house and joined his fellow kelpies outside and begged them to avenge him. They in turn asked who did it, and the water horse said, "It was I." From this the kelpies concluded he had spilled boiling water on himself, and the whole group repaired to the loch, never to return.[24]

In Loch Boisdale, South Uist, I recorded two anecdotes of an even more sophisticated nature. These stories were told about the *each uisage* (Gaelic for kelpie).

He's supposed to be a very fearsome monster who lives in—oh—certain rivers or little mountain pools or in the sea in some places and he can assume human form and become a very handsome young man with an eye for the ladies also. And there are several stories told about him. Apparently he's in his monster form and here's one of his stories. Oh, he came upon this beautiful girl down near the shore and he fell in love with her, but he knew that if she once thought that he was, you know, an *each usage* she'd have nothing to do with him. So he changed himself into a most handsome young man and they met there every so often. He courted her and one day they were sitting above the sea talking to one another—the warm sun streaming down—and he grew drowsy. And he fell asleep with his head in the lady's lap. And she was stroking his hair and thinking how very happy she was—all the joy he had brought her and she felt, you know, that gritty feeling of something rough and she looked down and there was sand in his hair and, even as she watched, his hair became seaweed and tangle [kelp]. And she looked down and his feet became hooves, and she knew at once what it was, you see; so she sort of just gently removed his head and fled, and it was the last he ever saw of her.

There's another story about this woman, you know, this kind of story a stepmother whose own daughter, you know, she was that pretty. She wasn't ugly to look at but she was very hardhearted and very, you know, sort of light. There was just nothing to her. And she was being courted by this very worthy young man, who she thought was very dour, and she wouldn't have anything to do—she trifled with him—she knew she had him and she flirted with all the other young men around. And the other daughter was a very pretty girl also. But sort of more—modest—you know, less forthcoming and she of course had all the hard work to do, being the stepdaughter and not the daughter of the mother. And she was sent down to fish, you know, to feed the family. She was sent down to milk the cows, to look after the cows, to do everything the other one would not do. And she was sitting fishing one day and, oh, she just wasn't having any luck at all and she daren't go home. She was too scared to go home because her stepmother would have whipped her and sent her to find food elsewhere. She didn't know where to go. She was still fishing there and she had for days been observed by this kelpie, this *each usage*, who had fallen in love with her. And he saw what a heart-of-gold she had—what a beautiful girl she was in every way. And he appeared one day to her in his human form and talked to her, and she didn't exactly pour out her woes but he gathered that she hadn't a very happy life —that things didn't go very well for her. And he said, "Well, what are you doing here fishing?" And she said, "Oh, I must catch food for the family." Then he said, "Well, give me the line and I'll fish." And of course he pulled in fish one by one. And she thought this was wonderful. And when her stepmother saw what luck she had, she sent her back straightway the next day to fish again, and he appeared again and he caught fish for her again. All this time she was falling in love with him as well. She was never aware that he was a kelpie, but he, in this supernatural form, was aware of everything that was going on in the villages all around and he knew the unhappiness that her sister had caused the girl—her stepsister—so he thought— well, if there's nothing else he could do, then surely he'd make her happy in some way. And it so happened that this girl, she discovered that he was a water horse and of course would never come back again. Her mother used to whip her and send her out fishing but of course she wouldn't go and it dawned on the stepmother what had happened and it was then really he determined to make her happy the only way he could. And there was a big dance in the village and he knew that her stepsister would be going and that she had an eye for the most handsome young man in the crowd—and

anyone she thought was a likely prospect, you know, the man in the richest
cloak or the man with the most beautiful sword, or anything like that—the
most likely. And he told his councillors down below, "You must prepare for
I am going up to the other world," he said, "and before the night is done
we shall have a mortal with us." And he told them all about this girl and he
didn't tell them very much about the other sister who he loved. But they
gathered jewels studded with rubies and his belt was crossed with diamonds
and emeralds. He had a long purple cloak that was braided with silver and
he had a gold garland around his head. And he gathered, they gathered him
up into a chariot with four white horses and sped him up to the surface of
the sea and he came ashore in a lonely spot and he went to the dance. And
the young man who had been courting the stepsister so earnestly had been
dancing with her and he was beginning to really think he had won her heart
at last when this tall and very handsome and richly robed stranger walked
in. And of course she had no eyes for anyone else after that. And he danced
with her and he flattered her and he courted her and the end of it was that
he took her down to the shore. And she was so bewitched she didn't know
what was happening until it was too late and he had taken her down below
the surface of the sea. And that was the last they saw of her. Nobody saw
her again.

Like many other pagan beliefs, the lore of the kelpie was adapted into
Christian mythology. Probably his malevolence toward mankind, his association with fire, his hoof and the fact that he is always male induced the
early Christians to associate him with the devil. As a devil he survives in
an old ballad still popular in America today, which tells how James Harris
returned from a voyage to foreign parts and persuaded his unfaithful lover
to run off with him to sea. Not until they were well offshore did she see
his hoof and then it was too late. Assuming his true monstrous form—

> He strack the top mast wi' his hand,
> The main mast wi' his knee,
> He stove a hole in the bottom of the ship
> And they sank to the bottom of the sea.[25]

Not only is the kelpie remembered in Christian song, but he early became associated with the church in both tale and art, as can be seen in
church sculpture extant today. There is a belief that on at least one occasion a kelpie hauled stones to build a kirk on top of a loch. Whether he
did this as a beast of burden or in his human form we are not told, but the
church soon became haunted and was abandoned.[26]

While the waterhorse is usually thought of as malevolent, the water bull is not. In some cases he actually protects people from trouble, as Campbell points out with a story from the island of Islay in the Hebrides.

On that island was born a bull of such a peculiar size and shape that an old witch recognized it as a water bull's offspring, and ordered it shut into a barn and supplied with a diet of milk for seven years.

About the time the seven years were up, a young island girl met a stranger, who asked her to comb his hair. This she did, and was horrified to discover that his scalp was covered with green seaweed. She continued to stroke his head until he fell asleep, and then she fled for the house. Looking back, she saw a horse following her.

Meanwhile the old crone observed what was going on and turned loose the great bull, who fell upon the horse. They fought furiously until at last the bull drove the kelpie back into the sea, where the fight continued. The next day the bull, all bloody and mangled, washed ashore, but the kelpie was never seen again.[27]

In Ireland the water horse is not unknown but seems to restrict its forage largely to lakes and streams.[28] Its activities are shared to a great extent with the water bull and with a beautiful white cow that has mythological as well as magical overtones. Of this last animal, I have told several stories in Chapter II. The fishermen on Tory Island say that such a white cow has always inhabitated a loch on the island, that it is still there, and further, that it appears every hundred years.

Sometimes one is startled at the response to an innocent question. In Fanny's Hole, Mulroy Bay, Ireland, I asked the MacBrides, "Did you ever hear of a thing called a sea horse?"

"Oh aye.'"

"Well, do these sea horses do anything?"

"Yes, I have heard of it. It had big wings on it, aye, and it was blue, blue, called pealogwill. They'll sink a boat, you know. Big wings on them, oh, aye, you know that some men are afraid of them. They are dangerous. The curragh men are afraid of them. They come up the bay and turn the boat [capsize it]. They are in there by the hundreds of them. That's all the gathering I know about them. I couldn't tell you about the sea horses. Ah well, it would be better to talk about crocodiles."

Far to the north in Scotland they still recall "The Blue Men of the Minch," creatures who inhabit the area around the Shiant Islands, but today the memory is dim. When I asked about the Blue Men I had the following reply, "You must mean 'The Blue Men of the Minch.' Aye, I have heard of them. They can raise great storms, they say, but I don't know a great deal about them, really." At the turn of the century they were a lively tradition. People on Skye had seen them, and at that time there was a popular story about them:

> A vessel was sailing between the island of Lewis and Na h-Eileinean siant [The Charmed Islands] in the channel called Struth nam Fear Gorm [The Stream of the Blue Men] when they saw a blue man asleep in the sea. They picked him up and bound him hand and foot so tightly he could not move. Before the vessel was clear of Struth nam Fear Gorm she was pursued by two more blue men. One said, "Duncan will be one." The other replied, "Farquahar will be two." With this the prisoner hopped up, snapped his lashings, dove overboard and swam away with his friends.[29]

Years ago the Blue Men were more closely described and their activities were far more dangerous. They were said to be winged; their bodies were painted blue and they liked to sing, but this seems to have been their only pleasant quality. They attacked boats passing the Shiant Islands, came aboard in numbers and demanded tribute. If they did not receive it, they caused terrible storms which could overcome the strongest vessel. One way a person could escape was to sing them a song that was better than their own, another was to pay a tithe in gold. Their leader was called Shony in the seventeenth century, and Martin Martin says that at Hallowtide the natives poured a cup of new ale into the sea to propitiate this god, who would then bring them seaweed (kelp) to fertilize the fields. After the libation a candle, specially lit for the occasion, was extinguished.[30]

The Blue Men are believed by some scholars to embody a folk memory of Moors caught by the Norse and brought to the area. Others think that it is a memory from the sixth or seventh century, when the islands were a retreat for blue-robed monks.[31] For variety's sake, the folk on the island of Skye believe they were some of the fallen angels.[32] A fourth possibility, and one that seems to hold more weight than the other three, is that this is a vestigal memory of the ancient Picts. These little people were replaced by the later Celtic invasions of the British Isles centuries ago, yet we know a considerable amount about them. They painted their bodies blue, lived in underground "brocs" and must have been excellent seamen, for remains of their culture are to be found in islands as remote as St. Kilda,[33] and some of their beliefs and activities may have been copied by the Celts. It is interesting to note that when they dwelt in the islands a considerable portion of their diet consisted of seal meat. Since the Shiant Islands are inhabitable, it is highly probable that remnants of this curious group (who, some people think, gave rise to the belief in faeries) may have held on in these remote and inaccessible spots long after they had vanished in the larger islands. Here, because of their aquatic qualities, they have become interwoven with the mermaid-merman-nuggle-kelpie tradition.[34]

Now that we have suggested some of the possible origins of the mermaid stories, it might be well to note down a few to show the variety one encounters.

These beliefs were still very popular in the nineteenth century. They were so popular that the Japanese made a good thing out of selling stuffed mermaids—the upper works of a monkey sewed to the after half of a fish—in Europe. Today, however, this popularity has languished, and it is only in the remoter areas of the English-speaking world that they are still accorded a degree of credibility.

Within the memory of living people a boat from the west coast went to the east coast of Scotland to fish for herring. One morning the boat was scudding off before a two-reef breeze with a great load of fish. Suddenly a mermaid appeared in their wake and followed them. One after another the crew threw herring at her, but the mermaid ignored them until a young lad threw her one, whereupon she sank and did not reappear. The vessel made port, and the skipper told the boy that he must never go to sea again if he valued his life. The lad took the advice and stayed ashore a year. Then one day a man was looking for a crew to take a small boat he had purchased home. The boy signed on, and the boat left on a clear bright day. They had scarcely cleared the land when a gale sprang up and the boat and her crew went down![35]

Actually, this is a rather tame version of a common story. Ordinarily when mermaids are sighted at sea the crew observe their motions intently—if they follow the ship or look at it, it is construed as an omen of disaster, but if they turn or look away from the vessel, the sign is considered favorable and the voyage will be a lucky one. Occasionally, too, when the mermaid pursues the ship a crewman will throw overboard a knife, and if she dives the vessel will escape destruction. The idea here, of course, is that cold iron will drive off evil spirits, and since sailors usually carried sheath knives, the iron was in the shape of a cross. Should this fail, sometimes she can be diverted by tossing out silver coins.[36]

Captain "Bob" Roberts told me that the town of Orford in England once had an excellent harbor but it now was a bad one, for it has silted in and a bar has made up across its entrance. Local tradition holds that this was because a mermaid had received ill-treatment and had plugged the harbor in revenge. According to an ancient work, a merman was captured there in the twelfth century, suffered many indignities and torture which ended up in neglect, and finally managed to escape into the sea.[37] It might be pointed out that a similar incident took place in Cornwall, where a mermaid plugged the harbor at Seaton.[38]

In Cornwall the otherwise excellent harbor of Padstow is choked with sand. Once it was under the protection of a mermaid and kept clear, clean and deep, until one day a fowler either for spite or sport fired a shot at her. He missed, but the merry maid was very upset. Raising her right hand, she swore that she would choke the harbor, then vanished.[39]

A number of years ago I sailed with a man who had no fear of the water. It turned out that he was a Manxman, and there was a belief on that island that apparently is still extant—that the islanders are descended from a mating between a human and a mermaid. The mermaid blessed the off-spring by making them immune to drowning.

At one time mermaids were said to be all about the island and to cause much trouble. One tried to strangle a shepherd, others carried sailors to their underwater haunts and in general were a nuisance. Finally there came a knight, who attacked them and pursued them very close. When it looked as if they might be captured one escaped by transforming herself into a wren, and since that time on the first of each year wrens are sought and killed on Man—for it is thought that at this time all mermaids transform themselves thus.[40] Memory of this story may have passed into North America, for in Chesapeake Bay the jenny wren is said to foretell a storm.[41]

When a mermaid was wronged, she did not just content herself with filling a harbor with sand but usually tried to dole out punishment that would fit the crime. In Scotland, for example, a mermaid was seduced by a youth at the mouth of a tidal cave; he promptly forgot about her, but she lured him back to the cave and chained him there with golden chains.

Near Land's End a story popular in the last century related that once there was a woman who bathed her child in a deep pool. One day the mermaids substituted one of their children for the infant, and the change-ling grew up to become a beautiful girl. But the people knew that she was of the merfolk, not only because she was greatly upset by going into a church or even by passing one, but because of her remarkable ability to swim in the surf.

A farmer living in the vicinity did not like the girl's parents, and in order to take revenge on them he persuaded a young soldier to seduce her.

This the young man did, and the girl pined away and finally died in child-birth just as the tide turned to ebb.

Shortly after this the pandering farmer ran into trouble. "The crops failed, the cattle died, hay-stacks and corn-ricks caught fire, cows slipped their calves, horses fell lame or stumbled and broke their knees" Eventually the farmer was turned out of his rents and became a drunkard.

At midnight on the anniversary of the girl's death, her seducer found himself on the beach where she used to swim. 'He heard beautiful music, and in searching for its origin he came face to face with a mermaid, who seized him and paralyzed him with a kiss. The tide rose and with it a storm. A great wave swept the seducer away forever, and at the same time the farmer was struck by a bolt of lightning and burned to a crisp.[42]

From the Middle Ages to the end of the nineteenth century there was a tale popular in Scandinavia, Scotland and Ireland about a mermaid who befriended a fisherman. It is sometimes called the story of the Gray Lad.

One day this fisherman, who was old, poor and childless, was out fish-ing and had had no luck, when a mermaid rose beside the boat and offered to make him prosperous if he would promise her his first-born three years hence. Since the old man had no children, he agreed, and the mermaid gave him three grains of corn for his wife, dog and horse, and three more to plant. As a result of these fertility pills his wife had triplets, the horse three foals, three pups from the dog, and three trees in the back yard.

Three years passed and the fisherman did well, but he could not bring himself to give up the eldest boy. The mermaid extended the time for another four years, and when he again failed to produce the child, for seven years more. Shortly before the final date, the old man told the boy his troubles, and the young man—the Gray Lad—departed on a journey, riding one of the foals and followed by one of the dogs. On his way he befriended a dog, a hawk and an otter, who said that if he needed them they would come to his aid. Eventually he came to a pleasant kingdom and got a job as a cowherd. Unfortunately, there was a three-headed mon-ster in the area that ate the cows, which kept the herd small and un-productive—but the boy, aided by his dog, killed the monster and recovered a large treasure. When the king discovered this he was very pleased, and the boy continued to herd cows until one day another monster appeared to ravage the country. The king, in order to save his herd, ordered his daughter to be given to the monster. The Gray Lad interfered and cut the heads off the ogre one by one, each time accepting a token from the girl. Later, when another person tried to claim the victory over the monster, the lad proved he had killed it by exhibiting the tokens, and married the girl.

Shortly after this he was swallowed by a sea monster (in some versions a mermaid). The girl sang; the beast came to the surface and exchanged the boy for treasures, and then proceeded to swallow the girl. In order to kill this creature, the boy had to go to an island and catch a white deer, inside of which was a bird, inside of which was a trout with an egg in its mouth. The dog he had befriended caught the deer, the hawk the bird, and the otter the trout. The boy extracted the egg and crushed it, thereby killing the monster.

Shortly thereafter the boy was hit on the head by a witch. Back home his tree began to wither, and his brother went after him; but he too was clubbed by the witch, and the second tree withered. The third brother, observing the two trees, came to the rescue, found the witch, killed her, and restored the other two.[43]

This story is of course a seagoing version of the Two Brothers story, one of the oldest and most widespread of all folktales. The author collected an almost identical version, minus the mermaids, from the Mohawk Indians several years ago.[44]

Today tales of mermaids are not easy to come by in the British Isles. Many people have heard of them, but few are inclined to talk about them. The case was somewhat different in Fanny's Hole, Mulroy Bay:

"Did you ever hear of a thing called a merry maid, Mrs. MacBride?"

"Ah, there was a man here who was married to a mermaid."

"No!"

"Aye. It was as far back as my, maybe, great grandmother or maybe further back—but I heard that when I was a little girl and it was always going out fishing on the rocks, you know—so—. Aye, and bathing too. Bathing—and he was a good fisherman."

Mr. MacBride: "There was a cove and there was a merry maid too in that cove."

Mrs. MacBride: "But he was out fishing, you know. There is something in a web that they have on the head and if you steal this web, you understand, you can take them away, you could take them away. But anyhow there came a day and she was sitting—oh, just combing her hair on the rocks and he saw her. And made a splash and took the web off her, then she made a splash out in the sea, and he went to her and got the web, or whatever she took off her. And before she came in she was going back with her tail—it's half woman and half a fish, and she was going along with her tail and he called to her and took her home and he kept her confined there two days—and he always kept under the turf stack—they had the peats— and he always kept this web, or whatever, hidden so she couldn't go any-where. So the little boy, when the father went away to some fair or somewhere—and the little boy was so curious that she was able to have a conversation some way—whether she was able to speak, I don't know, but anyway, he understood the mother and she would understand him. And he took her to the peat stack that the father had hidden this web—and she got it and she left, and they have never seen her more."

J.C.: "And she left the child as well?"

Mr. MacBride: "She had to go. She was compelled to. There was something to that net."

Mrs. MacBride: "Aye, aye, I've often heard—ah—I had an uncle, now he's dead, and I heard him say out at Dewey—away from Dewey, if you know where Dewey is—there's an aunt of mine and a tower beside the house now—in the lowest house in Dewey down on the point. This, anyhow, this uncle of mine and another man seen her sitting combing her hair— yes."

H.P.: "I'd like to see that."

Mrs. MacBride: "So would I. There were fairies and everything in this country. Ah, but I don't know. They're gone."[45]

Unfortunately, the traditions of the mermaid, the faery and the water horse have deteriorated even more in North America than in Ireland. Why this should be is hard to say, for there was considerable belief in these beings among the American Indians from Maine clear down to Florida and up to the Pacific Northwest coast, and where a climate has been established for a certain type of story, related stories often thrive. The Neptune family, hereditary chiefs of the Penobscot in Maine, believed that they were descended from a half-man, half-fish who lived in a hole under Indian Island and who could foretell danger to the tribe. This creature drowned those who fell into the water and plugged up their eyes, ears and mouth with mud. He was last seen before the cholera outbreak in 1949.[46] His name—Hapodamguen.[47]

In 1610, Captain Whitbourne, on a voyage to the new world, put in at St. John's, Newfoundland, where he was approached by a strange creature swimming toward him "looking cheerfully as it had been a woman, by the Face, Eyes, Nose, Mouth, Ears, Necke and Forehead." When the good cap-tain backed off in some alarm, it turned around and tried to scramble into a boat belonging to William Hawkridge, but was given a clout on the head for its pains. Like Captain Whitbourne, "Whether it were a mermaid or no . . . I leave it for others to judge."[48]

In the same century John Smith came upon a lovely mermaid in the West Indies, where they had previously been seen by Columbus. While Columbus did not appear to be entranced by their beauty (and may, indeed, have encountered either a manatee or a seal), Captain John found the lady remarkably attractive. She had "large eyes, rather too round, a finely-shaped nose, a little too short, well-formed ears, rather too long, and her long green hair imparted to her an original character . . ." He was startled on further examination to discover that this beauty from the waist down "gave way to fish."[49]

We have already mentioned Mr. Mitter's experience with a merman in Casco Bay. Not long after that, Captain Rouleau with three French vessels off Nova Scotia encountered a merman, which they tried to catch with ropes but failed. "He brushed his mossy hair out of his eyes which seemed to cover his body as well—as much as seen above water, in some places more, in others less." After clearing his view, he dove and was seen no more "to the great dejection of the fisherman.[50]

The eighteenth century seems little more productive than the previous one in the discussion of mermaids in North America. In the nineteenth century Bassett says that stories of mermaids were not at all uncommon in the United States. He records one story from a Negress, who said she was rescued by mermaids, taken to an underwater palace and later put aboard a ship by them. Another tale tells of a mermaid who climbed into an American fishing vessel and had her hand chopped off. She sank with a sigh and was seen no more.[51]

A somewhat more interesting tale was told in Maine. Captain Kittridge told Harriet Beecher Stowe:

> Once when I was in the Bahamas—it was one Sunday morning in June, the first Sunday in the month—we cast anchor pretty nigh a reef of coral, and I was just a sittin' down to read my Bible, when up comes a merman over the side of the ship, all dressed as fine as any beau that ever ye see, with cocked hat and silk stockings and shoe-buckles, and his clothes were sea-green and his shoe-buckles shone like diamonds. . . . He came up to me and made the politest bow that ever ye see and says he, "Captain Kittridge, I presume," and says I, "yes sir." "I'm sorry to interrupt your reading," says he; and says I "Oh, no matter, sir." "But," says he, "if you would only be so good as to move your anchor. You've cast anchor right before my front door, and my wife and family can't get out to go to meetin'. . . ." He was such a gentleman, I wanted to oblige him. (And moved the anchor.)[52]

Years before this, in Cornwall there was a story about a mermaid who came to church now and then to listen to the singing of the choirmaster, Mathew Trewhalla. Year after year she came and her looks never changed nor did her marvelous voice fade. Eventually she enticed the choirmaster to join her and they vanished into the sea, never to be seen on shore again—although he could occasionally be heard singing in Pendower Cove. Several years after he had vanished, a sea captain let go his hook in the cove. A mermaid came aboard and asked him to shift his anchor, for it was blocking the door of her house and she could not get in to see her children and her husband, Mathew Trewhalla.[53]

Some of these anecdotes die harder than others, and Mr. Mitter's experience is certainly one. Not many years ago a fisherman was hand-lining by himself in a dory just off the Newfoundland shore. At noon he stopped fishing and started to eat his lunch, when much to his surprise and annoyance he discovered a merman about to climb into the boat. He tried to shoo it away with no success, so he grabbed the fish gaff and bashed it on the fingers, after which it acquired a lively interest in other things.

Nor was this the only merman around the area, for about the same time two men were hunting in Cat Arm (Bay) when they saw a creature in the water and shot at it. Whatever it was sank, but a short time later a dead merman with a black beard and hair washed ashore nearby.[54]

On still another occasion a man was caught in a small boat in a heavy gale. When the situation became most critical a mermaid appeared, climbed onto the gunnel and conned the boat safely through the breakers to shore.[55]

Both mermaids and mermen occur frequently in the earlier literature of not only Newfoundland but Prince Edward Island, Cape Breton and Nova Scotia, and now and then someone still reports seeing them. An Indian shaman is believed to have transformed a girl into a mermaid on Prince Edward Island,[56] and a mermaid was kept in thrall by stealing her shell in Nova Scotia.[57]

In this same general area there also seems to be a living tradition about kelpies, but these creatures have become largely confused with the devil in recent times. Two anecdotes should suffice. In one a handsome, well-dressed stranger appears near the shore and enters a tavern where he plays cards, but he is soon recognized when a player drops his cards and discovers his opponent has a cloven hoof. Were it not for the emphasis on personal beauty and the fact that the event was set near watery surroundings, one would think he was dealing with a devil story.[58]

From the same source comes another story. In this case a man saw a beautiful white horse standing in the road. Unable to resist temptation, he climbed aboard and rode down the road. Suddenly the animal balked and began to swell up. The rider struck him with a whip and the creature rang like iron. As soon as it felt the whip, however, the satanic steed bounded off through the air and finally the rider, by the utmost exertion, managed to throw himself to the ground, where he landed with such force he broke his bones.[59]

Perhaps the last great stronghold of these merfolk is the West Indies, where they flourish today as actively as ever they did in the Old World, albeit in a somewhat different form. Nearly every lake, stream and cove in the islands has been the habitation of one of these creatures within the past forty years, and it is only during the last decade that they have begun to desert their homes—driven out by "gasoline fumes."[60]

In May 1971 a man on one of the Windward Islands dreamed a strange dream. A mermaid came to him naked because she was so hot she couldn't wear clothes. She said the island people had used her ill, and unless something was done—and promptly—the drought the island was enduring would continue and she would cause the sea to boil and kill the fish. The man awoke in consternation and told his neighbors, who immediately organized a sacrifice consisting of fowls and sheep which they killed and threw overboard. During the ceremony one chicken died with its feet up, which was taken as a good omen and indeed it must have been. The rains came the following day and the sea did not boil.[61]

The belief in merfolk in the Caribbean area is preserved there largely among the blacks, and in the stories about them[62] they appear as a curious amalgam of African water deity and Scotch-Irish-English mermaid.[63] They come in two types. Faerymaids are female and live in fresh water; mermaids are male and live in salt water. The homes of both are in caves under the water, where life is conducted much as it is on earth—except on a grander scale. The creatures are usually recognizable by their long blonde hair, blue eyes, fair skin and golden comb. Very often they have a cloven hoof in addition to a tail, or in lieu of it. Besides the preceding names, they are called Mama Alo or Mama Jo—names also applied to them in Africa.[64] This peculiar amalgamation of beliefs is to be seen in stories like the following one about Terracomo and Anansi (these heroes are tricksters who are very popular among the Island people as well as in Africa):

> Bo Hawk went out over the sea to steal rice. He invited Brer Terracoma, Brer Terracoma didn't have any wings, so dey make up wings wid clay and wood. Hawk told Terracoma to carry one bag because he don't have any

wings and he will not be able to carry many load. He still carry about fifty bags which Bo Hawk have only one. Whey they was comin' a hurrican set in. Brer Terracoma was too deep loaded, he couldn't fly. When Bo Hawk told him, "Fly high!" Brer Terracoma fly high. Sir, he can't come—he have too much load. He told him to drop some. An' still he wouldn't drop it. The storm came on, pierce him an' wash off his wings. Bo Hawk clear out an' Brer Terracoma drop on a broad stone in the sea.

When he dere he see Brer Sharapan. He tell Brer Sharapan, "Please to haist me out!" Brer Sharapan say, if he ketch he swallow he. Brer Merry-maid come, and Brer Merrymaid carry him to shore. Ven carry him 'shore, Brer Terracoma cast off one of Merrymaid breast and he carry it home and boil it wif de rice. And after he find it very fat and sweet, he invite many friends to see if they could ketch the other breast.

Brer Merrymaid was very active. So she lay down like she's dead. So de men dere say, "If she's dead when they took him he weel keek." An' dey went an' took him wid a stick, and haist his foot an' keek, and dey clear out an' say dat dead man canot keek. So dey don't succeed de other one. There ended the story.[65]

Both mermaids and faerymaids are dangerous, and those that resemble Indians are considered the most malevolent. One of the things they seek is a man's shadow, and once in possession of it the person bereft is likely to go mad, for shadow, soul and sense to the West Indian are inexorably linked together. Sometimes, too, they fall in love with mortals and carry them off to the caves by "parting the waters." Should the unwary eat anything in these caves, the result is similar to what happens to mortals who eat food in faeryland: they can never return to earth.

These merfolk have the power of transformation and not infrequently come ashore in the guise of cats. As such they approach their victim and abscond with his shadow—for which reason stray cats in the West Indies are not accorded the best of treatment, but rather are ill-used and some-times killed.

Unlike their northern relations, these creatures are not overly feared, for they are somewhat slow-witted and can be easily duped. (In one case, knowing that faerymaids love beauty, a victim caused a faerymaid to trans-fer her affections to him by making a flower garden which captivated her heart.) When duped they can be made to grant various gifts—gold, silver or special powers. Sometimes, too, they come to mortals for help and re-ward their benefactors accordingly. One is reminded of the English mer-maid story when we learn that a rather run-of-the-mill doctor delivered a mermaid's wife in their undersea cave and in return was granted super-human skill as a physician.[66] Before leaving these West Indian creatures, I should like to include two tales out of a large number collected there to give an idea of the variety found in them:

> This is the story of a girl that was courtin' with a fish and every time she come her mother didn't know about it and every time she come she selling her cake she says, "A chez a Mini Bon Bon," and Mini Belle is the name of the girl. She say, "Mini Belle, Mini Belle, Mini Belle-O." And one time the fish was damaged by the brother because the brother went and he sang the song, the very song and when the fish come he damage the fish so then when the sister came to meet this Mini Belle, to meet Oshun all the thing she can give no appearance of Oshun because Oshun was killed by the brother so she keep on singing and she cannot see Oshun so she go down until she come to the bottom of the sea and then she became a merry maid of the sea.[67]

In Grenada I met an old sailor who had encountered a beautiful mermaid. "The lady was settin' down an' she was combin' her hair, the purtiest hair you ever seen." He and his friends tried to get the comb because they knew that if they had it, they could "get millions, for if ever you have her comb she must do whatever you ask of her to get back her comb." Unfortunately the attempt failed and the pretty lady was never seen again. He then told a less typical story:

> In the old days you would see the river comin' down heavy [in spate and] you'd hear music comin' down that river an' we could see it comin' down sittin' up on a table, sailin' down on a table with her and she playing this music in a cloud and she'd keep on playing until she reach the mouth and then the table gone and she stop playin' and she gave tea. Now I saw this mermaid personally.[68]

Most of the stories told and remembered today in North America concerning mermaids and kelpies are humorous and greatly diluted in comparison with the Old World tales. Southern Negroes tell of a brown horse that lives in cliffs along streams and foretells disaster, yet if a sick horse hears one of these animals neigh, it will recover. They also tell about a mermaid that lives in a stream and climbs out now and then to ride on car radiators.[69]

From New England comes the story of two Indians fishing in Muscongus Bay in a canoe. The Indian in the bow got a bite and hauled up a mermaid with blue eyes and blonde hair. He examined her minutely for a while and then extracted the hook and threw her overboard. Up to this point the Indian in the stern had said nothing, but he had observed what went on, and now he spoke. "Why?" The other Indian baited his hook and cast his line. "How?" he asked.

Christine Kennedy of Broad Cove, Cape Breton, told me that at certain times and for certain reasons, like guarding a treasure, or during a storm, tiny people were seen in the surf wearing red caps and sometimes singing. She also related that many years ago some fishermen were walking along the beach in the twilight. One looked out and was surprised to see a beautiful white cow standing in the water with the waves breaking against its breast. He called to his mates, and when they looked again the cow wasn't there.

It is well to end with this somewhat prophetic story, for mer people as real entities are vanishing. They are becoming comic, and the stories about them are losing strength and vitality. Soon, except as fantasy, they will vanish like the white cow of Broad Cove. Yet when they do, we will have lost something very old and precious.

As we have pointed out, the yarns that make up the rope of stories about the merfolk come from many areas and the cable itself stretches back in time, perhaps past our present comprehension. Belief in Dagon and in Lilith from the Near East have merged with Celtic faery lore, which in turn has become confused with what may be a belief that is older than any of them and is preserved in the wheel at the back end of the nuggle. If this is correct, we have, among mermaid stories, the northern versions that are distinct from other versions in the motif about the magic garments—something that may be anchored not only in the high latitudes but back in Neolithic times or before.[70]

"Done gone flukes!", whaling, Bequia

CHAPTER X

MONSTERS, SEA SERPENTS AND ENCHANTED ISLANDS

"Now put me into the barge," said the King...
"for I will unto the Vale of Avilion to heal me of my
grievous wound; and if thou hear never more of me,
pray for my soul."

—Sir Thomas Malory, *La Morte d'Arthur*

THE idea of sea monsters and sea serpents is anathema to the scientific mind. Yet men have believed in them since the earliest recorded times, and still do so, though perhaps hesitantly. Actually, if we examine the word "monster," we find no problems. It means primarily a huge creature; after that it seems to imply both the idea of rarity and that it is of a species unknown to the observers. Finally, it may connote savagery, ugliness or deformity. We hear of "monster births" where children are born deformed, but we also hear hunters talk of a "monster bear," and whalemen talk of Moby Dick as a "monster whale." It is a fact that Moby Dick was said by Melville to have a crooked jaw and to be an albino with a truculent disposition, but it was his vast bulk that gave him the sobriquet "monster." In short, under this rubric, anything that is large and unknown to the observer could be called a monster for want of a better, more definable term.

What has been said of monsters could be applied to sea serpents with equal facility. The phrase connotes only the idea of a large marine ophidian creature. A ribbonfish or a huge eel, along with the sea cobra and the oarfish, could be called a sea serpent. Even a long strip of kelp might pass for a sea serpent under proper conditions. The idea that sea serpents are saurian, breathe fire, emit smoke and are relics of an age that vanished millions of years ago is a figment of the vulgar mind.

To complicate matters, popular belief persists in confusing the two and insisting that the sea serpent or monster is only one ancient, lonely creature. In respect to this definition, its adherents are harking back to the remnants of nearly forgotten mythology, wherein one ancient worm from the past lurked in the offing to slay the unwary until destroyed by a hero like Beowulf.

No group of people has a corner on the belief in such unusual creatures. It is worldwide, running from the Orient through India and Africa to Greece, the entire Mediterranean and up into Scandinavia. Tales of serpents and monsters were popular even among the American Indians and the Eskimo. Scholarly thought seems to indicate that these beliefs sprang up somewhere in the East and gradually spread across Europe, but there is also a possibility that these creatures, as they appeared to the Celts and the Germanic people, were part of a large independent northern mythos. It may be that enchanted islands, lands beneath the sea, seals, Finns, kelpies and merfolk are really the frayed strands of a tapestry of mythology far greater than we presently recognize—a tapestry that may have been old in Megalithic times. Bits and pieces, greatly altered by the impact of Christianity, have survived to the present.

The popularity of the belief in these creatures in Scandinavian countries is scarcely to be rivaled elsewhere in the world, and stories about them have continued to flourish most tenaciously in the area dominated by the Vikings in early times—places like Greenland, the Orkneys, the Shetlands and the coasts of northern Scotland. So strong was the concept of sea monsters in early times that the Norse went so far as to design their long ships to look like firedrakes.

Much of our knowledge of these earlier ideas is based on the accounts of Bishop Olaus Magnus of Sweden in the middle of the sixteenth century,[1] and later on the work of Bishop Erick Pontoppidan, who wrote *The Natural History of Norway* in 1755. Both of these men devote long pages to the drew, the krake, Leviathan and the whale, all of which appear as aliases for our subject.

The popular concept of monsters and sea serpents in more modern times undoubtedly harks back to beliefs widely held in the early centuries of the Christian era, beliefs made plausible by the appearance of the Norse long ships with their dragon heads and tails, with the oars like legs, shields like scales and sails like wings. This concept was reinforced by tales popular in the Middle Ages—tales of knights and squires bound on search-and-destroy missions against dragons and monsters wherever they could be found. These activities are epitomized in the early period by Beowulf slaying a dragon, in the Middle Ages by St. George running one through with a lance, and later by Spenser's Red Cross Knight in the *Faerie Queen*. Such creatures are what the ordinary person has in mind when he talks about monsters, and especially about sea serpents.

There can be no doubt, either, that the discovery from time to time—from the Middle Ages through the eighteenth century—of fossilized bones of great prehistoric creatures did little to dispel these beliefs. If they lived once, went the rationalizing, was it not possible that they still lived—in the vast deeps, somewhere in a cave or in a remote jungle fastness? Was there not one, somewhere, alive and well?

But these creatures, no matter how fascinating to the landsmen, are not exactly what the seaman thinks about or has thought about for many centuries. The majority of reports dealing with marine monsters and serpents simply indicate a creature of great bulk and unusual properties that may or may not display violence toward men. Of the two, the sea serpent is the more stereotyped. It usually is depicted as a large snake. It moves rapidly by undulating vertically, is about forty to sixty feet long, has a head sometimes like a snake, at other times like a turtle, lion or horse. Far back at the other end it has either a reptilian or a fishlike tail. It is usually covered with scales, and often it is said to have a mane like a horse extending at least part way down its back. Although in earlier times it attacked ships occasionally, in modern times it has seldom attacked ships or men, and has invariably eluded pursuit. In short, its descriptions are narrow—as narrow as those concerning flying saucers, and the number of sightings of U.F.O.s in this century.

Descriptions of monsters, unlike those of sea serpents, vary so widely that they defy any attempt at cataloguing. Some of them would fit the description of a whale or huge shark, others a giant squid or cuttlefish, while still others suggest a saurian akin to a dinosaur. Some reports describe them as attacking ships and men, while others describe them as placid. A short definition would be: "A large creature of unknown species, presumed dangerous." None has been found or caught that could not be identified by biologists as a member of a known species. Therefore those "in hand" are not monsters.

When we begin to examine the facts about the creatures, we come to some surprising conclusions. Sea serpents and sea monsters have been sighted all over the world and with a good deal of frequency up to the present time,[2] with by far the greatest number in the smoky seas of the higher, colder latitudes. Some have been seen further south, like the one encountered by Captain Trelawney of the Boston brig *Daphne* on September 20, 1848. At the time he estimated his position as 4°11′ south latitude, 10°15′ east longitude, which would place him almost within the port of Mayoumba in Gabon, Africa—an area noted for its rainfall and poor visibility.[3]

Not only are these monsters seen in areas where visibility is often restricted by fog, rain or snow, but they seem to have a propensity for certain places. One such spot in European waters is the northern coast of Scotland and the adjacent islands. In North American waters the area adjacent to Cape Ann, Massachusetts, seems to be a frequent haunt, and in Canada, Newfoundland, Labrador and British Columbia are popular. John Josselyn recalls seeing one at Cape Ann in the seventeenth century sunning itself on the beach "coiled like a ship's cable," with a head like a young lion.[4] Another was seen in 1700 about fifty miles south of there, off Martha's Vineyard.[5]

In all of these places the water is deep "steep to" the shore, the tide runs hard and the sea is greatly encumbered with off-lying reefs and ledges, many of which are covered with weed.

At this point it is germane to mention the fact that from time immemorial seafaring people have been conditioned to accept a large number of beliefs, and among them the belief in sea monsters or sea serpents is and was a lively one. Moreover, they have heard detailed, vivid descriptions of these creatures. It is also well known that during periods of exhaustion or great strain one is given to hallucinations, yet these hallucinations are based on some kind of learned response. One must recall that when Joshua Slocum was caught in a great gale in *The Spray*, he was abetted by one of Columbus' crew in a red hat, and when Manry was caught in similar circumstances in *Tinkerbell* a few years ago, he also saw "visitors." But his visitors were from the Midwest because he had been conditioned to inland life; Slocum had been raised for the sea.

Holding these things in mind, one can understand how, when brains are tired, when the visibility is poor and when eyes ache with the strain of searching for land, the wash of a tide rip over a weed-festooned rock, a bit of debris in the water, or anything else unexpected could readily be taken for a sea serpent or a sea monster.

Another point to be borne in mind is that for sundry reasons—the bottom, the currents or the abundance of food—basking sharks, turtles, whales, an occasional cuttle fish squid and porpoises tend to congregate in these places. It is not at all unusual to see whales off Gloucester, Massachusetts, or in the Orkney Islands, where they were hunted until recently. Basking sharks are common on the west coast of Ireland, the Hebrides, northern Scotland and Newfoundland. In all these areas the porpoises are very abundant, and they have a way of humping through the water one after another that, under conditions of moderately poor visibility, would make them look like the body of a great undulating snake. Given this much, the mind could fabricate the head.

In 1948 the author encountered a very large leatherback turtle in the Gulf of Maine. It was calm and in dense fog. The creature was first heard snorting, the waves were heard lapping on its back, and the animal was seen close aboard in the mist. Its head—greatly enlarged by the fog—was raised, while from its jaws drooped great gobbets of kelp on which it appeared to be feeding. A certain amount of biological acumen was required to keep me from imagining I was looking at a sea monster.

Of course, these are rationalizations of monster and serpent sightings in recent times, i.e., since the seventeenth century. In very early times such stories may have been a kind of allegorical explanation of natural phenomena. We have already seen how the Corryvreckan was believed to be the home of a sea hag, and in northern Ireland the "Rooten Wheel" was thought to house a witch who sucked the water up at its bottom,[6] while the Klobotterman was believed to inhabit the great maelstrom off Norway. Then there is that long and involved tale from the Hebrides, about the Gray Lad—really a variant of the Two Brothers story—one version of which is given in the previous chapter. Certain aspects of the story bear consideration here.

A smith (in Celtic folklore often an intercessionary between human kind and otherworld creatures) was very poor and childless until he was befriended by a mermaid, who promised him great catches of fish if he would promise to give her his first-born child. He agreed and shortly after his wife had triplets, his mare gave birth to three foals, his dog three hounds, and three trees sprang up in the yard. Through one way and another the smith kept his first-born out of the clutches of the mermaid until he had grown to a lusty lad. The boy then went off to seek his fortune and had numerous adventures and gained great wealth and honor. Finally he met a princess who was about to be fed to a dragon who lived in the loch (in Scotland the term means either a lake or a bay, as "Loch Awe").

The lad fought this creature on three different days and killed it during the last encounter. The third encounter, which is identical to the other except for the monster's death, described the arrival of the creature:

> Then the tide began to rise and the clouds to gather in the West and the dark squall came down and the sea ran East and the waves waxed great and gurly, green and blue and black. . . .
> Then she saw the dragon coming up the Loch with the spindrift flying, steaming and spouting, roaring and raving. . . .
> The dragon landed . . . and trailed himself up the sand and sank in it, vast and heavy he was.

Then the hero and the dragon fought so fiercely that sand and mud and pebbles were hurled about in every direction, but at last the creature was slain. "And the dragon was a pool of water and a heap of sand."

Of equal interest to us here is the arrival of the hero on the scene before the battle is joined. The girl looks up:

> Then they looked West and they saw the squall, and they looked East and they saw the same. And they saw a rider riding through the sky in a glittering green garment on a yellow, golden-brown palfrey, with a bright, gleaming, glittering, bright sword of light in his right hand, and when they saw him they [the fourteen soldiers sent by the King to guard her] all fled to their lairs as was their wont.[7]

After slaying the dragon the Gray Lad routs the King's cook and fourteen craven members of the King's guard, who pretend to have killed the dragon, and marries the King's daughter. His adventures continue and he is swallowed by the mermaid, rescued by his wife, who is herself swallowed and rescued by the Gray Lad, who finds the mermaid's heart in an egg inside a fish, inside a duck, inside a ram, inside a wood, under a house on an island in a lake.[8]

As one examines the foregoing, it is not difficult to see its possibilities as an explanatory myth about the weather. There is nothing in the description of the dragon or its death that could not easily be associated with a waterspout—spindrift, high winds, big seas, a driven tide. When the monster comes ashore it sucks up sand and rocks and then it collapses into "a pool of water and a heap of sand." Then the arrival of the hero who puts to flight the craven fourteen is very possibly an extended metaphor about weather signs that indicate clearing. And it is not beyond the pale to conceive of the fire-breathing, smoke-wreathed, yelling firedrake as an approaching weather front.[9] (It might be added that within a century people in Scotland still measured distances by using the monster's grave as a starting point.)

This is one explanation, but there is still another, for the tale closely parallels an actual event. In the story the hero chopped off one head of the dragon on each of three successive days, killing it with the removal of the third head on the last day of the battle.

On Monday, April 25, 1875, a group of Irishmen were fishing in a curragh off the west coast when they spotted a huge cuttlefish lying on the surface. Although the only instrument of destruction aboard was a knife, the crew decided to kill it because it was good "as bait for coarse fish." They paddled up silently and slashed off one arm. This aroused the creature to great activity and it rushed off. When it stopped, the curragh ran in and another arm was sliced off. These tactics were continued until most of the arms had been lopped off. The crew then went after the head, which they severed, and the body sank. The arms measured eight feet in length and fifteen inches in circumference. Thus, through the folk process, the story of the Gray Lad could possibly be a romanticized account of a similar experience centuries ago.[10]

There are, interestingly enough, many accounts of similar encounters with giant squid in Newfoundland and Labrador in the Folklore Archives of the Memorial University of Newfoundland. One of these tells how a giant squid several years ago attacked a small boat and very nearly dragged it under. The narrator ascribed the squid's actions to the color of the boat's bottom, which was red and therefore attracted it.

Over the centuries the mythological aspect of these tales has become lost, for as fast as pagan beliefs fell into the hands of Christian missionaries, they underwent great change. Since Christ and His Apostles from time to time controlled weather and stilled the waves on Galilee, what was more natural than to have a local "saint" like Columba do the same thing?[11] Eventually the tail began to wag the dog, until St. Gilbert, with a single arrow, is said to have slain a fire-breathing monster called Dhub Ginthais near Loch Fyne when it came to burn Dornoch. And further south in England about the same time it was popularly believed that St. George had skewered the Great Orm with a lance.

Another anecdote of a little different importance comes to us from the edge of history. Sometime between A.D. 550 and 590 Cholm Cille was traveling through the land of the Picts. When the great saint arrived at a certain river, he saw being buried a man who had been bitten by a "water beast" while swimming. Despite this fact, the saint ordered one of his men to swim across the river and get a boat on the opposite shore. The man did so, but before he was halfway across—

> . . . the monster, whose appetite had earlier been not so much sated as whetted for prey, lurked in the depths of the river. Feeling the water above disturbed by Lupne swimming, it suddenly swam up to the surface and, with gaping mouth and with great roaring, rushed towards the man swimming in the middle of the stream. . . . The blessed man who was watching, raised his holy hand and drew the saving sign of the cross in the empty air; and then, invoking the name of God, he commanded the savage beast and said: "You will go no further. Do not touch that man; turn backward speedily." Then . . . the beast, as if pulled by ropes, fled terrified in swift retreat, although it had before approached so close to Lupne as he swam that there was no more than the length of one short pole between man and beast.[12]

This is the first appearance in print of the most famous of all sea monsters, the Great Orm of Loch Ness—better known as the Loch Ness Monster (familiarly, "Nessie"). Since this creature is to other monsters what the Flying Dutchman is to other ghost ships, we should pause for a glance at its characteristics.

Until recent times Loch Ness was a remote lake not easily accessible to the public. It lay in a geologic fault that roughly divided the Highlands of Scotland from the Lowlands. Tradition says the lake has no bottom, and indeed it is deep—over six hundred feet, narrow, and about twenty-four miles long. The water is so stygian that one can see only a few feet beneath the surface. Most of the time it is shrouded in mist or rain, hail or snow, and sharp squalls roar down from the barren blunted hills surrounding it, making it doubly treacherous to navigation. Even on a bright day much of the dark tarn lies under the brooding shadow of the high hills. If anything is needed to enhance its gloomy prospect, one need but recall that one of the most treacherous mass murders in the annals of Scottish history occurred close by—the Glencoe massacre. Out of the lake runs a tiny rill, the river Ness, and because it is so small an outlet for so vast a body of water, there have arisen a number of beliefs that the lake is connected with the ocean by subterranean passages and that its bottom is salt.

This, then, is the lair of the Great Orm of Loch Ness. In order to protect themselves, their homes, and their herds, the folk have sacrificed cattle and sheep to the creature in the deep since the days of Cholm Cille. Who could ask for better proof of its being than the fact that the carcasses never returned to the surface?

There are some other interesting aspects of this gloomy lake. The water is bitter cold, and many people have drowned while swimming in it and their bodies are rarely recovered. Some say also that the lower reaches of the lake are populated by schools of eels of such shocking size that few divers will go down there, and it is believed by some of the people that it is these eels that devour the lake's victims.

According to one informant, about a quarter of a century ago a couple and their children went boating on the Loch. The woman was wearing a necklace valued at four thousand pounds. Much to their dismay, the boat sank and they were forced to swim for it. When they got about halfway to shore they realized they had left the children, and the mother said she would go back after them because she was the stronger swimmer.

It turned out to be an unfortunate choice, for she sank before reaching shore and her body never came up. Her husband was a wealthy man, and either out of love for his wife or because of the value of the necklace he hired two divers to search the lake for the body. One was a local diver and the other a German. Both went down and both came up. The German said, "Your wife is down there and if you want her you can get her. I will not go down again." The local diver also came up but in a much worse state and had to be taken to an asylum, where he remained for many years.

To make matters even more interesting, the narrator concluded his story by saying that the Brahan Seer (an ancient prophet) had predicted a great monster would be caught in the lake during the present century and when it was cut open its body would contain a valuable necklace.[13]

No matter what it does to the dead, after being exorcised by St. Columba, Nessie did not bother the living until 1969. In fact the worst act I heard ascribed to it was that in 1966 it ruined some fishing for two anglers by scaring off the salmon.[14] On August 19, 1969, the *Scottish Daily Express* had a story as follows:

A fisherman told last night how he and a friend used a shotgun and oars in a fantastic battle with a sixty-foot monster which struck their boat on Loch Morar, Invernesshire.[15]

They believed the brown, hump-backed giant bit a large chunk from one of the oars . . . and only vanished under the dark waters when they scared it away with a blast from the gun.

Since the early tale of St. Cholm Cille, there has been a continuous string of references to sightings of Nessie. Unlike other monsters who seem to have slipped from fashion, this one seems to be enjoying its greatest popularity in the present century, particularly from 1934 to the present, during which time hundreds of people have reported sighting it—doctors, lawyers, bankers and fishermen among others. It has been photographed numerous times and once was sketched by a recording fathometer on the Scotch fishing vessel *Rival III* of Peterhead, as well as being detected by sonar. Interestingly enough, the pictures, the verbal descriptions and the fathometer recordings all are largely in agreement as to the general size, shape and activity of the creature or creatures.

The monster is variously reported as being between twenty and forty feet long. It has been sighted most often early in the morning, most frequently near the ruins of Urquhart Castle, but it has also been seen ashore at night. Both afloat and ashore it travels with great speed and is believed to swim at about eighteen or twenty knots. Those who have seen it ashore describe it as a saurian with short heavy legs on the after-end and smaller ones forward. Water reports agree that it has herpetological characteristics. They say it has a head the size of a football attached to a long neck; there are humps on its back, it floats reasonably high in the water and has a long tail. Most agree it proceeds by vertical undulations and leaves very little wake.[16]

So far, it has eluded all efforts to capture it. Indeed, it seems to be in league with the Fates, for ashore it leaves no tracks on the stony ground, and when recently a submarine was employed by some Americans to try to kill it, the vessel filled and sank to the bottom of the lake.

With this much evidence compiled about it, one might think science would accept the creature's existence, but its very elusiveness has made it suspect. The pictures have been questioned as to their authenticity. I was told the fathometer recording was a trick done to pass the time while the *Rival III* lay fog-bound in port, and the similarity of verbal accounts indicates the possibility of collusion. Further, it has been pointed out that the rumor of the monster serves as a splendid tourist attraction for the area. Beyond this, scientists ask many hard questions. How did it get there? What can so vast a creature find to eat in a relatively small lake? How can it have survived so long alone, and if it has a mate, why aren't there many monsters? And so the battle rages. It is not likely that science will accept the thing's presence until it is dead on a dissecting table, and it is not likely that its advocates will agree that it does not exist until the lake is drained dry. Neither event appears likely in the foreseeable future.

However it turns out, the folklorist is one who tends to the theory that there is sometimes a very thin line between belief and actuality. There is little doubt that to many of the people who live in the area, both literate and illiterate, the monster is a reality. They speak of it as commonplace and it fits into their lives like the weather.

Loch Ness, although the most famous, is not the only spot where sea monsters have been sighted. In recent times they have been noted frequently on the California coast, from Monterey and San Clemente Island clear north into British Columbia.[17] All of them have been described in roughly similar terms: forty to seventy feet long, serpentine, dark in color—brown and gray—maned or at least possessing nubs along the neck, and with a head like that of an eel or snake with very prominent eyes. They are shy of man, move at a great rate of speed, leave little or no wake, sound without a splash. None has been captured, nor have they harmed anyone. A further word or two must be said of one sighted off Vancouver. This has been variously described as having a head like a camel's, a snake's and a seal's. It was said by one observer to have flippers and by another to be coiled in the water. A third said it devoured a crippled duck.[18]

A somewhat different creature appeared at Teague Creek in Chesapeake Bay not many years ago, but whether to describe it as a sea monster or some sort of spectre is open to debate. A small vessel took shelter there one evening, and during the night a monster came aboard. It appeared as a great snake, slithered down the ventilator and could not be found below. In the morning its muddy tracks were clearly discernible on deck.[19]

If the waters of the Pacific Coast have become a popular haven for sea monsters in this century, the New England coast was equally popular in the previous one. Actually, the area seems to have been visited by the creatures ever since Josselyn saw the one at Cape Ann and Mr. Mitter chopped the arm off the "merman" in Maine during the seventeenth century. But none of these serpents raised the excitement of the one that broke water in Gloucester Harbor in August of 1817. Not only was it seen in the harbor but offshore as well; further sightings were made over subsequent years from Provincetown to Nahant. What is most interesting in these sightings is that on most occasions the beast was seen not by one or two seamen but by scores of people ashore and afloat. Moreover, it was seen by naval captains, ministers, artists, authors and the flower of New England society.[20]

The creature caused such a considerable flurry that a number of depositions were taken from people who had seen it. Most of the comments were similar, especially as to size, color and head shape. One account should suffice for all:

> I Solomon Allen, 3d. of Gloucester in the County of Essex, Ship-Master depose and say: that I have seen a strange marine animal that I believe to be a serpent, in the harbor of said Gloucester. I should judge him to be between eighty and ninety feet in length and about the size of a half barrel apparently heavy joints from his head to his tail. I was about 150 yards from him when I judged him to be the size of a half barrel. His head formed something like the head of a rattlesnake, but nearly as large as the head of a horse. When he moved the surface of the water, his motion was slow, at times playing about in circles, and sometimes moving nearly straight forward. When he disappeared he sunk apparently directly down. . . . I saw him on the 12th, 13th and 14th of August, A.D. 1817.[21]

During the nineteenth century the creature harmed no one and eluded all attempts to capture it. Apparently it survived to return again just prior to World War II, for in 1969 Lawrence Geller of Plymouth, Massachusetts, interviewed an aged fisherman, who told him that he had seen a creature thirty years before off High Pine Ledge (near Plymouth and in a vicinity noted for large sharks):

> I saw a serpent with three heads between the waves. It was a light grey in color. He was headed away from us so we couldn't see his head. He was pretty big. . . . I used to laugh when they talked about sea serpents, but when I saw this one I was convinced. He was at least sixty feet high out of water . . . . The water was all greeny where it went down.[22]

These present-day creatures are but pale and anemic shadows of their forebears popularly believed in during the Middle Ages and earlier. Yet the Norse krake, so popular in medieval times and described by Magnus, Pontoppidan and others, may have been but a mild exaggeration of the actual giant squid or cuttlefish, which have been found to exceed sixty feet in length.[23] But if the krake was big, there were even bigger monsters— so large that early historians were convinced they were biological sports, for if they were able to breed they would soon fill up the ocean. When a traveler in medieval times went to sea he never knew when he would encounter one. Especially to be feared was the monster called by the Jews Leviathan, which was not restricted to the Mediterranean environment.

Modern science tends to correlate Leviathan with the whale family,

but his size and characteristics were such as to make Moby Dick a puny
representative of the race. This great creature was described variously as
being as large as three football fields and as containing over four acres.
His hide had a rough, gravely appearance, and on it grew plants and trees.
Sometimes he lay beneath the surface and the sailor, finding the bottom
close, cast anchor. The flukes became fouled in the folds of the gravely hide,
which annoyed the creature, and he would sound—taking ship and crew
along with him. At other times he came to the surface to take the sun.
Mariners would mistake him for an island, go "ashore," dig pits and build
cook fires. These would rouse the creature and he would dive, taking all
hands with him. It was said many men could stand in his eye socket, and
a horse and rider could gallop up and down his "swallow" without difficulty.
For some reason the beast seemed particularly attracted to the clergy, one
of the early travelers who encountered him under a different alias being
St. Brendan, whose voyage typifies the experiences noted as happening to
most early explorers.

In his youth Brendan had a vision of the Land of Promise, and upon
being assured by an angel that he would find it, he set out with a party of
monks in a large curragh. They sailed east forty days and found a rocky
island, where they landed and were greeted by a great hound and fed, but
no human was seen. Next they came to a green island full of huge sheep,
where it was never winter but always summer. An old man told them to
seek further to find "The Paradise of Birds." Again they set out, and
their ship—

> . . . was driven by storms till they saw before them another little island, and
> the Brothers went to land on it, but Brendan stopped in the ship. And they
> put a fish in a cauldron and lighted a fire to boil it, and no sooner was the
> fire hot and the fish beginning to boil, than the island began to quake and
> to move like a living thing; and there was great fear on the Brothers and
> they went back into the ship leaving the food and the cauldron after them,
> and they saw what they took to be an island going fast through the sea, and
> they could notice the fire burning a long way off that they were astonished.
> . . . Brendan . . . said, "It is a great fish, the biggest of the fishes in the
> world, Jascoyne his name is, and he is laboring day and night to put his tail
> into his mouth, and he cannot do it because of his great bulk"

Next they found the Paradise of Birds and learned the birds were really
fallen angels who did not go all the way to Hell. They prophesied Brendan's
future activity, and the party then set out for the "Island of the Silent
Brotherhood" where God gave everyone white bread to eat. After a stormy

passage they landed there, remaining until "Little Christmas" when they put to sea again. Once more they made heavy weather of it, but on Easter they were able to celebrate mass in a peculiar way, for "They sailed to where the fish Jascoyne was lying. And they found upon his back the cauldron they had left there a year ago and they kept the Feast of the Resurrection there upon the fish's back."

And so their voyage continued from enchanted island to island, and on the way:

> There came after them a horrible great fish that was swallowing their ship and that was casting up such great spouts of water out of his mouth that they had like to be drowned, and he was coming so fast that he had all but reached them. And then they called out to Jesus Christ to help them . . . [and] there came another fish bigger than the first out of the west and made an attack on him and beat him and . . . made three halves of him.

Next they came to a little island full of fruit and took on a forty-day supply, then—

> they went sailing through storm and through wind. And of a sudden there came sailing towards them a great monster and made an attack on their ship and had like to have destroyed them . . . and the little bird that had spoken with them . . . came at the monster and struck out one of his eyes with his first attack and the other eye with the second, and made an end of him.

Following this escape, they sailed in clear water for eight days before a strong southerly wind, and after another week came to an island full of stench and smoke; and as the ship drew near it they heard a noise like thunder. Shortly thereafter they were attacked by demons and learned they had come to the rim of Hell, so they kept off to the north until they raised "a hill on fire" with clouds upon it and smoke. Here they lost one man. Then a gale drove them south seven days, when they encountered a ghost sitting on a rock. The sea had worn off all his flesh and only bones were left. Around his neck were two tongues and a cloth. The man was Judas, and the cloth and the tongues were symbols of his only two good deeds in life—once he had given food to priests and once he had given a cloth to a leper.

Next they reached the island of Paul the Hermit, who had been nourished for forty years by an otter. And they went on, celebrated Mass again atop their friendly fish, and at last, through storm and wrack and fog, they came to the Land of Promise. "Clear it was and lightsome . . . and the trees were full of fruit . . . and the apples were as ripe as at harvest time . . . and it was never hot nor cold." Finally they reached a river which "is the Mering that divides the worlds for no man may come to the other side of it while he is in life."

Having come to the end of his quest there in the Land of Promise, Brendan turned again for Ireland and at last he landed there with great rejoicing, having been forty years cruising, and soon died.[24]

This story is a curious melding of fact and fancy, Christian and Celtic mythology. If we disregard courses steered and content ourselves with the experiences of the voyage, much of it will stand up under scrutiny. The island of eternal summer, the edge of Hell, the clear water, the rock in the sea could perhaps be based on experiences in the tropics, where volcanoes were still active. The pursuit of the monster and his overthrow by another might reflect an encounter between a whale and a killer whale. Even Jascoyne might be derived from an experience of dragging in the fog during a heavy run of tide. In such cases the land seems to leave the boat rather than the other way around.

Out of the pagan past comes the dead man on the rock with his two tokens, and the otter that fed Paul those forty years. Likewise, out of Celtic lore comes the Land of Promise with its apples always ripe and its expression of all the hopes and vain dreams of a people living out their lives in rain and sleet, cold and misery, with black bread and dulse as diet— and little of either. To the Irish of the Middle Ages and before, the voyage of this northern Ulysses proved the reality of those enchanted islands which were so much a part of early northern mythology.

The idea of enchanted islands is by no means the sole property of northern peoples; like the belief in sea monsters, it is extremely ancient and worldwide in diffusion. Such lands have been seen by travelers in all ages of which we have a record—barring the present century—and today we may still believe in them, for the latest chart of the island of Antiqua, B.W.I., states it has been "reported moved 1½ miles." Moreover, some very important people have had strange experiences with them. Alexander the Great was one such person who ran aground on an enchanted island on his way to sack India. Among the Celts, with their beliefs in the Islands of the Dead and a Paradise beyond the sea, such tales seem to have found very fertile soil in which to develop. It will be recalled that when King Arthur had his mortal hurt, he first returned his sword to the water goddess who had given it to him, and then was loaded onto a barge and rowed off to the west, to the Island of Avalon where apples (the fairy fruit) grew, there to remain and be healed of his wounds.

Enchanted islands seem to be of a limited number of types. First we have the island that can never be found again. Usually it is shrouded in mist, the directions are faulty, it is under a spell or it moves about. Such, it will be recalled, was the beginning of Inishbofin, and such was Brendan's Land of Promise. Next we have the islands that rise and sink at will. We then encounter islands of glass and islands of ice, which in all probability are the same thing. Finally we have a large number of islands that are peopled with demons or strange creatures, harbor a sorcerer, are beset with dangers or have an atmosphere dangerous to man.

That such things exist is reasonably easy to prove if we accept the limited frames of reference of the time. A mariner is blown off course. He has no navigating equipment. After a few days he comes up with land which appears out of the fog. He goes ashore and returns home again. The possibility of that land being found another time is remote.

Until fairly recent times the phenomenon of icebergs was but dimly understood and their appearance in the paths of Old World travelers (with the exception perhaps of the Vikings) was infrequent. When they were seen, they were usually shrouded in mist, and it was not uncommon to find strange creatures on them—nervous Arctic foxes anxiously watching their island shrink, polar bears, seals, perhaps a skua or even an Arctic owl. When the light struck them, they gave off a beauty beyond most things in this world. According to observers they have—

> all known styles of architecture, cathedrals with pillars, arches, portals, and towering pinnacles, overhanging cliffs, the ruins of a walled city, pyramids and obelisks, castles with towers, walls, fortifications and bridges . . . trees, animals and human beings. . . . One resembled, at first, a cluster of Chinese buildings, then a Gothic cathedral of the early style. . . . It was curious to see . . . its vast interior now a delicate blue, and then a greenish white. . . . An age of ruin seemed to have passed over it leaving only to view the inner cliffs, one a glistening white and the other blue . . . as the July heavens. Water streamed down . . . in little rills . . . glistening like molten glass. Veins of gem-like transparency, blue as sapphires crossed the mass. And at sunrise and sunset their ridges have the shape of flames. And with it all the booming of the sullen sea in the hollowed crevasses at its base.[25]

One island in particular that qualifies as magic or demon-haunted is Bermuda, of which an adequate contemporary account is given in Shakespeare's *The Tempest*. Actually, the island merits much of what has been said about it. First, it is located over four hundred miles off shore. It rises precipitously from great deeps. It is frequently shrouded in rain, and squalls roar off it. Its harbors are good but tortuous to enter. It has no fresh water and had no human inhabitants. It made up for this lack by having unusual creatures and plants on it, including a monster spider which, according to John Smith, spun webs suitable for weaving into ship's cables. The hazard of the place in early times is beyond imagination. A vessel on a wild night is running for her life hundreds of miles off shore, for days in deep water and no known land between her and the coast of Europe. There are no lights, no fires, no warning when suddenly beneath her very bows rises a coral reef (the only one of its kind that far north in the world) eighteen miles long. A vessel in company a few miles east or west of her scans the sea at daylight, but no trace is ever found of the ship or crew.

Like Circe's Isle, Bermuda was full of swine and goats put there by early explorers but, as every sailor knows, swine and goats have an unfortunate connection with the devil, with witches and warlocks. Perhaps they were sailors transformed after they were shipwrecked by witches like Caliban. Sylvester Jourdan, Sir George Somers and Captain Newport (whose body is buried there), Richard Norwood, Juan Bermúdez, all warned of the dangers, and Hakluyt gave the opinion of prudent seamen when he wrote:

> For the Islands of the Barmudas, as every man knoweth that hath heard or read of them, were never inhabited by an Christian or heathen people, but ever esteemed, and reputed, a most prodigious and inchanted place, affording nothing but gusts, storms and foule weather; which made every navigator and mariner to avoid them, . . . as they would shunne the Devil himselfe.

Moreover, the woods were haunted and the islands themselves were seldom seen.[26]

There are several other plausible reasons for less-tutored people believing in such fabled islands. Clouds at sea, especially in the tropics, resemble islands; mirages may deform or contort some object into a weird shape; great masses of weed floating in the sea can look like land, especially if the visibility is poor. On top of this, in various places sandbars rise up to the surface and then sink again. The action of great tides may lead mariners not accustomed to such phenomena to believe in floating islands. Now and then, too, volcanoes erupt and bring forth islets, some of which remain while others sink.[27] Finally, all along the west coast of the British Isles and

Ireland—along the whole Atlantic coastline of Europe, for that matter—flotsam has come ashore carried by the wind and the action of the Gulf Stream drift. Some of it has come incredible distances—colloidal sand from coral in the Caribbean or a bit of bamboo. Now and then in the Outer Hebrides a malaga nut (called Mary bean) is picked up and treasured after a voyage from South America. Not knowing of other continents, it was only natural for the people to think of islands.[28] These ideas undoubtedly lay at the back of the minds of explorers like Cook, who went in search of that fabled area called Terra Incognita—moved by then further west into the Pacific.

Ashore, in ponds and marshes, people were accustomed to seeing floating islands of weeds and refuse that were capable of bearing the weight of a man for a short while. Why should not larger ones exist in the ocean? Belief in such islands, floating, enchanted and glass, served a twofold purpose. It explained why a vessel sailed over the rim of the ocean and never returned, and it gave those at home a hope that perhaps the crew were not deceased but under a spell, or living in a spot from whence they would someday, somehow, return.

Belief in these islands was sufficiently strong that they appeared on charts done by the best cartographers; Gummer's Ore lay off Stockholm, Eynhallow and Heather-Bleather near the Orkneys. Off Killybegs, Ireland, lay O'Brazila, to which the Crown gave a patent in the seventeenth century. Further south and further offshore lay the Green Islands of the Dead (Fiddler's Green). Further west still lay the Isle of Demos in the St. Lawrence entrance. To these we might add the more solid Sable Island and Bermuda. Some of these bear discussion, for as they are located in different regions they reflect not only the popular thinking of the times, but the dominant culture of the area as well.

Gummer's Ore ties the Norse krake and the enchanted island belief tightly together. Men spent their lifetimes looking for it, but only a few were fortunate. Fishermen could detect it by sounding on the bottom, for it rose before mighty storms, bringing with it great shoals of fish. If a mariner timed it right, a tremendous fortune was to be had in the fish, but if he stayed too long and the krake breached, he, his catch and his vessel would be overpowered and presumably devoured. Therefore, when the soundings reached a certain level it was time to clear out. When the krake surfaced, Gummer's Ore could be seen in the offing as small islands of a rounded shape and several high peaks.[29]

Somewhat different is Eynhallow, in that it is a real island. Lying in the tide-run waters between Rousay and Pomona in the Orkneys, its name is Norse for "Holy Island," and according to accounts it was the site of one of the earliest monasteries in the area. At any rate, the island was thought to belong to the sea folk, and was supposed to pop to the surface from time to time. It was popularly believed that if a man had the courage, and held steel in his hand and went for the island without regard for anything else, the place would lose its enchantment. Many tried and were lost in the tide races, until one man fixed his eye on the island when it came up. He disregarded "the roaring roost," as the tide race is called, held his steel, won to the island and seized it from the sea people, who still make the water boil around it.[30]

To this day Eynhallow is believed to be partly enchanted. It is said that neither iron nor steel will remain on the island overnight and that no rat can survive there. Indeed its clay is proof against rats, and its soil is put under corncribs and new houses on other islands to keep out rats and mice.

Nearby lies Heather-Bleather. As yet it has not lost its enchantment but lies wrapped in mist and sea fog. Once there was a young woman who vanished from her island home and was never heard from again. The years rolled on and she was all but forgotten when her father and brother became lost in a heavy fog while fishing. At last their boat grounded and they went ashore to a white house, where the woman turned out to be no other than the long-lost daughter. While they were there her husband and brother-in-law arrived in sealskins, which they took off on coming into the house. When the father and her brother left, the woman gave them an iron knife which would allow them to come to the island whenever they wished. Unfortunately, the knife fell overboard, the fog rolled back, the years trudged on, and no one has gone to Heather-Bleather since.[31]

O'Brazila, many leagues to the west and south, represents little more than a streamlining and embellishment of the voyage to the Land of Promise undertaken by Brendan. This island lay southwest of Killybegs and was still thought to be under enchantment as late as the seventeenth century. On clear days people ashore could sometimes see the island on the horizon, but usually it was shrouded in fog. Eventually, after many had tried to find it and failed, a Quaker had a vision of the place, built a brand-new vessel for the voyage and set out, but as one might suspect of a Quaker in Ireland, he had no luck. At last, on March 2, 1674, a Captain Nisbet, bound for Ireland from France with a mixed cargo, ran into a cloudbank following a bitter cold night. After three hours the fog cleared and his men found themselves close to an island, with a storm driving them onto it. Accordingly, they anchored in three fathoms and four of the crew went ashore. They passed through a wood and came to a most pleasant green valley where they saw colonies of black rabbits and other kinds of beasts—save swine—fruits and vegetables, but no people or dogs. In the distance was a handsome castle, but no one was at home. That night all save one went ashore and built a fire for supper, but such a roar went up that they all fled back to the boat. The following morning the crew met an ancient man and his ancient followers. The old man said the island had been enchanted by a magician, but now the spell was broken and it would henceforth be visible. The people provided for the skipper's every need and the vessel was put away for Killybegs, where it landed laden with silver and gold. Unfortunately, the old man was wrong about the enchantment, for the island has not been seen since.[32]

This same island, under the name of Hy-Brazil or Tir-n'an-Og, is supposed to have been visited by Ossian at an earlier date. That hero is said to have married its queen, but he was forbidden to stand on a certain stone. One day he did so, and thoughts of his home overwhelmed him. His queen allowed him to return to Ireland for one day, providing he did not dismount from his black horse. He forgot the charge, dismounted, and his years were upon him. He immediately became a middle-aged man, an ancient, and a wisp of dust blowing down the road.[33] It requires little imagination to see the threads that make up the tapestry of this tale.

If this story has been forgotten at Killybegs, it is still remembered a little further south at Aran and elsewhere along the shore. For some reason the coast there has a reputation for mirages, and the people see not only islands and cities but ships as well.[43] In Aran they say Hy–Brazil can be seen every seven years. The stories of former times contained more character than those of the present.

About three hundred years ago two fishermen were caught in a storm and driven south from a shallow bank off Aran called the Yellow Bank. In the morning they were close enough to an island to see sheep grazing on it, but were afraid to land thinking it was a Wizard Island. At about the same time another boat was more daring, and when the fishermen discovered they were alongside an uncharted island they went ashore. From the island they could see the Irish coast quite plainly. A man told them the place was enchanted and they left, but not before one of them received a book on medicine with instructions not to open it for seven years. He obeyed and became a great healer. A similar story has a different beginning.

A man named Lee was kidnapped and taken there by its occupants and then allowed to go home.[35]

Two thousand miles west by south of Killybegs lies the Gulf of St. Lawrence. For a century before Captain Nisbet visited Hy-Brazil, seamen in this region—near the Straits of Belle Isle—were aware of a terrible island called Isola de Demoni. In fact, the whole of the coast of Labrador (known locally today as "the Land God gave Cain") at this time was believed to be infested with such repugnant creatures as walrus, bears and griffins vying with each other to torment civilized man, but the Isle of Demons seems to have been their capital. Father Thevet writes:

> True it is, and I myself have heard it, not from one, but from a great number of sailors and pilots with whom I have made many voyages, that, when they passed this way, they heard in the air, on the tops or about the masts, a great clamor of mens' voices, confused and inarticulate, such as you may hear from the crowd at a fair or market place; whereupon they well knew that the Isle of Demons was not far off.

He goes on to tell how he himself has seen these demons torment the natives until they came to him for relief. By repeating the Gospel of St. John he was able to rout these fiends, who were very handsome to look at but were so malicious they had driven out all the inhabitants.[36]

When Roberval the explorer sailed by this island, he had on board a niece who, despite all he could do, persisted in a passionate affair with a young man of his company. This action enraged the Viceroy, and he put the girl ashore there with her old nurse and four guns. Before he sailed, the young lover dove overboard with two more guns and ammunition and swam ashore. There they were solely tried by the demons, but the Virgin Mary interceded and drove the imps back. These creatures howled and tore at the dwelling, but could not get at the lovers. The girl became pregnant and the fiends redoubled their efforts. Still the girl resisted them, and although she shot three white bears that tormented her, her bullets were of no avail against the demons. Eventually these fiends made away with her lover, her nurse, and her offspring. Two years and five months went by. A small fishing vessel passing by saw smoke, closed the land, found the girl, and brought her back to France.[37]

Sailors and travelers from Europe passing this general area were well aware of these enchantments, and as they crossed the smoky seas around Newfoundland, they saw on numerous occasions enchanted islands (no few of which were obviously icebergs). John Josselyn was such a man.

June the first day in the afternoon, very thick foggy weather, we sailed by an enchanted island, saw a great deal of filth and rubbish floating by the ship, heard Cawdimawdies, seagull, and crows (birds which always frequent the shore), but could see nothing by reason of the mist, when we were past the islands, it cleared up . . .

The fourteenth day of June, very foggy weather, we sailed by an island of ice which lay on the starboard side three leagues in length, mountain high, in form of land. We saw likewise two or three foxes or devils skipping upon it.[38]

One cannot help but wonder what Josselyn would have thought had he seen the sight another shipmaster encountered off Cape Horn in a more enlightened age. The *Marco Polo* hit a berg in March 1861. When it hit, its crew saw a man lying on top of the ice as if asleep. He was hatless, a signaling staff was by his side, and his hair blew in the wind. In all, the sight seemed to support the proverb that what the sea wants the sea will have.[39]

Returning again to North America, we will pick up another island, this time a real one—Sable Island off Nova Scotia. It is cucumber-shaped, and many fishermen have been caught in the bight there and have been lost, while other vessels have run foul of it and gone down in thick weather or in gales. This island, too, was thought to be enchanted and to have on it supernatural people who could be detected as moving lights at night. There may be some foundation in fact here.

At about the turn of the sixteenth century the Marquis de la Roche sailed for America. Among others, he had on board forty convicts, whom he put ashore at Sable Island while he went in search of a suitable place to plant a colony. One thing led to another and the Marquis did not return. The convicts made houses out of an old wreck, clothes out of skins, and for food ate seals, fish and whatever they could get. Five years went by and the convicts, by preying upon one another, reduced their ranks from forty to twelve, which number were rescued and carried back to France.

From what has been said of monsters, serpents and peculiar islands, it becomes relatively obvious that most of these places and creatures inhabit waters dangerous to navigate. Many of the serpents and monsters may indeed have a basis in fact, and some can be understood as solar myths long forgotten in their entirety. In their time, they satisfied the needs of people who went to sea and gave them reasonable explanations of what otherwise seemed unreasonable. They served their purpose well. Today they are pretty well relics of the past, and we learn more of them from records than from living informants. Poe said that science with its "peering eyes" had "driven the hamadryad from the wood" and left him without a dream beneath the tamarind tree. The great deeps have been plumbed, much of the ocean floor has been wire-dragged; the location of the last island has been pricked on the chart, its geology, flora, fauna, climate and economic worth computed to the last grain, flea and farthing. There is little space left for a sea dragon to hide and less for an enchanted island to find seclusion. We know now that Ossian could not have lived four hundred years, and there are no fairies. Still the imagination of man is hard to kill. We have flying saucers, we have gremlins. If the Land of Prester John is not here on earth, may not the Land of Promise yet lie beyond the stars? Even the mathematician gives us hope, for he tells us that the law of probability indicates strongly that there must be life elsewhere in the universe. Hurrah for Positive Science!

℞ CHAPTER XI ℘

SUPERSTITION, CUSTOM AND BELIEF

Superstition is a quality that seems indigenous to
the ocean.
—James Fenimore Cooper, *The Red Rover*

IT has often been said that men who follow the sea are the most superstitious lot of people on earth.[1] It has also been said that a man who goes to sea without a reason would go to hell for a holiday.[2] Before we can accept the first statement, and to give a better understanding of the present chapter, we must attempt a working definition of "superstition." To do this, we must also show its relationship to custom and belief.

For the purposes of this chapter, a superstition may be defined as an open-ended conviction held by a number of people over an extended period of time. By open-ended I mean that the person contemplating the superstition is left with a choice—he can accept it or reject it. For this reason, superstitions often begin with "when" or "if" or a phrase implying choice. The person who follows the superstition usually expects he will be rewarded, while the one who disregards it can expect to be penalized. Hence, "See a pin and pick it up/And all the day you'll have good luck" is followed by "See a pin and let it lay/And many a time you'll rue the day."

A second characteristic of a superstition is that it requires some action on the part of the believer. He must spit if he sees a black cat, knock on wood if his hopes are not to be dashed, cross himself before passing a graveyard.

Finally, a superstition is generally expressed through some kind of a mnemonic device, most often a rhyme or pithy saying which not only helps one to remember but may, in the cases of a rhyme, also be efficacious in making the superstition "work."

Opposite: The shipwright, Neil Cameron, Crinan, Scotland

Belief, unlike superstition, is rarely open-ended, and does not necessarily require any action on the part of the faithful. It seems to concern itself more with tangible objects than does superstition and is not necessarily set in a mnemonic framework. In Scotland it was once thought prudent to hoist a he-goat to the masthead to procure wind;[3] in Newfoundland an upside-down hatch cover meant bad luck,[4] a knot in the painter a long voyage;[5] and, as we have already seen, to most sailors a red sunset means a good day on the morrow. If you lower the goat, turn over the hatch, untie the knot, you are not assured a calm, good luck, or a speedy passage. In the case of the sun, the sailor cannot choose the color nor is he told that a nonred sun means a poor day.

Very often a belief has an attendant act. For example, it is believed in Newfoundland that if you spit on the first fish caught and throw it back, you will have good luck for the rest of the fishing. But as time goes on, the act may outlive the belief and the reason for performing the act may be forgotten. Few seamen today know why they salute the quarterdeck when they step aboard a man-o'-war, why a broom is hoisted to the masthead after a successful catch, why a man gives money to the first person he meets after a promotion or why the whistle is blown leaving port. Should he faithfully observe all these acts, no blessing will attend him, nor will he be penalized if he disregards them. Yet he does them and such acts I refer to as customs. Customs come close to habit.

Of course there are gray areas between these three definitions where one is hard pressed to identify the material as belonging to one group or another, but at least a platform has been established from which one can begin to sort things out. Furthermore, if one accepts the above concepts of superstition, custom and belief, it becomes apparent that the sailor is by no means as superstitious as he is belief-ridden.

The number of beliefs, customs and superstitions prevalent amongst seamen is so large, so varied and so contradictory in nature that at first glance it seems impossible to make rational sense out of them. Close scrutiny, however, reveals that they can be classified under a number of headings. Further, it is possible not only to find reasons for their origins but to recognize the efficacy of these concepts on the people concerned. If some of the items mentioned seem to conflict with others, it is not so much a matter of conflict as it is an adaptation of material to fit a specific environment.

Perhaps the largest single body of lore concerns the supernatural and, in particular, the dead. Living as he does a hazardous life where no man can be sure of seeing the sun rise on the morrow, it is only natural that the sailor should be inordinately concerned with the spirit world, and this concern is augmented by sea conditions, where fog, ice, mirage, exhaustion, bad food and isolation from normal living enable a man to see, to hear and to feel things not ordinarily experienced by other mortals.

I have long contended that fear of oblivion has always been a driving force in human life, and it is certainly so in Western society. In order to avoid this hazard, man has attributed to his dead comrade a spirit that can roam the world and help or hinder the living. These ideas can be seen in Greek mythology, wherein Charon ferries the dead across the river Styx, and it can be seen in Celtic lore, for it must be remembered that after the great battle with Mordred, King Arthur was placed on a barge and carried away to Avalon, there to be healed of his wounds. Even before this, there was a belief that the fisherfolk on the coast of Brittany every night ferried all dead souls across the sea to an island—which some think may have been England, and which the Irish believe to be the Islands of the Dead,[6] specifically a group of rocks off the west coast of Ireland called today the Cow, the Calf, the Heifer and the Bull.

I am indebted to Sean O'Sullivan of the Irish Folklore Commission for a translation of a seventh-century Irish tale about these islands. It seems that an ancient king or god named Morgan wants to know how his foster son died. A poet tells him how it happened, Morgan refuses to believe it and is cursed by the poet, but the dead man comes from the "Tigh Dhuinn" (the present Bull Rock) to prove the poet wrong. In more modern times, according to O'Sullivan, the legend is preserved in the story of a dead man coming back from there to settle a dispute over a will.

Sailors when they die, especially if they die at sea, are said to go to Davy Jones' locker, which is a euphemism for the devil and hell, but if they are decent chaps they are believed to end up in Fiddler's Green, an under-sea paradise not unlike Faeryland (the words "fiddler" and "green" both are associated with faeries).[7] For that matter, it is not greatly different from the underwater home of the mer and sealfolk, thus linking Christian and pre-Christian concepts together through the picture of Paradise.

An interesting example of this confusion of ideas is to be found in two long Irish tales—told here in abbreviated form.

Sixteen men left port in a vessel. When they failed to return, they were presumed lost at sea. However, after a short time they began to be seen around their home village at night. At first they were quiescent, but as time went on they became bolder and the villagers realized that they were not dead but captives of the faeries. One day one of these prisoners accosted a man named O'Boyle and told him that they were indeed faery prisoners, but not wanting to become permanent residents in the faeries' underwater kingdom, they had refused to eat any food there. Instead, they had been foraging nightly in the village for unsalted food and were nearly starved. They could be saved, he told O'Boyle, if he could muster enough men to fight the faeries on a certain night in November. To assure the villagers of victory, they should each be armed with a black-handled knife, anoint both themselves and the battlefield near the village of Kilgalligan with a mixture of hen manure and holy water before the fray, and bring a priest.

O'Boyle spread the word and recruited a goodly company, including a priest who applauded the entire venture. Just before the battle the priest proved to be a coward and refused to come. Seeing this, many of the rescuers lost heart and the plan had to be abandoned. The fatal hour came and passed, and the sixteen forlorn men were seen marching down to the shore with the faeries, weeping bitterly. For awhile a few of the men were seen about the village, but at last they, too, vanished forever to their green-and-gold world beneath the sea where time is unknown and the wind never blows.[8]

The second tale comes from a little island off the west coast.

One November night a woman of Shark Island, coming home at the late hour of the dead, grew tired and sat down to rest, when presently a young man came up and talked to her.

"Wait a bit," he said, "and you will see the most beautiful dancing you ever looked on, there by the side of the hill."

And she looked at him steadily. He was very pale and seemed sad.

"Why are you so sad?" she asked, "and as pale as if you were dead?"

"Look well at me," he answered. "Do you not know me?"

"Yes, I know you," she said. "You are young Brian that was drowned last year when out fishing. What are you here for?"

"Look," he said, "at the side of the hill and you will see why I am here."

And she looked and saw a great company dancing to sweet music; and amongst them were all the dead who had died as long as she could remember—men, women, and children, all in white, and their faces were pale as the moonlight.

"Now," said the young man, "run for your life; for if once the faeries bring you into the dance, you will never be able to leave them any more."

But while they were dancing, the fairies came up and danced 'round her in a circle, joining their hands. And she fell to the ground in a faint, and knew no more until she woke up in her own bed at home. And they all saw that her face was as pale as the dead, and they knew that she had got the faery-stroke. So the doctor was sent for and every measure tried to save her, but without avail, for just as the moon rose that night, soft, low music was heard round the house and when they looked at the woman she was dead.[9]

The idea expressed in the last two stories—that the dead often do not vanish completely—is a very popular one. They often return in corporeal form to haunt the spot where they died. Should it happen that they were lost at sea through drowning or some other mishap and did not have a decent burial, one could be almost certain that as spirits they would remain at or return to the spot where they were lost, sometimes to frighten, sometimes to help their old shipmates or others in the vicinity.

Because of the ever present possibility of their return and the uncertain reception ghosts give their friends, seamen want no truck with them. In Scotland an old man died on the island of Muck, and his body lay above ground eight days before a vessel could be found to transport it to the graveyard.[10] Years ago in Bermuda there died a sea captain who made an unusual request. He loved the island so much that he asked that his heart be buried there and his body shipped back to England. His son complied with his wishes, removed his heart and buried it on the island. Knowing the crews' reluctance to carry a dead body on a ship, he hit upon an interesting ruse. He pickled the body in a barrel of rum and brought it on board without the crew knowing about it. Halfway across the ocean someone found the rum, bored a hole in the barrel and drank his fill. The dead man arrived home in a dry coffin.[11]

In many parts of the world, and particularly in the Canadian Maritime Provinces, seamen thought that merely mentioning a dead man's name would bring him back among the living, and therefore they avoided speaking of dead comrades; and when they found it necessary to do so, they never referred to them as dead. Sailors in Nova Scotia and Newfoundland, for example, always place "poor" before a dead man's name when it is necessary to speak of him.[12]

One way, of course, that one can protect the living from the dead is to give the corpse a decent burial with all the attendant flourishes. The body is washed, clean clothes are put on it, and it is carefully sewed up in a canvas shroud by the sailmaker, as described in an earlier chapter. Weights are attached to the feet (in the old days a twelve-pound shot), the corpse is placed on a platform covered with a flag, and the ship hove to. The crew is mustered aft and the captain or mate reads the burial service. The body is then either lowered over the side or slipped overboard feet first. But things do not always go as planned. Captain Dean MacFarlane, from Carriacou in the West Indies, recalled a sea burial:

I left here [Carriacou] going to Guyana. I had a fellow aboard called Sigette Patrice. He was a fellow who used to drink a lot. A lot, a lot, a lot he used to drink. One day he come to me and told me if I had any money to give him to let him buy a bottle of some kind of tonic for him to drink. It is the truth now. I handed him a hundred dollars. I said, "It's all the money I have. I have no small change." He went and buy a bottle of Seven Seas you know and he had it on the boat and we left for Guyana.

Well, we had about two days going up. Well, I was around the latitude of Pamaroon but not near land—I mean, away outside you know. The night he just say he feel bad an' he went to start the pump. That's the steam pump and there's a line you're pulling that this pump should start and after he start the pump he leave and he come back aft, you know. Aft there behind the wheel box, an' he lie down there an' the feller that was on the wheel call up an' say, "Is Uncle (we used to call him Uncle Sigette, you know) dying or what?" And when I went to see what happening he was throwing up but it was all blood. All blood and the same time a kind of hooking up like, and so on, and I call up his son. His son was the engineer aboard. I call up the son and I say, "Boy, there is something wrong with the father."

The boy come and by the time the boy did come the boy call him, "Dad, what happen?" and so on and sit down and put the head on the boy. He was a dead man. He dead. Well, I decide that it was Saturday night and I decide anyhow that I would force her for Georgetown, make Georgetown tomorrow you know. Well, after a little while a scandal in the cabin. The engine. Something wrong with the engine. The engine, it break something. The boy went down. He leave the father there. Dead there, and he went down. And the boy fighting all the ship and you know, the engine never work. Engine never worked! And when he was back here they said he had told the people that he would like to get a sea grave. He told the people straight that he wanted to give nobody trouble. That he would like to get a sea grave.

The engine wouldn't work no more. Something wrong with the engine and we haven't got the parts aboard. The wind come and haul in south. I couldn't get no course more than about south-by-west and very light. The boom just jocking. Well I go in on the shore. I go in on the shore an' when I did make shore I make Pamaroon but I did not make shore with him because Saturday–Sunday evening we didn't raise no land yet because the wind wasn't blowing and the engine not working; so we didn't raise no land and the man—you know how it is—was beginning to swell up already big and so on. So I decided. I said, "Well boys, you know we'll have to do something." I called to the son and I tell him. I say, "Well, what can we do, boy? I'm sorry. He's your father and we would have really tried to give him a grave ashore, but you see he cannot rest here. We can't do any better." He was crying but he said we couldn't do no better and I had a Dutch fellow on board the boat and the fellow say yes he could bathe him.

He took a knife and run it in the clothes he had on and the son went in his grip and got out his pajamas and they put them on and I had a mattress cloth and we shove him in it and we tie him up nicely and we sew him up in canvas and so on and the mate have his prayer book and the mate was ready and everything, and when everything was ready he was well put away you know, and I put the ship to the wind. We didn't have much wind and the ship come up and the ship stop. Just bumbling there you know. We had no wind and just bumbling light and the tide was so strong, and of course I knew the tide was strong and bound down and I put a rope both in his head and tail and lower him overboard and the mate' read over him, read the sermon and so on and we draw the rope and we let him go.

But there is one mistake I made. You see I made a mistake that we did not remember, as everybody was so sad and all crying, crying for him. I never remember to tie a sinker on him. Well, after they let him go he would not go to bottom. He float. The men kept watching and he kept going and we watched him a while and he was gone. We could do nothing else. That's how he goes. We gave him a sea burial and the mate reading as if it was ashore you know. Read a regular little sermon and so on, and we lowered him down but we really should have put a sinker on him. Whenever you are going to bury a man out at sea you must put a sinker on him and when you let him go he goes. It doesn't matter if he make bottom or where he make. You must put a sinker on him. We could see him after we gave way to go and that was wrong. We should have put a sinker on him.[13]

There are two points of interest here. The story supplements nicely the song "Pappy You Done Dead" by Nathan Phillips, and it also strongly implies that the failure of the ship to reach port was owing to the spirit of the dead man.

Although Captain McFarlane was obviously upset by his oversight, such mistakes are sometimes the source of much amusement. On a certain island in Maine an old woman died in the middle of winter. The ground was hard and the men were reluctant to dig the grave. Moreover, it was discovered that no wood was available for a coffin, so the old lady lay stretched out in the corner while friends and relatives decided what would be best to do. Eventually, someone suggested, "Why not bury her in the schooner's foresail?" "Too big," was the reply. "We could two-reef it." Accordingly the foresail was double-reefed and the corpse sewed into it. But before any more could be done the granddaughter began to cry bitterly. "I n-never thought to s-see the day that poor old g-granny would go through hell in a t-two-reef fors'l." An English version of this tale has a ship's passenger weighted down with a sinker made of coal and the comment is, "I never thought that the old lady would have to carry her own coal to hell."[14]

In the West Indies, where spirits constantly elbow the living for room, there is an interesting custom having to do with dead sea captains that in many ways resembles the old Norse practice of disposing of a shipmaster by placing his body in his ship, setting her afire and letting her sail out to sea with the corpse.

Sometime between one and seven years after a sea captain has died, his family hold a "stone fête" for the erection of his tombstone; however, this is not done until they are sure the body has moldered away. The man's family prepares a great feast and everyone is invited. A large barrel is rigged out like the captain's own vessel, with an anchor chain attached. A bos'n is selected and musters a crew. A cargo is taken aboard and the ship "sails" for a certain point, where it is discharged and another cargo loaded. The ship sails again. Eventually she is "cast away" on a reef and lost, or "sunk" at sea. The sham crew spend the entire night drinking rum, singing songs and dragging the mock ship through the crowd. At the appointed time they fall upon it with sticks and chains and beat upon it until it falls to pieces. With the demolition of the barrel, the dead skipper's shade is released and presumably he will trouble the living no more.

In line with superstitions and beliefs of the dead, a curious practice was carried out until recent times on the island of Bequia in the Lesser Antilles. In days gone by when transport on the island was poor, the dead were often carried to the graveyard by boat. At such times the oarsmen used "de dead stroke:" One stroke would go through the water; the oars were feathered and the next stroke went through the air. The oars were again feathered and the third stroke went through the water. In this way both body and spirit were conveyed to the burying ground.[15]

Should a man lose his life at sea without any funeral rites, it was a general and popular belief that he would haunt the area, returning to his old ship when it passed the spot where he was lost, or that he would climb aboard another ship should his own fail to return. This was especially true when a vessel foundered with all hands. To illustrate this point, consider a tragedy that took place a century ago.

The *Haskell* was a new schooner out of Gloucester, Massachusetts, when she anchored one night on Georges Shoal. Astern of her lay the *Johnston*. During the night a gale sprang up and the *Haskell* parted her cables and fell off to leeward. The *Johnston* yawed, and before anyone on either vessel could raise a hand, the *Haskell* struck her amidships and the *John-*

ston went down with her crew. The *Haskell*, only slightly damaged, returned to Gloucester.

Shortly after this event the *Haskell* returned to Georges and dropped her hook. Sometime during the midwatch the crew were appalled to see twenty-six wet and ghostly men crawl over her rail. No word was spoken—but one man went aft to the wheel, others stood by the halyards. The rest unwound fishing gear and lined the rail to fish for ghostly fish. There they remained until dawn, when they vanished. Every time the *Haskell* went to Georges the fishermen came aboard, until eventually no seamen could be found to go in her, and she lay alongside a pier in Gloucester until she fell to pieces.[16]

On another occasion a schooner, the *Northern Light*, drove down on Georges Shoal in a gale of wind. Before she was aware of where she was, she had white water all around her and it seemed impossible that the ship could survive. When all hope of saving her had been abandoned, twenty dripping sailors piled in over the rails, drove the master and crew to the fo'c'sle, then took over the ship. The only sound heard by the crew was the wail of the wind in the rigging and the roar of the seas boarding her. Next morning they were astounded to find themselves under full sail, jogging toward the twin towers of Thatcher's Island. The day was pleasant, the wind light, and no one on deck.[17]

As the foregoing story illustrates sometimes these shades are helpful to distressed mariners and either warn them of impending trouble or save them in their hour of need. Joshua Slocum, it will be recalled, once had this sort of aid when he became exhausted during a severe gale: one of Columbus' crew, complete with a red hat, came aboard and took command until Slocum could get some rest.[18]

The *Vesta Pearl*, a coaster from St. John, New Brunswick, was a schooner built in the nineteenth century. She carried a crew of five, but her captain had died and she was believed to have a poltergeist aboard. Unlike most poltergeists, he was often helpful, though he could be seen only by the helmsman. When the vessel needed reefing and all hands were called, the man at the wheel could unfailingly count five men reefing. Despite his helpful nature the poltergeist was feared, and the crew always slept ashore whenever they could.[19]

In Ireland there is a story of two sailors who were fast friends. One day as they were standing under Erris Head, one sailor vowed that someday, be he alive or dead, he would help his friend in a desperate hour. Seven years passed and one of the sailors was sent aloft to the crow's nest with another tar. He looked down and, much to his surprise, he saw his friend standing on the deck urging him to come down. The man aloft hesitated for fear he would be court-martialed, and the man on deck suggested that he might drop his knife and go after it without much jeopardy. This he did, and had got about halfway to the deck when he heard a cry and looked up to see the crow's nest tumbling down on top of him. Despite all he could do, he was carried along with the wreckage and lit on deck. His shipmate was killed, but he was only slightly injured as he was further down the mast and did not have so far to fall. Unknown to the sailor, his friend had died some time before. It was not the quick but the dead who had fulfilled the promise.[20]

From Nova Scotia, where ghosts are very frequently encountered, comes an interesting tale of a somewhat different nature. A vessel was fishing off Georges one wild winter day when one of the crew encountered a stranger at the chart table writing on the slate (kept in the old days to serve as a rough log). The startled crewman called the captain, who came down—but the man had vanished. However, someone had been there, for the slate had a message: "Change your course to NNW and in a certain time you'll see a vessel turned on its side with the crew hanging to it." The vessel's course was reluctantly altered, and after the required time they came on a wreck with sixteen men hanging to her, whom they picked up. One man had been lost.[21]

Down in Chesapeake Bay there is a slightly different story. A waterman saw a skull appear suddenly on the side of the pilot house. The startled captain called his mate and he, too, saw it. The skipper altered course immediately in the direction the skull was looking and arrived in time to pick up some survivors from a wreck.[22]

An example of a ghost visiting a friend or relative is to be found in a tale told by Judge Hadlock of Seal Harbor, Maine. During the "gale of '98" Ames Hanson was fishing on the Grank Banks in a new schooner and his brother in an older vessel. Shortly after midnight Ames went to the captain and said, "Captain, my brother's gone."

"You're crazy! How do you know?"

"I seen him walking towards me on the water an' he said 'Goodbye'."

"Nonsense, that warn't nothin' but a dream."

"No, sir, it wasn't. My brother's gone." And so it proved to be, for neither his brother nor the schooner he was in was ever heard from again.

But even dead men who have been buried properly are believed to make themselves seen from time to time, as either ghosts or poltergeists, sometimes to help or hinder the living. The skipper of the pilot boat in Sunderland, England, dropped dead on deck a number of years ago, and his shade has been reported seen on board from time to time.[23] Two yachts, one belonging to David Kayll, an Englishman, and another to an English charter captain in the West Indies, were plagued by poltergeists. In the first case the owner had changed the head (toilet) and a skylight. The ship was plagued with blocks and chains that rattled, accompanied by strange bumps and heavy footfalls on deck. In the latter case the problem arose after the vessel's rig had been altered to a more modern design. In the morning halyards would be found twisted around the mast aloft, with shackles still secured and wired shut. The luff of the sails would be twisted without having been removed from the mast and, among other things, food would be removed from one place and stored in another. In both cases the boats had been owned and designed by extremely exacting people who required everything "just so." They were bought and altered after the original owners had died. In the former case, the problem was resolved by selling the boat and passing both the ship and her troublesome crew on to someone else to deal with. In the latter case, the present owner plans to restore the vessel to her original rig and is sure this will solve his problems. Indeed, since his plans have been made known the visitations have become markedly less frequent.[24]

The dead are believed either to travel from the spot where they lost their lives to visit the quick, or to return to the spot where they died should they be buried elsewhere. In the Caribbean many stories are told of shipmasters who unwittingly carried such people, called *la jablesse (la diablesse)*, from one island to another, thinking they were real people. When the vessel reached port, the *jablesse* paid the skipper and went ashore. As soon as he disappeared the captain became aware of his folly. Instead of the pay he thought he had received, he would discover that he had a pocket full of leaves and goat manure.[25]

According to Malcolm MacDonald, engineer on the *Girl Vivian* of Frazerburgh, Scotland, there was an ancient cemetery called Uig on the island of Lewis in the Hebrides. Years ago it was the custom of the people to pasture their cattle in the graveyard overnight, and leave an old woman to guard them. On one particular night an old lady was guarding the cattle and whiling away the time by spinning. Just at midnight (the hour popularly believed to be the one in which the dead begin to walk) she was somewhat surprised to see all the graves open and the ghosts emerge. All hurried off in different directions. Shortly before daylight, the shades returned and the graves closed over them—all except one, which remained open.

The old woman determined to find out where the spirits had been, and she placed her distaff (shaped like a crucifix, which no ghost may pass according to popular belief) across the grave. Just on the verge of light the last little shade appeared and rushed to the grave, only to find her way barred. She pleaded with the woman to remove the distaff, but the old lady refused until she had learned where the ghost had been, who she was, and why she was late. The ghost told her:

"I am the daughter of the King of Norway and many years ago I was sent by my father to Scotland. On the way the ship sank in a great storm and my body was washed ashore here, and was buried in this grave. Every night we dead must return to the place where we died. It is very far from here to where I was drowned and that is why I am the last to return. Let me into the grave and I'll give you a valuable present."

This satisfied the old woman and she removed her distaff. The little ghost gave her a pure white stone with a hole in it and tumbled back into the grave. It was this stone that eventually became the property of the Brahan Seer, the most widely acclaimed of all the Scotish prophets: he used it to see into the future. Just before he died he threw it into a lake. I have mentioned this seer earlier, and will say more of him later.[26]

In another version of the same story, the ghost tells the old woman that if she will remove the distaff she will tell her where to find a treasure. It is located, she says, under a bunch of tangle (seaweed) or a bush on the beach. The old woman hurries to the beach but can never find the right clump of tangle.[27]

So far the discussion has centered on people who have lost their lives accidentally. The attitude of the dead toward those who have caused their death is another thing altogether. The ghosts of murdered persons are believed to be ready, willing and able to get revenge, and are not particular in selecting their victims. On the coast of Cornwall, where wreckers lured ships into the breakers by displaying false lights and killed what survivors remained, it is still considered very poor practice to visit the scene of a shipwreck. In Scotland seamen will not even go near a vessel that has been cast away for fear of the attending spirits. According to the late F. Rollins Maxwell of Duxbury, Massachusetts, there used to be creatures called "Yo hos" on Cape Cod. They were the spirits of drowned seamen, and on dark nights they could be found crying "Yo ho" in the fog, and displaying a light. The unwary ship captain, thinking the light and the

cry came from distressed sailors, would go to the rescue, only to find himself trapped in the shifting sands and currents off that cape the French
called Cap Malebarre.

To suppose that vengeful ghosts inhabited only the coastline would be
incorrect: neither man nor vessel could go so far that they would be out of
reach of an irate shade. There is a folk song called "The Ship's Carpenter,"
wherein a carpenter murdered a girl before going to sea. Much later, when
the vessel was far from land, Willie went into the hold and there he saw
a beautiful woman. He attempted to take her in his arms, "But he drew
back in awe and surprise/For flashes of lightning rolled forth from her
eyes."[28]

Another phenomena that bodes no good, in either the Old World or the
New, is a strange phenomenon known as the Spectral Funeral. Creighton
mentions it and I have collected stories about it in Scotland, Ireland and
the West Indies. Usually the story runs that a man walking down the
road, often in company with a friend, suddenly steps aside. He is asked
why, and he replies that he is giving way to let a funeral procession go
past. His friend, of course, sees nothing. Very often he recognizes by the
composition of the funeral party that it is the funeral of a certain living
individual. It is then generally believed that the person in the coffin is
marked for death and will die before many days have passed.

One evening a MacBrayne's steamer (a company about which the
rhyme was composed "The World's the Lord's and all that it contains/Ex-
cept the Western Isles and they're Macbrayne's") tied up at an outport and
the captain, an abstemious man, stepped ashore for a short visit with his
wife. To reach home he had to climb a flight of stone steps, and halfway
up he was suddenly jostled by a funeral procession. He tried to get clear,
but before he could the mourners were upon him. His nose was bloodied,
his clothes torn, and he was hurled down the steps. Badly mauled and
completely terrified, he managed to crawl to his door and get into the
house, where his condition was none the best for several days. He an-
ticipated that some dread calamity lay in store for either himself or someone with whom he was associated, and the villagers agreed with him. As
of this writing, however, nothing has happened that could be directly
associated with the event.[29]

It was popularly believed that the dead took other forms, especially
those of birds. Sea birds in general, and petrels and albatross in particular,
were thought to be restless spirits of drowned sailors. This is not surprising,
for sea fowl do not act like land birds. They can drink sea water, they

need no dry spot to perch or roost; some varieties seem never to come ashore. Many have a wild and plaintive cry. The albatross, more than any other bird, can soar seemingly forever without moving a feather, and even in the wildest weather the petrels can be seen walking on the water—a feat undoubtedly tried by many but accomplished only by Christ and St. Peter, from whom they derive their name.

As the Ancient Mariner learned, it is extremely bad luck to kill one of these birds, and sailors watch for them as they are considered helpful in various ways. In an otherwise prosaic log, Captain Coggeshall, a nineteenth-century shipmaster, records seeing fourteen strange birds following the ship just before he reached Cape Horn, and notes that they trailed him all the way to the harbor entrance of Valparaiso.[30] On more than one occasion this writer has been kept from running ashore in thick weather by the crying of the gulls on the rocks in the small hours of the morning. Although I do not hold with the belief that it is good luck to have one defecate on you, as most sailors think, I am reluctant to harm them.

Sometimes these birds act as forerunners of coming events and, as with dreams, the only problem is to translate their meaning.

In Chesapeake Bay a waterman went gunning one stormy day on a marshy point. He had not been long in his blind when he saw a foul duck fly over the blind, and he killed it. Two more came by and he killed them. These three birds fell behind the blind on the marshy point, and he left them there to pick up later. He shot a couple of other birds and decided it was time to go home. Search as hard as he might, he could not find the three ducks that had fallen behind the blind. He surmised they either had been crippled and swam away or had been grabbed by some water creature, and thought little more about it. That night a terrible gale sprang up and it blew three days. When it was over he went out to his blind. There in the shallow water on the marshy point, exactly where the birds had fallen, lay the bodies of three drowned sailors.[31]

Interestingly enough, a similar tale is current in Newfoundland. In this case the hunter shoots the birds and when he goes to pick them up, he sees the three corpses staring up at him from the bottom.[32]

Sometimes the birds take an even more active part in the lives of seamen than squawking and warning them off rocks or of future events. According to the account of Captain Johnson of the barque *Ellen*:

> Just before six o'clock in the afternoon of September 12, 1857, I was standing on the quarterdeck . . . beside the man at the helm. Suddenly a bird flew around me, grazing my right shoulder. Afterward it flew around the vessel,

then it again commenced to fly around my head. It soon flew at my face, when I caught hold of it and made it a prisoner. The bird was unlike any bird I had ever seen, nor do I know its name. The color of its feathers was a dark iron-grey; its body was a foot and a half in length, with wings three and a half feet from tip to tip. It had a beak full eight inches long and teeth like a small hand saw. In capturing the bird it gave me a good bite on my right thumb; two of the crew who assisted in tying its legs were also bitten. As it strove to bite everybody, I had its head cut off and the body thrown overboard.

When the bird flew to the ship the barque was going a little north of northeast. I regarded the appearance of this bird as an omen and an indication . . . that I must change my course. I according headed to the eastward direct. I should not have deviated from my course had not the bird visited the ship and had it not been for this change of course, I should not have fallen in with the forty-nine passengers [of the sunken ship *Central America*] whom I fortunately saved from certain death.[33]

Finally, it may have been the belief in birds as good omens that caused Admiral Rodney to take special care of a bantam cock that sat on his poop and clapped its wings and crowed with every broadside in the famous Battle of the Saints, which won for England control of the West Indies.[34]

Earlier I mentioned the fact that many seamen were reluctant to go near a wreck for fear of its attendant ghosts. It may be that stories of ghosts and evil spirits were built up as a kind of deterrent to those who would destroy vessels or plunder distressed mariners on the beach. If so, the following tale certainly must have had a telling effect on its auditors.

Long ago in Shetland there was a violent gale, and the following morning a fisherman rose early and walked the tide line to see if anything useful had come ashore. Before he had gone very far, he came onto the debris of a ship that had gone down during the night. Spars and cordage lay about in profusion, and just above high-water mark lay a well-dressed man. No one was about, so the fisherman stripped him of his valuables, dragged the body down to a lower level, went home and hid his small treasure. Then he joined his fellows in a hunt for survivors from the wreck. When they came to the spot where the body had been, the fisherman was startled to find it had vanished. The body-robber surmised it had been washed back into the sea and held his tongue.

That night there came to the fisherman's house a strange and beautiful gull of a kind he had never seen before. The bird uttered strange cries and beat and beat and beat against his window all night. Nothing the fisherman did could drive it away: And so it continued night after night.

The fisherman tried every device he knew to drive it off or kill it, but he failed. The bird continued to cry and beat on the window until the man went mad.[35]

Closely associated with the dead and the supernatural is the belief in the efficacy of dreams. Until fairly recently no one ever thought to understand machinations of dreams and the folk still attribute them to a sort of border world between reality and the supernatural. Sometimes dreams may be taken literally. At other times it is believed that the reverse of the dream will come true; e.g., to dream of a wedding means that a funeral is in the offing. On still other occasions it is necessary to interpret the dream—even to the extent of having to go to a fortune teller, a witch or some other person versed in the art.

Neal Cameron of Crinan, Scotland, told a story of a simple dream. It seems that Lady Campbell ordered a man named Archie to take a bundle of papers to the keeper on Fladda Light, about five miles away. The wind was blowing a gale from the south:

> . . . that wild that the pilot didn't want to go, but the word of a Campbell was law in the land in those days and Archie the Pilot had to go in his little boat, the *Alert*. [Campbells were, and still are, not highly esteemed in the highlands. In fact there is a saying about them; namely that "there are but three pests in Argyllshire, the bracken, the rabbits, and the Campbells. The bracken is a pest and the rabbits a misfortune."] It was flood water, and his wife was making oatcakes. She looked out the window and saw him on the port tack. She went to turn the cakes and when she looked again she could see nothing but the sea. And from that day there's been no hide nor hair of that boat found.
>
> Now my grandfather was very fond of Archie and he took his loss, which he considered needless, very much to heart. One night he dreamed that he walked to a certain point on the island where he lived and there lying on a rock was Archie the Pilot's cheese-cutter bonnet, his plaid and all. The old man was so impressed he woke up and found himself in a great sweat. He went back to sleep and dreamed the same dream again, and a third time. The dream was so sure that at first light the old man got up, went to the place he had seen in his dream, and there was all they ever found of Archie—his cheese-cutter bonnet lying on the rock in the surf. My grandfather brought it home and for fifty years it hung from one of the posters of an old box bed in our home and there I have seen it many years.[36]

These dreams apparently can occur to anyone. A member of the Royal Ocean Racing Club told me that he had a strange dream racing across the channel many years ago. When he was called for his watch, he told his friends that he had dreamed about a man he knew slightly who was in trouble. His name was Bobby Lowen, and in the dream Lowen was just entering a French harbor. There was smoke or fog around him, and a French trawler was mixed up in it somehow. It subsequently came out that at the very hour of the dream the man in question was entering a French port when his stove blew up, trapping him below. A French trawler came to his assistance, but he put out the fire and made port unaided.[37]

At St. Coombs on the Moray Firth lived the greatest "snapper" in all of East Scotland—Captain Jimmy Buchan, known the length and breadth of the country for his courage, his strength and the deperate way he drove himself, his crew and his ship. Captain Buchan persisted in attributing his great success to a dream. It was a dream of the dead—the most significant of all dreams.

On the east coast of Scotland it is the custom never to leave port on Sunday. One must wait until one minute into Monday morning. While waiting for the appropriate time, Captain Buchan stretched out in his cabin and went to sleep. Presently he dreamed that the vessel was underway and steaming full speed down a river bound to the sea. Ahead the sun was just rising. The Captain looked aft and saw his dead sister-in-law in a skiff, rowing furiously after him. He kept going straight into the rising sun for eight hours, while the rower slowly gained on him until at last she was alongside. His sister-in-law stood up in the skiff and offered him a piece of golden cake which she had baked; but just as he reached for it, it fell in the water. She cut another slice and offered him that, but it too fell into the sea. Then she offered him the rest of the cake in one lump. The Captain took it and had a bite, and it was the sweetest cake he ever ate "and yellow as gold." The taste was so delicious that the skipper awoke and discovered it was time to get underway.

He went into the pilot house, and as soon as they cleared the harbor entrance he said to his helmsman, "Hold her east and give her all she's got." After eight hours of steady steaming he gave his next order. "Stop her, lads, and shoot your nets and dinna be discouraged." The nets were set and hauled back, and they were empty. "Never mind, boys. Shoot your nets again and dinna be downhearted." Again the nets were set, and again they came back empty. "Now, lads, go below and I would have you eat hearty and have a wee dram, for we shall shoot again and there will be nae rest aboard this ship this day."

After the meal the nets were shot a third time, and this time they came back so full of fish that it took "fourteen lifts" to empty the bag completely;

and the vessel returned to Peterhead so deep laden with fish that any sort of hard weather would have sent her to the bottom. "Ach noo," said Captain Buchan, " 'Twas the greatest catch of fish ever to be landed in Peterhead and for mony the day after."[38]

A very similar dream ordered the life of Athneal Ollivierre, the head harpooner of the Bequia whale fishery, Bequia, St. Vincent, West Indies.

Athneal's wife was a person who, as is sometimes the case, had a reputation for having dreams that came true. It was his habit to get up every morning at five-thirty to milk his cow. He would then come in and have his breakfast of two eggs and then depart for the whale fishery, arriving there about six-thirty.

On this particular morning he came in from milking and instead of two there were four fried eggs on his plate. He asked his wife why, and she told him that after he had gone to milk the cow she had dozed off and met an old woman (Athneal's dead mother—dead for twenty-one years) who handed her four eggs and said they were for Athneal. Accordingly she got up and cooked the four eggs and insisted that he eat them. As he was going out the door, she told him, "I think you will have good luck this day." And so it proved, for that day they took whale.

As a result, Athneal interpreted the dream to mean he would catch four whales that season, and that is the number he brought ashore. But the dream cycle didn't end there.

Toward the end of the whaling season people began telling him of their dreams—that they had dreamed that they were, or someone was, bringing him something. Then Athneal had a dream himself: he was leading his cow down the road and she

> . . . began behaving so badly I gave her a lash and knocked the old bitch down, but the calf started running down the road and I saw old Joseph Ford [stroke oarsman in the whaleboat] coming, and I called to he to turn it and he did, and as it flew past me I gave it a lick and knocked it down.

On April 1, 1971, shortly after the dream, the boat steerer, Arlington Richardson, had fallen sick and old Joseph Ford was promoted to his place. They had not been at sea long when a fishing boat came flying downwind with news of a cow and a calf whale. They went for them and Ford skillfully got ahead of the calf and Athneal killed it. The cow was another matter. "It behave very badly," attacking the whaleboat and knocking the harpooner overboard twice. Then it stove the boat, and Athneal dove overboard and swam to the other boat, climbed aboard, picked up the whale lance and killed her dead with a single thrust. "It happens just like my dream."[39]

Many dreams, or objects in them, seem to recur frequently, and these objects have been formularized. In Scotland, to dream of sheep is a sign of good luck; while to dream of swine, especially in the room, or of blood, is a warning of death.[40]

On the island of Bequia the number of sheep a whaleman sees in a dream is the number of whales he'll see in a season. Strangely enough, to dream of a policeman is fortunate. To dream of something green means good luck, and corn indicates coming money. To dream of a white child swimming in the sea is good luck, but to dream of a black child or black people, even for blacks, is a precursor to misfortune.[41] To list the objects, ideas, colors that are good and bad in dreams would be to compile a dictionary on the subject.

From the foregoing material one can depict the importance that the mariner's dreams take. It seems obvious that they play a large part in ordering their lives and ordering their attitudes for better or for worse.

Another omen that borders on the supernatural is second sight, called by some, extrasensory perception. This comes in two forms, one of which can be easily explained, but the other is baffling. Any shipman worth his salt is attuned to his shipmates, his vessel, the sea, and the weather to a degree that is not readily understood by landsmen. A good skipper of a sailing vessel can lie in his bunk asleep and know by the myriad sounds his vessel makes, by her motion, by the wind in the rigging, and by her angle of heel exactly how hard she is being driven and how fast she is going. He can sense anxiety in his crew, and he can look at the sky and predict a blow. His knowledge is based on actual sensory perceptions, but he is so used to them that he often finds it impossible to sort them out or even articulate them. This is one type of second sight.

The other is the kind wherein a man is believed able to predict the shape of coming events. It is most prevalent both in Scotland, where people inordinately good at it are called "seers," and in the Canadian Maritime Provinces among people whose ancestors came from the Scottish highlands. However, it is by no means restricted to these areas.

In Scotland, the greatest of all the people possessed of second sight was a man named Coinneach Odhar, better known as the Brahan Seer. Among other things, he "saw" the coming of the Caledonian Canal, the introduction of sheep into the highlands, the coming of the telephone, the destruction of a church and the collapse of a family. He was burned to death for his predictions in 1692.[42] But if he was the greatest of the seers in Scotland, there are many there today who predict the sex of unborn infants, the coming of strangers, the death of friends and enemies and other more immediate and less pretentious things. Nearly every community has one person who is believed to be more gifted in this way than his neighbors. To him the sailors go for all sorts of advice—what boat to buy, where and when to go to sea. This advice is usually followed, and disaster frequently attends those who ignore it. There was such a man living on the island of South Uist in 1968. He said he had "the gift" from his father and he sometimes felt it was a curse. Although he was reluctant to talk about it, he admitted that many people on the island consulted him before taking any important steps.

Shortly before I met him, some fishermen had come to him and asked if he thought they should buy a certain boat. The price—always a matter of importance in Scotland—seemed right, and they needed a vessel. Unfortunately, the vessel in question belonged to the seer's close friend. At first he refused to venture an opinion, but at last his conscience forced him to speak, and he said they should not buy the vessel on any account. He gave no reason. The fishermen took heed of his warning and refused to buy her. The owner asked why not, and they said, "——said not to," thus making an enemy of a close friend. The seer would only say he had "seen something in the vessel." Long afterward, we heard the ship had sunk.

This power is believed in not only in Scotland but in Ireland as well. Years ago there was a large fishing fleet operating out of Inishbofin Island on the west coast.

October 28, 1927, was a day of mist and rain, but there were mackerel around the island and it cleared up toward evening. Most of the boats at that time were drifters and they preferred to fish at night. When it seemed to clear, the fishermen were determined to go, and five boats put out with five to six men in each boat:

> and they had just set their nets when they heard this terrible noise coming, and of course they suspected right away that it was a storm. It came along in great force and some of them broke away from the nets and more held on and between all we lost ten men. One boat held on to the nets until it eased off—it lasted about two hours—and came in in the morning. . . . But all the men that had the yoke [caul] survived. . . .
>
> Now in Cleggan there was an old man—a great old seaman himself, and he didn't like the weather at all, and he got on his bicycle—they had no cars in those days—and he rushed off to stop them but they had gone. He was too late.

Well, I know a man—he's still alive yet—and a man that never told lies. His brother-in-law came to him that night—him that was out fishing. You see this man wasn't out and he came to him while he was looking after his own boat. He had tied the boat down and he was just going away from her when this man came and tapped him on the shoulder light-like and says, "I am drowning," he says, and he turned around quick and he just saw the shoulder of the person going from him. And that was one of the men that was lost. Oh that happened for sure, and it weren't the only one that night. There was a young boy and he saw the crew, the full drowned crew come into the kitchen.[43]

Over two thousand miles from the Hebrides, on Bras D'Or Lake, Nova Scotia (actually an arm of the sea), lived a man named McNeil. He was standing on the shore one day when two young men approached him inquiring where they could hire a boat for the day. He advised against it. "If you go out one of you will not come back at all and the other will almost not come back." The warning was disregarded and they went to sea. The boat capsized, one drowned and the other was picked up by a passing boat, more dead than alive.[44]

One day on Cape Breton a man was walking along the beach when suddenly on the sand before him he saw a drowned man in a blue suit. Two women were standing over the body. He looked again, and he was alone on the beach. Two years to the day on the spot where he saw it, two women discovered a drowned man in a blue suit.[45]

Sometimes, apparently, this ability can be induced. In Scotland when a vessel was missing, a strong-minded girl would be persuaded to go to sleep while a friend kept watch. Her spirit would go forth and find the vessel and return with the news. There was, however, an element of risk involved, for if the wind should change while she was on the quest she would go mad.[46]

Although it is strongest in certain people, the power of second sight can come to anyone. A sailor walked into a public house in South Uist and had a drink. He had another, started to drink it, turned pale and bolted out the door. He could be heard being sick outside. After a few minutes he returned, pale as a ghost, and said, "I saw something but I don't want to talk about it now." He paid his bill and left. Within the month the barkeep was dead. When he heard about it the man said, "It was to be expected: when he served me that night I was sick. I looked at him and it wasn't him. It was a skeleton serving me. And I was sick right then."[47]

Concern with the supernatural is by no means restricted to quick and dead people, but flows over into the sea, into ships and into many other items. As to the sea, the sailor's attitude toward it is peculiar to say the least. First, the sea is regarded animistically. The real seafaring man genuinely loves the sea. He believes in a kind of spiritual purity in the "being" Sea. For this reason, as stated earlier, he fears to travel with a murderer, a man with unpaid bills, a thief or anyone who does not have, or seem to have, a kind of moral integrity. The sea does not want such people trammeling up her placid bosom and could cut out some good flesh at the same time it takes the proud. Moreover, he feels that the sea is against all those who pass over deep waters. He believes its attitude toward him varies from indifferent to cruel and malevolent, and he accepts it. At times the sailor will curse the sea and at times he will try to assuage her malevolence with gifts, for he knows the best he can expect from her is indifference.

Even in our present-day, enlightened society, we know less about the ocean than we do about the rest of the world. It is sufficiently untrammeled even now so that if it were to dry up, there would still be a good many acres of the bottom devoid of beer cans or Coca-Cola bottles. We are not even sure we have discovered and classified all that lives in it. Because of his nature, man seems determined to rationalize the unknown. The folk rationalize through personification and animism; the sophisticated rationalize by the use of science. The folk believe that the marks on a haddock are the thumb and finger prints of St. Paul[48] and are content. The scientists see the marks as protective coloring and rest easy. Fortunately, neither has thought to ask the question, "Why was the haddock singled out for this?"

In Ireland and in some parts of Scotland there yet lingers a belief that was popular throughout northern Europe until recent times. This is the belief that "what the sea wants, the sea will have." Should a man fall overboard or a ship sink, the people are at best reluctant to pick up any survivors, and in some areas will not pick them up on any account. Neither will they search for missing vessels. Only when the bodies are washed ashore,[49] no longer wanted by the sea, will they bestir themselves to pick them up and "give them a grand funeral."[50] This belief appears to extend to the Caribbean, for there the fishermen seldom say where they are going or for how long, and when they do not return only the merest kind of a token search, if any, is instituted.

Furthermore, if the sea wants a person and he is rescued, it is believed to be but a temporary salvation, for the sea will take him in the end—and maybe his rescuer as well. Although the saying is little known today, its ramifications stretch far. One tale comes from the Carolina coast.

Many years ago a man came ashore from a wreck at Cape Hatteras, where he decided to remain and make a living as a fisherman. In this respect he was very fortunate, for he was never known to catch "trash" (nonsalable) fish or to have his nets damaged. When other men would not go, he took his little boat out and always came back with a big haul. His name was Quawk.

One day a storm sprang up and, against all advice, Old Quawk put to sea and returned with a big haul. He had long been considered an atheist, and he proved it on this occasion, for he gave God a round tongue-lashing and said in part, "With Satan's help and protection I will put out to my fishing grounds [again] and I will come back with an even bigger haul." So saying, he pushed off a second time. "As he sailed into the gale a mocking laugh was heard and he was never seen again."[51]

If the sea takes some because it wants them, it takes others because they are unfit to travel on its surface. Countless stories and sea songs are based on this theme. A typical example is to be found in the fate of Captain Glen, who quarreled over a woman and killed a nobleman. The king pardoned him, but the sea did not. On his next voyage his crew fell sick, a tremendous storm sprang up, some of the crew were washed overboard and the ship was in immediate peril of founding when the bos'n informed the crew of the master's activities. The Captain was immediately thrown overboard, and instantly "The wind was calmed, so was the sea/And we arrived at High Barbary."[52]

In Ireland there is a story about a ship that sailed for a foreign port. On the way she hit bad weather and a big sea broke over her. When it drained off, a coffin was lodged on deck. The captain wanted to throw it overboard but didn't dare, and so it remained until the crew became used to it.

One day one of the crew on a bet got into the thing to see if it fitted him. Instantly a huge rogue sea cockled up and broke over the ship. When the vessel freed herself, crewman and coffin were gone and never seen again. It was not until the vessel reached Africa that the captain learned about the lost crewman. There was a warrant at home for his arrest on a charge of murder.[53]

Even a whole population can incur the sea's wrath. For instance, men from a certain island in the Hebrides are considered poor risks at sea. The reason is an interesting one. Once the people were great sailors, but about a hundred years ago a Spanish vessel went ashore there. Instead of helping the distressed sailors or leaving them to their own devices, the islanders fell upon them, clubbed them to death, cut off their fingers for their rings and robbed the bodies of valuables. After this cruel and inhuman act, men began to be lost at sea and to die from falling over cliffs at a rate quite out of proportion to the losses suffered on the other islands. Since this has continued year after year, the people of the neighboring islands have come to the conclusion that the inhabitants are cursed.[54]

I have already mentioned that the sea does not like debtors, and in the winter of 1970 I was startled to learn that the belief is still viable in the Windward Islands. Speaking of a vessel that had recently gone down, my informant said, "You know he run off without payin' for de kyargo." The fact that she was overloaded and only kept together "by the maggots holding hands" never crossed his mind.

Another character that the sea does not appear fond of is the braggart. Already mentioned is the policy regarding saving ships, and we can easily add to this the story of the Flying Dutchman (discussed fully elsewhere) who swore, and in a sense boasted, that he would go around Cape Horn no matter how long it took. Captain Coggeshall, writing about the engagement between the U.S.S. *Constitution* and H.M.S. *Guerriere* does not attribute the victory to the superior size of the *Constitution* or even to the skill of her commander as much as he does to the fact that Captain Dacres boasted that he would bring the Yankee to his knees in less than an hour.[55]

If the sea swallows some because she wants them and others because they are unfit to be on her, there are some she destroys who are unfit for either land or sea. Thus convicted pirates were always hanged over water, and three tides were allowed to pass under them before they were cut down, and they were buried on the beach between high and low water.

Many years ago a Scandinavian fishing vessel was wrecked at Loch Skiport in Scotland and the entire crew died—most people think by drowning, but some think by foul play. The crew consisted of six men and one woman. All were buried on a small island, and all the male corpses have long since moldered to dust. The woman's corpse would not stay interred and was finally buried above ground in a cairn, but the bones fell out of the cairn and may still be seen, I am told, scattered about the island.[57]

From Nova Scotia comes a similar story. A vessel went ashore one night on Mud Island, and in the morning the crew of twenty-six men and one beautiful woman were found dead on the beach. The natives buried them there and forgot about it. Years passed and the island began to erode. One day some fishermen went clamming there and dug up some bones. Then they dug up something else—the woman, unchanged in any respect from the day she was buried. She was so remarkably preserved that the clam diggers put her on display until the government took her away and reburied her. Again she was dug up and again she was placed on exhibit until the government took her off and buried her secretly.[58]

George Carey tells a somewhat similar story from Chesapeake Bay. Here a sea captain murdered a black man and buried him on a sandspit. The next time he sailed by, the man was lying on the surface. He buried him again, but he could never get him wholly under. Some part, an arm or a leg, always stuck out.[59]

Taken collectively, all the characters that the sea wants or does not choose to have cruising on her surface could be called Jonahs—a group going back to biblical times and including such august names as St. Paul and Commodore John Byron (grandfather of the lame poet), who experienced so many hazards and encountered such bad weather wherever he went that he was known as "Foul Weather Jack." Seamen believe that these people bring misfortune upon their shipmates and were formerly in the habit of throwing them overboard. Currently such actions are not viewed with favor, but that does not mean the belief is dead, for sailors are reluctant to sail with "an ill-favored man," and when they are sure one is aboard, they will set him ashore.

Except for the larger ships, vessels are usually operated on a family-unit basis, or at least on a local basis, being manned entirely by one nationality and very often by people from one town. Should an outsider be aboard, that is the man who they believe brings the bad luck. Further, not being altogether convinced of the popular belief that all people are alike, the mariner tends to blame his tribulations on anyone different. Thus anyone with physical characteristics materially different from the rest of the crew is looked upon askance. Black men, red beards, white men, men with blue eyes or brown, chinless men, men with narrow heads, are all believed to be Jonahs by groups where these features do not predominate.

A slightly different reason can be found for making deformed people the scapegoats for misfortune. The devil is popularly conceived as being lame and humpbacked, and there is always the chance that people with these characteristics are either in league with or are the Old Boy himself. Cross-eyed and squint-eyed men are somewhat different. The eye has long been thought to be "the window of the soul," and among people of Scottish and Irish backgrounds there still remains a considerable belief in the "evil eye." Since this belief is also common in Africa, it is not surprising that it has survived in the West Indies.

There can, I think, be little doubt of the validity of much of this

material. Aboard a jumping vessel there is no room for the physically handi-
capped. Moreover, the long periods of confinements, to say nothing of the
efficacy of closely-shared cultural experiences, tends to stress the worth of
homogeneity among ship's crews over heterogeneous ones.

Closely associated with "what the sea wants" is the idea that what
belongs to the sea, or comes from the sea, must return to the sea. In Scotland and Ireland ships' ballast may not be taken from the sea, for the ocean
may rise at any moment and claim it. By the same token, clothing may
not be dyed with colors made from sea plants. As far as ballast is concerned,
the idea is probably a good one, for sea stones are usually smooth and
round and given to shifting with the rolling of the ship; while stones from
inland are more angular and less easily rolled about.[60]

If some men are considered Jonahs, there are others who are thought
to be "lucky," i.e., less likely to attract the malevolent attention of the sea.
Amongst white Anglo-Americans, blonde seamen with blue (thought to
be farsighted) eyes are believed to make good sailors. As stated earlier,
men who are born with the caul are thought to be safe from drowning.
To this end, within fairly recent times, cauls could be purchased for a
modest sum; and even today some sailors carry a dried one in their pockets
to ensure they will not drown.[61] It will be recalled, too, that Manxmen are
drown proof because they are descended from the merfolk. Such a belief,
whether it be true or false, can be helpful to a sailor, for while others
worry about being washed overboard, he can proceed about his business,
secure in the belief that he at least will not end in the sea.

But all men cannot come from the Isle of Man, be born with a caul,
or have blue eyes and therefore be immune to ocean hazards. For safety,
well-being and prosperity, those less fortunate depend on charms. These
are so numerous and varied that only a few can be mentioned here. All of
them seem to derive their efficacious properties from rather simple rules.

In Roman Catholic areas sailors like to wear amulets of various saints—
especially St. Elmo, patron of the sea, and St. Christopher, patron saint of
travelers, and St. Nicholas. (Since recent papal decree has, in a sense,
revoked the license of some of these holy people, one wonders if their
protective properties will vanish). In the Shetland Islands we learn that
otter skins are good protection for the sailor, while in Scotland seamen
feel that, among other things, the right front paw of a seal made into a
purse, a "Mary Bean" (Brazilian malaga nut), especially a light-colored one,
and white stones with holes in them are auspicious. In both Scotland and
Ireland, dirt from the graves of certain saints is held to be lucky—e.g., the

earlier discussed clay from the grave of St. Cummin.[62] In New England and the Maritime Provinces we learn that smooth stones with a ring around them, called "lucky stones," bring good fortune. Sailors from the neighborhood of the Elizabeth Islands in Massachusetts like to carry "lucky bones" (bones taken from the male horeshoe crab) to keep them safe at sea.[63] Seamen on Chesapeake Bay prefer to keep horse chestnuts in their pockets, or certain bones found in the blue paddler crab.[64]

We have already seen how on St. Stephen's Day the people of Ireland beat the bushes along the roadside to catch wrens, which they tie to a broom near the hearth to keep out faeries. Others are plucked except for the terminal wing feathers, taken to church, blessed, and then thrown out into the cold to ensure a good year (by making sure the faeries stay away).[65] On the Isle of Man these wrens' feathers are greatly esteemed and kept in sailor's purses[66]—another possible link between the belief in faeries and the belief in merfolk.

Fishermen in the West Indies, although they believe in these kinds of charms, like also to secure the help of Obeah men (conjuremen) to ensure good luck and safety at sea. Usually they are given charms by these people in the form of a combination of aromatic oils to anoint the body and the boat, or a scarlet amulet to be carried about the person. For the West Indian believes that evil spirits are affected by smells. To this end the West Indian sea captain throws his dirty undershirt to leeward in order to dispel a storm.[67]

Two other items that seem to be thought highly efficacious among almost all Anglo-American sailors are the knife, preferably with a black handle and a guard, and either a silver sixpence or its counterpart, a dime. According to James Buchan, a Scot, it is best if the coin is given to you.

Finally, of course, one must notice the power of the priest and prayer. Before a ship went to sea, the minister often called for the prayers of the congregation to bless the efforts of those about to embark. Today, from Shetland Island in the north to Tobago in the south, the priest or minister can be found blessing the boat, the crew and the gear. Moreover, the holy man is often called upon in times of stress to drive away misfortune with bell, book and candle. Two stories, one from the Island of Harris and the other from Portsmouth, Dominica, illustrate the age of some of these activities as well as the manner in which paganism and Christianity meld together to help mankind in his hour of need.

Martin recalls that early in the seventeenth century the people of Harris propitiated a "sea-god" named Shony on "Hallow-tide."

The inhabitants round the island come to the church of St. Malvay, having each man his provisions along with him; every family furnished a peck of malt, and this was brewed into ale; one of their number was picked out to wade into the sea up to his middle, and carrying a cup of ale in his hand, standing still in that posture, cried out with a loud voice saying, "Shony I give you this cup of ale, hoping you'll be so kind as to send us plenty of sea-ware for enriching our ground for the ensuing year," and so threw the cup of the ale into the sea. This act was performed in the night time. At his return to the land, they all went to church, where there was a candle burning upon the altar; and then standing silent a little time one of them gave a signal, at which the candle was put out, and immediately all of them went to the fields, where they fell a-drinking this ale and spent the remainder of the night in dancing, singing, etc.[68]

In April, 1971, Carleton Maglorie of Dominica told my wife and me:

I can remember one time there was a big shark in this harbor, a huge, big, big shark. It's big—about half of this boat, a big, big shark. It is always cruising on the beach where children is bathing on Sundays. It always come on Sundays—cruising on the beach. Once it make a leap at a little child. It hurt her. Then the people went to the priest and tell it to the priest. They could have gone to the dealer [Obeah man] but on the line of the sea they got the priest. Then the priest make a Mass and he said that he will come down here when he knows when that thing will be around. Then on Sunday they put up notices that nobody must bathe in the sea. Then you see it coming across the beach and cruising—you can see the tail passing—it's under water, you know. It's swimming all around and the waves was beating, and the priest come. And as the waves was beating the priest checked seven waves. He checked one when it beat, two when it beat, three. Checked four and five, and then the seventh wave he say, "Stop." And the wave stop beating. Then he open a book—a big sort of book and he read some kind of a prayer, a sort of a prayer, he do some kind of a thing. He make some sign on the sea and he say, "I am calling you on the shore. Put yourself on the shore." And all of a sudden you see the fish. It pop up in the air, and it come right ashore—wrecked itself on the shore; and the priest tell the people to destroy it. And they destroy it and he take a piece of the shark and bring it to a dealer and the dealer tell him that the fish was sent by somebody for a certain child of an enemy. And the priest go to that person that send the fish and throw him in jail. And he was in jail for a lifetime, and he die.

As we examine these charms we discover certain things. They are rare, or hard to come by, and anything that is different is thought to contain magical properties. Some of the items are connected with the dead and are usually considered powerful in the otherworld. Some are items that are marine by nature. The people believe that if they possess these objects, the qualities of the object will transfer themselves to the owner. In the case of the knife and the coin, we are dealing with iron and silver, and both of these materials are connected with the faery world. Finally, spirits are thought to be susceptible to odors and therefore it is reasonable to believe that strong-smelling charms will either drive away spirits or replace evil ones with good ones (if the smell be pleasant).

Charms, of course, are used more broadly than just to ensure good fortune. They are also used to preserve good health and cure sickness. This is most frequently done through the use of sympathetic magic or through the idea of transfer; or sometimes through polarity. Since sharks have an abundance of large, sharp teeth, a shark's tooth has long been thought to be good for children to teethe on. Fish skin in the bottom of a boot will help warm a sailor's foot because fish are cold. Turtles live to great age, and if you eat their flesh or keep a bit of shell about you, "it will make you strong, strong in your old age" (West Indies), but if you eat fish heads you will be stupid because fish don't have sense enough to swim out of a net and "what you eat you are."[69]

This of course moves us directly to the realm of marine folk medicine, which appears to observe the same rules as those already mentioned. Because of their isolation, seamen are not prey to the wide variety of sicknesses that appear on the land. Although they have other diseases, their chief complaints seem to stem from diet, from living conditions, and from the hazards of their work. Seasickness, lacerations, suppurating wounds, bumps and contusions probably predominate in their complaint chest. Scurvy is another plague, and exposure to constant wet and damp conditions leads to sore and aching joints, cramps, and sometimes colds or respiratory infections.

Of all maladies, the one that is perhaps the most uncomfortable, and is quite capable of killing a person—seasickness—is the one taken most lightly. Salt water, dry biscuits, tea, pickles and dried fish are all suggested remedies, and the sufferer is always advised to steer clear of sweets. At the same time, there usually is some wag aboard who will induce the tenderfoot to swallow a lump of salt pork on a string and after five minutes haul it up, or suggest he stick his finger down his throat, or quaff a bumper of diesel oil and fish gurry.

Scurvy, the real killer aboard ship, was brought on almost exclusively by diet, and cures for it had been found as early as the time of Captain Cook. The trouble was that Jack Tar simply refused for a long time to eat anything more delicious than ship's biscuit and salt meat. He had never had much fresh meat, fruit or vegetables and found them quite unpalatable. Eventually he was induced to eat onions and potatoes, and to drink lime juice (to the extent that English sailors are still called Limeys and their ships Limejuicers).

Another great annoyance to seamen living in wet or damp clothing for a long time was salt-water boils. To prevent these, for years it has been the practice in Newfoundland to wear copper or brass bracelets. The thinking behind this is, I suppose, that the boils start where the skin is discolored by chafing, and the bracelets discolor the wrists through the action of salt upon them. I am informed by Professor Halpert of the University of Newfoundland that it works.

In order to ensure good health, strength and long life, it was popularly believed that one should drink iron water. An old sea captain from Pond Island, Maine, was in his nineties and had every intention of making a hundred. To do this he would drink a cup of rusty water, which he dipped out of a well-stirred rain barrel with some rusty ballast lying in the bottom.[70] In Newfoundland, sailors swallow shot for the same purpose.[71]

Although sometimes prescribed to remove wrinkles and often associated with faeries, rainwater was not looked on favorably. It was believed to promote worms and to be most unhealthy. If one takes the time to examine an old barrel of rainwater, he will very quickly see the reasoning behind the belief.

For most ailments requiring antiseptic treatment, the three best items were rum, tar and urine. Rum was used to restore hair, disinfect wounds, ease "the misery," kill worms and keep one from catching cold. Today in the Windward Islands, Jack Iron (the "Jersey lightning" of the Caribbean) is good for colds, for strains, to disinfect cuts and to ensure longevity. Tar, applied hot and allowed to cool, will prevent bleeding or act as a poultice; and when chewed is good for the teeth. Aboard old-time sailing ships, a barrel full of urine was kept lashed to the foc's'le. Sailors used it to wash their clothes and hair. The one it bleached, and the other it drove lice from. Below decks the aroma was overpowered by more noxious smells, while topside it was blown off to leeward.

As a matter of interest, excrement has long been used medicinally by the sailor. Hen and cow manure are thought to make excellent poultices, and I was informed in Maine that "nanny-plum tea is the best kind of thing to straighten you out."

Of all cures perhaps the most persistent and most popular were those that had oil as a basic ingredient. Usually the oil came from sea creatures, but even lard and kerosene were used. Oil extracted from seals, porpoises, whales, fish and even sea birds was used to ease strains, prevent colds, stop headaches (along with fish skins wrapped around the head), act as a laxative and promote long life. The very best seal oil came from baby seals and could be extracted in two ways—either by boiling the fat over a fire or through solar extraction.

Over the centuries the "seat of life" has been located in various parts of the anatomy—the heart, the lungs, the brain. Each organ in turn has been probed by medical science and this role discredited until the seat of life has just about left the body and found a new and tenuous home in the "intensive care ward," where it divides its time between dials, vials and tubes. At one time, long ago, it resided in the liver. There are many tales which center around this particular belief, and it is interesting to note that the Grand Banks fishermen always threw the cod livers into a barrel when they gutted the catch. Every morning they would dip up a cup of the liquid and drink it down—and remained, in spite of the dismal climate, healthy and pink-cheeked. From this, medical science discovered the virtue of cod liver oil.[72]

Whale oil has qualities that make it unique. Among them is the fact that it does not cloy, that it will not grow rancid easily, that it is an excellent preservative. Moreover, it comes from the world's largest animal, which in the sea is supple as a snake and "moves faster than a sprat." All of these things make it desirable as a medicine taken internally and externally. In 1969 the first sperm whale in over thirty years was landed on the island of Petite Nevis by the Bequia whale fishermen. An old man badly crippled with arthritis had himself transported there at considerable personal expense, hazard and discomfort. A kind of sling was rigged and he was immersed in the case oil in the whale's head. After a considerable immersion he was hauled out, taken home and reported he felt much improved.[73]

Before leaving the subject of medicine, there is a final belief to be mentioned. Pirates and old-time sailors are so often pictured with earrings that this ornament has become a kind of identifying characteristic of the group. But the earring is prized not as much as an ornament as for its therapeutic value. Among sailors there was a belief that by piercing one ear you would improve the sight in the opposite eye. To this end, sailors had both ears pierced to improve their usefulness on watch, and the skipper pieced the ear on the side opposite to the eye used for the telescope.[74]

Earrings are still worn by sailors, and in North America and the British Isles they are worn by those who have crossed the international date line or the equator. In the West Indies they are worn usually in one ear, and the idea here is no longer to improve vision but to insure good health. The idea has gone ashore and has been taken over by high steel workers in the United States, who wear one after surviving a dangerous fall.

No matter how healthy a person is or what precautions or curative measures he takes, he is not likely to survive if he doesn't watch "the signs." To be sure, the majority deal with the weather, but there are a tremendous number of items that spell bad luck or disaster for ship and crew, as well as an occasional odd thing that presages good luck. In general terms, anything that is different from the normal expectancy for that thing is taken to be portentous. For example, land birds at sea, sea birds ashore, albino creatures, creatures that act out of character with their kind of species, are held as prophets of things to come. A quick sampling might not be amiss.

Pigs, chickens, pigeons, cats, rabbits, foxes, women (particularly virgins, whores, witches, brides, women with empty pails or barefoot), tailors, ministers, priests, churches, flowers, kingfishers, howling dogs, tolling bells, holly wood, cards, dice, walnuts, insane people, empty buckets, brooms, boathooks, pointing at a ship, crows flying in front of a boat, insects, bluebirds, funerals (spectral or real), coffins (real or imagined), rainbows, shooting stars, sharks, porpoises, flying fish, salmon, stowaways, umbrellas, are only a tiny listing of the innumerable items that the sailor must observe if he would learn about the future. The list does, however, give a feeling of the variety. Each item mentioned here has numerous stories illustrating its value. We can retell only a couple, but first a bit of analysis is in order.

Almost every item mentioned can fall into one or more of three categories. Most important, they are detrimental to the ship in some way: cards, dice and women can only lead to trouble at sea. The item does not usually frequent the sea—for example, crows, pigeons, bluebirds—and therefore is thought to bring some kind of warning. The items are connected with the world of the supernatural. Foxes, hares and cats are shapes in which witches can appear. They do unusual things. Hares go mad in March, foxes are too clever to live, and cats carry static electricity in their fur and are familiar with the devil. Ministers, churches and bells all deal with Christianity (a ship's bell is supposed to toll her knell when she goes down). Since the sea is not Christian, it tries to do away with them. The more categories the item fits into, the more viable the belief.

Maine and Massachusetts have had witches for a long time. John Josselyn records there were many large "bottle-bellied" witches, "mostly Quakers," about whom all kinds of tales were told. One of them appeared to a sailor twenty leagues out at sea and he gave her a clout with an axe. Ashore, at that very moment, a woman long suspected of being a witch dropped dead.

More recently a witch near Falmouth, Maine, was annoyed by a fisherman, and warned him he'd be sorry. When he went to launch his boat to go fishing, there sat a large dog in the bow and refused to move. The fisherman got his gun and gave it a double charge of rock salt—which gave the creature a sudden interest in distance. Back in the village, the woman who had warned him nearly died from wounds at home.[75]

In 1971 a fisherman in Saint Lucia told me that the next-door neighbor was a *Gagé* (a kind of witch). She always was begging fish from him, and when she did not get any, she gave his wife fits. He went fishing and brought back "a nice piece fish." Only he sprinkled poisonous powder on it first. "She don't ask for no more fish. In two days her head grow small, small, small and her mouth big and red like fire—and she dead. My wife don't have no more fits."

Usually witches are old people—certainly they are today. Further, they are poor. They can be detected because they can't cry, have no cuticle, can't say the Lord's Prayer, don't bleed, are insensible to pins thrust into them in odd places. In brief, they are people suffering from the infirmities of age, malnutrition and isolation. Since they are different from their neighbors, they are witches. Of course this is not always true. Sometimes men, especially in Scotland, can work sorcery, and young women are said to be able to fly out of their bodies to seek information about ships. Nor, as I have implied, are they easily distinguished in the West Indies, but certainly the foregoing information would serve to identify a large number.

If witches are disliked, so too are sharks. These creatures are great scavengers and will follow a vessel for miles. Among seamen they have gained a reputation similar to the one landsmen attach to wolves. If one cruises by a ship little is made of it, but when they follow a ship in large numbers or for a long time, it is looked upon as a sure sign of death. Sailors will go to considerable effort to be rid of them.

Years ago a vessel was annoyed by a very large shark that would not leave it. Hooks proved of no avail, nor anything else. Eventually it bit one of the crew, and the bos'n decided to take a hand. He procured a shoat and persuaded the sailmaker to fashion a small canvas pouch. This he partially filled with sand. Next he persuaded the smith to heat a small cannon ball white hot. The piglet was then transported to the rail, killed and disembowled. The blood and entrails fell into the water, and the shark rushed in to partake of the meal. Meanwhile the shot was dropped into the pouch, the pouch into the shoat, and the belly sewed up. It was then thrown to the shark, which took it at one gulp.

The crew lined the rail, but for a moment nothing happened. Then the shark suddenly began to bestir itself. Faster it swam and faster. It jumped out of the water, dashed along on its tail, and finally flung itself ashore, much to the amazement of the natives on the beach. The crew rowed over and discovered that the shot had burned a hole entirely through its belly and fallen into the sea.[76]

The longer one deals with these items, the more stories he hears about them, and the more he checks the stories against personal experience, the less likely he is to deride them.

There is a popular belief that an umbrella aboard ship is unlucky. Apparently it is not a very old belief, for the log of a privateer in 1812 recounts "spread-eagling" one of the crew for stealing the skipper's umbrella. In the summer of 1966 my wife brought such an item aboard the boat in Copenhagen. I put it ashore, and she put it back aboard. For the entire summer we had gales, fog, engine trouble, head winds and sickness aboard. At last, through a number of astounding coincidences, we ran aground in the English Channel. The weather began to deteriorate and the prospects looked very bleak. The ship lay over and the umbrella tumbled out. I stuck it in the sand alongside. The tide rose, the vessel floated, the wind moderated, and the rest of that summer and all the next were trouble-free.

The items listed in this chapter do little more than skim the surface. Hundreds of beliefs have been left out and even many categories; the belief that certain days are lucky and unlucky, birthmarks, fishing lore and many others. It is rather obvious, I think, that if sailors didn't believe in them, they wouldn't have so many. It is obvious, too, that if they didn't work— at least part of the time—sailors would abandon them. It could be argued also that, with so many beliefs, some are bound to hit the mark. This is undoubtedly true.

At the same time, these items fill up a vast void in the seaman's life.

There can be little doubt that those which cannot be proved to have any logical basis may indeed have a tremendous psychological value. When the omens are bad, why struggle? Conversely, when the omens are good, one has a chance and keeps trying. When all visible means have failed, a man may yet succeed by trying invisible ones. Sometimes they work, sometimes not.

A fishing vessel once took shelter from a storm in Chesapeake Bay by running up a creek. The weather continued bad for a couple of days, and supplies ran low. The mate said to the captain: "You gotta do something."

"What do you want me to do. I've tried everything!"

"You ain't tried prayin'."

"All right, I'll try that, then," and for about two hours before turning in he prayed for the weather to abate.

Next morning the skipper awoke and poked his head out the scuttle. "How is it?"

"Bout as I expected. A little mite worse."[77]

Sailors have a saying, "When you come to the end of the line, bend on another one." These ideas may do just that and provide the extra scope that will bring ship, cargo and crew to port.

One may not conclude without pointing out that when these items prove to be beneficial, it is not without a couple of nudges from the believers. When a dream comes true, one is more likely to remember it than if it fails. If the dream does not work and the ship founders with all hands, who's to know? Moreover, when people believe in these things, they are reluctant to go against them, especially when it costs them nothing to conform. I once asked an old captain, "Do you think Friday is a bad day to start a voyage?" "I certainly do." "Did you ever sail on Friday?" "Sail on Friday? Hell no. Who'd think of sailing on Friday?"[78]

" 'Tis the whiskey under the peat that makes the profit," Galway hooker, Killala Bay, Ireland

REAVERS, PRIVATEERS AND SMUGGLERS

"My Lord, I am innocentest of them all, but I have
been sworn against by perjured persons."
—CAPTAIN WILLIAM KIDD

IT is one of the ironies of history that the role of pirate should be better
recalled than either of the most dangerous trades on the ocean—privateering and smuggling. It is doubly ironic that the man whose name is best
remembered as the archetypical pirate—Captain William (not Robert)
Kidd—was indeed "the innocentest of them all." It is triply ironic that a
miscreant so foul no sink or drain in Hell is vile enough to contain his
remains should have been knighted for his deeds—Sir Henry Morgan. But
such is fate—when abetted by money and politics.

Of the three professions, the one least remembered is that of privateer,
and of it a word must be said, for some remarkable men were on its rolls
and some of the greatest acts of courage and ship handling were performed
by privateers.

Contrary to popular belief, a privateer was not a pirate (or reaver,
as they were called in Scotland) or a buccaneer; for the pirate preyed on
all flags, a buccaneer on all but his own nation's, and a privateer only upon
those of a country at war with his own. Further, he had a license to do this
—which he purchased from the government—called "a letter of marque and
reprisal," which empowered him to go in search of enemy shipping and
capture it if possible or else destroy it. This "commission" differed from "a
letter of marque," which merely permitted a merchant ship to carry
ordnance to protect herself.

In an age when personal safety and longevity have become for many
people life's chief motivation, violence, war and the rumors of war have be-

315

come anathema. The possibility of modern push-button wars has served to reinforce these views, and it is with some temerity that I mention privateering. Still, when one reads Captain John Smith's account of a sea fight long ago, which he bases on numerous experiences, it helps to explain why men were excited about going privateering. The following is a complete chapter from his 1627 book, *A Sea Grammar*:

How to manage a fight at Sea, with the proper tearmes in a fight largely expressed, and the ordering of a Navy at Sea.

For this master peece of this worke, I confesse I might doe better to leave it to every particular mans conceit as it is, or those of longer practice or more experience; yet because

Many bookes of the Art of War for the land, none for the sea.

I have seene many bookes of the Art of Warre by land, and never any for the Sea, seeing all men so silent in this most difficult service, and there are so many young Captaines, and others that desire to be Captains, who know very little, or nothing at all to any purpose, for their better understanding I have proceeded thus farre; now for this that followes, what I have seene, done, and conceived by my small experience, I referre me to their friendly constructions, and well advised considerations.

A saile, how beares she or stands shee, to wind-ward or lee-ward, set him by the Compasse; he stands right ahead, or on the weather-Bow, or lee-Bow, let flie your colours if you have a consort, else not. Out with all your sailes, a steady man to the helme, sit close to keepe her steady, give him

To give chase.

Wast clothes.
Top armings.

chase or fetch him up; hee holds his owne, no, we gather on him. Captaine, out goes his flag and pendants, also his waste clothes and top armings, which is a long red cloth about three quarters of a yard broad, edged on each side with Calico or white linnen cloth, that goeth round about the ship on the out sides of all her upper workes fore and aft, and before the cubbridge heads, also about the fore and maine tops, as well for the countenance and grace of the ship, as to cover the men for being seene, hee furles and slings his maine yard, in goes his spret-saile. Thus they use to strip themselves into

Fighting sailes.
To hale a ship.

their short sailes, or fighting sailes, which is onely the fore saile, the maine and fore top sailes, because the rest should not be fired nor spoiled; besides they would be troublesome to handle, hinder our sights and the using our armes; he makes ready his close fights fore and aft.

How to begin a fight.

Master how stands the chase? Right on head I say; Well we shall reatch him by and by; What's all ready, Yea, yea, every man to his charge, dowse your top-saile to salute him for the Sea, hale him with a noise of trumpets; Whence is your ship? Of Spaine; Whence is yours? Of England; Are you a Merchant, or a man of War? We are of the Sea; He waves us to lee-ward with his drawne sword, cals amaine for the King of Spaine, and springs his loufe, give him a chase peece with your broad side, and run a good berth ahead of him; Done, done, We have the wind of him, and he tackes about, tacke you about also and keepe your loufe, be yare at the helme, edge in with him, give him a volley of small shot, also your prow and broad side as before, and keepe your loufe; Hee payes us shot for shot; Well, wee shall require him; What are you ready againe, Yea, yea. Try him once more as before, Done, done; Keepe your loufe and loge your ordnance againe; Is all ready? Yea, yea; edge in with him againe, begin with your bow peeces, proceed with your broad side, & let her fall off with the wind, to give her also your full chase, your weather broad side, and bring her round that the sterne may also discharge, and your tackes close aboord againe; Done, done, the wind veeres, the Sea goes too high to boord her, and wee are shot thorow and thorow, and betweene wind and water. Try the pump, beare up the helme,

How to fling a man over boord.

Master let us breathe and refresh a little, and sling a man over boord to stop the leakes; that is, to trusse him up about the middle in a peece of canvas, and a rope to keepe him from sinking, and his armes at liberty, with a malet in the one hand, & a plug lapped in Okum, and well tarred in a tarpawling clout in the other, which he will quickly beat into the hole or holes the bullets made; What cheere mates, is all well? All well, all well, all well; Then make ready to beare up with him againe, and withall your great and small shot charge him, and in the smoke boord him thwart the hawse, on the bow, mid ships, or rather than faile, on his quarter, or make fast your graplings if you can to his close fights and sheare off. Captaine we are fowle on each other, and the ship is on fire, cut any thing to get cleare, and smother the fire with wet cloathes. In such a case they will presently be such friends, as to help one the other all they can to get cleare, lest they both should burne together and sinke; and if they be generous, the fire quenched, drinke kindely one to another; heave their cans over boord, and then begin againe as before.

A consultation & direction in a sea fight, & how they bury their dead.

Well Master, the day is spent, the night drawes on, let us consult. Chirurgion looke to the wounded, and winde up the slaine, with each a weight or bullet at their heads and feet to make them sinke, and give them three gunnes for their funerals, Swabber make cleane the ship, Purser record their Names, Watch be vigilant to keepe your berth to wind-ward that we lose him not in the night, Gunners spunge your Ordnance, Souldiers scowre your peeces, Carpenters about your leakes, Boatswaine and the rest repaire the sailes and shrouds, and Cooke see you observe your directions against the morning watch, Boy, Holla Master Holla, is the kettle boiled, yea, yea, Boatswaine call up the men to prayer and breake fast.

A preparation for a fresh charge.

Boy fetch my cellar of bottels, a health to you all fore and aft, courage my hearts for a fresh charge, Gunners beat open the ports, and out with your lower tire, and bring me from the weather side to the lee, so many peeces as we have ports to beare upon him, Master lay him aboord loufe for loufe, mid ships men see the tops and yards well manned, with stones, fire pots, and brasse bailes, to throw amongst them before we enter, or if we be put off, charge them with all your great and small shot, in the smoke let us enter them in the shrouds, and every squadron at his best advantage, so sounds Drums and Trumpets, and Saint George for England.

How a prise doth yeeld, and how to entertaine him Sea-man like.

They hang out a flag of truce, hale him a maine, a base, or take in his flag, strike their sailes and come aboord with their Captaine, Purser and Gunner, with their commission, cocket, or bils of loading. Out goes the boat, they are lanched from the ship side, entertaine them with a generall cry, God save the Captaine and all the company with the Trumpets sounding, examine them in particular, and then conclude your conditions, with feasting, freedome, or punishment, as you finde occasion; but alwayes have as much care to their wounded as your owne, and if there be either young women or aged men, use them nobly, which is ever the nature of a generous disposition. To conclude, if you surprize him, or enter perforce, you may stow the men, rifle, pillage, or sacke, and cry a prise.[1]

To be a great privateer, a man required many talents. In the first place, he had to have tremendous courage and great prudence, to know when to fight and when to run. He had to be an excellent ship handler, able to carry sail beyond the point where it seemed possible a vessel could bear it, and he had always to be able to maneuver his ship in such a way that he could capture a prize, sack it and get away before being overtaken by a superior vessel. He had to be an expert navigator, for he might remain on station in hostile waters for months at a time without once going ashore. He had to be a psychologist supreme to deal with unruly crews, sometimes fed up with cruising, sometimes overanxious for or overfearful of combat. Finally, he had to know when and where his quarry was likely to be found. An English writer said in 1778 that a privateersman was "a reckless dreadnaught, a daredevil collection of human beings ... ready to obey any order ... a sort of half-horse, half-alligator with a streak of lightning in his composition, with a super-abundance of whiskers as if he held his strength in the composition of his hair."[2]

When possible, a privateer liked to travel in company with a companion. Then when a convoy was sighted, one commander would expose his vessel to the patrol ships, who would immediately give chase. The decoy had to be fast and weatherly enough to escape the more heavily armed escorts and, if he knew his business, he saw to it that he stayed just out of extreme range and did not increase his distance markedly. This gave the pursuers heart, and before they knew it they were miles away from the convoy. Meanwhile, the other privateer would move in and attack the merchantmen, either cutting up the ships at long range with her Long Tom (rifle throwing a nine- to eighteen-pound ball) or sailing alongside one, delivering a broadside and then boarding through the thick smoke.

The first privateers apparently appeared as early as the thirteenth century in England, but they began to flourish around the close of the sixteenth century, when the idea caught on among the French and the Dutch.[3]

A little later on, there was a privateer in England named *The Terrible*. Her commander was Captain Death and the first officer was Mr. Ghost. Although she was eventually captured, her career was meteoric

enough to warrant a song about her, which was still popular in 1814 when
it was copied down by an American prisoner of war at Forton Prison in
England.[4]

Although privateering began in the Old World, it came to fruition in
the New during the American Revolution and the War of 1812. Prior to the
Revolution, North America, because of its isolation from Europe, its many
harbors and its sparse population, and because most of its commerce was
carried on by sea, had spawned a host of pirates; and to insure the success
of any commercial venture merchantmen had to have a reasonable turn of
speed and an arsenal sufficiently strong to beat off attacks by marauders.
Nearly every vessel that left port had aboard a cutlass or two, some
muskets and a "great gunne" or a couple of swivels. Moreover, the crews
were middling fair in their ability to use them. Further, because the British
trade laws forbade Colonial ships to carry a great many commodities,
smuggling had become attractive. Hence the Yankee skippers had long
been accustomed to running their vessels dark and silent through the night,
to eluding pursuit by revenue cutters, to entering and leaving harbors in
weather wild enough to make a landsman cower in his bed—all excellent
training for a privateer.

So popular was the business that by the end of the American Revolution there were 3,000 armed Colonial vessels at sea, and a conservative
estimate would indicate that this force comprised about 120,000 tons of
shipping, 90,000 men, and 18,000 cannon. These vessels captured or destroyed a total of 3,379 British vessels. The booty taken included every
conceivable item from shoes and salt beef to powder and crowbars, and
there can be little doubt that this material contributed substantially toward
providing the needs of the army.[5]

In vessels with such intriguing names as *The Young Hawk, Jack's
Favorite, The Tartan, Rattlesnake, Hornet, The Weasel, Loyal Sam, Thinks
I To Myself Thinks I, Revenge, Black Joke* and *The Bill of Rights*, Ameri-
can seamen roamed the four oceans led by audacious skippers like John
Paul, Miller, Murphy, Reid, Boyle and Barney.[6]

During their lifetimes these men gained such fame that legends
circulated about them throughout the waterfronts of America, but probably
because their deeds were done mostly away from home, the tales about
them are preserved largely in print, and the folk have begun to forget them.
That we may gain insight into their activities, a few brief remarks about
them have been included.

The career of John Paul, the Scot who later added Jones to his name, is too well known to be recorded in any detail here. Every schoolchild knows of his battle with the *Serapis*, of his retort when asked if he surrendered—"I have not yet begun to fight"—and of the disgraceful manner in which he was treated by American politicians. Not so well known are his activities before his famous engagement with the *Serapis*, when he tormented the British in the old *Ranger* and attempted to sack Edinburgh in the *Bon Homme Richard*, about which two stories are still told in Scotland.

It seems that word of Jones' activity had spread all along the coast, and when he appeared off the Firth of Forth the laird of the castle mistook him for a British man-o'-war. Either as an act of patriotism or as a device to ingratiate himself with the British, the laird sent his servant out in a small boat with a keg of powder and a letter requesting the captain to use said powder to destroy the Yankee pirate. Jones took the powder, wrote a thank-you note saying the powder would be used to good advantage, signed it, and sent the servant back with it to the laird.[7]

While this was going on, word came to Edinburgh of Jones' intentions and position. The town was in dismay. There were neither sufficient ordnance nor troops in the area to repel the American force, and it seemed as if the town must fall. About the only thing that could save Edinburgh was a westerly gale, and that seemed unlikely. At any rate, word of the predicament reached the old bishop, and he decided to take stern measures. He ordered a chair and proceeded down to the shore. The tide was out, and the old man marched out onto the flats until his feet were wet. There he planted his chair and there he sat down. Raising his eyes and voice he prayed, "Lord, I have served you well over forty years. Either send a gale to drive away the pirate who is coming to attack our town or I will sit here until I drown. Amen." The tide turned; the water rose to the old man's ankles. Up it came and there sat the Bishop grimly confronting the sea. The water reached his chest. Then the wind hauled west and blew a gale. The old man rose, retrieved his chair and went ashore.[8]

It is hard enough to beat up the Firth of Forth in a close-winded yacht in a heavy breeze. For Jones it was impossible. Every hour he was delayed was an hour in which relieving forces could draw closer. After a day and a night, John Paul Jones and his keg of powder squared away and departed in search of other game.[9]

Another skipper in a warmer clime also had a brush with the English. Captain Miller in *Jack's Favorite* sailed into the West Indian harbor of St. Barts. He had not been there very long when a British sloop of war, the

Subtile, arrived. Since the harbor was neutral the Englishman could do nothing, but he was irate to think of an American "pirate" in the same harbor with him, and he swore an oath that he "would follow and take the damned Yankee Privateer if he went to Hell for her." Such oaths have never been considered wise by seamen, but when *Jack's Favorite* cleared port the *Subtile* was close astern. Miller, feeling there was little to be gained from engaging a man-o'-war, shook out all his canvas and attempted to outsail the Englishman, who did likewise. At this point a tremendous squall sprang up, but both vessels continued to carry all the sail they could lug. When it blew itself out *Jack's Favorite* was sailing on an empty sea. Miller immediately went about and retraced his course, but all that was ever found of the *Subtile* were a few hats floating in the sea.[10]

Captain Staples of New York in the *York* made a nearly fatal error by mistaking a British man-o'-war, the *Lord Somers,* for a merchantman and engaging her. It was not until the Britisher opened his ports that Staples realized his mistake, and then it was nearly too late. The *York* received terrible fire and was badly cut up—and Staples was mortally wounded. He was carried below and attended by a surgeon. Staples asked if his wound was fatal. When he learned it was, he sent for the first lieutenant, Mr. Burch, and made one of the remarks for which seamen have from time to time been famous. Staples told the officer that he was mortally wounded and that the ship was in desperate straits. Then he turned over the command, saying, "I am too far gone to speak. Take care of yourself and do the best you can." Burch did. The *York* was got clear and limped back to Baltimore.[11]

That these commanders were made of sturdy stuff can be seen in the action of Captain Champlin of New London. In an engagement with a frigate off the Surinam River, his vessel, *Joel Barlow,* was badly mauled (as was the frigate) and he was shot through the shoulder. Loss of blood forced him to retire to his cabin, where he overheard his officers suggesting that they surrender the vessel. Champlin drew his pistol and cocked it. "Tell the officers and men that if anyone dare strike the colors I will immediately fire into the magazine and send us all to Hell together."[12]

The *General Armstrong,* after a long and highly successful career under her commander, Samuel Reid, put into the neutral port of Fayal for water. While the operation was in progress a small flotilla of British men-o'-war hove upon the scene. They were the British armed brigs *Carnation* and *Plantagenet* and the frigate *Rota.* Suspecting he might be attacked, Reid had the *Armstrong* rowed in under the shore and placed springs on his cable to enable him to veer his vessel at will. As he was doing this he was attacked by boats from the *Carnation*, which he shot to pieces. Fearing a similar attack, he moved the privateer still closer to shore and awaited events.

Reid's appraisal of the affair proved correct, for about midnight, under a full moon, the *General Armstrong* was attacked by twelve boats. The result was catastrophic. Many were sunk by cannon fire, and those who reached the privateer and attempted to board were cut to ribbons. After forty minutes what was left of the boarding party fled.

Next morning the *Carnation* took up the attack but was so severely damaged she was forced to retire. By this time it became obvious to Reid that he could not escape. The *Rota* and *Plantagenet* were moving in, and several of the *General Armstrong*'s guns were out of order. Reid ordered the vessel scuttled and he and his crew escaped to shore.

The English had won the day, but it was one of the most costly battles in the entire annals of the British Navy. When the smoke had cleared away the Americans had suffered 2 killed and 7 wounded (one when his over-loaded musket blew up), while the British lost 120 killed and 180 wounded, including the captain of the *Rota*—who lost a leg, but preferred to let on it was from "being tred on by an ox" rather than admit it was from American gunfire.[13]

At the expense of a pun, Captain Boyle began his meteoric career in the *Comet*. In 1812 he ran the blockade of the Chesapeake on a wild night and showed up off Brazil. Off Pernambuco he fell in with three English vessels and a Portuguese brig "large enough to hoist the *Comet* aboard." The four mounted fifty-four guns, but the *Comet* managed to destroy the entire fleet.

Boyle next proceeded to the West Indies, eluded the frigate *Surprise*, captured three larger vessels, and played cat and mouse with the armed brig *Swaggerer* until he became bored with the game and proceeded to capture another vessel, after which he returned to Baltimore through the blockade.

The privateersman then took command of the brig *Chasseur*, which carried sixteen twelve-pounders and a crew of one hundred. In her he made a cruise to the English Channel, taking eighteen valuable prizes on the way. Boyle, however, was greatly annoyed at Admirals Cochrane and Warren, who declared the entire coast of the United States blockaded. To get even, Boyle made a similar proclamation, declaring that the *Chasseur* was blockading all of England—which proclamation he had posted on the bulletin board at Lloyds of London.[14]

Of all the men who sailed under letters of marque and reprisal, none was equal to Joshua Barney of Maryland in skill, color or success. A man in every way cut out to be a legendary hero, he lies buried in a cemetery in Pittsburgh, where he died of a wound received defending Washington, D.C.—almost unknown. His picture hangs in the United States Naval Academy, an alley is named for him in Newport, Rhode Island, and an inhospitable bit of shingle near New Bedford, Massachusetts, is known as Barney's Joy.

When he was fifteen, Barney found himself in command of a sinking merchantman in the wintry Atlantic. He saved the vessel and returned home with a handsome profit.

When the Revolution broke out he joined the Navy, and as a masters' mate of the *Hornet* was the first officer to fly the American flag. He then set out to take part in the attack on Nassau under the command of Ezek Hopkins and in company with a Scot named John Paul Jones. Barney's vessel met with foul weather and put back to Baltimore, where the young man, now sixteen, joined the *Wasp* and his career blossomed.

In all, Barney was the victor in thirty out of thirty-five pitched battles, was thrice imprisoned and twice escaped (once disguised as a girl), was shipwrecked twice, served as a commodore in the French Navy, and put down at least one mutiny. Of them all, four events are of interest here. The first is a ridiculous incident that took place when he was in the *Rossi*. Barney had had a successful cruise, having taken 1.5 million dollars worth of enemy shipping in ninety days, and sailed into Newport to refit. The people of that town were delighted. They lined the waterfront waving handkerchiefs and cheering. They even gave him a naval salute from the fort. Not to be outdone, and to show his appreciation, Barney ran out his guns and fired a broadside. Unfortunately he had forgotten that the guns were shotted, and the result was that the town was severely battered and one innocent bystander lost a foot.[15]

On another occasion Barney was bound for Bordeaux in a small privateer with a load of tobacco. On the way across he captured a vessel loaded with a cargo of crowbars, some of which he took into his ship. Shortly after this he was pursued by a large British privateer named the *Rosebud*. Barney tried to get clear, but the *Rosebud* was a better sailor and slowly gained on him until he was in reach of the *Rosebud*'s Long Toms. At this point Captain Duncan and Captain Barney made a discovery. Barney's ship had no stern ports, so she could not return the Englishman's fire, and all the *Rosebud* had to do was to lie astern and pound the American to pieces.

During the night Barney had a hole cut in his stern and a six-pounder mounted in his cabin. He also had a canvas dodger designed and fitted to cover this new gun port. Next morning the *Rosebud* again commenced firing from astern and Barney allowed her to come very close. At the opportune moment he dropped the canvas, ran out his gun, and delivered a charge into the bows of the unsuspecting Englishman. What made things even more shocking was that instead of loading his six-pounder with conventional ammunition, he had crammed it full of crowbars. The result was catastrophic. Forty men were killed, the rigging was shot away and the *Rosebud's* mast so damaged she had to break off the battle to save herself, while Barney went on to Bordeaux to sell his tobacco.[16]

The other two events in which Barney participated were his destruction of the *General Monk* in twenty minutes with the *Hyder Ally*, termed one of the most brilliant naval battles of the War of 1812[17] and his defense of Washington, D.C., when he held the entire British army at bay for six hours.

In March 1782 Barney returned from an eighteen-month stay in Europe and immediately took command of the *Hyder Ally*, then being converted to a sloop of war mounting sixteen six-pounders. To help obtain a crew, Philip Freneau had written a poem about her and her new commander—and was soon to write another about her remarkable action.[18]

On April 8 she got under way to escort eight merchantmen to sea off the Delaware Capes. Unfortunately the wind hauled ahead and the fleet anchored inside the Capes. There they were discovered by the frigate *Quebec*, which could not get at them owing to her deep draft. Accordingly, Captain Rogers in the *General Monk* (originally the *General Washington* before being captured and renamed), a frigate mounting twenty twelve-pounders with a crew of 120, was ordered to attack the fleet with the aid of some privateers. Rogers was known as a formidable officer, having sent in over sixty prizes and defeated an American frigate. Moreover, his crews were well trained.

Two of the English privateers refused to join the action and another, the *Fair American*, distinguished herself by running aground. Rogers bore down on the *Hyder Ally* alone with the intention of boarding. Barney meanwhile climbed on top of the binnacle and instructed the helmsman that he should repeat all commands and then execute them in reverse.

When the *General Monk* was close aboard, Barney bawled, "Hard aport." The helmsman threw her hard astarboard; but Rogers, hearing the order, ordered his helm adjusted to meet it and was surprised to find the *Hyder Ally* across him. Before Rogers could do anything, the Britisher was locked into the Yankee at an angle where his guns could be brought to bear. The American ship then proceeded to pour in twenty broadsides in twenty-six minutes—a remarkable feat even for a seasoned crew. Hat and coat riddled with shot, Barney maintained his position on the binnacle with sword in hand until a round shot hit his perch and knocked him down. At the end of twenty-six minutes the *General Monk* struck, leaving over a third of the crew killed or wounded. Barney then hoisted British colors on both vessels, thereby fooling the *Quebec* long enough to allow him to slip past her with his prize, and Joshua Barney returned to Philadelphia and a wild reception.[19]

Barney's final action came on shore during the War of 1812. The British had begun their march which ended in burning the Capitol. The American army had broken and fled in panic, leaving the way clear to Washington. The British marched through the little city of Bladensburg, with the extreme heat their sole annoyance. About a mile outside town there was a small hill and atop it waited Joshua Barney with five naval guns and six hundred men. As in the *Hyder Ally* affair Barney exposed himself, this time on a horse for want of a binnacle; and, although severely wounded in the thigh—a wound which caused his death later in Pittsburgh —he refused to dismount until his horse was killed under him.

The six hundred men and five cannon could not be dislodged, and for six hours the attack on Washington was halted. At last the commander collapsed from loss of blood, the ammunition gave out, and the bluejackets were forced to surrender.[20]

Strangely enough, the affair with the crowbars has remained in oral tradition, while the rest of the events with which Barney was associated are largely forgotten by the folk and the historian—while lesser men like Davy Crockett and Ethan Allen are remembered by both.[21]

If deeds like the ones mentioned have become buried in the dust of time, one would expect the same fate to befall lesser men, but this is not the case. All along the Eastern seaboard the privateers have left a thin but tenacious trace. In Maine there are the earlier mentioned Bunker's Cove, Bunker's Ledge, the Bunker and Bunker's Whore. To these we can add Morris' Mistake, Bowen's Ledge and Beals' Island—all names derivative from privateering days and about which stories are still told.

Captain Bunker, unlike Barney and Reid and the others just mentioned, seems to have concentrated his energies along the Maine coast. Here he could lie concealed behind a convenient island and pounce on coastal shipping as it went by. His favorite spot was a tiny blind cove on

Roque Island. When he was waiting for a coaster to sail by or was pursued by men-o'-war, he would anchor in this little bay and secure his stern to the shore. He would tie spruce trees to his mast and remain so well hidden that the English vessels would pass by only a few hundred yards away without detecting him. This stunt of tying foliage to the spars appears to have been very popular, for it was practiced in many places. Drake is said to have done it at Drake's Pool near Crosshaven, Ireland, and an English fleet is said to have hidden from the French by tying palm trees to its masts while it lay in Marigot Bay, St. Lucia. (The fact that there is scarcely room for two frigates in that cove does not seem to have occurred to anyone.)

Bunker's greatest deed, and the one which probably gave him legendary stature amongst the folk, was his seizure of an English supply ship. The people on Mt. Desert Island were very near starvation, thanks to the effective blockade by the British during the Revolution. Down in Tenants Harbor, half a day's sail to the southwest, lay a British ship bulging with food. On Christmas Eve it began to snow, and out of the snowstorm came Bunker (in a canoe, with one helper) to cut out the supply ship and sail her to Mt. Desert—where she arrived on Christmas Day, and supplied the whole island with a Christmas dinner, and a good many dinners thereafter.[22]

It has often seemed to me that a satisfactory definition of a patriot is a successful traitor and *vice versa*. The same relationship holds true between privateer and pirate. Properly speaking, of course, a pirate is one who preys on all shipping. In point of fact, such is not the case. Sir Francis Drake was a pirate according to the Spanish; as late as 1926 John Paul Jones was called "pirate" in the *Encyclopaedia Britannica*, then an English publication. Henry Morgan, a homicidal psychotic who practiced murder by every conceivable method upon the entire human race, through prudent application of a fortune in gold obtained by torture and extortion became a Knight. He eased his declining days by hanging those of his former friends, colleagues and associates whom he had not already hanged, poisoned, drowned, stabbed, shot, crushed, marooned or roasted.[23] On the other hand, the mate of the *Quedah Merchant* was proscribed a pirate and the cargo of his ship was divided amongst Massachusetts dignitaries to defray the cost incurred by his trial. Just before he was hanged, he warned people against coming to Boston with too much money "lest they be hanged for it." Finally, after two hundred years it was discovered that one of the most notorious of all pirates was in fact an innocent privateer who was hanged because he had stumbled onto some embarrassing political intrigue. His given name was William Kidd, but after his death it was corrupted to Robert Kydd.

The popular concept of Kidd to this day is that he was an atheist, a murderer, a man who seized any and all vessels on the high seas; and that he amassed a great fortune which is buried somewhere (I will have occasion to speak of this later). Perhaps the best way to measure his image in the public eye is to quote selectively from the still popular, scurrilous broadside written about him.

> My name is Robert Kydd, as I sailed, as I sailed.
> My name is Robert Kydd as I sailed.
> My name is Robert Kydd, God's Laws I did forbid
> And much wickedness I did, as I sailed.
>
> . . . My parents taught me well to shun the gates of hell
> But against them I rebelled . . .
>
> . . . I had a Bible in my hand at my fathers great command.
> But I sank it in the sand . . .
>
> . . . I murdered William Moore, and left him in his grave
> Not many miles from shore . . .
>
> . . . And being cruel still next my gunner I did kill
> And his precious blood did spill . . .
>
> . . . My mate took sick and died which me much terrified
> When he called me to his side . . .
>
> . . . I was sick and nigh to death when I vowed with every breath
> To walk in Jesus' ways . . .
>
> . . . My repentence lasted not and my vows I soon forgot
> Hell is my just lot . . .
>
> . . . I spied three ships from Spain and fired on them amain
> Till most of them were slain . . .
>
> . . . I had ninty bars of gold and dubloons manifold
> And riches uncontrolled . . .
>
> . . . Then being o'er taken at last and into prison cast
> And sentence being passed, and I must die.
>
> . . . Now to Execution Deck where the many thousand flock
> And many there will mock, and I must die.
>
> . . . So it's up a rope I go, with my friends all down below
> Saying Bill we told you so . . .

... Come all you young and old, you are welcome to my gold,
For by it I have lost my soul ...

... Take warning now from me and shun bad company
Or you'll go to hell with me . . .[24]

Actually, the correct story of Captain Kidd is a tragic one. Because he had been a loyal, competent and courageous sea captain, he was chosen to command the *Venture Galley* and go in pursuit of Thomas Tew, a one-time friend and associate who had been proclaimed pirate and was thought to be in the vicinity of Madagascar. En route he was empowered to pursue and capture such vessels belonging to enemies of England as fell in his way. Earl Bellomont was one of his sponsors in this venture, and the Earl hoped to make some money.

Kidd's voyage was unfortunate from the outset. In order to recruit a crew he had to go to the prisons before he found enough men to man his ship. He had not been at sea long when a mutiny broke out led by the bos'n, named Moore. Kidd belted him over the head with a small oak bucket worth six shillings. Moore fell down an open hatch and was killed. Next he ran into a fleet of ships belonging to the East India Company. In order to enhance the coffers of the Company, they had been chartered to the enemy and were doing a thriving business under French colors. Kidd, upon discovering who they were, seized them as hostiles, which act at one stroke made him wealthy, cut severely into the East India Company's profits and threatened to expose the Company and its backers in the worst possible light.

Eventually Kidd returned to Newport, Rhode Island. He knew he had been proscribed a pirate, but he sent word of his arrival to Governor Bellomont in Boston, alleging that he had hidden a ship load of goods in the West Indies and had a large cargo of gold with him. Bellomont promised to help him if he'd give up the French passes taken from the Indiamen and the gold. Kidd then sailed out of Newport, but returned after three days with an empty ship and surrendered himself and the French passes to the Governor.

Once he was in custody, Bellomont's attitude toward Kidd changed. Within a few days he found himself in prison, then in double irons. In this condition he was transported to London's Newgate Prison and eventually tried for the murder of William Moore. An act such as this in Kidd's day was scarcely considered reprehensible, but he was summarily convicted.

He was then tried for piracy, and again the conviction was swift. Kidd had based his whole defense on the two French passes that he had given Bellomont, but when his trial began the passes had vanished, and only Kidd seemed to know anything about them.

Kidd's ignominy was not yet complete. On May 23, 1701, he was marched to Execution Dock and there hanged with six companions. At the first attempt the rope broke and the wretched man fell to the ground. Another rope was found and this one proved stout enough. Kidd was hanged and allowed to dangle while three tides passed under his body before his remains were cut down and encased in an iron cage. He was then hung up as a warning to others to lead more prudent lives. He was still swinging there when Benjamin Franklin visited London years later, and the shadows of his life, real or fictitious, still serve as examples of what evil men will do for fame and fortune. Even the French passes, when they were found two hundred years later, could not do his memory much good, for the mark of pirate lies too heavily upon him to be eradicated by simple facts.[25]

Of quite a different character was Ned Lowe, a freebooter who flourished after Kidd. He appears to have been a misanthrope with an especial hatred for Puritans. Whenever he captured any of these unfortunates, he prepared tortures for them. He sliced off their ears and their noses, broiled them before their eyes and made them eat them.

Rather than go on the grand voyage to Africa and beyond, Lowe contented himself with acts of piracy from the West Indies to the Grand Banks of Newfoundland. Most of his activities therefore were confined either to fishermen or simple traders and his booty was small. Still, because of his atrocities he was feared perhaps more than any other pirate.

Eventually he overstepped himself by seizing a vessel from Block Island, Rhode Island, and maiming the crew before cutting them adrift in their lifeboat without oars, sail or provisions. At this time Rhode Island—"that hotbed of Quakers and Baptists"—was considered immune to the attacks of pirates, for it was here that their contraband was traded and it was here that many pirates lived—men such as Thomas Tew, Irish, English, William Avery—and it was here that Kidd had come because he knew he would not be molested by the authorities.

Instead of vanishing, the fishing boat with her maimed crew were found, and the hue and cry went up. Lowe escaped, only to be subsequently marooned by his own men, but twenty-six of his crew were brought to

Newport. They were tried, found guilty, hanged on Long Wharf, and buried on nearby Goat Island between high and low water.

The story was still told along the waterfront in this century that these twenty-six men were the epitome of evil. Twenty-six men were captured, brought in, tried and convicted of piracy, and sentenced to hang. They were then lodged in jail in double irons and under double locks. The night before the execution there were twenty-six prisoners, but when the guard came for them there were only twenty-five. Neither the window nor the door had been forced, but there was a strong smell of sulfur and smoke throughout the jail![26]

Pirates were thick not only in North American waters, but in Europe and the British Isles as well. One was a German named Stoertebeker. He plied his trade in the North Sea and the Baltic, but two stories about him are still extant in Grenada. When he was finally captured with his entire crew, they were tried and all were condemned to be beheaded. The judge, as was customary at that time, told Stoertebeker that he could make one request before he died and that it would be honored. The skipper's wish was an unusual one. He asked that his crew be lined up in a row, that he be beheaded standing up, and that all the men he could run past after the headsman's axe had fallen be set free.

On the appointed day the crew were lined up and the captain's head was severed from his body. The headless, spurting trunk staggered past fourteen of the crew before it finally fell to the ground.

Before he died, the authorities tried every way they knew how to find out where his treasure was hidden, but to no avail. After his death they searched in vain. There was none aboard his ship and there was no map or clue to its whereabouts. At last, when his ship was destroyed, the gold was found inside the masts.[27]

The criteria by which the folk select objects to be retained in their memory passeth understanding. They retain "The waiter roared it through the hall/We don't serve bread with one fish ball" with the same facility they preserve "The wind shall blow through his bones forevermore." The only reasonable explanation is that the event or the individual about whom they speak was involved at that time in circumstances with great emotional impact. Over the years the environment of the event has been forgotten and only the flat doggerel remains. Such is the tale of the reaver of Loch Boisdale, and why it should remain when other stories have been forgotten is a complete mystery.

At the entrance to Loch Boisdale in South Uist there is a tiny islet called Calvay. Should one land there, one can just make out the ruins of an ancient fort built by Ian Brecht (Ian of the Spots—" 'Tis a term usually applied to a cow, but this fellow somehow survived smallpox"). There he lived with his crew, and everyone in the islands was terrified of him. One day he left his fort and came onto the main island to go for a walk. Eventually he came to a pleasant place on the south side of the island and sat down in a little hollow and fell asleep.

There was an old woman there tending cattle, and she noticed the pirate dozing in the glen. Above him on the side of the hill was a huge boulder. The old woman crept up to it and gave it a great shove. The boulder plunged down the hillside and crushed the pirate where he slept. An old woman had done what the rest of the community had been unable to accomplish. "And to this day the place remains 'Brecht's Hollow'."[28]

A series of stories of far greater magnitude surround the figure of another pirate, this one a female who resided in the west of Ireland. Her name was Grace O'Malley, but she was commonly called Grana Weil (spelled variously Granny Wale and Granuaile) Queen of the West, or "the Great Sea Pirate."

Female pirates were not unknown, of course. Two famous ones were Mary Reed and Anne Bonney—both street women who had turned to piracy for a better living and did well by it for a time. Mary Reed was hanged; Anne Bonney was sentenced to be hanged but the execution was deferred until after her child was born. Before the noose could be fitted to her neck she was again pregnant, and so she persevered and saved her life. Her character can best be measured by an event which took place in prison. Her husband, Captain Rackham, was sentenced to hang for piracy, and his last wish was to see his wife. Said Anne Bonney, "Had you fought like a man, you would not need to be hanged like a dog."[29]

There are two sides to the life of Grace O'Malley—the historical side and the one preserved through oral tradition. It is worth while to give both sides that one may better understand the working of the folk mind in developing a legend. Since the historical one is briefest, it will be set down first with an occasional comment.

Scholarship says she was born on Clare Island in 1530, daughter of Dubhdara (Black Oak) O'Malley, lord of the region in Connacht known as The Owles. While still a young girl she climbed a cliff and killed a brood of eagles that had been harrassing the sheep on her father's island. During the struggle with the birds in their eyrie she was severely gashed in the forehead and bore the scar the rest of her days.[30]

In 1550 she married Donald O'Flaherty, who was killed in battle on the Aran islands—but not before Grace had borne him three children—one of whom was named Murrough—and had built a castle. After his death she married a man named Burke, better known as Iron Dick. He, too, had a castle and as soon as he died it became the property of his widow. By Burke she also had children—one of whom, named Tibbot of the Ships, was born at sea.

Grace had a keen interest in castles and ships and amassed enough of the latter to have a fleet and to acquire numerous strongholds, either inheriting them through marriage or by building them herself. Among others she built one at Inishbofin to protect her fleet which she kept in the little harbor there. This woman of the O'Malley's had long been "potent on land and sea" and she did her best to live up to her reputation. According to William O'Brien, this "gracious and charming" lady (despite her scarification and a long life at sea) had just given birth to Tibbot when she was attacked by a Turkish vessel. She instantly left her delivery berth and rushed on deck, a blunderbuss in each hand, and drove the enemy off.[31]

After a long life of warfare, some as a pirate, some against England, she retired from the roving trade and went to visit Queen Elizabeth. This was in 1593. At that time her children and her brother were in English hands, and she represented herself as a penniless and broken woman while she sued for the release of her family and a pension for herself. Elizabeth bowed at least in part to these requests, and referred to Grace as "an old woman" (but three year's Elizabeth's senior). But since charity was never one of the virtues associated with the Queen, it is doubtful Grace O'Malley was as helpless as was pretended, else Elizabeth would have given her nothing.

On her return to Ireland she was slighted by the owners of Howth castle, and revenged herself by kidnapping the heir. Finally her son Tibbot became a peer of the realm. This is the historical side; the folk memory follows.[32]

In the West of Ireland there is a saying to the effect that all law belongs to God and the O'Malleys and God isn't always there. Black Oaks' daughter was truly a chip from the tree.

Grace was born at sea and as a child received a severe wound in the forehead while killing a marauding group of eagles who were carrying off sheep on Clare. After she recovered from this wound she attempted to go to sea with her father and when he refused she disguised herself as a boy and went anyway. Once out to sea she revealed her identity and performed so well he allowed her to go with him thereafter. (When one realizes that these crews were made up almost entirely of family members, this tale becomes quickly apocryphal.)

Her first husband, Donald O'Flaherty, was killed in an attack on the Aran Islands, but after him she had a succession of husbands all of whom came to sudden and untimely ends, but not before their wills had been drawn leaving their property to Grace. One husband, named Burke, she married agreeing to make him Lord of the Castle on Clare after a stipulated period. However, before the time was up, Burke, ate something that did not agree with him and she became mistress of his castle at Achillbeg opposite her own at Clare.

These castles that she acquired one after another spanned a considerable stretch of sea coast. Each was in sight of another, and should an attack be started against her at any point from Aran Island in the south almost to Tory Island in the north, a bale fire would be lighted and seen by the next castle, which would ignite its fire. In a matter of moments the coast would be ablaze; the fires would be seen at Clare and Grace's ships —so powerful that Queen Elizabeth wanted no part in attacking them— would rush to the rescue.

By her various husbands she had numerous children—one was born at sea whom she named Mweedn, "Child of the Sea," and lived, according to my informant, to become "a great admiral." However, she does not seem to have been an exemplary parent. Once while she was being rowed in a large curragh from the castle at Achillbeg to the one at Clare, a storm blew up and the sea became very rough. One of her sons by Burke fell overboard, but he grabbed the gunwale of the curragh with one hand and started to pull himself back aboard. Whether she believed the old adage about "what the sea wants," or feared he might upset the frail boat, or had some other reason is not known, but no sooner had he grabbed the gunwale than she chopped off his hand. The startled youth said, "But I was only going to get back aboard." "If you had been a true O'Malley," said his mother, "you'd not have fallen overboard in the first place," and she rowed away, leaving the maimed youth to drown or bleed to death.

If she was harder on her children than most mothers, she was a better sea fighter than most men. One story tells how she defeated the Spanish pirate, Don Bosco of Inishbofin, and another claims she took a Spanish fleet off Clare. (Whether or not Grana Weil did these things would be hard to prove, but the facts behind the tales are identifiable. Oliver Cromwell's fort stands on the site of the one built by Bosco—of whom little else is known save that he was "a Spanish pyrate." It is also a known fact that some of the shattered Armada went past Clare, that one ship sank near there, and that the O'Malleys put hundreds of Spaniards to the sword, but whether this was an act of Grana Weil or Dubhdara O'Malley would be hard to prove.[33]

Perhaps her greatest victory came in a battle with a Spaniard off Shark Island near Inishbofin. Granuaile was no longer young and she was tired, so she turned in and went to sleep. Outside her cabin the battle raged furiously and the Spanish began to dominate. When things looked hopeless, one of the Irish crew hurried to the cabin and woke up his commander. As soon as she heard how things stood, Grace grabbed her sword and pistol and rushed on deck in her nightdress, gray hair streaming down her back. A Spaniard, not knowing there was a woman aboard, saw this apparition wreathed in smoke coming at him sword in hand. He spread the alarm and the Spaniards, convinced they were looking at a ghost, threw down their arms.

Her fame spread abroad and reached the ears of Elizabeth, who immediately invited her to come to court. Three stories are told about her reaction. One says she refused to go on the grounds that she was superior to Elizabeth. A second story has it that she went, and appeared in court stripped to the waist, which startled the old Queen no end. (However, since she was sixty-three at the time it's not likely that she set a fashion precedent.) A third tale says that she went to court and, being very tall, contrived to place herself in a position where Elizabeth was forced to look up at her—an act that the old sororicide found very disquieting.

One story (of many) says that, on her return from visiting Elizabeth, she stopped at Howth Castle near Dublin for lunch. The porter refused to admit her for some reason and the O'Malley retired in rage. As she was leaving the castle she saw a child with his nurse and, suspecting that he was attached to Castle Howth, she kidnapped him and held him for ransom. It turned out that he was indeed the heir to the castle, and his parents, realizing the futility of attacking Grace O'Malley in her home territory, agreed to ransom him. The tribute that Grace exacted was that the gate of Howth Castle, henceforth forever, be never locked and that there always be an extra place laid at the table—both of which things, according to my informant, are still faithfully performed.

After the old lady finally died, she was buried on Clare Island and a tombstone erected with a little niche in the top where her skull was placed, and where it is supposed to remain to the present time. During the present century some English scientists were said to have come to the island to steal the head. They had hardly got into their boat when a terrible storm sprang up. It continued until the culprits put back to the island and restored the skull to its niche.

The people of Clare were very much disturbed by this act and, to prevent its happening again, they hid the head of Grace O'Malley and substituted the skull of a child in its place. It turned out that they were prudent, for another group of Englishmen did steal that skull and take it to London. Naturally, the sea made no objections, and the inhabitants inserted another set of head bones in the niche.

In the west of Ireland the stature of this woman has grown tremendously. In Inishbofin it is said that she started a castle, and a huge pile of jumbled rock is pointed out as its remains. She is also supposed to be responsible for a tremendous natural fissure in the island, which the natives say was dug by her to make a canal but was abandoned at the same time she abandoned the castle.

Granuaile is still very viable. To make polite conversation one day in Galway, I asked a taxi driver if he had heard of this remarkable woman.

"Grana Weil? You mean Mother Ireland?"

"No, the other one."

"Oh, you mean Grana Weil, Queen of the West, the Great Sea Pirate?"

"Yes, that's the one. What do you know of her?"

"Well, I know she was a grand, great woman. Queen Victoria invited her to her Diamond Jubilee and she came in a dress without no top."

There is more to the legend of Grana Weil. I am referring to her treasure, but before talking about this aspect of her life a few words are necessary about treasure in general.

To the average person, treasure and pirates go together like ham and eggs. But to seafaring people, and to the folk in general, this is not entirely the case. Besides being pirate booty, sometimes "treasure" is something cast up or occasioned by the sea—ambergris, for instance, or a sunken wreck loaded with money or some other valuable commodity. Treasure also meant money or valuables hidden away for safekeeping.

When one studies treasure lore, one soon discovers that it divides neatly into four parts. First is the lore of how and when to bury it. Second is how to find out about it. Third comes how to get it,[34] and finally what are the results of finding treasure. Each of these aspects has a number of fascinating stereotypes with it.

Of them all, the stories of ambergris are the most stereotyped. Ambergris is almost always discovered, not recognized, and is wasted, allowed to rot or taken from the finder by a trickster. Captain Erling Taubs told me of a man who found several hundred pounds of it on his island in the Pacific. He fed it to his hens, and when only an ounce or two remained discovered it was ambergris. The people of Bequia recall finding some, but they didn't recognize it immediately and it all rotted away. In New England a large lump came ashore and the natives, disliking the smell, burned most of it before they noted their error. In Rhode Island some was found and taken to the local druggist, who said it was some waste material which he would dispose of to save the finders effort; shortly thereafter he retired from mixing potions and began living in a manner to which he had long felt he should be accustomed.

In North America there are myriads of treasure stories—stories dealing with sea treasures and treasures of highwaymen far from the ocean. Of them all, three of the best known and most interesting are those of Kidd's treasure, Lafitte's and the treasure of Oak Island, Nova Scotia.

When Kidd sailed into Newport, he reported that he had aboard a large treasure in metal. He had, he said, another in perishable commodities hidden away in the West Indies. It will be recalled that he then left Newport for three days and returned with his ship empty. It has been assumed by most people that he buried a treasure of great worth somewhere and that it still lies hid. This treasure has been reported in innumerable places from Oak Island, Nova Scotia, to Charleston, South Carolina. Not only that, but it is also supposed to be buried somewhere along the Hudson between New York and Albany, and I have even heard it said that he buried it in a wretched little gap in the mountains near Bristol, Vermont—an area three hundred miles from the sea and largely unexplored in Kidd's day. Between these cardinal points the "very spot" is located in every out-of-the-way place imaginable in Maine, Massachusetts, Rhode Island, Connecticut, New York, New Jersey, Nova Scotia, Newfoundland and the Labrador coast.

If Kidd had a treasure and did in fact bury it, there are certain logistical facts that must be observed. The first is the matter of the three days. About the best a vessel of those days could do was around seventy-five to one hundred nautical miles per day. And Kidd's vessel had a foul bottom. It would take a decent period of time to anchor, secure the ship, dig the hole, return to the boat and get under way. At the most, he had a little over a day for going or coming, and a whole day occupied with burying the treasure. It could not, then, have been stashed away much west of Gardiners Island off the tip of Long Island, or east of the extreme end of Cape Cod. In point of fact, it is probably hidden on Gardiners

Island—where lived Lion Gardiner, a close friend of Kidd's—or Fishers Island, Block Island or one of the Elizabeth Islands in Buzzards Bay. All were sparsely populated, had fairly adequate harbors, and were not too far from Newport.

These islands have been spaded over by treasure seekers, as has a good part of the rest of the northeast of North America. Aside from some treasure recovered immediately after his capture, to this day no one has acknowledged finding it, none has turned up, and there is considerable likelihood that none ever will.

Interestingly enough, great stimulus was given the Kidd legend during the 1930s, shortly after the discovery of the French passes in the Public Records Office. After two hundred years a large desk and three huge chests belonging to Kidd turned up. Each and every one contained a secret compartment, and in each compartment was discovered an "authentic" map of what was thought to be a treasure island. Unfortunately, the latitude and longitude of the island had been improperly worked, but the caption stated that it was located in the China Sea—which, through the peculiar machinations of the human mind, has led some people to think the island lay off the New England coast.[35]

Kidd, of course, is not the only pirate who ever buried treasure. Even Ned Lowe is supposed to have buried a treasure which he got from "a Spanish galleon." It lies under a large flat rock on Pond Island, Casco Bay, Maine. In all, it contains three large bars of silver, a trunk full of silver and a trunk full of gems. Its location was revealed to a seeker by an Indian fortune-teller, who said he should share it with a friend. The greedy wretch tried to get it all and was frightened off at the last moment.[36]

Rather than having an ephemeral location for the Kidd treasure, that on Oak Island in Mahone Bay, Nova Scotia, is quite definitely located. It is simply rather hard to get at, though people have been trying for about two hundred years.

The story of Oak Island began when three men visited the spot in 1795. There were two peculiar things about the island. On it stood a grove of ancient live oak trees—trees that do not grow naturally north of Virginia. Also, there was a kind of red clover not found elsewhere in Nova Scotia.

The attention of the three discoverers was drawn to one of the trees, for a huge limb had been sawed off, from the stump dangled a block, and the dead wood was badly scored by a rope. Under the limb was a depression. Digging down ten feet, the treasure seekers came to a platform of thick wood, which they dug out. Every ten feet they came to another. Most were wood but one was of putty, another of charcoal. At ninety-five feet they found a rock, with writing on it they could not read. They tossed it aside and dug on. It was a Saturday, and when they returned on Monday the pit had sixty feet of water in it. All efforts to bail it proved fruitless.

Over the years many people have tried to get through this barrier of sea water, which comes from a false beach built on a platform of fiber resembling coconut husks, and all have failed. After many years a drilling rig was set up and bored down to a depth of 155 feet. At 110 feet the bit struck a platform with a twelve-inch void beneath it. Then it went through four inches of oak, then a layer of iron, dropped 40 feet and struck cement. One boring brought up three links of gold chain, another produced something with which the driller made off in great haste, and a third recovered a bit of parchment. It is thought that there is a treasure room at the bottom of the shaft—a room at least 40 feet high and 15 in diameter, filled with gold and soggy parchment.[37]

After all the intense work and hundreds of thousands of dollars, these are the only three things ever taken from the pit, yet people have been digging there ever since the end of the eighteenth century.

Perhaps the greatest mystery is not what is there, but how and why it got there. Writers feel that the live oaks and coconut fiber indicate that the people who put it there came from the south. The layer of putty and the block point to sailors. The deep pit, the false beach and the elaborate waterworks to flood the hole indicate a long operation by many men directed by skilled engineers—a feat scarcely possible for an ordinary ship's company. The stone with writing and the platforms indicate perhaps a plan for retrieving the treasure, with directions on the slab. Local residents call it Kidd's treasure. Thoughtful writers feel that it is a Viking treasure.

Kidd can be ruled out, and it is difficult to imagine Vikings with this much loot or this kind of engineering skill or the necessity for such an elaborate burial.

Thoughtful writers also tend to lump the live oaks, clover, coconut fiber, sawed-off limb, and ship's block into a single package. But it would seem reasonable to suppose that the live oaks were there before the treasure. Unless he were Noah, one would not expect a ship's captain to transport and transplant a grove of live oaks four feet through, plus this much gold and fiber in one load! It would be more reasonable to suppose that the site was chosen because of the trees or the isolation of the island, and that the block, limb and treasure were of a later date. The Royal Navy was quartered in Halifax during the American Revolution. They cruised to the Gulf of

Mexico and South America. They took prizes. They had sappers and engineers aboard, and they had big crews. Could this not be a treasure dating from the American Revolution?

Although people of considerable note have tried to get this hoard, the folks of Chester, Nova Scotia, say it is not worth the effort. The gold, indeed even the island, is haunted. There are several guardians of the treasure pit. One is a great stallion with fiery eyes that neighs and charges up and down the island. Another is a great slobbering black hound, strongly reminiscent of the Irish Devil Dog, that roams the place at night. A man in a red coat is said to stand guard, and a pulling boat with eighteen oars rowed by spectral oarsmen patrols the waters nearby. These creatures appear only when someone is close to the treasure; so one would assume that their duties are not exhausting. Offshore, when the treasure is about to be uncovered, the *Teazer* burns as she does before a storm.[36]

Less than two years before this writing, according to an article in *The New York Times*, a man and his sons were after the treasure. They were so close they cabled friends to come and witness the event. They entered the hole for the final *putsch* and they never came out. A rescue party found them dead in their tunnel.[39]

Another famous treasure may lie in Tobermory Bay, where a Spanish galleon blew up. I say "may" because there is some doubt—first as to whether or not a Spanish galleon was lost there; and second, if there was a galleon lost there, as to what ship she was. If she was the *Florencia*, there may be a treasure. If she was the *San Juan Bautista*, as some think, there is none.

According to the people of Mull, there are three stories about the treasure wreck—which indicates that the event probably did take place. One states that, scudding off before a great gale, badly in need of food and water, a refugee from the Armada disaster slipped into Tobermory to refit and restock. The Scots were not interested in supplying the fugitives with necessities until it was discovered that the vessel had guns aboard. Since the Macleans and MacDonalds were currently at war, the Macleans promised the galleon food and water for the use of her soldiers. This was provided, but a rupture occurred between the Scots and the galleon's people. The Macleans took three Spaniards prisoner, and the Spanish captured a young lad of the Maclean family. When things seemed hopeless as far as provisions were concerned, the vessel was readied for sea. Young Maclean, finding this out, blew up the ship along with himself, and she sank in deep water in the harbor.[40]

There is also a story that states she was not blown up at all but was wiped out through sorcery—the same witches who were supposed to have sunk the Armada being employed to destroy the galleon.[41]

It was said that on board there was a Spanish princess, a great gun designed by Leonardo da Vinci, a large quantity of gold, and a crown for the young woman, who was supposed to become the ruler of Albion after it was captured. And around the neck of the princess was a chain with a medallion, also by da Vinci.

For centuries the wreck lay there. After the first attempt to salvage her only a few relics were found—among them a great gun which is in the possession of the Duke of Argyll and is presumably the da Vinci model. Over the years the hulk settled into the mud, but in the early part of this century salvage work was started, using pressure hoses to blow away the silt. It is said that a diver was operating one of these hoses when something struck him. In the murk he could not see, but he clutched the object and surfaced. He held a skull and attached to it was a chain and the medallion struck so long ago.[42]

Another story clings to this wreck. It tells that the ship came into Tobermory and blew up. Aboard was a Spanish princess, who was killed; but her body was recovered and buried across the Sound of Mull in a little cemetery at Kiel. Later the body was dug up and taken back to Spain for burial there. However, there is a ghost that haunts the area—the ghost of the princess seeking her fingerbone that was inadvertently left behind when the skeleton was shipped home. The restless shade seeks the fingerbone because of the ancient belief that only the complete body can enter the celestial kingdom and sit at the Lord's table.

These treasure stories are well known. There are others not so well known, but equally fascinating, that must be mentioned. Foremost among these are anecdotes concerning Granuaile, who has amassed so many legends that they could be said to comprise a cycle.

The people on Tory Island say there is a treasure buried on the north end of the island close to a great chasm known as Balor's Prison. All are agreed on this point, but there is some divergence of opinion as to who buried it. Many hold to Grace O'Malley, but others think it was put there by Balor of the Evil Eye. At any rate, it remained hidden for many years until an Englishwoman and her son found it during the present century. They dug it up and prepared to carry it back to London, but before they could leave the island both fell sick. No one knew what was the matter, but they grew hourly worse and it appeared that they were both about to die. The islanders said the disease was brought on by the treasure, and in a desperate bid to save themselves the finders returned it to its resting place. The disease slackened slightly and they were carried home, but whether or not they recovered is not known. The islanders think they died.[43]

The Queen of the West also buried treasure (nine tons of it) on Inishbofin, where it lay hidden until the nineteenth century when some of it was found, but most still remains buried. What was found was discovered in an interesting way and started a curious series of events. According to Captain O'Halloran it happened in the following manner:

Well about this treasure that was got here on the island—mind you all this is true. This man that got it—well, it wasn't him that got it really—twas the lad working for him—in the field. They were working in the field, you see—doing a bit of forking or something like that. So it was the boy that hit it. He hit against this thing with the spade you see he was digging with, and he didn't know what it was. But he thought it was something funny. He knew it wasn't a stone. Anyway, in the end he called the boss and he came of course. So between the two of them anyway they got around it and they dug it up. Of course the boss knew what it was. The lad didn't. He was young at the time, you see. And he had a family of his own too, you see [the boss]. So he was all excited about the money, natural enough, and he hid it until the night came and then he took it home and nobody ever knew he had it. And he threatened the lad and told him not to tell, you see—that he had done wrong and wasn't supposed to be working there anyway, and so on. And I don't suppose the lad knew what it was anyway.

But, however, he decided to send his son away to school to learn navigation and to make a sea captain out of him, and he decided then to build a boat. She might be maybe a hundred ton or so—thereabout. She'd be a fairly big boat at that time. And they got her—he got her—built right over there now where I was telling you [pointing to the head of the harbor] and anyway when the boat was finished he himself the captain of the boatwrights that built the boat they had a dispute over the boat and I think it was over money. It was. He didn't want to give him the remainder of the money until the boat had made her first voyage.

So all right. The son was made a sea captain (and he didn't want it at all) and he came back to Inishbofin and the boat was fitted out ready for sea. So on this evening he was ready to leave it came on very strong from the southeast. And the son said it wasn't fit to leave though he was bound for Jamaica. He was to get a cargo of rum or whatever out there. Cheap rum out there and bring it in and make a good profit out of it, and he had aboard the rest of the treasure money to pay for it.

However, this son left and went—the father compelled him to go, to leave, so he did go. He went out of here and went out between Shark and Bofin—down that way—a fair wind you see. Now he had just gone and the father got sorry. He feared for the boy and he sent a boat out from the north side of the island, you see—one of those ordinary rowboats—in the north side of the island, thinking they'd overtake him and bring him back in again and stop him. But they were late and they did not stop him and he had passed down and the night and the evening was getting worse and worse and he was lost that night on Blacksod that night going down to Flat Inishkeg Island—going down. And he had the remainder of the gold with him now in the boat. He had a certain amount for buying the stuff and there it was. Years afterwards there was a fellow supposed to be gathering seaweed down on Inishkeg Island—you see you use seaweed for manure for the [garden] and he was supposed to get the gold—the remainder of the gold on Inishkeg. So that finished it.

Now the man that built her was supposed to have cursed her into the water and said that she shouldn't turn (and I suppose she couldn't) because he didn't treat the lad right that found the treasure, and he never gave him any. They say he was well out of it anyway. That was the first and the last of her. Her name was the *Raven* and it was supposed to be Grana Weil's treasure, they say it was. There's supposed to be a bit more of it buried here too.

I know where it is supposed to be—some of it—and it will remain there for all of me and I don't suppose it mightn't be there at all. I know places where they did dig for it and this man here on the island he had a dream one night about this gold—where it was—and he was supposed to follow a brier. You know what a brier is? Tis a big long rod that grows in the ground and it's very parmy [handy]—you see—we call it a brier and there's plenty of it growing here on this island. He was supposed to follow the brier down and to be careful not to cut it and to bring something alive with him. That's anything alive—even a fowl or a hen or anything like that because around this gold all the time there is supposed to be a serpent. And when they find the gold, in order to get rid of the serpent he'd have to throw something to the serpent alive, you see, and then he could take the gold.

Fair enough. All went on very well and there was an old fellow on here—on the island—supposed to be an old fellow. He used to be sellin' stuff. They called them peddlers—I suppose you never heard the name before, a peddler. They took him with them—of course it couldn't go well, you see. They took him with them to throw him to the serpent when they would meet the gold; so they didn't tell him what they wanted him for but they took him with them. And they were digging away and true enough the brier was there and they were very careful. They continued on it and they were very careful. They continued on and they went down fairly deep and didn't they happen to cut the brier with the spade and that finished them. They couldn't ever get the brier again after that. As soon as they cut it, all went.[44]

There is still another treasure story of Inishbofin that bears repeating. This is not a buried but a sea treasure. Years ago there was a three-masted vessel named the *Royal Oak*. It is believed she lost her rudder on a wild night off the west side of the island. On that side there is a narrow, deep cove about the size of a large clipper ship. There were no lights on the island to warn anyone and, under the circumstances, it is doubtful if anything could have been done if there had been. The ship drove forward, slipped into the cove bow first and took the ground, where the terrible seas made almost instantaneous work of her. Fortunately, her bowsprit projected into the peat of the island and all hands walked ashore.

The *Royal Oak* was said to have aboard a treasure of great value, and the government sent divers to Bofin to salvage it. The divers arrived, descended to the wreck—which was not very deep—found the treasure and came up immediately empty-handed. Once ashore, nothing could induce them to return to the sea, and they refused to say why, other than that there was something down below they could not or would not face. People on the island say it is a serpent that lies coiled about the gold guarding it, and although they are very poor they prefer poverty to bearding the serpent.[45]

Another pirate of interest here is Jean Lafitte, who like Barney was responsible for discomfiting the British, and like Kidd became involved with politicians—in this case Andrew Jackson, who placed a price on his head after he no longer needed his services. Lafitte is said to have buried much treasure. Apparently he had little interest in recovering the loot, for if the tales be true, one of his favorite devices was to fill up the barrel of a cannon with gold, plug it and drop it overboard.

Sometimes Lafitte buried his treasure ashore. In one case he reportedly buried a large quantity of gold and silver near Galveston. To mark the spot he stuck an engineer's staff in the ground and went his way. (This was a long iron rod with a small cup for holding a compass at the top). People searched for many years, but in the high grass and knowing little more than that the treasure was near the Lavacca River, they were literally looking for a very valuable needle in a haystack.

One day a rancher sent a boy out to drive the cows home for milking, but they wandered and he had some trouble finding them. When he finally came up with them, it was getting late. The cows were fractious and with the typical perverse nature so ingrained in the breed, they persisted in going the wrong way. The boy lost his temper and looked around for something to stimulate their interest in going to the barn. Finding a persuader, he picked it up and applied it to the cattle with enthusiasm, and soon the herd was in full career for home.

When they arrived, the farmer noticed that the cows were breathing hard and turned to the boy for an explanation. The boy told what had happened and said he had used a rod on them, and showed it to the farmer. It was the engineer's rod with the little cup on the top that the boy had pulled out of the grass to brighten up the herd. What with running here and there, the night coming on, and the country a little strange, he had not the faintest idea where he had found it.[46]

Generally speaking, treasure stories seem to fall into a series of patterns and the following one is no exception. On the Island of Bequia a woman had a dream. In the dream she was told by her dead mother that if she would get up and go down to the shore and walk along the beach, she would find an iron rod buried in the sand amongst the mangroves. Usually, when treasure is revealed in a dream, the person is warned not to tell anyone, but this was not the case. She got up and, fearing the jumbies, jack-o'-lanterns, and other supernatural creatures of the night, she called her sister to go along.

The two women proceeded along the sand and one sister, not believing much in dreams, wandered off looking for coconuts. The other went on to the mangroves, and there before her sticking out of the sand was the iron rod. The woman snatched it out and began to dig. Suddenly the sand began to bubble and, overcome with excitement and fear, the woman rushed away to tell her sister, taking the rod with her. She had trouble finding her, and when they tried to retrace her steps to the place where the rod had been, they could not find it. Try as they might, the spot where the rod had been planted eluded them, and eventually they gave up.[47]

Although most treasure stories end in frustration, now and then one hears of a successful hunt. A man lay asleep on the island of Petite Martinique in the Windward Islands, and he had a dream. In the dream a dead woman appeared to him all dressed in white. She stood at the foot of the bed and looked at him. "Get up," she said, "and follow me through the prickly bush and I will show you a treasure." The man awoke and was afraid, and he was also afraid of what the neighbors would think if they saw him tramping around in the thorny bush in his nightshirt at two o'clock in the morning. He stayed in bed.

The next night he dreamed the same dream. "Get up," said the shade, "and follow me through the thorny bush and I will show you a treasure, but you must not tell anyone." Again the man awoke and again he did not go. The dream occurred a third time. "Get up and follow me a little way through the thorny bush. After a little way I will turn and come toward you. When I smile, dig and the treasure will be yours. Nobody will know you even went outdoors."

This time the man got up and went outdoors. He picked up a spade and followed the white-clad figure that went before him. He went scarcely a hundred yards when the apparition stopped, turned around and smiled. The man immediately began to dig and soon unearthed a treasure of great value. With it he built a schooner and prospered until he became one of the richest men in the islands. The ghost never appeared to him again.[48]

Often the dead appear in person rather than in a dream—especially in the British Isles and Ireland—to lead someone to a treasure. There are at least three tales in England: one in Northumberland and two in Wales. In the first, a white lady tried to pursuade a child to go with her and offered him treasure as a reward. The child, as a result of this conversation, was nearly frightened to death. In Wales, a white lady was so grateful for being spoken to that she showed a man a treasure. In another case, the white lady gave half a treasure to a man for speaking to her, but when he wanted it all, she nearly tore him to pieces.[49]

Such beliefs have been carried to North America, for Creighton mentions a sailor with a knapsack who shows people treasure that can be had by killing a baby and letting the blood fall on a special rock. Creighton also mentions that ghosts transformed into animals will help one find treasure.[50]

In Nova Scotia the people sometimes resort to another means of finding buried treasure. They use a divining rod, but they have no better luck, apparently, than those who rely on dreams and shades. One man found a treasure in Cape Breton in this manner, only to be chased away by a flock of headless crows guarding it. Still another man found one in the same area. Just as he was about to drag his hoard out of the hole, he looked up and discovered a huge millstone directly over his head suspended by a thread. Apparently he paused long enough to determine it was revolving at one thousand revolutions a minute, but only after he had developed a lively interest in distance.[51]

A third aid to finding treasure that is especially popular in Ireland is faeries, about whom there are numerous stories, but faery gold does not seem to come from the same source as other treasures. It has usually been left by otherworld creatures or produced by magic, and therefore is of little interest to us here.

The fourth and best-known way to find a treasure is with a chart or "plan"—as a chart is called in the West Indies. Tales about treasure found in this way are so numerous and well known as to make it unnecessary to retell any, but it is interesting to observe that nearly all these charts are obtained either from a secret drawer in a desk, or in a chest discovered accidentally, or by befriending some old hulk who wanders in out of the weather and gives his benefactor a chart of hidden wealth on his deathbed. Almost always there is something wrong with the chart and a good part of the tale is concerned with making the plan intelligible. (This was the device used by J. Fenimore Cooper when he wrote *The Sea Lions*.)

Before treasure can be found it must be created, and there is as much lore connected with this as with finding it. People in the United States usually think of treasure as meaning pirate loot, but the West Indians and people abroad point out that any money or jewelry buried for safekeeping is treasure, and hiding it must be done according to a formula. I was told innumerable times in the West Indies that it must be buried at night (logically enough) and in secret. For even the smallest cache a sacrifice has to be provided—usually a chicken, sometimes a goat—augmented with rum, rice and incantations. The blood is poured on the spot and the body of the sacrifice is often buried with the pot.

For larger caches, like a whole ship's cargo, more involved rituals were indulged in. Under these circumstances, human sacrifices were made. Often the person to guard the treasure would be beheaded or hanged and the body thrown face down atop the treasure and the blood liberally sprinkled about. The spirit of this sacrifice would guard the treasure, and before anyone could seize it, the guardian had to be placated—often with blood. If not, the guard might take any means to assure that the treasure remained buried.

I was told on the island of Bequia that on pirate ships they used to draw lots, and the man with the unlucky lot was killed and buried with the treasure. Old Bill Wallace, a famous islander, was for a long time disturbed by a man who kept wandering near a certain tree beside his house. Old Bill finally dug the ground and discovered a skeleton buried face down. He dug further but found nothing; so he reburied the skeleton, apparently face up, and never was bothered again.

The treasure having been properly buried and its whereabouts correctly charted, one discovers that there is an equally large body of lore connected with the act of recovery. First, any instructions must be followed explicitly—especially if they come to the hunter in a dream or through a ghost. Generally one should go for treasure after nightfall, preferably in the dark of the moon; and the best time to work is between midnight and dawn. A silver spade is helpful, and often a sacrifice is required. Most important of all is that no one speaks—and there are hundreds of stories about people who endure much to gain a treasure, only to lose it by saying "I've found it!" as their pick strikes the chest or the container is about to be lifted—at which the chest drops through the earth and vanishes forever. (I have yet to hear of anyone who ever had two chances at a treasure.)

Now and then there is a story about someone who found a treasure, but the failures outnumber the successes. One of the great drawbacks to treasure hunting is greed. The following story, collected in the winter of 1971, illustrates both.

One day toward the close of the nineteenth century a French yacht sailed to the island of Mayero in the Windward Islands and anchored. The skipper went ashore and asked the owner of the island for permission to dig for treasure. He told the owner that he would give him one-third of the treasure if he would agree. The owner said no, he wanted half, but the captain said that was impossible. He had had great difficulty obtaining a plan of the treasure and had come too far to settle for less. Anyway, he said, the treasure was so large that there was no way in which the islander could spend his share in his lifetime. The proprietor held out for half and the deal fell through. However, before returning to his boat, the man asked to see the island, and the two wandered all over it. Finally the captain asked for a drink of coconut water, as he was very thirsty. The owner obliged, and after drinking the stranger threw down the empty coconut, whereupon they went back to the shore and the skipper said he would not bother with the treasure, he couldn't find it anyway. The vessel made sail and vanished over the horizon. The next morning the greedy landlord discovered a great hole where the skipper had thrown the coconut. Scattered around the hole were a few gold coins—left as proof that the treasure had really been there.

This brings us to the fourth stage of buried treasure—what happens after one finds it. It is almost universally felt that such a hoard is unlucky. Time and again I have heard the folk say, "I wouldn't trouble myself about buried treasure. No good ever come of it. It only brings trouble." Strangely enough, this point of view has extended itself to smuggling and even to rum-running in the United States. Moreover, the folk can give numerous examples of what happened to people—sometimes famous ones—who obtained their fortune in this manner.

The reasons for this are rather simple. Obtaining money without hard work is antithetical to the Christian ethic. Moreover, treasure does not really belong to the finder but to the burier. Much of it has been obtained illegally. If it belongs to anyone, it belongs to the ghost who guards it or to his lord, Satan. Thus it is that a serpent guards the treasure in Inishbofin and a slobbering hound runs on Oak Island.

In order to keep a treasure and enjoy it, elaborate rules have been set up. The people in Dominica, for example, believe that if you find treasure and if you would keep any of it, you must invest it all in some enterprise immediately, or else you must return half of what you found. In the former case, the finder stands to make great profits or lose it all. In the latter, he will live out his days better with half a loaf than with none.

This brings us to a very brief perusal of piracy's country cousins— smuggling and bootlegging. For many people smuggling is a way of life. The smuggler feels he is performing a service to his community rather than commiting a crime. After all, he is supplying his friends, at a price they can afford, with goods that otherwise are either unobtainable or extremely expensive. The fact that he is breaking the law never enters his head. If he thinks about it at all, he feels he is depriving politicians living far away of a portion of their income, and in doing so he is helping his neighbor. He may be right.[52]

For smuggling to flourish, certain conditions are essential. First, there must be protective tariffs that make certain commodities exorbitant. Second, there must be a source of supply for these commodities reasonably close by. Finally, there must be facilities for bringing in the contraband. With these things in mind, it is not surprising that Scotland, Cornwall, southern Ireland, Maine and the region around New Orleans are the scenes of many smuggling stories.

It is interesting also to note that stories about smuggling flourish in proportion to the intensity with which the attendant laws are enforced and the severity of the penalties attached to them. Scotland and the United States are full of stories. On the other hand, smuggling is carried on at a great rate in the West Indies. For one island there, it is the only source of revenue. There are many laws against smuggling, but they are seldom enforced and the penalties are nominal. Several months of intensive research in the area brought only a minimum number of stories to light. One concerns the island just mentioned.

It seems that a new administration had taken office in Grenada and there was an intense effort made to stop the illegal traffic that was flourishing, especially in alcohol and tobacco. The police commissioner ordered his minions to go to the island, search it and bring in any contraband and smugglers they could find. For one reason or another, the minions never seemed able to "reach up" to the island in question. The commissioner redoubled his efforts and went to a neighboring island, where he ordered the police to proceed to the smugglers' nest immediately. The police resigned. His hackles up, the commissioner decided that one should never send a boy to do a man's work, and commandeered a boat to ferry himself across. When he arrived and dropped anchor, he was surprised to hear a drum beating and to see a big crowd on the beach. He was even more surprised when a delegation put off in a small boat and came aboard. The delegation was most polite. They asked after his health and said the whole island hoped he would come ashore for the entertainment. They would be crushed if he didn't. The commissioner asked what entertainment. The delegation said it was a funeral (always a festive event on the islands). Who had died? Nobody yet. The people had worked all night preparing a feast, warming the drums and digging a hole. It was exactly the right size to fit the commissioner and they hoped he would not disappoint them. His Excellency pulled up his anchor and returned to Grenada. The laws against smuggling remained on the books, but the torpor about enforcing them returned.

In St. Lucia an old man who had at one time been in the smuggling trade told an interesting story about his career. His gang put into Dominica one night and were unloading when they were discovered by a woman. She demanded she be given a "share" in the contraband, but the captain gave her only two bottles, and she went away. Shortly thereafter the police arrived. They knew just where to look and found the remainder of the cargo under the *dachine* (a kind of vegetable), arrested all hands, and secured the ship. The captain and entire crew were thrown in jail, with the exception of my informant, who managed to escape.

Instead of fleeing from the country or hiring a lawyer, he went to an obeah man, who told him all would be well. As each man stood before the judge he was to say "Freedom." The obeah man also identified the informer as the woman who wanted a share of the cargo. Accordingly, then, the crew came to trial; each man said "Freedom" as he stepped before the bar, and the judge set each one free. In the courtroom was the informer, and my narrator pointed his finger at her and said "Freedom." Instantly her lip began to swell until it was the size of a pumpkin and was so heavy that it bent her neck. It was reckoned that with her new lip, she was one of the ugliest people on the island—so ugly in fact that the hamlet where she once lived is today known as Pays Bouche.

This capture of the smugglers seemed to have done something to the law, for the next time the captain and his crew were in the vicinity they were again taken by the police. The vessel was searched but nothing was found, and the officers were very rude to the ships' company. Among other things, the police chief told the smugglers exactly what they could expect to happen when they were caught. He then demanded food. Such arrogance was intolerable. Moreover, such zeal on the part of the constabulary could ruin a good comfortable trade. Drastic measures were needed, and drastic measures were taken. A nice piece of fish was found and cooked to a turn. It was heavily seasoned, as West Indian food is wont to be. It was also liberally sprinkled with poison. The policeman ate and departed—on a longer journey than just to the shore. "After that we have a good time for a long time," said my informant.

Years ago there was a little sloop named the *Artful Dodger*. She was to pick up a load of liquor and tobacco at Martinique and land it on an English island. All went well until the last moment, when it was discovered that a revenue officer was hiding under a propped-up rowboat on the beach waiting to catch them redhanded and receive a large reward. As soon as the captain found out how things stood, he had himself and another man rowed ashore. They sneaked up on the rowboat, kicked the supports from under her and sat on her keel, with the revenue officer neatly pinned inside. As the cargo came ashore they regaled him with a running account. "Two hundred cigars, one keg of brandy. . ." When the cargo was all ashore and on its way, they lashed the boat to the beach with lines fastened to pegs and went about their business.[53]

These stories about tricking the law are rather common. The foregoing tale occurred in the nineteenth century. A story with a similar plan is told of the rum-running days in Rhode Island. A bootlegger had just landed a huge cargo on the beach and was busily engaged in loading it into trucks when one of his men came dashing back down the road. "The deputy sheriff is up at the crossroads waiting." "Well," said the leader, "go up and see how much he wants to clear out. I don't want to kill him lessen I have to, but I won't pay no more than three thousand." His henchman went back and approached the sheriff, who stated he knew what was going on and was there to uphold the law—no matter what. "How much would you want to go somewhere else?," asked the bootlegger, reaching in his pocket. "Well, when you put it that way, I just might move along. Do you think five dollars would be too much?"

A story very similar to the story of Cutter Rock also comes from

Rhode Island. At the head of Narragansett Bay, off a spit called Popasquash Point near Bristol, lies a mud bank awash at extremely low water. A smuggler in the employ of John Brown came into the bay in 1772 and was ordered to heave to by a cutter called the *Gaspee*. Since Brown's vessel had a cargo of contraband aboard and was known as a smart vessel, her skipper crowded on the sail. Drive as hard as he would, he could not shake the Crown's vessel, and he was rapidly running out of room. But the old man knew the bay and he eased his vessel over the shoal. The *Gaspee* fetched up and was aground until the next tide. The smuggler kept away for Providence, where he spread the news. As a result, Brown outfitted a whaleboat, and that night, before she could be floated, they attacked the British.[54]

According to one tale still popular in the area, a man named Bucklan saw the British officer on the quarterdeck silhouetted against the moon. "Hand me up my goose gun, Tilly [Tillinghast], and I'll kill the son of a bitch where he stands." So said, so done. The *Gaspee* was taken and burned, and this event (along with several others) has often been called the first battle of the American Revolution.[55]

During the rum-running days an identical stunt was pulled on the Old Bull, a rock awash further down the bay. A Coast Guard cutter pursued a rumrunner named the *Black Duck*. When the *Black Duck* came to the Old Bull she turned out her stern light—which she had neglected to do during the chase—dodged around the rock, and relit it. The Coast Guard, as one might expect, kept straight ahead. Only their bottom stayed on the horns of the Old Bull. The rest of the ship and her crew went down in deep water several boat lengths beyond, and the *Black Duck* proceeded leisurely "up river" to unload.[56]

Perhaps one of the most unusual escapes of a smuggler took place many years ago in the Hebrides. According to Mary MacClennan, it happened as follows:

My great-great-grandfather came across from Kintail to settle here and he had three inns. He had one at Gramisdale, which is in the north of Benbecula; one at Loch Eyhort, which is just a little bit southeast of it; and another at the south end here [South Uist]. He used to make his own whiskey and smuggle it across. He used to make his whiskey over in Kintail days and he used to spend his nights dodging revenue cutters, you know, across the Minch where he ran his whiskey across, and this time there was a frigate chasing them. They were close and they couldn't really make much speed so they slipped into Loch Tarbert—East Loch Tarbert in Harris. There was a very narrow inlet into the Loch and while they were able to get through, there wasn't enough room for the Government boat and they had to anchor outside for the night. During the night of course they [the smugglers] couldn't get outside or slip past the mouth of the Loch anyway, so they [the people on the frigate] just sat back until morning. But when the morning appeared there was no sign of any boat. Everything gone, and what had happened was that my great-great-grandfather had gone ashore with a big crock of whiskey, you see, and he gathered a crowd of cronies and got them all boozed up and borrowed every horse and everything in the district, and it's a very very narrow neck of land that divides East Loch Tarbert from West Loch Tarbert and he got his boat dragged away with his whiskey before the others were up.[57]

Today most of this activity is dead. Pirates are found only in remote areas in the China Seas—if at all; privateers have been outlawed since the American Civil War, with the somewhat questionable exception of Count von Luckner and the *Sea Adler*. Smuggling continues, but at a greatly reduced rate, and most of it is now done by aeroplane and motorboat. Much of the romance of buried treasure has been lost with the advent of new and improved methods of finding it. What chance, for example, does a lone ghost have of protecting his hoard against a laser beam or a suction dredge? Who needs a plan when he can obtain a metal-detecting device? Who does not know that dreams are but jumbled recordings of personal experience?

Still the old heads remember, the old hearts believe, and in the remoter outposts of the English-speaking world their children listen and they too will believe, remember, and hopefully repeat. When the light is dim, thunder mutters in the west and the sea growls on the shingle, it is difficult not to believe as you sit in a ship's cabin or in a shack by the shore and hear an old man tell these tales. It is then that cold science and the madding crowd do not count for much and one can escape for awhile to the land of dreams—or is it reality?

CHAPTER XIII

LEGENDS AND TALES

"For God's sake let us sit upon the ground and tell
sad stories of the death of kings."
—Shakespeare, Richard II

Along with singing and scrimshaw and horseplay, a tremendous source of entertainment for seamen was the telling of stories, particularly tales and legends. Many of these have been mentioned elsewhere, but it is necessary to devote some time to this particular means of shuffling off spare time, because to a seafaring man tales, and particularly legends, have a significance beyond mere entertainment. As a good Christian reads about the vicissitudes of Job or the exploits of David, so the sailor delights in his yarns. To him they carry almost a religious significance. From them he draws solace and learning.

The question arises immediately as to what is a folktale and what is a legend. Until some kind of distinction can be made, it is difficult to talk about them.

Actually there are three kinds of folk stories. At one end we have myth (which in this chapter does not concern us) and at the other, legend. In the middle stands the tale. Each genre has a number of criteria that are applicable to it, and with these in mind one can judge which category a story falls into, just as one rates a diver by points. The perfect dive is worth ten points and, unless the diver lands on the diving board, any plunge is worth something. As dives are seldom perfect, so tales and legends rarely incorporate all the points.

Both a tale and a legend are true, but the kind of truth is different. Although the terms may have broader meaning elsewhere, in this chapter the tale is involved with explanatory facts and the legend is concerned with

Opposite: The Spanish Prisoner, Duart Castle, Isle of Mull, Scotland

historical events. While a legend may tell about a person being drowned, a tale will tell why the wind blows.

Legend and tale both deal with time, but while the legend is concerned with "clock time" the tale is concerned with "geological time"—if I may invent a term. In this regard, then, the tale is far older than the legend and often has a formulaic beginning as "long, long ago" or "once upon a time." The eleventh-century story of King Canute trying to hold back the tide is ancient for a legend but would be young if considered as a tale.

While the tale is widespread and seldom localized, the legend is restricted in space and concerns events in a definite locality. When the tale is so restricted, it is for the purpose of explaining some otherwise incomprehensible local phenomenon.

The legend deals with characters within the matrix of the times, but the tale tends to paint them with strokes that are larger than life. To do this it often incorporates magic, otherworld or supernatural elements in the story. Tales are often about gods, demigods, goblins and demons. On the other hand, the people within the framework of legend are real people and the events in which they took part really happened. It may be that over the years the peripheral details have become adjusted to the degree that we no longer recognize the main story, but behind the superfluous material lies a hard fact. It does not bother me very much when I hear a legend and learn that the source hasn't been "documented by a trained historian." There are too many legends extant that trained historians have been unable to disprove, to make me reject one for which there is no source. Who knows? Proof may come tomorrow.[1]

During the long night when part of the watch shelters under the lee of the longboat, or during the time below, the crew like to tell stories. Most of these concern themselves with personal anecdote—about storms an individual was in, about shipmates he has encountered or excesses ashore with whiskey and whores. I have not found that politics, religion or intellectual acrobatics ever take up much of a sailor's time. After observations on the weather and ship's business have been covered, Jack Tar's mind wanders to the past or ahead to the next liberty when he will make the grog shop and the whorehouse jump.

I have found that sensitivity is usually a result of ease and luxury. A seaman's life does not permit it. What the sophisticated person finds cruel, the sailor often finds funny. But if he is crass, crude and cruel, he is also generous; he is tough and he has courage. Speaking of this, Professor

Herbert Halpert of the University of Newfoundland made a penetrating remark: "When you learn what the fishermen endure and the things they do in their lifetime, courage has no meaning."

As a result of their life, then, seamen tend to paint things large. The details of their dockside excesses must be gargartuan to retain a place in their memory. Living next to danger and sudden death, they recall only those items that are so fraught with peril, so violent or so heinous that they seem unbelievable to a landsman. An anecdote illustrates the point.

As I heard it the original story was longer, but the bit here will suffice. During a heavy fog off Sandy Hook two vessels hail each other. A frail voice squeals out, "Ship ahoy. What ship is that?" The answer comes back in a tired, roaring bellow, "The steamship *Ocean Monarch*. What ship is that?" "The yacht *Betsy Ann*. Where you from?" "Bombay. Where you from?" "Sag Harbor. How long have you been out?" "One hundred and eight days. How long you been out?" "I've been out all night!" It is difficult to see how either party could empathize with the other. But to return to the task.

Formerly tales and legends were popular at sea, if we are to judge by the numbers that have survived in print. Today, however, they provide only a very modest part of a seagoing narrator's repertoire. (Should one wish to gain some insight into the earlier stories, one need only examine the books by Bassett, Skinner or Rappaport named in the Bibliography.) In point of fact, with modern means of entertainment and with the invention of motor power, which shortens almost any trip appreciably, the need for homegrown diversions has waned markedly.

Perhaps the best known of these tales was the one about the salt mill. Long ago there were a poor man and his wife who lived in a small house. It was almost Easter, and there was no ham in the house and no prospect of getting any. The man's wife was insistent, however, that ham be provided for dinner. This was the situation, and to solve it the husband went into the forest to think how he might get a ham. There he met a wizened little man who asked for food, which the man gave him. In gratitude for this, the little man asked him what he would like most to have and was told, "Ham for Easter Sunday." The little man then told his benefactor that if he went to Hell and offered the devil some bacon, the devil might give him a certain quern that would grind anything its owner asked. All one needed to do was say, "Grind——," and the little mill would continue to grind out the desired object until the command, "Grind no more——."

With this information the poor man returned home, took up the last flitch of bacon in the house and set off for Hell. After some difficulty he found the place and viewed with interest the various devices used to discomfit the wicked. He saw the quern in a corner and met the devil. The devil saw the bacon and wanted it. The poor man bargained successfully and at last obtained the magic mill, which he took home.

Just before he reached home the man decided to see if his new machine worked. He set it on the ground and said, "Grind ham." Immediately the mill began to whir and one grand fat ham after another popped out. Satisfied, he said the magic words, the mill stopped, and he went home to delight his wife with the Easter ham.

Thanks to the magic mill, the man and his wife prospered mightily. At last he gave it to his brother, who was a farmer. The first thing the farmer did was command the mill to grind soup, and before he could stop it he had a river of soup running out of the kitchen. After that he ordered it to do various things and soon became very rich.

One day a sea captain came to the farmer's house and saw the mill in operation. He was fascinated with the possibilities of such a machine and determined to have it and to learn how to make it work. Hs asked the farmer how to start it and the farmer told him. That night the captain stole the mill and put to sea on a fishing trip.

When they arrived at the fishing bank they caught a large number of fish and, being in need of salt to preserve the catch, the skipper got out the mill and ordered it to grind salt. The mill began to whir and it wasn't long before he had plenty of salt. But the problem was how to stop it. Without the magic words he was powerless to control it. The mill filled the cabin and then the companionway and finally the hold with salt until the overloaded vessel foundered, taking the mill and the crew with her. And there to this day the mill lies on the bottom grinding salt. If you don't believe this story, you have only to taste the sea water.

In the Old World this story has nearly died out in oral tradition, but it is still popular in the West Indies, where it has become a formula story attached to the Anasi cycle of tales. These stories often deal with magic, and they are always told in a peculiar manner. At the beginning the narrator says "Crick" and the audience answers "Crack." In order to be sure everyone is listening, from time to time the teller will interpose a "Crick," and if the audience is on its toes it will roar out "Crack." Further, at intervals during the story the speaker will sing a verse in patois, which serves as a kind of chapter break within the tale. Moreover, these stories employ a vocabulary not used in common speech. And when the narration is over, the teller will signify it by a set phrase—either "And that is the end of my story" or "The wire ben', and my story end."

One night in Carriacou, while searching for stories about magic, I told a story about the Brahan Seer and how he threw his magic stone into the sea before he was burned alive. I was startled when our informant, Captain Charlie Bristol, came up with the following tale:

Crick!

Crack!

Now there is a man, he—ah—he was a faery man. The man had a mill. Well, this mill that he have, heh, he stole that mill and he get himself on a ship—on the ship filled up with passengers—going on the ship and they all bound for somewhere. Now, whiles going they have no salt and he take the mill but he can't control the mill because why? He haven't the final sense of the mill before the mill was got it to him. The mill—to get the mill going—

> Moulez-moi qu'arondé
> Moulez-moi qu'arondé
> [sung nineteen times, faster each time]

Crick!

Crack!

So the mill, so they say, they had no salt but the mill operating anything that they ask the mill for is because the mill would operate it to the time. . . . Well, they ask the mill to give the ship salt because food cooking. There is no salt and the man hear de voice, "Start de mill"—this moulez-moi qu'arondé—. Now he tell the mill he want to get salt, he going to start the mill. Moulez-moi oh qu'arondé. He tell the mill he want salt so the mill going grind salt now. As sea water or water for operating going salt. That is only for the food they want condiment they want in salt for the ship. Well, I'll tell you, Mr. Man going tell the mill, "Warandez"—the mill name is Warandez, so any time he say "Warandez" the mill have to answer and give him whatever he ask. So anything he ask if it is anything so the mill have to operate it to suit him, because it is a faery mill. So the traveler say to the mill he want salt and it start. He tell the mill to arondé, 'Moulez-moi qu'arondé [sung twelve times]

Crick!

Crack!

That mill start to grind salt, heh. The mill grind salt until the ship get loaded with salt. When he came by to stop the mill he have no way to stop the mill with. The mill grind salt until he sank the ship and every individual have gone with that mill.

When you see you take a thing—you rob something and you knows nothing about it, it would always bring error for many that do not know have fallen in error and so many lifetimes gone, but, still it is better to know of operating than to know not the way of operating.

Crick!

Crack!

That is the end of my story.

Despite the fact that the seaman feels strongly about the "purity" of the sea and recognizes that it does not tolerate murderers, debtors, cripples, braggarts and any number of undesirable persons (excepting practical jokers and whoremasters—almost sailors' avocations), he also knows that the sea will kill him if it gets a chance. This trait he ascribes, and has ascribed since time immemorial, to omnipotent beings that dwell within its depths. Formerly these were beings like Poseidon and Shony, but with the advent of Christianity these were replaced by the devil and his imps.

Looked at from one point of view, there is nothing inconsistent in this dichotomy. If Satan wants the wicked, what is more natural than that he take them from the element into which he has been cast by God? If in his search he drowns the good to get the wicked, it is little more than what the surgeon does—cut out the good flesh to get at the proud. The fact that the devil and his minions reside within the sea's depths does no more in the sailors' eyes to change her personality than childhood diseases corrupt the child.

Surrounding the concept of Satan is almost a whole cycle of tales. In one he is connected with the Flying Dutchman, in another he is attached to corposants. Stories are told of how the devil brings storms, and particularly important is a great cycle of stories of his brushes with innumerable saints, who always overcome him in the end. He is seen in waterspouts, in the sunset; and sometimes a great hand is said to rear itself out of the sea, clutch a vessel and vanish with the ship and all that is in her.

One of these tales about Satan dealing with a saint bears a brief retelling. Like Noah, Satan built a great ship in which to place his captured souls. This he made out of wood grown in Hell. It was a fine ship, but it smelled of sulfur and smoke—and in her the devil literally raised hell, destroying vessels, spreading disease, loading aboard the damned, and carousing all night. So great was the havoc and so wild the revelry that it eventually came to the attention of St. Elmo, who put a stop to it. First he set the ship afire and then, not fully satisfied, he knocked such a hole in her side that she went down like a stone, very nearly taking Lucifer with her. Had he not been a strong swimmer he might have "gone bottom" and thereby dealt Christianity a mortal blow. However, he made shore, but to this day his vessel burns beneath the water. It is said that this burning is the cause of phosphorescence in the sea. It is also said that the phosphorescent lights are the devil's torches and that he is looking for the wreck of his pride and joy, apparently to salvage her.[2]

In Scotland there is a considerable body of lore surrounding a strange being, the King of Lochlann. "Lochlann" was an ancient name for Norway, but it was also a term applied to a mythological region in the North.[3] Today there does not seem to be a clear-cut distinction between the mythological and the actual kingdoms. As a result, the misfortunes of this King (or kings) loom large in Hebridean legend and tale making. We have already seen how his son was swallowed in the Corryvreckan, his daughter cast away on her way to Scotia, and a number of his other children turned into seals. And the King had still other children who do not seem to have fared much better. These stories must once have been long and involved, but today they survive almost as anecdotes. The following story was told to us one night in the Outer Hebrides:

> Once long ago the sun and the moon were equally bright. The sun ruled part of the time and the moon the rest, and it was always daylight. The moon was a woman and she met the King of Lochlann, who slept with her and together they had a flock of children, mostly daughters. For some reason Sun became jealous of Moon—probably because she had so many offspring—and cast a spell on her which dimmed her brilliance and made her very much secondary to the sun. Not only did Sun dull her light, he went further and transformed all her children into swans. And this is the reason, as almost anyone can tell you, that when the birds are asleep the swans can be seen swimming or flying across the path of the moon, their mother.

In Ireland tradition dies even harder than it does in Scotland, and although the tales of the King of Lochlann are well known, the Irish stories are from their own past—a past rich in tales and legends of remarkable length. Although the longest tale I have collected in Ireland took over three hours in the telling and dealt with "the time of the giants," there are stories that take twenty-four hours to recount—and there are still both people to tell them and a ready audience.

Among these ancient tales is a cycle dealing with Fion (Finn) the

Fair. This remarkable youth was born under difficult circumstances and was reared precariously in the wilderness, but grew to be a mighty man excelling in all things—especially fighting. One of his better-known adventures concerns a salmon and helps to explain why the salmon, among all fish, is so important amongst the Gaelic people. (In Scotland, to mention salmon is bad luck; but in Ireland it is sufficiently popular to be struck on coins.)

> And then he said farewell to Crimall, and went on to learn poetry from Finegas, a poet that was living at the Boinn, for the poets thought it was always on the brink of water poetry was revealed to them. And he did not give him his own name, but took the name of Deimne. Seven years, now, Finegas had stopped at the Boinn, watching the salmon, for it was in the prophecy that he would eat the salmon of knowledge that would come there, and that he would have all knowledge after. And when at the last the salmon of knowledge came, he brought it to where Finn was, and bade him to roast it, but he bade him not to eat any of it. And when Finn brought him the salmon after a while he said: "Did you eat any of it at all, boy?" "I did not," said Finn; "but I burned my thumb putting down a blister that rose on the skin, and after that, I put my thumb in my mouth." "What is your name, boy?" said Finegas. "Deimne," said he. "It is not, but it is Finn your name is, and it is you and not myself the salmon was given in the prophecy." With that he gave Finn the whole of the salmon, and from that time Finn had the knowledge that came from the nuts of the nine hazels of wisdom that grow beside the well that is below the sea.[4]

Standing midway between these tales and legends are a vast number of stories about saints—especially in Scotland and Ireland. None is better known than the stories about Cholm Cille, alias St. Columba, who was a king in Ireland at one time. As King he wanted a certain holy book and went to war for it.[5] The result of the war was three thousand young men killed, which so upset the King that he had a nervous breakdown, and when he recovered he vowed to become a holy man and spread Christianity to the people of the north—a reaction not often encountered among statesmen.

Accordingly, the distressed monarch traveled to the west of Ireland, embarked in a curragh with some companions, rowed up the coast, crossed into Scotland and founded a monastery in Iona. On the way he visited most of the islands and harbors in the west, and from Iona he ranged widely through Scotland. In his travels he had many adventures and performed many miracles, some of which have been preserved by Adomnan in his *Life of Columba.*[6] Many more have been preserved at various points where he landed along the coast, and even inland—for it was he who ordered the Great Orme of Loch Ness to cease and desist from eating people. Some of the stories about him, like most hagiographic reports, concern his deeds, while others are inspired by his presence. In Fanny's Hole, County Donegal, we were told about the holy man's visit there. According to Mrs. MacBride:

> Cholm Cille was a man of war—he loved war—but he was a saint and he went to Iona to do penance, and where that is I'm sure I don't know, but probably it is somewhere in Scotland. And on his way there he stopped at Mulroy Bay. Cholm Cille, you know, was from Doonwell where there is a holy well. People used to go there on crutches and return without them. But anyway, there were two fishermen at Mulroy Bay and they saw him coming. It was for salmon they were fishing and they had two in the boat, but they knew that Cholm Cille was the great one for begging. Always asking for something, and they knew he was going to ask them for salmon— and if they did say they had some, he would be wanting them. So they agreed, the two of them, they would tell him they did not in spite of the two grand salmon they already had in the boat.
>
> Well, he came and he asked them and they said, "No, we do not."
>
> St. Cholm Cille then said, "That is a great pity. If you do not have any, from now on you will catch many in Mulroy Bay, but if you do have some, never a salmon will you nor anybody else catch in the Bay again." And he went his way.
>
> Now from that time until about twenty years ago no salmon ever was caught in this bay and then some men were out in a boat and a salmon jumped and one of the men caught him (he was a Protestant, you know) and as he caught him he said, "St. Cholm Cille was wrong." Just then the salmon gave a great leap out of him and he was back in the sea. St. Cholm Cille was right after all, for never the salmon has been caught in this bay from the day of the curse to this.

As mentioned earlier, St. Cholm Cille also visited Tory Island not far from Mulroy Bay, where Balor of the Evil Eye, an ancestor of Finn, once had his close. At the time the island was full of pagans under the leadership of a man named Dougan, and when they saw the holy man coming they gathered on the shore to prevent his landing. The saint, however, talked to Dougan and at last he was told he could land without strife. At the time Dougan had a monstrous black hound famed for its violent nature. When Cholm Cille landed the dog was on a cliff, and as the holy man started up the bank the beast sprang at his throat. So powerful was the spring that the hound's feet sank into the living rock and his tail split a boulder as he took off. The mighty saint merely raised his hand. The devil dog came to a sudden stop in midair and tumbled to the rocks below, its neck broken. For those who doubt, the split rock and the beast's footprints are still to be seen in the stone beside the landing place.

Also on the island, but kept hidden even from the natives themselves, is a most dangerous rock known as a cursing stone. The good saint left it there to protect the people, for they had no other defense, and it has served them well. On the stone was written in Latin, "Turn me over easy and don't hurt me." Should anyone molest another or should the island be in danger, all one need do is place a hand on the stone, turn it over, and mention the name of the offender. Blood will run from the stone and the offending mortal will drop dead. The last time the stone was used was September 22, 1884.

Tory Island had been backward about paying its rents, and H.M.S. *Wasp* was sent with a small detachment to collect. The islanders got word of what was happening and carried the stone to the beach. Just at sunset the *Wasp* was seen in the offing, and the stone was put to work. That night a fog rolled in, and in the morning the *Wasp* was not to be seen. The crew eventually washed ashore as corpses but the ship was never heard of. After that, rent collecting became a haphazard event and the stone was hidden, for it was considered too dangerous a weapon to be available to all.

These cursing stones appear to have been popular in Ireland at one time, for according to Professor Seamus Delargy, there were two at Kilcummin Roads far to the south, but the people were so in awe of their power that they cast them into the sea.[7]

Saints of course are not the only people who stand midway in the transition between tale and legend, nor is God the only source of magic. Neither are Ireland and Scotland the only places such stories are told. The late MacEdward Leach related to me the following tale, which he collected in Cape Breton in 1949. As one reads it, he is at once struck with the New World quality of an Old World idea.

> Years ago living in Cape Breton was a Scotsman who had one son. His wife died and he married a woman who had two children of her own, whom she brought with her when she moved under the new roof. The stepchild she despised. She would feed him only scraps, make him sleep on a pallet and gave him all kinds of hard and dirty work to do, while she gave her own children the very best of everything.
>
> Now it so happened that her two children were very musical, and she went to every effort to see that they played well. She had a piper teach them and bought them both excellent bagpipes, but when her stepchild

wanted to play she at first refused to allow it and later gave him a miserable little chanter that would scarcely play.

One day the stepmother sent this boy out into the woods to cut firewood while her children stayed home and practiced the pipes. For his lunch she gave him two pieces of bread.

The boy had not been in the woods very long before he saw a very small old man sitting against a tree. The little man said he was starving and asked for something to eat, so the boy gave him his bread. The little man ate it all and asked for more, and was told that was all the boy had and it was really his lunch.

Then the little old man said, "What would you like to do most in the whole world?" The boy answered, "I would like to be the greatest piper in the world," and he told the old man about his chanter and his hard life at home.

"Put your fingers in my mouth," said the little old man, "and think piping music." The boy did. "Now go home and tomorrow you will be the greatest piper in the world."

The following day a man came to the door and told the woman he was from a circus and was looking for a piper to play between the acts. The woman was very pleased and brought out her two sons. They played for the man, and they played so well he couldn't make up his mind. While he was thinking about it he noticed the boy. "What about him, does he play?" "Oh no. He can't play at all. All he has is a miserable little chanter."

"Well, let him try anyway."

The boy took his chanter and played the sweetest music the man had ever heard and so he was hired at once, and they went away to the circus where he became the greatest piper in the world.

Now it happened that a new steamship was launched a few years after this in Sydney [Nova Scotia], and they wanted a piper to entertain the passengers and they hired this boy.

One day in the winter the steamer ran into a terrible storm. She sprang a leak and started to go down. It was before the days of wireless and the captain didn't know what to do when the piper appeared on the bridge. "Warm my hands," he said, "by blowing on my fingers and I will save you." The captain did this and the piper started to play. He played distress music and he played so loudly that the people ashore twenty-six miles away heard it and sent out boats and rescued everybody.

The owners of the steamship were so grateful they gave the piper a great reward and he retired to a little valley. His name was Campbell and the place where he lived is still called Pipers Glen.

Cursing stones and pipes are not the only objects about which stories revolve. Almost anything one can mention probably has a story about it somewhere, and one object that has a considerable body of lore attached to it is the bell. But let us speak first of two other producers of sound.

Armada anchor, Inishbofin, Ireland

From earliest times the spirit world has been thought to be moved by whistles and by rattles. Very often these rattles were made from special materials (in Carriacou I was informed that a good "chac-chac" [rattle] had to contain a certain red seed—the same seed a person uses when he wishes favors from the devil). To most members of the folk community, ghosts and spirits live in a silent place and move about in the long, still watches of the night. The folk also believe that spirits are wraithlike—"I come like water and like wind I go." To bang rattles and to whistle create noise which is intolerable to spirits. Besides this, whistles and whistling use wind, and the spirits are often wraiths moving as air.[8]

After rattles we are confronted with bells, a slightly more developed device than a handful of red seeds in a calabash.

Bells have long been popular in folklore, and usually they are in some way connected with the otherworld. When a man drowns, the last thing he is supposed to hear is a bell; when a ship sinks, just before she goes under a bell is supposed to toll; when a healthy man hears bells in his ears, he knows a friend has died. Why bells are so important is not easy to say with conviction, but one may speculate.[9]

Like rattles before them, bells are associated with religious rites, and at weddings, funerals, and excommunications they play an important part. Bells are usually constructed of metal, especially iron, silver, gold or bell metal. Of these only two, gold and silver, are found in the free state. The one is white like the moon, the other yellow like the sun, and by the ancient process of transfer the folk have ascribed to these two metals the qualities they believe held by the sun and moon. Iron, of course, is found free in nature only in the form of meteorites, which came from the land of Athanasia. Moreover, iron was the atom bomb of its day, for when man learned to work it he had a terrible weapon with which to overcome his enemy. To those who believe faeries and otherworld creatures are really people who were wiped out by invaders, it is only natural that the sound of iron on iron should be disquieting. Or, as one ancient writer put it "The ringing of bells exceedingly disturbs the spirits."[10]

Bell buoys, gong buoys and "groaners" (whistling buoys) are not the only sounds the seaman hears. Far from it. He listens to magical bells heard in the air and beneath the water to give him the weather. Should a storm occur, bells are rung to drive away the wind, and if it is a hurricane the bell is rung backwards. Sometimes, too, bells were used to cure madness. A small bell hung on a gravestone in Scotland was used for this purpose. It was also tied on top of a lunatic's head and kept there; in the morning the patient was dunked in a holy well and pronounced cured. Another bell, this one in Ireland, was thought excellent for relieving pains of childbirth. Originally it fell out of Heaven, but before alighting in County Donegal the clapper had a change of heart and returned to Paradise.[11]

Now and then it is interesting to note parallel stories. I have already mentioned the wonderful bell of Caher Island and how it nearly destroyed the people who tried to lug it off. On the southeast coast of England there was a similar bell belonging to a holy man named St. Gove—a friend of all sailors. St. Gove lived a life of great asceticism, but he did allow himself the luxury of a lovely silver bell. Pirates stole the bell and made off with it, but hardly had their anchor come clear of the ground when a gale sprang up and all hands, along with the bell, were lost. The bell, however, did not remain down long but returned to the place whence it came and entombed itself in a rock. To this day when the rock is struck the bell is said to ring.[12]

Scattered around the waters of the world are a number of bells that continue to ring—usually as a warning of coming storm. Jones mentions a shipload of bells sent to Forrabury to rival those of Tintagel. The master of the vessel carrying them boasted about his ability as a seaman, and the ship went down. Also in Cornwall, according to an informant, is a city which fell into the sea because of its wickedness, and to this day the bells toll beneath the water when a storm is brewing.

When Columbus came to the New World, he put into Kingston Harbor and moored his stern to a silk cotton tree to ride out a hurricane. (I was told this story and shown three links of a chain by Mrs. Wilson of that place in 1956). From then on the harbor, one of the few decent anchorages in the island, was to be populated by an increasingly wild and riotous lot. Under the command of Mansfelt, whom Henry Morgan poisoned, and then under the command of Morgan himself, the town of Port Royal became one of the wildest and most depraved seaports the world has ever known. Pirates and buccaneers with pockets full of Spanish loot and retinues of female captives indulged themselves in every kind of debauchery known up to that time. Despite this, the town had a priest and a large church, although there is no evidence that either had much business. And while the church was not on the agenda of most of the inhabitants, many of them complained that the bell in St. Paul's was inadequate and a larger one was installed through, ironically, public subscription.

From time to time the minister and others tried to warn the people to mend their ways, but to no avail. At last God took a hand. At eleven o'clock on June 7, 1692, Port Royal was struck by a series of earthquakes followed by a tidal wave. By noon it was over and Port Royal lay with "full fathom five" of water over it. Contrary to local belief, only a quarter of the population perished, but the treasure there exceeds imagination. Local stories say that the town simply went down all standing and the bell remained in the belfry. There, before hurricanes and other cataclysmic events, it tolls dully to warn mariners of impending danger. And although the bell has been recovered along with vast amounts of treasure, the seamen in the area still believe the bell rings in times of danger.[13]

This story leads quite naturally into the historical legend as such, and also into a discussion of the authenticity of legends and legendary heroes. In recent years historians have looked askance at historical legends, and some have gone to considerable effort to point out that, because they cannot always be substantiated, they are suspect and invalid. Actually, the legend is one of the chief devices used by the folk to transmit history.

There is also a feeling current among scholars that legend (folk history) is invalid because it neither stresses the correct or important things in the historic past nor interprets them properly. Using this as a measuring stick, many histories written in the past would suffer heavily. In fact, Gibbon's *Rise and Fall of the Roman Empire* stands on rather boggy ground if analyzed in this way. But if history is the preservative of the past interpreted in the light of the historian's culture values, then the folk come off surprisingly well, for their culture values are different than those of the intellectual.

For an item to survive—particularly orally—it must have a significance larger than others. In legends, this usually is embodied in a protagonist, be it a person or an object, a saint or a sinner. To the Anglo-American folk, the hero must demonstrate great strength, must endure great hardship, must have great courage. When he wins he may boast about it, but when he goes down he must go down bravely, overcome by a sea of troubles.

Lord Raglan in his book *The Hero*, which attempts to prove that Christ did not live, gave a list of all the qualities the great heroes had in common and demonstrated that this was ridiculous. The fact is that if they did not have these qualities, they could not loom large amongst the folk any more than a statesman could stand among his peers without guile. I shall discuss a number of folk heroes in this chapter. All of them were large men, all of them were strong men, all of them had great courage, all accomplished impossible tasks and died—if dying were part of their story—like Beowulf, combating overwhelming odds. None was noted for his intelligence, his wealth or his family connections.

When a man or a story is remembered by seafaring people as outstanding, one must know what is commonplace. Since shipwrecks and rescues take up a large segment of seamen's legends, two brief examples of commonplace rescues might be in order.

A number of years ago a freighter took ground on Blackwater Bank off the east coast of Ireland. It was blowing hard and a terrible sea was running outside; when the people of Rosslear saw the rockets going up they launched the lifeboat and made for the wreck. Unfortunately, before she got clear of land the lifeboat was twice swept by seas. Once she lost two men and once one. Each time she put back for more men, and more men were willing to go.

When she finally reached the freighter, the weather was "that wild" she couldn't get alongside. The crew of the stranded vessel had gone into the rigging and seas broke clear across the hull. For a time the lifeboat coxswain studied the situation, then he worked around to windward of the wreck and waited his chance. When a big sea rolled up, he opened his throttle and roared across the deck of the freighter on the crest of the comber, picking up survivors as he went. This he did three times before returning to port with all the survivors. The only comment my informant made about the story was, "I can't understand it. That coxswain would not go to sea again from that day to this."

Before rescue work was put in the hands of the Internal Revenue Service in the United States, it was done by the Humane Society, and the annals of that organization contain many accounts of rescues just as miraculous. Once off Long Island, in January, a boat was launched and swamped sixteen times before it finally cleared the breakers on the seventeenth try. At Cape Cod in January 1866 the schooner *Christina*, with a crew of five and a hold full of coal, took the ground on Hawes Shoal. This was on a Sunday in a blizzard. By that night all hands had been driven into the rigging and the master had frozen to death. Mate Tallman hung on and watched the spires of his hometown of Osterville, when he could see them through the snow. One by one his crew froze to death, the cabin boy going last. Tallman eventually became encased in ice and frozen to the rigging. At last the weather moderated and a lifeboat took him off on Thursday. Tallman lost his feet and fingers, but survived.[14]

These are the kinds of events that are commonplace. I should like to illustrate these remarks with two stories, one from the sixteenth century and one from the eighteenth. Both have been treated by "trained historians" and preserved by the folk as well. The first concerns the Spanish Armada, the other an important wreck on the Scilly Isles.

A onetime fisherman, the son of Peig Sayers, the great Irish storyteller, is an old man now, and he lives in a little hamlet called Vickarstown on Dunmore Head, the westermost point in Ireland. Before him lies the Blasket Sound and beyond that the Blasket Islands, where he was born. His name is Michael Guheen, and he is one of. the last of the Irish filés. I visited him one wild day and he told the following story:

This is the kind of story I hear about that prince they call the Prince of Spain, and he was fighting that time against England, against the mighty power of England and the old people say he was a kind of madman to be fighting against the British Empire because he knows always that he must give up at the last, the final field, but he was forced to go into Smerwick Harbour in the beginning of the year, in the springing of the year. In spring, in January maybe, or maybe after January, and at that time the weather used to be very bad on the western coast of Ireland, heavy seas, heavy rain, constant storm always. But ere they took shelter in Smerwick Harbour and they was staying there with the Irishmen in there at the total force that was there that was—by somebody at that time I don't know why it was (further to the man) but I hear it was and his men they were fighting against the Spanish. They will not let them go in and land and they had to stay out in the harbour.

But later on there came the news that they were boxed up altogether by the English frigates outside the harbour, the mouth of the harbour. Then the Prince told the admiral that they have to make it away, to dash out and break through the cordon that was out in the mouth of the harbour. Well, as I say, they blockaded them and starved them to death of hunger. Their enemy was inside worse than the enemy outside. Well, the admiral told the people to fight their way out but they wouldn't do it and the Prince went then on the admiral's ship and when the Prince went on the admiral got courage and they fought their way through the British frigates that was out at the mouth of the harbour and they sailed away. They have only galleys, some kind of frigate that work with sails at that time. There was no steam-ship nor anything like it but sail and they went out sailing and the wind was coming northeast and it commenced walking on and they were fighting their way through the British frigates and there was nothing left after the battle only six ships.

Six of the Spanish left out, went through the blockade. And they worked the tide, the waves and the wind until they came as far as the road in yonder Blasket Sound and that place was terrible that day and they [I] heared the old people say that it was the worst day they ever saw. That hurricane came down from the Southland. High winds and wharfs and trees and the place was terrible with swells. Swells going up to the sky and foam. And the seethe and the surge and their sails were torn to rags until they came to the Blasket Strand.

And when they came to the Blasket Strand there was a heavy current passing through a little gap there and they call it "the Ebb Tide" and it was a very bad place but they insist that they were stranded. They don't know the right place to anchor and they left their anchors out in the middle of the Tide and the tide was so strong they drifted, drifted down and they had to let their anchors go. Six anchors, a steel anchor, a copper anchor was left there in the Blaskets between Dunmore and the Blasket Island. They let the anchor go and they were smashed to smithereens in the Goub. Six of the ships. And the old people and the young people of the Blasket Island that time went running down to the Goub, the heaviest point to Dunmore and they used to stand there with ropes and warps trying to save some of the crew, but there was no living soul saved. They was all smashed and sink.

Then the *Queen of the Rosarie* the Admiral's ship passed through the Blasket Strand and they anchored too but it was no good. They were drifting and in a very few minutes they will be smashed to smithereens on the Goub. But they took out and they cleared the Goub by a small sand and they went out sailing close toward Sley Head. They once got direction toward Sley Head and a big rock in the middle of the Blasket Sound between Dunmore and the Goub of the Blaskets and that rock is there with a kind of a table stone with flat broad top and not very dangerous at all but when the ship struck that rock—the old people say she didn't—that rock didn't make her any harm. But a big heavy squall came and the ship was upside down, turned upside down and all the crew were drowned only a young lad, about eight years of age he was. He was the son of the Admiral and he tied himself to a tub—a barrel, a little barrel and he tied himself with a rope on the barrel and the barrel was thrown in at Coursa Rahn Neu—Comino Strand—and he was got there in the morning and they took him home and they nourished him; they gave him nourishment and care for a day or two and then he told the story. But it was very hard to understand him. They didn't understand a word from him because he was a Spaniard and spoke Spanish and they were not able to understand any Spanish at that time.

But then he went to Cork. He went there to the office, the British office, and he told the story and after that they were looking for the Prince and some other corpse and a few days later the corpse of the Prince was got. On the side of Dunquin cliff and brought him up on sheets and bound him up in the sheets and later interred him here in the garden of Vicarstown and they buried him there and that's what the old people say anyways. They buried him there but they say; I heard from an old woman on the Blasket Island—she was eighty-four or eighty-five years—that she could put her finger on the place where the Prince of Normandy is buried. He ended on the Blasket Island, where the castle, Pierce's Hotel was and she knows that there was another Spanish sailor put in the same grave.

But as long as the people around her couldn't understand any Spanish maybe the Admiral is buried here in Vicarstown and the Prince is buried on the island, but only for the boy they wouldn't have known the Prince. The Admiral will be there. He gave the story when the Prince of Spain is buried here in Vicarstown in a patch of land in a garden, a little garden and that the news after some time when he was buried I heard my old mother say that people came from Spain, gentlemen from Spain, to visit the grave and when they saw the place where he was buried, here in Dunquin, they said he was buried in the wildest and the most beautiful place that he could find, or any other body could find but they left him there. They didn't take him at all. They left his bones there to rotten. And that's the story of the Prince of Normandy and they said, and more will say the same thing, that he was a damn fool to be fighting [the British]."

All the events in this legend happened, although two incidents several years apart are confused. Ricalde had been in Smerwick Harbour on another trip to Ireland a few years previous. He had had to run for his life and had probably come down through the Sound, for it is a long haul out around the Blaskets.[15]

According to historians, this is what happened when Admiral Cloudsly was returning from a successful cruise to the south with fifteen ships: On October 22, 1707, in thick weather, he was off the entrance to the Narrow Sea (English Channel). He called a conference to establish his position. All agreed on the course to steer except the sailing master of the *Lennox*, who had invented an improved form of navigation. He said the proposed course would set the fleet on the Scilly Isles. All his expostulations served only to annoy the admiral, who already had a reputation for hitting the beach. The sailing master was rebuked and the vessels sailed off on the course they had decided upon.

The weather worsened and a gale sprang up. Scudding before it, the whole fleet piled up on the Scilly Isles about eight o'clock at night and over two thousand men were drowned. The admiral was one of the few to reach shore, and he was summarily killed by the islanders and buried after they had cut off his rings. Later he washed out of his grave and was reburied in Westminster Abbey, where the curious may view the final resting place of this imprudent man, and one can dive for his treasure—which has lately been located and is being recovered. All this is documented history.[16]

Here is how the folk remember the event:

According to a tale told in Cornwall, Cloudsly in the *Association* had set his fatal course when a sailor on board who had come from the Scilly Isles went aft and expostulated with his leader, saying if they pursued the course they could run ashore. The admiral flew into a rage and ordered the man hanged for insubordination.

Just before the man was to be turned off he recited Psalm 109 and said no one who saw him hang would live to tell about it. The hanging went as scheduled, the body was put in a hammock, shotted and thrown overboard. Instantly a storm sprang up and the corpse appeared looking at the ship which it followed until she drove ashore. The admiral washed ashore naked on a hatch with a little dog. He was dead and was buried in a grave which refused to stay filled and on which no grass would ever grow.[17]

Now the filé told another story that is not historical in the same sense. It does, however, give an example of how ancient tradition keeps on and modifies itself to newer traditions. At the same time it shows how surroundings can sometimes shape a story. To this end a few remarks are pertinent.

A short distance from Vicarstown on the shore road to Dingle are to be found a large number of beehive huts thought to have been built and occupied by early Christian hermits. They are made of stone and have a number of compartments deep in the ground. Beyond these one can see the Islands of the Dead, where the souls of all the departed were believed to go after passing through Ireland. This is one segment of the story. Another portion concerns itself with the idea that the dead will help you, coupled to a belief in ghosts and in the satanic power of underground beings. There is also a tradition about the "hounds of Hell" (normally black) that long for the souls of men. (Mourners shouldn't cry over a corpse at a wake, so hell hounds won't hear and come and tear the soul to pieces.) And finally, the story reflects the great immigration of Irish to America.

About twenty years ago a farmer was digging in a field above the beehive huts when he accidentally exposed a great tunnel leveling into the hill. Before he could explore it, rocks began tumbling down the side of the mountain and he was forced to run for his life, leaving the tunnel open. Shortly after this two men were found dead near the spot, their clothes and bodies all torn to shreds. They were so badly mangled that people were afraid to go there after dark.

A year went by and another man was killed on the same spot. Some said it was robbers after his gold, but that was not true, and as a result of this killing no one would go near the spot beside the tunnel at night.

One evening a very brave man was drinking in the pub and he said he was not afraid of anything and he was going to go home past the cave. The pub-keeper argued with him and begged him to stay. He even offered to put him up free for the night but the young man wouldn't listen. He asked the young man, "Please just wait till cock crow," but the man refused again and set out walking for home.

He had not gone very far before he met another man in the road and they walked on together, but neither spoke a word. After they had gone a little way the bold young man was surprised to see water coming out of his companion's boots and he could hear it squish every time he took a step. He thought this strange but still did not speak. At last they came to a very lonely spot in the road and the stranger spoke.

"Are you afraid?" he asked.

"A little," was the answer.

"You must not be. You are now in the worst bog, but I am with you and as long as I keep a hold of you, you will come to no harm."

They kept on going and in a little while the man asked again if he was afraid. Again the youth replied, "A little." The stranger told him he must not be afraid but must keep up his courage. He told the brave boy that soon they would come to a spot in the road where there were two dogs, one on each side of the road and they would try to tear him to pieces, "But as long as I am with you, you will be safe."

Sure enough, they had not gone far when they came upon the dogs. On one side of the road was a great white bulldog with a collar and on the other side another—and as they came closer the great bulldog with the collar sang a wicked Irish song,[18] and the other dog also. And the stranger said, "Now you must have courage. Keep up your courage and do not be afraid, for I am with you. Have courage."

When they came closer to the two dogs they lurched at him and showed their teeth and looked horrible, but the dogs did not touch them and the stranger guided them through safely, and when they had got through safely the stranger told the young man that he was indeed brave and that he had known him when he was only a baby although he wouldn't remember him. His father would though. . . . "I want you to tell your father that his uncle from America has saved you." He had died in America and had come all the way across the ocean to save him.

"I came a long way to save you. God sent me that long way just to save you. That is why there is water in my boots."

The young man asked him if he wouldn't like to come to his house for a drink.

"No, I have been there before. Just tell your father that it was your uncle that saved you and not to expect any more letters or money from America for I am dead."

With that the man vanished away and the bold lad staggered into his house "and fell into a swoon upon a swoon upon a swoon" in the doorway. His father thought he was dying and sent for the priest. The priest came and the man confessed to him and told him the whole story. The man was sick a fortnight but finally recovered.

The priest came to the spot where the cave was in all his vestments and had an open-air high mass and closed the tunnel with a great stone. From then on it was safe to go by there any time of the day or night. But a few years later they took all the stones from the tunnel and used them for building a new road and no one was ever bothered again.

The preceding story also indicates that seafaring people have a romantic turn to their nature, and they like a yarn that has a happy ending and that proves God's in heaven (far away), and all is really right with the world. Hugh Miller recorded such a tale from Scotland, where wrongs are long remembered and righted, if at all, after generations.

Two fishermen bound up Moray Firth in a wild night took shelter in a little cove with a cave at the head of it. To their annoyance they discovered three men there before them—three men with whom they had been mortal enemies for many years for while William Beth (one of the two) languished in a Dutch prison Eachen of Tarbat married his sister and claimed his property. Eventually Beth returned to Scotland and on the death of his sister turned Eachen and his two sons out of his lands. As a result bad blood had flowed between the two families for many years, and they were now shipmates in a cave before a fire made from wrecks.

Probably because Beth and his son were outnumbered that night they tried to bury the hatchet but as the gale rose so did memories, and the two men left the cave and slept in the boat (pursuant to the Scotch belief that evil will not follow one into the sea) leaving the cave to the Tarbats.

When morning broke the gale was down and old Tarbat made his way home but nothing more was heard of Beth and his son. Not even a scrap of wreckage came ashore, and as the years passed they were forgotten by everyone but a young girl who had been in love with Beth's son and his widow who gradually fell upon thorny times until after five years she was at death's door. And as she gradually declined, so did the elder Tarbat.

Finally five years later, Beth's widow had a dream in which she descended to the sea floor and saw a cave with bones in it and heard a voice saying, "Go home for you will see your son again before you will live here with me."

That afternoon Eachen Tarbat visited her and a great gale sprang up. The old man was terribly distressed, for his two sons were at sea and they could hear distress guns firing above the gale. Toward morning the gale broke and the old man started for home only to find the bodies of his two sons dead on the beach. The shock was too much and he was barely able to reach home before he collapsed.

The next day a man appeared at the cottage with a story. The elder Beth and his son had been blown far to sea in the storm five years ago and then were picked up by a vessel bound to Central America. There the two had amassed a fortune in gold and there the father died. His son had survived and returned to Scotland to his mother and his girl. The man with the story was young Beth and he wanted to see Eachen of Tarbat.

The old man was delirious and kept saying he could not pray, that he was haunted by the spirits of the Beths. He denied that he was a warlock and had raised the storm five years ago—that he had done any harm to anyone. But the ghosts of his delirium still haunted him and at last he admitted he had cut the rope that held the vessel fast. At that moment the door opened and in walked Ernest Beth. The old man looked, screamed, and died.[19]

From the Grand Banks comes a tale from the nineteenth century. It has nothing to do with admirals, armadas or treasure, and is not about an event or a person of much significance to the writer of history. Yet this man's story is preserved in legend because it contains elements in common with the previous three stories.

The story begins in a salt banker late in the year. In those days the technique of fishing was as follows: early in the morning the mother schooner would jog up to windward, dropping off her dories one by one. Each dory contained two men, a doryman and his mate, and was equipped with a compass, a beaker of water, a tub of trawl, a bailer, some bait, a fish billy and a horn. After the last dory was dropped, the schooner, manned by the skipper, cook, and a boy, would heave to or jog back and forth at the weather end of the long line of nineteen-foot dories that stretched away over the horizon. At the end of the day she would swing off and run down the line under easy sail, picking up her flock one by one and hoisting them aboard.

Next to being run down by a passing steamer, the chief thing the fisherman had to fear was the weather. Should the wind change, the schooner could find herself to the leeward of her dories and be forced to beat up the line, a long and slow process. Should it breeze up, come thick of fog or a spate of snow, she might well miss a dory which would be "astray"—the most dreaded word in a doryman's life, for it is nearly three hundred miles to the nearest land and all against the prevailing westerly.

To lessen this hazard, the schooner was equipped with a great horn which she blew when she swung off to pick up her men, and blew constantly in thick weather. In their turn the little dories blew, but in wild weather it was hard to hear the horns. This was especially true in snow, which not only muffles and gives false direction to the sound but also obscures it by the hiss each flake makes as it hits the sea.

And that is what happened to Howard Blackburn. The wind changed, it began to breeze on, it snowed, and the month was December. Howard and his dorymate blew their horn and listened, but all they heard was the hiss of the snowflakes and the rising wind. Two lonely men were astray in the North Atlantic and there was no chance for them except Newfoundland, and that was no chance at all.

Nevertheless, they threw over the catch to lighten the dory and headed for Newfoundland. First Howard would row and his mate would bail, and then the roles would be reversed. On they rowed, and on and on. After a time Howard's dorymate gave up and froze to death. Blackburn kept rowing, pausing now and then to bail. It wasn't too hard at first but then his mittens iced up. In knocking the ice off he lost one overboard, but he kept changing the one he had left. Then he lost that one and his hands began to freeze. Realizing what was in store, Blackburn shaped his hands to the handles of the oars, dipped them in sea water and then held them up in the air until he had two frozen hooks to slip over the handles of the oars. On he rowed through storm and snow, through dark and day, and slowly, slowly the great gap to the land closed. He rowed through his skin, through his flesh and his sinews. At the end he was rowing through the bleaching bones of his hands.

On Christmas Day Howard Blackburn rowed his icy dory into a cove on the coast of Newfoundland. He found a shack built out over the water and he rowed to it. He made sure his dorymate was stowed properly and secured the dory to a piling. He crawled into the shack, which was deserted, but there was a stove ready laid and a supply of firewood. There were even matches—but Fate was not through with him yet. He could not strike a light with his frozen, broken hands, so Howard Blackburn gave up and lay down to die.

At that time the owners of the shack, who lived a distance away, discovered they were out of wood, and it being Christmas decided to fetch some from the shack. They harnessed the team and went to the camp. The first thing they saw was the dory and her cargo, and then they found Blackburn and carried him home.

He lost his hands and his toes, but Blackburn lived. Not only that, he built a little schooner and sailed her to England to take part in Queen Victoria's diamond jubilee, using hooks for hands. Moreover, the people of Gloucester gave him a saloon, which he kept, and he became "the greatest whiskey rectifier" in Gloucester. He survived until his saloon was closed by prohibition, when he died, supposedly of a broken heart. The law succeeded where Nature had failed.[20]

In Nantucket they still tell the story of the whaleship *Essex* which in certain ways is not dissimilar to the story of Howard Blackburn.

A century and a half ago the *Essex* was fishing whales in the middle of the Pacific Ocean. The boats were out chasing and the mate was aboard when a great sperm whale came up and looked at the ship. He studied her briefly and then charged. The first time he struck her in the chain plates, but the second time he met her "head-on-head," and the *Essex* went down before they could get anything out of her beyond navigational gear.

The whaleship gone, there was nothing for it but to try for South America, over three thousand miles away. The entire crew of twenty men were in three whaleboats, each measuring 35 feet in length by 6½ feet in beam. Almost without food or water, the boats worked slowly east. After thirty days they landed on deserted Henderson Island, near Pitcairn, but not knowing where it was they pushed on for South America. Their plight was made worse by a shark following them.

On the forty-eighth day a man died in the mate's boat. Another died on the eighty-second day, and they ate him and survived until picked up after ninety-seven days at sea. The other two boats fared even worse. Before the two remaining survivors were picked up just short of the South American coast, they had eaten four of their number. Three had died of starvation, but the fourth one, Owen Coffin the captain's nephew, was killed and eaten after lots had been drawn to see who should serve as food.

With the peculiar irony that seems to accompany fate, the ship that picked up Captain Pollard was the whaleship *Diana* out of Nantucket, Zimri Coffin, master. According to the legend he was the father of Owen Coffin.

The story does not end here. Captain Pollard commanded another ship which went down after striking a reef in the Pacific. He was picked up and ended his days as a night watchman in Nantucket. Mate Chase grew old and is said to have hidden great supplies of food in his attic lest he become hungry at any time. Shortly before he died he was interviewed by a young man who asked him if he had known Owen Coffin, an ancestor. "Know him? Why, young man, I et him."[21]

It was the story of the *Essex*, coupled with other tales and bits of maritime folklore, which a strange young schoolteacher turned whaleman collected and turned into one of the greatest literary legends of all time— *Moby-Dick.*

Legends are not always of the magnitude of the ones referred to so far. Very often they are mere anecdotes, such as the one told by John Leavitt about the crew who refused to pump. Instead of putting for shore as they expected or even raising a row, the old man laid the vessel's head to sea and said, before going below to his stateroom: "All right, boys, go ahead and throw the pump brakes overboard. I've got just as many friends in Hell as you!"

Very often these short anecdotes revolve around a single person—

a local hero or folk hero. Usually these individuals are somewhat insular—that is, they are known only in Maine or Chesapeake Bay. There are many of them, and they survive the test of time remarkably well. Down in Chesapeake Bay there are Lickin' Billy Bradshaw and the Reverend Joshua Thomas—one of the few preachers who became a hero to mariners.

On Tangier Island the watermen tell many anecdotes of the days of this great man. One tells about his assistant, a young man whom Joshua Thomas never allowed to preach a sermon. The young man became despondent, until one day his superior told him to prepare a sermon for the following Sunday. The young man was delighted, and he worked up a real humdinger and committed it to memory. Sunday rolled around, and the young minister found himself in the pulpit struck with a bad case of stage fright.

"Now I have a grand sermon for you today. One that has a message, and I want you all to study the sermon and see what you can learn from it. The text is, "And he cast forth seven anchors . . ." At this point the young minister's mind went blank. He gazed wildly about but there was no help. Truly his God had forsaken him. "And he cast forth seven anchors . . ." Nothing. "And he cast forth seven anchors . . ." Still nothing. Desperate, the young man repeated the phrase seven times, at which point an old skipper in the back of the church bawled out, "Thet's right, Reverend. We got the point. That's forty-nine anchors he's put down already, and God knows there ain't no vessel goin' to drag with all that ground tackle."[22]

Down in Maine there is Horatio Leathers, who lived near Portland, a blacksmith who could lift a barrel of sugar to his shoulder and walk off with it, or hold an anvil at arm's length. He knocked an ox senseless once when it resisted being shod. Further east is Fred Carver, master of the maggoty schooner *Yankstebooden*, who used to bite chunks out of "cattle" (oxen) when he was angry.

Still further east, "down Machias way," lived Barney Beal, of Jonesport. Barney was a huge man who liked to sit in a rocking chair and put his hands palm down on the floor. He never sought trouble, but when it came he always managed to stop it. Once in Portland he threw two men through the side of a house when they crossed him, and he killed a dray horse there by punching it between the eyes when it threatened to run over him.

Barney lived around the time of the American Revolution and the War of 1812. One day he was out with his seine net when a British man-o'-war sailed by and ordered him aboard, for they were looking for men to impress (the activity that political folklore tells us caused the War of 1812). Barney paid no attention and continued to fish, so a boat was manned with twelve men to go and get him and his crew. All hands were armed and Beal's companions became nervous, but Barney waited until they were close enough. Then he stood up, threw the purse seine over the whole outfit—sailors, boat, oars and guns—hauled in the strings and bagged the lot. He then rowed ashore with the entire net load and marched the prisoners to Thomaston jail, more than a hundred miles away.

After many experiences Barney met his death in a manner that is still in doubt. One version is that he tried to haul a loaded dory onto a dock. He got it as far as the timber head when something inside broke and he dropped dead. Another one has it that he picked up a 500–pound anchor and slipped. In trying to catch himself, something broke inside and he died.[23]

Only slightly different was Captain Parker "Stutterin'" Hall, who was known from New York to Eastport. Stutterin' Hall was not overly large nor was he known for strength, although his temper was feared by man and beast. His fame seems to have begun because he always sailed alone except for a cat, no mean feat in a big coasting schooner. Rumor had it that he had quelled a mutiny in his youth by killing the mutineer and he had never had anyone on board since.

Aside from the fact that he knew by heart the course and distance between every lighthouse and landmark from New York to the Canadian border, his chief bid for fame seems to have been his wit, his speech impediment and his eccentricities.

Once down in Northeast Harbor the wind was fresh from the northwest and the moon was full. A young man came up to him and said, "Well, Captain Hall, I suppose you'll be leavin' for the Cape tonight?"

"N-n-no," said Captain Hall.

"Why Captain, it's a beautiful night. You just might make a record passage."

"Y-young m-m-man," said the Captain, "When I was a b-boy down on the Cape we used to make nail scoops outen the skulls of m-men w-w-who tried to make r-record passages."

At Matinicus Island the old man grounded out against the wharf and started selling vegetables and fruit. On the quarterdeck stood a magnificent barrel full of apples—twenty-ounce pippins. The storekeeper bought vegetables and asked for some apples. The old man produced a barrel of rather wretched-looking apples, and the merchant was upset.

"How about them twenty-ounce pippins?"

"N-no, n-not for sale."

"Why not?"

"I'm k-k-keeping 'em fer bait."

One night Captain Hall was lying in Holmes' Hole, now Vineyard Haven, when another vessel came in and anchored close aboard. The newcomer was deep-laden with stone, and Hall had a big load of lumber.

The two skippers hailed each other and Hall went to the other vessel for a chat, leaving his schooner more or less in charge of the ship's cat— a large, black, ornery creature. Parker had scarcely sat down on the other quarterdeck when the cat emerged from the fo'c'sle and after glancing around in a furtive manner set out over the deckload of lumber bound aft.

Parker paid no attention until the creature had crossed the lumber pile and started to leap onto the quarterdeck. He had watched the whole procedure surreptitiously, and when the cat crouched to spring the Captain said, "G-get f-f-f-forward, you black bastard." The cat turned about and disappeared back down into the fo'c'sle.[24]

Today the climate is not good for the preservation or creation of tales and legends. With the advent of radio and other media, shocking event follows shocking event in such profusion that each is buried under new ones in our consciousness almost before it has happened. Moreover, with shorter trips and the addition of radio, there is less time to while away in the fo'c'sle and less necessity to do so. For tales the climate is even worse than it is for legends, because one of the basic requirements for the tale —the connection with magic and the otherworld—is shrinking. In a time when Hell and faeryland lay at the bottom of a well and when Heaven lay just beyond the clouds, it was easy to believe in the intercession of otherworld creatures, but today when we have bored into the earth thousands of feet, and sent space ships into the farther reaches of space and found neither imps nor angels, it becomes harder to believe in the ingredients so basic to the tale.

Still, in the more remote, less-enlightened areas of the English-speaking world both are still told and believed in. Indeed, legends are still being made and may continue to be made for some time.

I have spoken earlier of Captain Buchan, the great skipper from Frazerburgh. His name is known to sailors from Peterhead to Stornoway as a desperate ship handler and a lucky fisherman. They tell how he would leave port in the teeth of a force ten winter gale to be "on the grounds" when it moderated, how he worked through the tortuous channel into the Wizard's Pool in the Outer Hebrides on a wild and stormy night in February. But the great story, the one that is well on its way to becoming a legend, is the one of a rescue and a tow one night off Norway. I had heard the story, and I asked the skipper about it one day in 1968.

Four year ago I was fushin' eighty miles west of Eggarsund and the *Alliance*, he was another beam boat, he was fushin, six miles to the southard of us.

So about four o'clock in the afternoon—it was in the month of February and it was the second week of February. And we seen it was goin' to be a wild nicht and of course we had had it a force ten forecast. So I called up this ship and I told him I was goin' to Eggarsun', that I was goin' to make for Eggarsun'. Now when I come up in the lee of him I seen that he was in difficulty so I went alongside of him and asked what was the trouble and he said that he had fouled up his propeller, he had the whole net in his propeller, in fact. He had tried to get his net aboard and the vessel had slipped back in the sea and had fouled the net. So this was a Wednesday night.

Now we took hold of him and it was at nine o'clock that we started to tow him of a Wednesday night and the weather was gettin' worse and worse and worse. In fact during that tow it reached force fourteen. Now we started to tow him with a nine-inch tow rope and it held for about four hours. We had ninety fathom of nylon tow rope and it failed. It held for four, no, seven hours. It broke at about three o'clock in the mornin'. Now it was real bad at that time. So we spliced the nylon tow rope again and we got it to hold through daylight and it broke again and it had become such a short line then we saw that it was practically useless. We next tried a cable again with rubber fenders [truck tires] in the bight to take the stretch, you know. We lost one hundred and thirty fathoms of cable with thirty fathoms of anchor chain. We thought that with the weight it might keep down and it wouldna' break. And hardly it kem tight.

And the weather noo 'twas force twelve and an easterly wind of course and we could just dodge—just a direct set practically into the wind. We figured out that was all we was doin'. Noo we towed that way but a short while and the cable parted. The weather noo was force twelve, mind you, and a reef lay two miles under his stern so we seen we must do somethin'.

Now the other captain called me up and he said we should use the ropes from the great sea net and in fact we hadna' much else left—and that is exactly what we did. We used twelve coil altogether, four coil that's at a time, two coil to a side we was using and doubled it gave us two hundred and forty fathom each side for a tow. But we had a problem. The sea was vurra bad and we couldna' pass the lines and the *Alliance* was not in a good condition. The sea had swept her clean and she had no boat. In fact, we had lost our boat and most of our fushin' gear overboard.

So I worked up under his lee to pass the lines aboard and just then a great Russian kem by. She seen us and she made us a kind of lee like and we got the lines aboard, but in doin' so we come together and I carried away the bulwarks forward and some other things, but it was superfucial damage really. I knew we couldna' leave them, and if we couldna pass the lines or tow them, we must ram them and take them in over the bows for we hadna wee boat—and if we had it would not have lived in that sea. But with the help from the Russian we did manage and got our lines aboard and started towin'.

Now this was Friday night and we hadna come four miles and the wind was force fourteen, but more to the north—and the ropes kept breaking and we replacing the rope by firing a rocket over his boat and making fast the ropes that way. And then our rockets were all used up so he said he'd use some and at the time we was layin' a short distance to leeward of him and standin' ready to haul in, and the rollin' was vurra heavy. Noo the first rocket he fired was a green type—there's two types, a red and a green type. It's a long-distance phosphorous rocket and 'tis fired with a gun, you see, and when he fired he put it right into the cabin, right through the clamp and it lodged, it buried in the planks in the inside of one of the bunks. At first we was afraid it would ignite and we had naught aboard to extinguish phosphorous, and we tried to draw it oot and we could do nothing with it. So we was forced to leave it there and we thought any moment it might go up.

So we towed right up to Sunday morning. That was from Wednesday night and we had only eighty miles to steam to Eggarsun'. Now we couldna make Eggarsun'. All we could do that time was face the wind more or less and we come in at last on Correrra Light, that's just off Fergusun'. So now the final part of this story was vurra comical also.

After that storm we went up under that lighthouse and you could see the rocks on each side of the channel and it was that narrer I didna dare go in. Being a single boat I wouldha gone on but I was not wanting to go on in case I was goin' against Norwegian laws; so we goes under the light-house and fires a rocket off and out comes a wee boat, a Norwegian fisher-man, an' he comes on board us and I asks him if he understands English and he says, "Cairtainly," he says, "I ham a Cockney." "What are you doin' down here if you are a Cockney?" "I was a commander here during the war." And he married a Norwegian girl and he was in the *Travell Light*.

And I says, "Well, can ye pilot me up that Sound?" "Well," he says, "this Norwegian fellow will do it." "I would chance it on my own like, but I would not fancy it towin' a boat alongside. I don't know the laws here, if I would be allowed to tow a boat alongside or astern, you see." So of course this Norwegian came and he started us up. So to go into the port we had a great deal of trouble from the wind, and of course there was a lot of workers there that came down like to see us, and he told us that the speed of the wind indicator had been away around about one hundred and thirty miles an hour an' we was towin' in that. Now it is an experience I should never like to have to go through again.

We lost about six thousand pounds in gear and damages, but the insurance paid for that and we got a good salvage price as well.[25]

If Jim Buchan will be remembered in Scotland for this feat of courage and seamanship, so will the story of a great swim be recalled for some little time to come in the West Indies.

Down in the Caribbean every year several hundred people "go bottom," for the ships are often old and cranky and invariably overloaded. However, the water is warmer than it is off Norway in the winter, the seas not so wild, and islands and rocks are sufficiently numerous that a strong swimmer does have a chance. Further, there is a living to be made turtling, gathering conch shells or snaring lobsters on the bottom. As a result, most people can swim. Sometimes when a whole boat is capsized or a fishing boat rolls over, the crew will dump out the rock ballast and hold the boat up with their hands while one of their members crawls aboard and splashes the water out with his hands.

Of all the islanders, the men of Bequia have the reputation of being the best swimmers. They dive to depths of eighty feet, they can swim miles without effort; but of all the swimmers there is one who stands out above the rest. We heard the story of his swim repeated the entire length of the Windward Island chain. Further, although the event took place in the recent past, it has acquired many of the characteristics of the legend. In some places the swimmer's name is not mentioned, in others the reasons for his swim are conflicting, and nearly every story contains some element about him not found in other versions. All are in agreement on the essentials—that he was in a boat that went down off Martinique and swam for three days before he finally came ashore, that he was long in hospital, recovered and returned to the sea where he performed further feats. For our purposes, a composite of these stories should suffice.

There was a man named King who was born with a caul, which enables a person to see jumbies [ghosts] and although it will not keep you from dying, it will keep you from drowning. This man was a very strong swimmer and he went with the other men in a big schooner (around fifty tons) to Martinique for a cargo. Now Martinique is a poor place to leave in the night, but as soon as the cargo was loaded the mate wanted to leave but the captain did not. Anyway, they hauled up the anchor and set sail.

Everything went all right for awhile until they were about twenty-six miles from Martinique, when they were hit by a very bad squall. It was cloudy so nobody saw the squall coming, and when it struck, the schooner capsized and went down. King had some flippers on board and he tried to get them but he didn't have time, for the vessel went down quick and one of the crew went down with her, which left three and they went swimming off.

King tried to encourage the others, but after awhile one of them said, "It's no use. I can't make it," and he turned on his side and they watched him go down. And this left two, and King tried to encourage the other fellow as best he could, but after awhile he went down and King was left alone hanging onto a little piece of plank that had floated up from the schooner when she sank.

Daylight came and he was all alone and very thirsty, and then he got sleepy and dozed, but the waves would splash in his face and awaken him, and he kept swimming.

On the second day he was very tired and thirsty, and he was nearly ready to give up when a bird saw him and flew down and started to light. He reached up and grabbed it and tore it in half and ate it raw, and this made him feel a little better. But then the sharks came, and he thought they were going to eat him, but just then a school of porpoises came along and began punching the sharks until the water was red with blood and the sharks went away, and the porpoises started pushing him along.

On the third day there was a woman working in her garden as he came ashore. He reached in through the breakers and a sea carried him up on the beach, where he collapsed. The woman looked down on the beach and she saw something in the seaweed at the edge of the water. At first she thought it was a coconut on a log and she didn't pay much attention to it, but when she looked again she thought it might be a turtle. So when her husband came home from work she told him about it, and he went down to catch it. When he got there he saw this man lying naked on the beach and he thought he was dead. He called some of his friends and they carried him to the house, and he was alive but in a bad way. He had been in the sea so long his skin had all come off and sea worms had crawled into his tongue.

They took him to the hospital and for three days he was unconscious, but eventually he recovered and came home for awhile, and then went back to sea where he had another experience. He was out on Tobago Cays diving and there was a Canadian diving there. The Canadian speared a grouper and stayed down too long battling with it. When he finally did come up, he just rolled over and went back down again. He had the bends. King saw it and dove in after him and brought him back up. He and his partner got him into their boat and gave him artificial respiration and took him to Carriacou, and from there he was flown to Grenada.

When he recovered he learned who had saved him and went to see King. He was very rich and had a large property in Canada. He told King he wanted to give him everything he had in the world, but King would take nothing. So they made a bargain, and every year King "has to go to Canada and live with this fellow for six months" and everything is given to him. He can't do anything. "And that is how King was trapped into going to Canada."

So long as men follow the sea, no matter how modern the ships or how sophisticated the gear, they will always stand in jeopardy of their lives. So long as there are men like these, there will be acts of courage and endurance that lesser men will look up to. And so long as men possess memory, no matter what the current fashion is regarding bravery and courage, they or those like them will be remembered. I count myself lucky in having met some.

"Hold fast!", Irish Lifeboat Service, Arklow, Ireland

CHAPTER XIV

SPECTRE SHIPS

"And then I saw the Flying Dutchman
come pounding o'er the lee."
— *Lines from ballad "Flying Dutchman."*
Perlach collection.

THERE is one corpus of legends and tales so old, so important, so closely related to one another that they have been included here as a separate chapter. Let's begin in the present century.

Just at dusk a trading schooner left Grenada bound for Tyrell Bay, Carriacou, about thirty-six miles away. The wind was light and it moderated still further and came more to the north, making it a long, slow beat for the schooner. About midnight she found herself to leeward of Kick-em Jenny Rock. The moon was up and the sea was moderate. The helmsman dozed peacefully at the wheel. Someone looked forward and yelled.

Under full sail came another schooner running without lights. She was close aboard on a collision course. The only way to avoid hitting her was to tack, and the schooner went about amid shouts and epithets hurled at the stranger. The trader had scarcely settled down on her new course when the other schooner again came bearing down on opposite tacks. Once more the ship was put about, only to be confronted by the stranger. Port tack or starboard tack, the strange schooner was always ahead, always bearing down and close aboard—and this continued all night.

Daybreak found the trading schooner, greatly delayed by all the tacking, still to leeward of Kick-em Jenny, but sailing alone on an empty sea. My informant told me, "They is a sperrit ship that sail there."

These spirit ships come into being in a number of ways. If a ship "goes bottom" without taking any of her crew or passengers with her, it is popularly believed that she will come up again and sail forever looking for a crew to man her. As insurance against such an event, some shipmasters in the area do not attempt to rescue all hands when a vessel is lost.

Actually there is a logical reason for the apparition that in this case appeared at Kick-em Jenny. There are two rocks, locally known as the Leeward Rocks, and according to Mr. Forchau of St. George, Grenada, these rocks look very much like a schooner under sail when seen in the moonlight. When the wind is light there is just enough current to keep a tacking schooner almost stationary as she approaches them. Thus when she sees one she tacks and is confronted by the other.

But ghost ships are not restricted to the West Indies. They appear all over the world. Scientists have gone to great length to explain their appearance. Some say that they are caused by the loom (fata morgana) of the sea. This seems to take two forms—to invert images or to distort images. These mirages are due to atmospheric conditions and are most commonly seen near sunup or sundown, often before the advent of a storm or bad weather. They have also been ascribed to a combination of eye strain, exhaustion and tension brought on by bad weather and overlong keeping of the sea.

In thick weather, too, actual vessels may be mistaken for wraiths. Off Land End, Nantucket Shoals, Cape Horn and other places where ships tend to congregate for a brief interval in their lonely wanderings, a ship or even part of her could well be sighted by a lookout and neither seen nor heard by anyone else, or her horn could be heard by only one person— suggesting that it was a spirit ship they had encountered.

There can be little doubt that anxious hours spent peering into fog and snow will cause seamen to see and hear almost anything they wish. Moreover, thick weather has a tendency to distort real objects into out-landish shapes.

I recall being awakened one foggy morning in Long Island Sound and being told we had a wreck ahead. When I came on deck it appeared to be a good-sized fishing vessel half sunk some little way off. Inspection revealed it to be a small, half-sunk skiff with a mast, less than a hundred feet away. Finally, such beliefs are augmented by occasionally encountering derelicts and abandoned vessels at sea.

Whatever the reason, the belief in the ghost ship is ancient, widely dispersed and still accepted. Of them all the Flying Dutchman is the best-known example. To fathom this tale would be a book-length task, but some remarks may be made concerning it, for of all the folktales in the world, this is one of the most complicated, oldest and most widespread. Further, its ramifications have spread far inland and changed more markedly than almost any tale of its kind.

Although there are many varied threads spun into the cable of this story, at least four seem to be outstanding. One is the story of the Wandering Jew, another of Ahasuerus the Antichrist. This legend has been adequately treated in a tome by George Anderson.[1] Disregarding numerous earlier antecedents, the stories were well known shortly after the death of Christ and reached fruition before 1600.[2]

Briefly, it seems that as Christ was carrying the cross toward Calvary a certain man railed at Him and told Him to move on. Christ looked at him and said, "I will go, but thou shall tarry until I return." Since that time the man has been a wanderer on the face of the earth, unable to die, unable to rest. This man during the Middle Ages became confused with another man, a cobbler named Ahasuerus, who was believed to be the Antichrist—a leader of the Powers of Darkness who had been present at the Crucifixion and who would strive with Christ when he returned a second time.[3]

The second thread in the tale comes from the Germanic story of "The Wild Hunt." In the beginning this was a tale about Wodin who, with his retinue, was said to pursue game across the sky.[4] Later this changed to a ghostly crew mounted on spectral horses following slobbering, yelling hellhounds in a mad pursuit of phantom game—usually boars or stags. Finally it became attached to various people who overindulged in their pastime of hunting. An English version tells about a man named Dando, a sensual priest who loved to hunt. One day he met the Devil, who stole his game and refused to return it. Dando swore he would ride to Hell if necessary to regain the quarry. Immediately he was placed on Satan's horse and away they dashed with the clamoring hounds to hell. Now and then he returns and can be seen tearing across the moor in wild pursuit of his prize.[5]

The third strand comes from the tale of a strange murder and penance from the North. For over six hundred years a spectre has walked the battlements of Castle Falkenberg crying "Murder!" The spectre is accompanied by two lights. Long ago two brothers lived there and courted the same girl. She married Walderan, and his brother Reginald took it very hard. After the wedding he secreted himself in a closet in the bridal bedchamber and waited. Shortly thereafter the bride and groom entered and hopped into bed. Before their expectations could be realized, Reginald climbed out of the closet and killed the bride. In the struggle he also killed his brother, who smote him on the cheek with a bloody hand during his death agony.

Since water would not remove the mark (of Cain), Reginald visited a holy man in the forest, who said he must make a pilgrimage to the North. Reginald immediately set forth and with him went two spectres—a white one on the right, a black one on the left. North he went with shade and shadow until at last he came to the end of the land. In the offing lay a great ship, and no sooner had the fratricide arrived than a wherry put off and when it reached shore the oarsman said, "We have been waiting for you." The fratricide and his companions got in and were taken to the vessel, which immediately got under way. Reginald and his two companions went below, where the black shade began dicing with the white for Reginald's soul. For six hundred years they have been dicing, and mariners to this day aver that through the spindrift and the foam they have seen the great ship with the dicers and Reginald pounding up to windward under full sail.[6]

The fourth great strand, which is perhaps the oldest and most resistant to change, is found in the ancient belief in the ability of the dead to participate in the activities of the quick. This, coupled to the almost universal belief that supernatural beings inhabit the turbulent waters about great headlands, completes the strand and hawser, for it is here, around Cape Horn and Hope, that the greatest of all the spectre ships appears.

Our story appears in many forms and guises, but three seem to comprise the root of all the others. The first is the story of Dahul (an Arabic name meaning Forgotten One) who turns up sometimes off Cape Finisterre. This man was a pirate and had as his chief consort no less a personage than the Devil, who came aboard as a stowaway. One day he struck the Devil a terrible blow and threw him overboard. Shortly after this he captured a vessel and found aboard a Spanish family and a priest. Dahul ordered the priest to be crucified and cooked the Spaniard's child. He then laughed at the priest's final agony. Suddenly the sky darkened and a great voice was on the deep: "You shall wander, Dahul, at the will of the winds, at the mercy of the waves. Your crew shall exhaust itself in endless toil. You shall wander upon every sea until the end of the centuries. You shall receive aboard all the drowned of the world. You shall not die, nor shall you ever approach the shore, nor the ships which you will always see fleeing before you."

Since that day the vessel has wandered. No one sleeps nor eats. She has no water and no hope. She is seen always before a storm and in the ominous quiet and half-light that precedes a great gale. She drives past under close reefs, her black hull half-buried in a smother of foam.[7]

The second tale concerns a huge, powerful Dutch captain named

Bernard Fokke, who drove his ships beyond the power of humans. To make sure his masts could stand the strain he encased them in iron bands. He was hard on his men and given to swearing great oaths. His ninety-day passages from Batavia to Holland were so fast and so regular that sailors believed he had made a compact with the Devil. However, time means money, even at sea, and his owners loved him. Eventually he failed to return and it was popularly thought the Devil had called him home. He may still be seen before an approaching gale driving his vessel around the Cape of Good Hope.[8]

The final story has two versions. The simpler one states that a Dutch sea captain, Vanderdecker (The Cloaked One),[9] tried his best to beat 'round Cape Horn but made no progress. At last he made a vow that he would never stop trying until he doubled the Cape no matter how long it took. He would "be damned" if he did. This was, of course, a direct affront to God, and he has been battling for his westing ever since. The old Cape Horners used to see him before storms in the vicinity of Table Bay, and when he appeared they knew that dire things waited in the offing.[10]

Our more involved story says that God appeared to Vanderdecker as he tried to force his way around Good Hope and told him to stop. The stubborn Dutchman drew his pistol and shot at the Master, but the bullet deflected and went through his hand. Vanderdecker attempted to strike God, but his arm fell useless and his Father cursed him. From that day forward he was to wander all oceans, never reaching port. He would drink gall, chew molten iron, never sleep, have always foul weather; gales would attend him, his body would become deformed, he would be the Evil One of the sea hated by all. Finally, whenever he was seen by a passing vessel, disaster would attend his passing. Having thus negated every hope and pleasure sought by seamen, the merciful Father returned to heaven. The courageous captain said only "I defy you," and since that time has been forced to endure the punishments in his ship the *Voltigeur*.

Through the interweaving of these three basic tales have come most of the Flying Dutchman stories. Gathered around these three stories are many beliefs that do nothing to lessen the fame of Dahul, Fokke or Vanderdecker. Not only do they bring storms, their ships bring plague, madness. They cannot be boarded. They are luminous; if you take letters from them you are lost. On their decks are seen spectres dicing for souls. They make no sound. The figurehead is a skeleton and spectres swarm over their yards. You can hear them many leagues away and so on. Should you doubt the veracity of their being, they were seen by no less than the two sons of the Prince of Wales![11]

So catching has the idea of the Flying Dutchman become that it has gone ashore and become part of both folk and intellectual endeavor, appearing as an opera by Wagner and as the theme of numerous poems and novels by Scott, Longfellow, Marryat and Cooper, to name but a few. Among many folk antecedents are "Peter Rugg, the Missing Man," who haunts the Boston Post Road in New England; the Hitchhiking Ghost, popular around large cities from Philadelphia to San Francisco; the Spectre Stage Coach of the nineteenth century, and most recently, a spectre bus, truck or automobile which is forced to wander the better-known highways of the United States.

Robert Flaws, a former student who spent two years as a cowboy in the West, informed me that there is even a steer that fits the bill. Like the Judas goat that leads the sheep to slaughter, there is also a Judas steer that is said to lead cattle on the long drive to the hamburger stand. Such a steer was Don Ramírez, an ancient longhorn who was fated to escape the butcher only to wander the prairie, gaunt and luminescent, stampeding cattle before storms and prairie fires.

Before closing, it is worth noting that the spectre of Vanderdecker's ghost stalked the courtroom in a famous trial in San Francisco a century ago.

In 1851 the firm of William Webb built the extreme clipper *Challenge*. With her they planned to establish a speed record to California and made Captain Robert H. (Bully) Waterman her master. She was a tremendous vessel and under her new commander carried almost 120,000 square feet of sail—a spread no other commander could make her bear.

If the ship was magnificent, her crew were not. They were scraped out of every sink and drain in New York. Further, they were interested in pay and not in ships or records. They apparently did not know Waterman's reputation and his five foot eight stature did nothing to enhance it. None, apparently, took the pains to note his gimlet eyes.

Waterman had been chosen to command for a number of reasons. He was known to be fearless, to be the most desperate sail carrier of them all in an age where the motto among sea captains was, "What she can't carry she can drag." Moreover, he had a record for fast passages from the Orient. In the *Natchez* he had made the passage from China to New York in seventy-eight days. He had circumnavigated the world in less than ten months. He had sailed 385 miles in twenty-four hours in the *Sea Witch*, and had gone anchor to anchor, Canton to New York, in seventy-four days.

To get the most out of his vessel Waterman had his halyards padlocked aloft (to insure that no one would lower the sails) and stood aft roaring at God to dare to capsize him. As for his crew, he feared them in proportion to his fear of God, and would flatten the first shirker or malingerer with a four-foot "persuader" he kept lashed to his wrist. Before shipping on, the crew of the *Challenge* might have done well to have studied their homework.

Going 'round the Horn five men were lost overboard from a yard, and on August 17 the crew jumped the mate "Black" Douglas and stabbed him. Single-handed, Waterman waded in with his persuader, saved the mate but disabled the crew. From then on things went badly, and the *Challenge* arrived in San Francisco after a passage of 108 days. The crew jumped ship, those able to jump, and charged Waterman with inhuman treatment and murder. Waterman meanwhile charged the crew with mutiny.

During the ensuing trial the counsel for the seamen attempted to create a bad atmosphere for Waterman. They pointed to his past records from the Orient, his quick returns to sea, his challenging God, and averred that in order to make his vessels bear more sail he cased their masts in steel. In point of fact they attempted to demonstrate that, like the Flying Dutchman, Waterman was either cursed by God or in league with the devil.

Waterman was acquited, but like the three spectre captains his career was ruined. He retired to a small ranch and died of peritonitis.[12]

Although the Flying Dutchman is the best known and most developed of all the tales of ghost ships, they are sufficiently abundant on the coasts of North America, the British Isles, Ireland and the West Indies to make them a hazard to navigation.

Nearly all stories about ghost ships seem to have certain things in common. They appear in certain guises, as fire ships, as flying ships—in which case they usually soar over land or across points—or as normal ships that do peculiar things or have odd characteristics. They sail backwards, they vanish as they reach land, they carry full sail when others are forced to scud under bare poles, they sail dead to windward under full sail; they proceed at a rapid pace under close reefs in a flat calm carrying a living gale with them. Sometimes their planks are gone and only their ribs remain through which the sun can be seen, their sails are threadbare or totally flogged out, leaving only the leach, luff and bolt ropes. No man stands at the helm and the crew are sometimes skeletons, sometimes nonexistent. Very often they are luminescent and pass in total silence.

Every one of these ships seems to have a purpose—usually to serve as a forerunner to warn or prepare those who see it for dire events. Most often they are seen before violent storms and appear in the gloaming, in fog, snow, sleet, rain or humid weather when the glass is low. (Which lends credence that they are indeed mirages.) Of those that predict storm, the fire ships are the most common. They also are seen before tragedy—a family death or the loss of a vessel.

In almost every case these are ships that have come to a sudden or tragic end—particularly if they have been lost through foul play. Wrecked vessels, scuttled vessels, vessels on which mutiny and murder have occurred or dark deeds have been committed, are most likely to become spectre ships. Vessels that have been wrecked with loss of life—especially if through negligence or incompetence—may become spectre ships, but ships that are scrapped or "towed up the creek" to molder away on some mud bank do not as a rule. It is not surprising then to find these apparitions thickest where wrecks have occurred or where wreckers have been active— at the mouth of the St. Lawrence, on Georges Bank, Cape Hatteras, the Hebrides and the Cornish coast.

Perhaps one of the most spectacular phantoms that we have to deal with is the fire ship. Although they may appear elsewhere their most likely habitat seems to be North America. A number appear in the neighborhood of the Gulf of St. Lawrence, but whether it is actually one ship seen in different places or a number of ships each in a different locality would be hard to say. Professor Ives mentions one in Cumberland Bay that is a "full-rigged ship" that burns brightly while the crew scurry around the deck, but he also suggests she is "a tops'l schooner" and "a steamer"—neither of which is "a full-rigged ship." One of his informants told him it was Kidd's treasure ship that was re-enacting her final hours.[13]

Another writer mentions "a small schooner" that appears at Cow Head near there and that has bright running lights. Every twenty years she piles up on a reef and vanishes and is believed to be Captain Kidd's treasure ship. Although the author does not say the vessel burns, the two stories appear close enough to make one wonder if we are not learning about the same vessel from two sources.[14]

Two fire ships that are much less controversial appear in Mahone Bay near Chester, Nova Scotia, and at Block Island, Rhode Island. The first, the *Young Teazer*, we have mentioned briefly before, but her full story bears telling.

During the War of 1812, there were two American privateers named the *Teazer*. The old *Teazer* was captured after having sent in at least one

prize valued at fifty thousand dollars. At the time of her capture she was
under the command of a man named Johnson. This man was paroled on his
honor and could not again bear arms against the Crown until a prisoner
was exchanged for him. Should he fail to comply with the terms of parole
and be captured, he would be hanged by the British.

Captain Johnson did not wait for exchange but joined the *Young
Teazer* and went on a cruise to Nova Scotia. Things there were dull and
they sacked the small town of Chester but acquired little booty—the town
already having been plundered. They tried it again at a later date and were
trapped in Mahone Bay by a man-o'-war. Captain Warren summoned his
officers aft to see if a plan could be devised to elude the enemy, but Captain
Johnson, probably preferring not to be hanged as a common criminal and
believing escape impossible, went below and blew the ship up, killing all
hands save six men.

In discussing the affair Captain Coggeshall had this to say about
Johnson:

> Had Johnson blown his own brains out, or tied a gun about his neck and
> thrown himself overboard, some would have mourned for him, and none
> found fault. By all events he was not one of the most amiable men living;
> on the contrary, the desperate wretch must have been possessed by the
> devil, to have plunged so many human beings into eternity without a
> moment's warning.[15]

Apparently the *Young Teazer* was scattered quite liberally over the
bay, for as late as 1948 fishermen were retrieving bits and pieces of her
which brought good prices from tourists in the town. But the *Young Teazer*
left more than souvenirs to be sold to tourists. She rises from her grave
and re-enacts her final moments. So frequently does she do this that the
natives pay scant attention beyond remarking, "It's the *Teazer* burning
again."

Usually she appears in fog or thick weather as a bright glow offshore.
Should the curious investigate, the glow fades away as they approach, only
to appear somewhere else. This glow often lasts for many minutes and
when it occurs it is generally—but not always—thought to be a forerunner
of bad weather.

In July of 1948 I happened to be in Mahone Bay and saw a glow in the
fog and was told it was the *Teazer* burning again, and was advised that a
gale was imminent. It arrived the next day.

Unlike most spectre ships, this one seems to serve two masters. There is the treasure on Oak Island protected by a phantom horse and a hellhound. Whenever anyone approaches this treasure the hound is seen coursing on the island, the horse appears and the *Teazer* is said to burn most brightly in the offing.[16]

Several hundred miles to the southwest of Mahone Bay lies Block Island. This tiny island has been the scene of many tragedies and nefarious acts, beginning when Captain Oldham was killed by Indians in the seventeenth century.[17] Pirates were thought to bury gold there and the inhabitants once had a reputation as wreckers, and until recent times there was a belief in Rhode Island that strangers could lose almost anything there that wasn't well tied down and carefully guarded.

During the eighteenth century a vessel named the *Palatine* was lost there under unusual and conflicting circumstances. One story has it that she was a German immigrant ship carrying religious dissenters to this country; the vessel had had a hard passage, ran out of food and water, lost her way and at last picked up Block Island. She came in, dropped anchor and sought relief. The passengers and crew were in desperate straits and one woman had gone mad. While her people were ashore the madwoman set the vessel afire and was burned to death in her.

The second story has it that the island wreckers lured her in by the age-old method of extinguishing the lighthouse and placing a false light around the neck of a hobbled horse that was allowed to browse along the cliffs. The vessel came ashore, the natives knocked the survivors on the head, plundered the ship and set her afire, with a crazy woman aboard. The rising tide freed the blazing vessel, which drifted offshore and sank.

Ever since that time the vessel is said to rise and burn before great storms and also on the Saturday that falls between Christmas and New Year's commemorating her loss.[18]

Out of this tale there grows another collected on the island many years ago. From the profits of this wreck, and others, the islanders built a vessel and loaded a cargo for the West Indies. The crew was made up of Block Islanders and the skipper was a Block Island native renowned for his ability to make a fast passage. The vessel sailed, reached the islands, sold her cargo, loaded another and set sail for home. All of this was done in super-record time, and she arrived off the island weeks before she was expected. At twilight the natives looked out and saw a sail in the offing. The light was killed, the false one set. The night was dark and wild. The vessel came in and hit the beach and the wreckers attended to the few survivors who managed to get through the breakers. When dawn came they discovered they had wrecked their own ship and slaughtered their own kind.[19]

All weather breeders are not necessarily fire ships. In fact fire ships do not appear very often in British or Irish waters. According to Captain James Buchan, a transport loaded with returning troops was coming into Stornoway after World War I. The day was calm and the weather pleasant for Stornoway (it wasn't blowing a gale). There was no reason for tragedy, but the steamer hit a rock in the harbor and went down with terrible loss of life. Since that time a white steamer is frequently seen coming in before an impending storm.

Along the Cornish coast, where wrecks, contrived and accidental, have been numerous, the waters, the air and the land are thick with ghostly vessels. They vary in design from a lugger that appears over a pool to a tub manned by a witch who caused storms to arise and now for her evil ways must continually bob around on the ocean.[20] Some of these are said to bring storms, others to follow them. Some are simply signs or messages from the dead. Still others come to bear away evil persons or to make sure promises made long ago and broken are kept at last. Some, too, are fore-runners sent by the otherworld to prepare the community for the news that a certain ship was lost. Others are bent on revenge.

It is said that years ago a pirate landed in Cornwall, where he gave up "going on the account" and turned to the more respectable business of smuggling. This soon palled and he set his talents to wrecking. He was very clever at this occupation, lured many ships ashore and murdered the survivors before gathering up the loot. At last old age caught up with him and he lay on his bed dying, but his end was not easy. The Devil kept coming into the room and the neighbors drove him out again and again until he entered in the shape of a fly and they gave up. Suddenly in the room the watchers heard the sound of breakers and a great voice cried out, "The hour is come but the man has not come." Outside people looked up and saw a black cloud coming from seaward. In it was a coal-black, full-rigged ship under full sail. She swept across the land and over the house gathering up the wretched man's spirit as she passed.

After this event the neighbors decided the man should still have a decent funeral. They put the body in a coffin and headed for church. On the way the procession was mysteriously joined by a huge black pig, and just as they reached the church the coffin was consumed by a bolt of lightning.[21]

Interestingly enough, an almost identical story appears in Labrador. Just before a pirate-turned-wrecker-and-smuggler died, people in the room heard the sound of waves and breakers and a voice saying, "The hour is come but not the man." At that moment a black vessel sailing on a cloud appeared and carried off the man's spirit. Omitted are the episodes of the pig and the coffin.[22]

Actually a good many of the ingredients in these stories are common motifs among seafaring people, as can be seen by the following anecdote.

One night a fisherman was walking between Inverness and Cromarty in Scotland. As he topped a hill he saw before him an ancient cairn. The moon was in-and-out between the clouds, and as he watched a strange thing happened. The gloomy heath became a gale lashed sea and the roaring of breakers filled his ears, although he was three miles from the sea and it was a calm night. Before his eyes he saw the cairn turn to a stag (pinnacle rock), and driving across the boiling sea came two great ships which sailed round and round the cairn.[23]

Does not this story help to explain the other two? Fog on the heath resembles waves, the "roaring" of the sea could have been in his own ears or the fact that it was so calm allowed him to hear the far-away rote of the sea. Things as simple as this, when the circumstances are right, assume immense proportions, spread widely abroad and die very hard.

Many years ago there was a good harbor at Orford near Orford Ness, considered one of the more dangerous points along the English coast. For one reason or another (some say an irate mermaid was responsible) a bar was built up across the harbor mouth and a haven became a cul-de-sac. According to Captain Bob Roberts, vessels trying to work around Orford Ness in heavy weather often find themselves in difficulty. At this point a small sailing vessel is seen close aboard and standing in toward Orford. The incautious master, eschewing the proverb, "When in doubt stay out," adopts its counterpart, "Any port in a storm" and follows the stranger in, only to be wrecked on the bar.[24]

Of all the stories about ghost ships none can match for sheer horror one told at the Isles of Shoals. It could be argued that it is a story of the quick and not the dead, but if so it certainly embodies a good deal of spectre ship lore in its makeup. It is a good story to set down here, for it has an identifiable background, and it is my belief that behind all folklore there is some kind of demonstrable fact.

Like many lonely islands, the Isles of Shoals have a long history of violence. Here today can be seen the graves of little children buried and left by their parents years ago. Here a mother strangled her child lest it cry and reveal her presence to hostile Indians. Along the shore walks the shadow of Constable Babb in a bloody smock, and a hooded monk is said to hurry along the shore when the wind blows east. The ghost of one of

Blackbeard's wives stands on a rock and wrings her hands. Two spectre pirates are said to fight in the church attic. Many ships have been lost here. Sometimes the crews made shore and in one case froze to death fifty feet from a snug house. It was a hangout for pirates. Years ago two men set out in a small boat from New Hampshire and on Christmas Day they were sighted coming into the harbor at the shoals, but they never dropped anchor. The vessel is still seen on moonlit nights before snowstorms beating into the harbor. And here occurred one of the most atrocious murders of the nineteenth century.[25]

In March, 1873, a man named Wagner found himself out of money in Portsmouth, New Hampshire. He had previously stayed with the Huntvet family on Smutty Nose Island (one of the islands in the group). Discovering that the male Huntvets were away from home, he stole a dory and rowed ten miles across the black sea to rob the family. He arrived at midnight and rifled the house. While he was so engaged he was surprised by the womenfolk. Two he knocked unconscious with an axe and then leisurely strangled them with a scarf. The third he wounded, but she escaped in her nightgown to hide in the snowy rocks. Wagner ate a hearty meal, conducted an unsuccessful hunt for the remaining witness and rowed back to Portsmouth. He was caught, tried and given a long prison term.[26]

In 1953 I heard the following story from a fisherman on a seine boat anchored there. He began by calling my attention to the fact that there were no "guinea boats" (a kind of nondescript vessel from Boston manned largely by Italian and Portuguese crews) in the harbor. He then remarked that formerly they used to come there in numbers and lie there for a month at a time fishing around the island during the day. In the evening they would sit around a barrel of wine and swap stories.

One night a member of one of the crews got drunk and went ashore. There he accosted the wife of a local fisherman and when she would not do what he wanted, killed her with a knife, returned aboard and next morning went back to Boston.

The murder was discovered and the islanders accused her husband of the crime; he was seized on his return, and despite his protestations of innocence the police hustled him aboard a waiting boat to go to Portsmouth jail. At this point a violent storm sprang up. All attempts at a crossing were temporarily abandoned and the police retired to a house with their prisoner.

By midnight the storm had reached its peak, and it was then that the accused man jumped through a window, fled to the beach, launched a dory and rowed off into the wild night. Although they searched all the islands and rocks from Gloucester to Cape Elizabeth, no one ever saw the man or his dory again.

Later on the fleet of guineamen returned to the island and learned of the murder. They suspected what had happened but said no word of their suspicions to the outside world.

A few weeks passed and one night it "came thick-o-fog": the guinea-men were all nested in the harbor for the night. About two o'clock in the morning horrible screams were heard from the foc's'le of one boat. Every-body raced below to see what had happened. A light was struck and there lay the murderer, his right hand severed at the wrist. So great was the consternation at this assault that one man forgot to mention he had heard the sound of oars on tholepins, and another that he had seen the figure of a man in oilskins rowing away in the fog in a dory.

After that no guinea boat was safe in harbor there. If the weather was thick or stormy, screams would be heard aboard one of the vessels and a man would be found mutilated in some way: ears would be severed, a foot cut off, the nose sliced off or an eye gouged out. And always in the gloom would be seen the wraithlike form of a man dressed in yellow oilskins pull-ing away in a dory. Between the roar of breakers or the mutter of thunder his oars could be heard against the tholepins. No one saw or heard him come but someone always saw and heard him depart.

For eighteen years these attacks continued but only against the one particular breed of fishermen. At last the guinea fleet gave up going to the islands and then the attacks stopped. My informant told me that they never came there any more for fear of the fishermen, and indeed I have never seen them there in all the times I have stopped at the islands.[27] It seems to me that the development of this story is self-explanatory.

Another dangerous ship is said to lie about in the vicinity of the Solway Firth, a spot well populated with ghost ships. In this case a bride and groom went to sea. As is known, it is very bad luck to take a bride to sea,[28] and it may have been for this reason that the girl and her husband were murdered and thrown overboard. Shortly after this the ship went down with all hands, only to reappear. Should you see her you know she is an omen of evil, for terrible disaster will visit your ship soon afterward.[29]

All over the English-speaking world there are ghost ships that portend death. Perhaps the most famous of these—possibly because she was im-mortalized by the poet Whittier, who had a keen interest in abolition and the supernatural—was the ghost ship of Harpswell, Maine.

During the war of 1812 there was a privateer named the *Dash*. Because of her extreme lines she has sometimes been called the first clipper ship, although she appeared nearly a quarter of a century before the *Anne McKim*. The *Dash* was so narrow that she had little room for stores—which meant that she could not keep long at sea, but her tremendous speed made up for this and she was a very successful privateer, although one is led to suspect also that she might have been a bit tender.

One evening after the war her skipper made a bet with another sea captain that the *Dash* could sail away from his ship any time. Accordingly a race was arranged around Georges Bank and back. First boat home—the winner. Away they went and the old *Dash* showed her stuff. By the time they were approaching the shoals she was already hull down ahead and going away under a cloud of canvas. At that moment a heavy squall struck, and when it cleared the *Dash* was gone forever. Whether she was lost in the shoal water, driven under or capsized, no one ever knew.

Shortly after this the *Dash* turned up in Casco Bay. She was seen with all sails set just at twilight, with the fog coming in, sailing backward toward the town of Harpswell where most of her crew came from. Before reaching the harbor she vanished into thin air. Shortly after this one of the family of a member of her crew is said to have died. From then on she appeared at odd intervals, always in the mouth of night, and always after her appearance the church bells tolled the passing of someone related to her crew. Eventually it was rumored and then believed that she would appear as a harbinger of death until all the relations of the sailors aboard the *Dash* were in the churchyard, or as Whittier put it, "And slowly where the dead ship sails, The burial boat shall row."[30]

Sometimes of course the spectre ship is a vessel of mercy quite different from the one at Orford Ness. Once two small vessels left together from Broadsea for Aberdeen. They had not been long at sea when they were caught in a heavy gale and became separated. Eventually the gale abated and one of the boats kept away for Aberdeen—a dangerous and somewhat difficult harbor to enter. When she arrived off the harbor entrance she was delighted to make out the shape of her companion ship ahead of her in the dark and followed her glibly into the harbor without harm or danger. It was only after she had tied up that she realized the other vessel was not still ahead of her and in fact had never actually been seen since the gale.[31]

Many of these vessels appear only once. These, usually but not always, are couriers from the other world that visit the living to tell what has become of their friends. When the British ship *Neptune* was wrecked at Gwithian she was reported seen as an apparition at St. Ives a mile and a half away. The day before she was lost she was seen off Cornwall. A boat put out to her with a pilot and came alongside. The pilot stood up and reached for her planking to steady himself before boarding, but he grasped thin air and fell overboard.[32]

The most famous of these vessels to appear in North America turned up in Long Island Sound during Puritan times. Captain Lambertson had a brand-new vessel under him, but he felt she was cranky and he feared for her safety. At any rate, during January, 1647, he took on board a group of Puritans and vanished from the world of the living. Great was the consternation among the pious Puritans and prayers were offered for her speedy return. These prayers were (perhaps) answered in June, six months later. Following a storm, the ship was seen coming dead into the eye of the wind under full sail an hour before dark. On she came until her crew could be distinguished and then her sails, her spars and masts and the vessel itself disintegrated and were no more.[33]

About the same time another ship departed from Salem, Massachusetts. She had aboard a young man and a lovely young girl. The crew were very unhappy about their presence, and the vessel vanished. Whether or not she would have been like the vessel already mentioned in Solway Firth we shall never know. She appeared, sailed backwards, one of her crew could be clearly seen pointing at something—indeed she had all the qualifications for a spectre ship—but a Puritan minister exorcized her and she hasn't been seen since.

So far we have been talking about vessels that are spectres on the sea. There are many on fresh water (Wilbur Bassett mentions two on the Great Lakes and Hunt has a small lugger on a pond in Cornwall). There are also spectre ships that float or fly through the air with the greatest of ease, and these are thought to be harbingers of storm or death. Bassett mentions them in the British Isles and the Carey collection in Maryland has at least one story about a phantom ship that soared across a neck of land in Chesapeake Bay.

In this case a woman had pressed and preserved an infant's caul so she would be able to see into the future, and she was rewarded on several occasions. One winter afternoon at five o'clock she looked out of her window and saw a ship under full sail sailing above the tree tops. Later she learned that at that exact instant her husband was drowned.[34]

Still another is sometimes seen in the Newfoundland area. This vessel is a large white steamer (not unlike the one at Stornoway). She is usually seen in the offing making for a harbor too small to hold her. Nevertheless, on she comes under a full head of steam, enters the harbor, runs up on the shore and keeps on going "cross lots."[35]

Not infrequently spectre ships appear for no particular reason. Apparently this is especially true in Scotland and in the West of Ireland. The ships are constantly being seen, rowing ashore, fishing, or just sailing by, manned and unmanned. Although such sights are commonplace, the identical craft and crew do not reappear very frequently.[36]

Two startling but harmless spectre craft belonged to pirates. One was Kidd's old vessel that has been seen engaged in mortal combat with another vessel in Long Island Sound. Another pirate vessel—we would think that of all ships the shade of a pirate vessel would betoken some kind of coming legend—that apparently was harmless appeared frequently in Galveston Bay and in the adjoining waters at the end of the last century—the *Fame*, a black-hulled, heavily armed tops'l schooner belonging to Jean Lafitte. The *Fame* was supposed to have gone down with seven million in jewels and gold aboard after Lafitte's death. The crew were drunk and most went down with her. She was seen on several occasions and once in '64 helped a blockade runner get into Charleston harbor. The most famous sighting of this vessel came in 1892 when she was observed by two ships. One reported he was nearly run down by her and that the crew looked like living dead men. Another man, master of the Norwegian *Fair Hilda*, reported that she had missed his ship by inches one afternoon while her crew paid not the slightest attention. What was most remarkable about her was that she was luminescent and as she swept past she cast no shadow.

Apparently this vessel was an ocean wanderer, for she was shortly thereafter reported seen off Central America.[37]

Less formidable than the *Quedah Merchant* (Kidd's ship) or the *Fame* was the ghost of the old clipper *Tennessee* that was said for many years to be seen working her way into San Francisco Bay only to vanish before reaching port.[38] So too with the Gloucester schooner *Alice Marr*. She was named for the captain's fiancée (a bad omen) and went to the Grand Banks never to return. On the anniversary of her sailing she was reported in the outer harbor of Gloucester but never reached port. Every year on the anniversary of her sailing she was supposed to rise from the bottom and appear off Gloucester, but for what purpose no one knows—unless it was to give some comfort to the bride-to-be, who eventually wore her wedding dress as her shroud.[39]

All of the ships mentioned so far have had real vessels as their origin. There are another collection of phantom ships that need passing consideration. These are death ships or devil ships, and have their beginnings in far older times than those of the Flying Dutchman and her consorts. Fortunately or unfortunately, these stories have become so diluted as, in many cases, to be simply ridiculous tall tales. We need only to recall the idea of a death voyage and note that for the Greeks this voyage was made in Charon's boat—a vessel so lightly built that she nearly sank when a live human came aboard. Moreover this vessel appears to have been constructed for the old ferryman and was not the fortuitous result of the loss of some fishing smack with a cargo of sardines.

Both the Celtic and the Germanic people had such boats as Charon's only they were larger and went upon the sea and not across a stygian river. One of these ships kept station off the west coast of Ireland, and it was her duty to load aboard all the dead of the world and freight them to Paradise. Another was under orders to scour the seas and oceans of the world picking up drowned sailors, while yet a third roamed the cold northern seas freighting German dead to their long home.[40]

All of these ships are large—larger than the Ark which measured only 525', and their length and width seem to say something about their creator's views of the dead which, unlike Christian belief which makes the soul miniscule, envisioned the human soul in lifelike proportions. Hence it was necessary to devise a floating pen big enough to hold them.

With the advent of the Christian faith these vessels either changed radically or vanished. For despite the fact that Christianity was spread by Apostles who were fishermen, Christianity is an agricultural rather than a marine theology. One adaptation of the older form was that Satan was supposed to have built a huge vessel of his own. With this craft the Evil One went about gathering up unshriven dead for his dark purposes until St. Elmo sank him.

Such tales can, I suppose, be taken seriously, but the other kind of tales into which these early stories degenerated borders on farce or the tall tale. In these the emphasis is on the vast bulk of the vessel concerned, and almost all the stories about her are really expanded metaphors attempting to make length and breadth, both abstractions, concrete. To this end relays of horses are kept aboard to gallop forward with messages and orders; the masts are said to be so high that young boys are sent aloft and descend as old men with long beards, and pass young boys bound up; restaurants are located in her blocks so the crew won't starve aloft. The vessel is so huge that she was unable to get through the English channel, even under the sure hand of the skillful, giant sailor Stormalong, and left her paint on the cliffs of Dover—making them white. She took one hundred years to come about and she went by many names in different countries: *Skid-baldner, La Grande Chausse, Fondre, Manningfual, Refanu, Roth Ram-bach, Pape Lucerne* and the English *Merry Dun of Dover.*[41]

Yet behind the comic there still seems to linger a belief in these devil ships. When the folk talk of a phantom ship or a ghost ship they appear to mean one thing. When they talk of a devil ship or spirit ship they mean something else again.

In the folklore archives of the University of Newfoundland there are all kinds of stories about ghost ships, including a ghost barge towed by a spectral tug which, so far as I know, is unique. They also have a few stories dealing with devil and spirit ships. These can be identified by their running lights, red and blue rather than red and green. A man saw one one night and recognized what she was instantly. Therefore when she drew near he was not surprised to see ghosts walking her decks. Unlike most skippers, he determined to ram the vessel and he did. When the two ships hit, the spirit ship vanished into thin air, crew and all, and was never seen again. The strange thing was that when the two boats came together there was no sound. The real boat, however, felt an impact and immediately took a heavy list.[42]

This concept of spirit ship is still viable in the West Indies, although down there it has become much more amorphous than it is even in New-foundland. Morgan McLaren of Windward, in Carriacou, told a tale which clearly illustrates the difference between the two kinds of belief. He was sailing, he said, one mild moonlight night when he glanced ahead and saw an object in the water which after close scrutiny he decided was a whale. He showed it to the rest of the crew, and they did not share his opinion of what it was but said it was a devil ship. They immediately gathered pots and pans together and set up a terrible din, which apparently caused the object to vanish. It is worth while, I think, to note that this ghost did not look like a real vessel as the spirit ship does. Moreover, the devil boat apparently is considered dangerous but can be driven away by making a racket by beating spoons on dishpans.

There is of course one more category of strange ships that must be touched on, for they are very numerous. These are what I would term mystery ships. From time to time vessels that are proceeding quite alone in the sea are encountered by seamen. There is no hand at the helm and no crew aboard.

Generally there is an explanation for what happened. The vessel may have stranded, the crew left her and she floated off. The crew may have died of disease. The vessel may have caught fire or sprung a leak and been abandoned only to have the leak stopped, the fire extinguished and the vessel continue on her lonely way. Some may even have been cleaned out by pirates, or swept overboard by a sea. But there is usually evidence aboard these vessels to tell what happened—water in the hold, wreckage, smoke-blackened holds and so on.

A few are found, however, that baffle the scholar and terrify the sailor. These are vessels that show no sign of trouble and yet the crew has vanished into thin air. The most famous one was the *Mary Celeste*, but her story is too well known to repeat. Another one, not so well known, should suffice to illustrate the type.

It was a pleasant summer morning in the month of July 1750 at Newport, Rhode Island. Some fishermen at Easton's Beach were working on their gear when they noticed a small brig in the offing standing toward the land. The vessel stood in for Rough Point and just before she hit the breakers came about and sailed over toward the rocks on the other shore. Again she tacked short of the breakers and sailed ashore on the sandy beach.

The startled fishermen went aboard and found one dog and one cat. The kettle was boiling on the stove and the table was laid for a meal that was hot on the stove. There was no sign of violence or confusion, but the crew had vanished and no trace of them was ever found. Ironically, the vessel and master both belonged to the town and were bound there from Honduras when the affair took place.

The vessel was refloated and renamed *Beach Bird*, and carried cargo for many years until she was eventually made into an armed galley by the British during the Revolution.[43]

This, then, is the shape of the spectre ship. It is interesting to note that few are steam vessels and that few have come into being recently. To support this one might note that neither the *Andrea Doria, Lusitania, Morro Castle* nor *Normandie* have stories built up about them. Each year they become fewer and fewer as the old traditions die and the old seamen go to Fiddler's Green. Yet, taken all together, they have survived modern times remarkably well.

In Dominica, where spirits are as thick as the jungle, the people say, "The jumbies (spirits) are going." When you ask why, you learn they don't like smoke, particularly tobacco smoke and the fumes from engines. Is it possible that there are still regions in the sea where the air is sufficiently pure to support phantom life?

EPILOGUE

THERE yet remain a few words about the preceding pages. Unlike a ship, which starts out on an ocean passage for a certain harbor and either sinks or arrives there, a book does not always end up the way it began. When this book was conceived, it was intended to be a general historical compendium of maritime folklore. But the bulk of the material became immense. Therefore the vision narrowed, and the prospect was for a similar study based on the English-speaking people.

This plan was put into practice, but before long I discovered I had so many tales from the quick that there was little room for the dead—or for many of the quick, for that matter. Accordingly the book was modified a third time, with the result that almost every item in it has been in living tradition within thirty years of the writing. Sometimes the modern version is markedly different from its ancestors and in many cases an effort has been made to point this out, and a good deal of time has been expended searching for explanatory reasons for the material that are acceptable to modern and, hopefully, semisophisticated man.

Another problem with the book arose when trying to decide what to include and what to exclude, for when it came time to write there were many more items before me than could reasonably go between covers and even some categories, although I hope not many, that went begging. Read on paper and then recalled in their environmental totality, many of these stories became fascinating again, and it was hard to exclude one and include another. For it must be remembered that folklore is not an item but an experience.

For folklore to be at its best, it requires a narrator and an environment.

As one looks at an anecdote on the printed page it may be very dull, but when recall is employed and the face of the narrator swims before you and the weather and the smell and a host of other little things, it takes on meaning and stature beyond the printed value. If the teller and times are propitious, a mean anecdote can become a great story.

Sarah Orne Jewett said years ago that the only thing worth writing about was the thing you could not forget. Before her Wordsworth wrote a poem "The Daffodils," indicating that he could say something interesting after all; and later Willa Cather said something to the effect that all human experiences were complete when a person reached age ten. The effect of them all is that good material must withstand a time test, and this was a prime factor in my selection. The material that I recalled most easily had first priority.

I once asked an old fisherman about a story. He thought awhile and he said in a slow, tired voice, "Oh, that was long ago I heard that. I can't remember exactly. Probably aboard a fisherman, somewhere—sometime—someplace." And that remark leads to another problem—the source. Good folklorists always give the particulars on their informants—name, age, occupation and so on, until the data are a cross between a police dossier and a health record. I never felt it was terribly important to know whether Bill or Fred Jones told the story, and few readers plan to swim out to the Faroe Islands to interview an informant. Unfortunately, I began collecting folklore before I knew what folklore was, and for many of these stories I have to reach back nearly forty years.

For those interested, the names of the informants have all been preserved. They have been used sparingly in this book for two reasons. It is possible that some will not enjoy the idea of being identified in a public document of what "educated" people call nonsense, and at the same time the same informant may become irate when he finds his name omitted and another's included. The names are available to responsible scholars—even though some of the stories have been with me a long time.

As one runs over the material in these pages, one becomes conscious that there is more small-boat lore in it than big-ship lore—by that I mean it has been collected from people connected with smaller craft. It is popularly thought that the clipper ship was the great carrier and creator of maritime folklore. This is incorrect. Clippers may have been excellent conveyances for creating sea chanties, for the work required it, but the crews were made up largely of a raggle-taggle bunch of men picked up by fair means and foul in saloons and gutters in every waterfront slum where big ships tied up. They were aboard, many of them, for only a single voyage, and left the ship nearly as ignorant as when they entered her. Further, the modern steamship is not much better, being manned by mechanics with little or no knowledge of the sea, and less interest in it.

Rather, the folklore of the sea lies in the small-craft sailor, the fisherman or the coaster, who is born with the sea in his ears, follows it all his life and dies with the turning of the tide. Here is where the traditions are made, and it is here they are preserved. It is toward these people that I have made my major thrust for information.

When one looks at the material presented here, it becomes immediately apparent that it stems from three sources: the Old World, North America and the Caribbean. Both the West Indian and North American material are derivative from the Old World. The Old World material is the most complete, the most aesthetically pleasing. The West Indian lore plays a more total part in their way of life than the other two, and the views are somewhat more archaic. At the same time, this material differs markedly from the others. This may be partially due to the environment, but is probably owing in considerable measure to the application of African attitudes to Old World beliefs.

Of the three areas, the material from the United States is the most fragmentary. This may be due in part to the lack of isolation experienced here, with an increased dependence upon science and methods of communication, and a more fluid way of life. As an illustration, in Ireland I met an informant who was living in the house occupied by his family for a millenium and a half, and I met storytellers who could tell a story lasting twenty-four hours. For better or worse, this would be impossible in the United States.

At the same time, one must not forget that in three centuries the United States has passed through the same ethnic development the people of the British Isles experienced over nearly two millennia. It may be that the lore of this particular occupation—seafaring—which has endured through the centuries and through great material change, could serve as a kind of laboratory to show what changes are wrought when cultures are in confrontation. By comparing the American corpus of material with that extant abroad, we may be able to measure what the culture there was like ages ago and perhaps make predictions toward the future.

One of the people who kindly read this manuscript complained that little differentiation was made between the credible and the incredible. To the landsman, there is a deal of difference betwen a story about a shipwreck that occurred on a certain day and place and another about a spectre that stalked a vessel in a storm. Hopefully, this book is written with the mariner's point of view in mind. To him the line between the real and the unreal is very thin, and he is credulous of the incredible. He has been conditioned to accept the idea that the spirit world interferes with the world of reality. He therefore makes little distinction between the two.

Perhaps there is, in a sense, more of the credible in the incredible than we would like to admit. The mind responds to stimuli. Where possible, it reacts in terms of learned response. Therefore, if a man has the sea really in his blood, he can sense the coming of a blow without knowing it. The knowledge is made manifest by a dead man coming over the bow, by a spectre ship in the offing. These may, in the scientific sense, be incredible but the reactions they engender are credible ones—to reef the sail, to head for shore, to alter course.

This book was not written or intended to be a study in abnormal psychology, although undoubtedly some will be able to find erotic interpretations of the material. It was intended to show the effect of custom and belief on human reaction, which has long been a deep interest on my part. Does the conviction in a belief provide the infinitesimal grain of endurance or despair that brings the man and the vessel to port or conversely sends all hands to bottom? In short, do these beliefs work, either on a real or a psychological level? Perhaps I have lived with them too long, but I think they do.

One last word. Perhaps it does not really belong in this work, but the collecting of folklore is to me not just fun, but a fascinating way of life. It has taken us many miles to many harbors in many lands. It has exposed us to a multiplicity of experiences, to different life values, different interpretations of reality. We have met good people and bad people, but few small ones. Through the collection of folklore we have been allowed to walk with mighty men.

NOTES

CHAPTER I

1. Statement purported to have been made by John Paul Jones. Capt. Robert J. Bulkley, *At Close Quarters, PT Boats in the United States Navy*, Naval History Division, (Washington, D.C., 1962) n.p.

2. Folklore and Language Archives, Memorial University of Newfoundland.

3. Alan Villiers, *Captain James Cook* (New York, 1967), p. 78.

4. Personal collection. For comments on the cowhorn, see Ethel C. Ritchie, *Block Island Lore and Legends* (Providence, Rhode Island, 1967) and "Block Island Cowhorn," 70.763, G. W. Blunt White Library (Mystic, Connecticut, 1971).

5. For an excellent discussion of seventeenth-century shipbuilding, see Captain John Smith, *A Sea Grammar* (London, 1627).

6. Personal collection.

7. According to Benwell and Waugh, there are several analogues to this story. In Cromarty Firth, almost across the bay from Buckie, was a famous mermaid who granted a boatbuilder three wishes: that he build unsinkable boats, marry the girl of his choice and a third wish which was never revealed. On the Mull of Kintyre on the west coast of Scotland a man named Mackenzie was also granted favors by a mermaid—to build boats that would not sink and from which no one would be lost. Gwen Benwell and Arthur Waugh, *Sea Enchantress, The Tale of the Mermaid and her Kin* (New York, 1965), p. 172.

8. Horace P. Beck, *Folklore of Maine* (Philadelphia, 1957), p. 129.

9. Frances Kay, *This—Is Grenada* (Trinidad, 1966), pp. 130–131.

10. Carey Archives, University of Maryland.

11. *Ibid.*

12. Personal collection. The beginning of ship construction is, generally speaking, analogous to house construction with one serious exception. More care is taken with the ship than the house, for should the house fall upon evil days the inmates have a better chance to escape than the seaman who finds himself overboard on a dark night because some careless person has failed to propitiate some spirit.

13. Personal collection.

14. Personal collection. This bell is but one of a number of "vanishing" objects held in awe by the Irish. One is the Cursing Stone of Tory Island, and another is the magic rock on Caher Island which has the ability to raise storms. Still another is the skull of Grace O'Malley on Clare Island (see Chapter XII).

15. Personal collection.

16. Personal collection.

17. See Peter F. Anson, *Fisher Folklore* (London, 1965), pp. 70, 83, for interesting analogues to this idea.

18. See Marion V. Brewington, *Ship Carvers of North America* (Barre, Massachusetts, 1962).

19. See Richard Lebaron Bowen, "Maritime Superstitions of the Arabs," *American Neptune*, 15:5–48, 1955.

20. See Brewington, *op. cit.*, Chapter III, "Frigates and Packets."

21. See John G. Lockhart, *Peril of the Sea* (London, 1924); see *Celeste.*

22. See Bruce Procope, "Launching a Schooner in Carriacou," *Caribbean Quarterly*, IV (1955), p. 123.

23. See Kay, *op. cit.*, for further details.

24. All the above material is from my personal collection, and both time and place have been made deliberately obscure.

25. Anson, *op. cit.*, states that if a vessel were launched stern first in Brittany, she would steer badly.

26. George S. Wasson, *Sailing Days on the Penobscot* (New York, 1949), pp. 117–121, has an amusing account of lubberly launchings in Maine during World War I, when shipbuilding was revived in the state after remaining dormant for a number of years.

27. Anson, *op. cit.*, p. 94.

28. Personal collection.

29. James P. Duggan, *The Great Iron Ship* (New York, 1953), p. 153.

30. Fletcher M. Bassett, *Legends and Superstitions of the Sea and of Sailors,* (Chicago and New York, 1885), p. 400.

CHAPTER II

1. George W. Stewart, *Names on the Land* (Boston, 1969), p. 292.

2. Horace P. Beck, *Folklore of Maine* (Philadelphia, 1959), p. 16.

3. *Ibid.*, p. 14.

4. Narrated by John Lorne Campbell, Isle of Canna, July 5, 1969.

5. Beck, *op. cit.*, p. 13.

6. Personal collection.

7. Beck, *op. cit.*, p. 15.

8. Richard Bauman, "Three Legends from the Ayrshire Coast," *Scottish Studies*, Vol. 8, Pt. 1 (1964), p. 33.

9. Stewart, *op. cit.*, pp. 176–82.

10. David Thomson, *People of the Sea* (Barrie and Rockliff, London, 1965).

11. Beck, *op. cit.*, pp. 18–19.

12. Alan Walker Read, "Folklore Factor in the Etymologizing of Place Names," lecture delivered before American Folklore Society, November, 1969.

13. Personal collection.

14. Patrick L. Fermor, *The Traveller's Tree* (New York, 1950), p. 185.

15. A. B. Taylor, "The Name 'St. Kilda,'" *Scottish Studies*, 13 (1969), pp. 145–58.

16. Personal collection.

17. Personal collection. This tale is remarkably like the tale of the Red Hand of Ulster—popular throughout Ireland and narrated to me by Sir Thomas Lipton many years ago to explain why a flag had a red hand on it. In Sir Thomas' version, however, the race was for prize money.

18. *Irish Coast Pilot* (London, 1954), p. 177.

19. Seaton Gordon, "Distinguished Scarba and its Whirpool," *The Times* (London, November 5, 1966).

20. Lt. Col. the Hon. Arthur Murray, *St. Columba and the Holy Isle of the Garvellaches—The Whirlpool of the Corrie Vreckan* (Edinburgh, 1950), p. 26.

21. Martin Martin, *A Description of the Western Islands of Scotland* (London, 1703; 4th edition, Stirling, 1934), p. 271.

22. Murray, *op. cit.*, records a somewhat similar story, p. 29.

23. MacEdward Leach, "Celtic Tales from Cape Breton," *Studies in Folklore in Honor of Distinguished Service Professor Stith Thompson*, ed. W. Edsen Richmond (Bloomington, Indiana, 1957), p. 43.

24. Personal collection. For a detailed account of Balor see Alexander H. Krappe, *Balor of the Evil Eye*, Studies in Celtic and French Literature (New York, 1927).

25. Thomas H. Mason, *The Islands of Ireland* (Cork, 1936), p. 58.

26. Obviously these stories are now fragmentary. There is little doubt that originally this tale was longer and connected to the numerous stories of magical cows like the one stolen by Balor of Tory Island from MacKineeley, on the mainland. See Alexander H. Krappe, *Balor of the Evil Eye*, New York, 1927.

27. Erwin G. Gudde, *California Place Names* (Berkeley, 1960), p. 243.

28. Mason, *op. cit.*, p. 60.

29. Personal collection.

30. Beck, *op. cit.*, pp. 178–80.

31. George F. Dow, and John H. Edwards, *The Pirates of the New England Coast, 1630–1730* (Salem, 1923), p. 376.

32. Charles H. Whedbee, *Legends of the Outer Banks* (Winston-Salem, N.C., 1966), pp. 44–56.

33. Back, *op. cit.*, pp. 17–18.

34. Personal collection.

35. Carleton Mitchell, *Isles of the Caribees* (Washington, 1966), pp. 72–75.

CHAPTER IIII

1. Joseph Conrad, *Mirror of the Sea* (New York, 1906), pp. 18–21.
2. *Ibid.*, p. 3.
3. Ernest Hemingway, *The Old Man and the Sea* (New York, 1952), pp. 32–33.
4. Jack London, *Jack London: Short Stories*, ed. Maxwell Geismar (New York, 1960), p. 76.
5. Carey Archives, University of Maryland.
6. *Ibid.*
7. William G. Saltonstall, "Just Ease Her When She Pitches," *American Neptune*, Vol. I, XV, 1955, p. 258.
8. Carey Archives.
9. Folklore and Language Archives, Memorial University of Newfoundland.
10. *Ibid.*
11. Personal collection.
12. Carey Archives.
13. *Ibid.*
14. Personal collection. See also Joanna C. Colcord, *Sea Language Comes Ashore* (New York, 1945), p. 5.

CHAPTER IV

1. Horace P. Beck, Personal collection.
2. Joanna C. Colcord, *Songs of American Sailormen* (New York, MCMXXXVII), p. 173. See also A. L. Lloyd, and MacColl, *Blow Boys Blow*, Traditional Records (New York) TLP, 1026.
3. R. Inwards, *Weather Lore* (London, 1898), p. 123.
4. *Reed's Nautical Almanac*, ed. Captain O. M. Watts (London, 1969), p. 815.
5. Frank E. Hartwell, *Forty Years of the Weather Bureau* (Bolton, Vt., 1958), p. 83.
6. Thiselton F. Dyer, *English Folk Lore* (London, 1878), p. 251.
7. *Ibid.*, p. 262.
8. Hartwell, *op. cit.*, p. 66.
9. *Reed's*, op. cit.
10. W. Richard, *Weather Lore* (London, 1839), p. 92.
11. *Reed's, op. cit.*
12. Inwards, *op. cit.*, p. 87.
13. Carey Archives, University of Maryland.
14. Beck, *op. cit.*, pp. 191–92.
15. Personal collection. For an English version, see *Reed's, op. cit.*
16. Personal collection.
17. Folklore and Language Archives, Memorial University of Newfoundland.

18. *Ibid.*

19. Personal collection.

20. Inwards, *op. cit.*, pp. 99–100.

21. John Josselyn, *An Account of Two Voyages to New England* (London, 1674), pp. 99–100.

22. See Chapter XIII.

23. F. Colón, *The History of the Life and Actions of Admiral Christopher Columbus*, in Pinkerton's *Voyages* (London, 1812), XII, p. 58; *The First Voyage Around the World by Magellan*, translated by Lord Stanley (London, 1874), p. 42.

24. Henry W. Longfellow, *The Golden Legend* (Boston, 1851), pp. 254–56.

25. William Falconer, *The Shipwreck: A Poem* (London, 1868), p. 145.

26. Richard Henry Dana, *Two Years Before the Mast* (New York, 1911), Chapter 39.

27. Personal collection.

28. George Gourlay, *Fisher Life: or The Memorials of Cellardyke and the Fife Coast* (Cupar, Fife, 1879), p. 26.

29. Richard Folkard, *Plant Lore Legends and Lyrics*, 2nd ed. (London, 1892), p. 494.

30. Beck, *op. cit.*, p. 202, 203.

31. Margaret A. Murray, *The God of the Witches* (London, n.d.), pp. 150–51.

32. From the rendering of Duncan McQuarrie, Tobermory, Island of Mull. See also John MacCormick, *The Island of Mull* (Glasgow, 1923), pp. 8–9, and *History of the Island of Mull* (Greenville, Ohio, 1923).

33. Personal collection. For an analogue see Thomas Hannah, *The Beautiful Isle of Mull* (Edinburgh, 1933), pp. 128, 131.

34. John G. Campbell, *Witchcraft and Second Sight in the Highlands and Islands of Scotland* (Glasgow, 1902), pp. 15–46.

35. *Ibid.*, pp. 15–16.

36. George Lyman Kittredge, *Witchcraft in Old and New England* (Cambridge, Massachusetts, 1929), p. 159.

37. *Ibid.*, p. 158.

38. Personal collection.

39. Folklore and Language Archives, Memorial University of Newfoundland. Also included in these archives is a story about a man who lost his ship in a gale brought on by throwing a five-cent piece overboard.

CHAPTER V

1. Jordan Silvester, *A Discovery of Bermuda* (New York, 1940), p. 8. Quoted from George Carey, "Enchanted Island Traditions," *American Neptune*, Vol. 29, No. 4, (October, 1969), p. 276.

2. Horace P. Beck, *Folklore of Maine* (Philadelphia, 1956), pp. 138–40.

3. Personal collection.

4. William Snaith, *Across the Western Ocean* (New York, 1966), p. 63.

5. William Falconer, *Dictionary of the Mariner* (London, 1782), "Lead Line." See also Stanton A. King, *A Bunch of Rope Yarns* (Boston, 1903), "The Lead Line," pp. 141–55.

6. Personal collection.

7. Carey Archives, University of Maryland.

8. Personal collection.

9. Personal collection.

10. Personal collection.

11. Folklore and Language Archives, Memorial University of Newfoundland.

12. For a complete version, see Thompson, Harold W., *Body, Boots and Britches* (Philadelphia, 1939), p. 194.

13. The above two rhymes may be found in *Now Is the Time for Fishing*, songs and speech by Sam Larner, collected and edited by Ewan MacColl and Peggy Seegar, Folkways Records, F.G. 3507.

14. Norman Duncan, *Dr. Grenfell's Parish, The Deep Sea Fisherman*, 4th ed., (New York, 1905), p. 35.

15. The translation of this is that there is grass or brush on the Head, not on the Souls. There is timber on the point but none on the Pole (Rocks).

16. Harry M. Lyndenberg, *Crossing the Line* (New York, 1957), p. 47.

17. Henning Henningsen, *Crossing the Equator* (Munksgaard, 1961).

18. Lyndenberg, *op. cit.*, pp. 15, 16.

19. *Ibid.*, pp. 15–18.

20. Henry N. Coleridge, *Six Months in the West Indies* (London, 1832), pp. 31–35.

21. Fletcher Bassett, *Legends and Superstitions of the Sea and of Sailors* (Chicago and New York, 1885), pp. 410–21.

22. Personal collection. For analogues, see William Doerflinger, *Shantymen and Shantyboys* (New York, 1951), p. 160.

23. Stan Hugill, *Shanties from the Seven Seas* (London, 1961), p. 535.

24. Falconer, *op. cit.*, "Punished," p. 362.

25. T. G. Wilson *The Irish Lighthouse Service* (Dublin, 1968), p. 57.

26. This story was told by a person living in Cohasset Harbor in 1948. Although it differs somewhat from the facts in the case, it is sufficiently close to the actual events to be counted a reasonable version of what happened. For a more accurate account, see E. R. Snow, *Storms and Shipwrecks of the New England Coast* (Boston, 1946), pp. 122–38.

27. Personal collection.

28. Personal collection. See also D.D.C. Pochin Mould, *West-Over-Sea* (Edinburgh, 1953), pp. 270–72.

29. For an excellent version of this story, see Robert Southey, "The Inchcape Rock." See also Alexander Hislop, *The Book of Scottish Anecdote* (Edinburg, 1883), p. 12.

30. Personal collection.

31. Personal collection.

32. Horace P. Beck, "Tales of the Banks Fisherman," *American Neptune*, Vol. XV. (1955), p. 129.

CHAPTER VI

1. For excellent discussions of the chantey, see Stan Hugill, *Shanties from the Seven Seas* (London, 1961); Frederick P. Harlowe, *Chanteying Aboard American Ships* (Barre, Massachusetts, 1962); Joanna C. Colcord, *Roll and Go, Songs of American Sailormen* (Indianapolis, Indiana, 1925); William M. Doerflinger, *Shantymen and Shantyboys, Songs of the Sailor and Lumberman* (New York, 1951).

2. This idea is supported by Roger Abrams of the University of Texas in a text of a forthcoming book.

3. Doerflinger, *op. cit.*, p. 51.

4. For full discussions of this aspect of chanteying and of chanteying as a whole, see Stan Hugill, *Sailor Town* (New York, 1967); Harlowe, *op. cit.*; and Richard Dillon, *Shanghaiing Days* (New York, 1961), as the best sources.

5. See Hugill, *op. cit.*

6. This is but one of many links connecting West Indian maritime lore with that of the Canadian Maritime Provinces. In Newfoundland and Nova Scotia a term often used when a vessel was carrying more sail than she could reasonably bear was, "Drive her, byes, drive her."

7. This is a popular rowing song on the island of Bequia, where whaling is still practiced, and dates from many years ago when there were several "fisheries" on the island, one of which, now defunct, was the St. Hillary fishery.

After some inquiries, I learned that the song was thought to have been composed about an ancient whaleman, Moses Osborne, who was still living on the island. I sought him out hoping to learn the particulars of the song. "I done meet up with that when I was first going in the fishery"—i.e., he learned the already popular song over sixty years ago. He had no knowledge of who had composed it or when or why.

8. Beside being an excellent account of an accident and sea burial in the West Indies this is a peculiar combination of chantey and fo'c'sle song. The spoken last line is most common in New England and the Maritimes.

9. Gale Huntington, *Songs the Whalemen Sang* (Barre, Mass., 1964), pp. 34–36.

10. MacEdward Leach, *The Ballad Book* (New York, 1955), pp. 697–98.

11. Charles Nordhoff, *Whaling and Fishing* (New York, 1895), pp. 1–11.

12. Of this song Professor Kittredge[*] says, "By far the most interesting thing in it is Allan's addressing his ship and the ship's intelligent behavior." Beyond this he makes little comment. The great ballad scholar, Professor Child,[†] is also puzzled by the "intelligent" ship. Obviously the rest of the song is equally puzzling to them, for neither man makes much comment on the story.

I have noted elsewhere that seamen to this day believe their ships to possess a kind of life—admittedly usually a perverse one—and they expect the vessel to respond to kind words or angry epithets. (Sometimes it seems as if they do.)

The song is obviously from the east coast of England and Scotland, between Peterhead and the Wash, and deals with the coal trade. The cog, translated by

Kittredge as "boat," is in all probability a cobh, a small vessel extremely popular in the area.

Young Allan finds himself in trouble, probably because of his boast. An easterly gale springs up and he looks for a haven. Realizing his predicament, the crowds gather on the shore and, in the absence of lighthouses and signal towers, fire canon, beat drums, etc., to warn him that the harbor entrance is too dangerous to enter. Allan keeps the gale on his quarter but still the ship is badly strained and begins to break up. To prevent her sinking he passes canvas around her hull to stop the leaks—a device known as frapping.

If Allan is in desperate straits, other vessels are worse off, for he passes flotsam—mattresses that remain afloat after the vessels have been torn apart. In the darkest hour Allan calls for help and the cabin boy takes the helm. Professor Child feels that this is an indication of inadequacy on the part of Allan, but there are many tales and stories about vessels being saved by young boys. This youth, however, may well be a supernatural being, for his vision is remarkable and he says that he has never had shoes on his feet or gloves in his hands.

Even with the superhuman efforts of the lad, things look dark indeed until the ship is promised a refit, including new golden rivits—at which time she displays interest and roars off into a safe harbor.

There is little in this song that is any way unusual to the seaman's eye.

English and Scottish Popular Ballads, ed. by Helen C. Sargent, George L. Kitteridge, (Cambridge, Mass., 1932), p. 547.

†*The English and Scottish Popular Ballads*, ed. by Francis J. Child, (Dover edition, New York, 1965), "Young Allan" Version C., Vol. IV, pp. 375–83.

13. Personal collection.

14. Sung by Mr. Sidney Luther of Pittsburg, New Hampshire. Recorded by Kidson in Yorkshire, England, from a sailor's daughter. (Words on broadsides. Kidson's tune seems hymn—not like Luther's.) *Helen Hartness Flanders Collection*, September 17, 1942, M. Olney, Collector, Disc. #640.

This song shows most clearly the affinity between the West Indies and New England and the Maritime Provinces. See also MacEdward Leach, *op. cit.*, pp. 196–97.

15. On July 10, 1777, the sloop-of-war *Ranger* was launched near Portsmouth, New Hampshire. Captain John Paul Jones took command and carried her to England, where she raided British shipping and engaged in amphibious attacks ashore. However, she proved a dull sailor and Jones did not remain in her very long. It is ironic that her turn of speed should be recalled at this late date and puzzling to know why her name was changed. As mentioned before, it is startling to note the accuracy of the navigation recalled in the song.

I collected a fragmentary version of this song in Dingle, County Kerry, in 1969—the first time that it has been collected outside of North America as far as I am aware. See H. P. Beck, *Folklore of Maine* (Philadelphia, 1957), pp. 173–74.

16. Fannie H. Eckstrom, and Mary W. Smythe, *Minstrelsy of Maine Folk-Songs and Ballads of the Woods and the Coast* (Boston and New York, 1941).

17. Elizabeth B. Greenleaf, and Grace Yarrow Mansfield, *Ballads and Sea Songs from Newfoundland* (Cambridge, Mass., 1933), pp. 230–31.

18. H. P. Back, *op. cit.*, pp. 204–05. See also MacEdward Leach, *Folk Ballads and Songs of the Labrador Coast* (Ottawa, 1965), p. 244–5.

19. Personal collection. Collected in Dingle, County Kerry, in 1969, this is typical of songs popular among fishing fleets to this day.

20. Personal collection. I first heard this song from Dr. Jeoffrey Bolt during a transatlantic passage in 1966. In England the Thames barges were similar to the American coaster of yesteryear. Although great cargo carriers in their day, they were nonetheless the butt of considerable amusement for deepwater men.

21. Collection of Helen Hartness Flanders. Hanford Hayes of Staceyville, Maine, sang this to Helen Hartness Flanders September 25, 1940. It begins on a phrase of the tune "The Dying Nun." Repeat the last two lines of each verse. See also H. P. Beck, *op. cit.*, p. 176.

CHAPTER VII

1. Jean Lipman, *American Primitive Painting* (New York, 1942), and John Wilmerding, *A History of American Marine Painting* (Boston, 1968), p. 28.

2. Herman Melville, *Moby-Dick* (Garden City, 1928), p. 12.

3. For an excellent discussion of these aspects, see Marius Barbeau, "All Hands Aboard Scrimshawing," *The American Neptune*, Vol. XII, No. 2 (April, 1952), pp. 99–122; see also Clifford W. Ashley, *The Yankee Whaler* (New York, 1942), pp. 111–16.

4. Rear Admiral Gerald Wells, *Naval Customs and Traditions* (London, 1930), p. 136.

5. Barbeau, *op. cit.*

6. *Ibid.*, p. 116.

7. *Ibid.*

8. Arthur C. Watson, *The Long Harpoon. A Collection of Whaling Anecdotes* (New Bedford, 1929), pp. 155–64.

9. Edouard A. Stackpole, *Scrimshaw at Mystic Seaport* (Mystic, Connecticut, 1966), p. 21.

10. William Falconer, *A New Universal Dictionary of the Marine, being a copious explanation of the Technical Terms and Phrases usually employed in the Construction, Equipment, Machinery, Movements and Military as well as Naval Operation of Ships: with such parts of Astronomy, and Navigation, as will be found useful to practical Navigators. To which is annexed a Vocabulary of French Sea Phrases and Terms of Art* (London, 1815), p. 79.

11. C. W. Ashley, *Book of Knots* (Garden City, N.Y., 1956), p. 148.

12. *Ibid.*, p. 2.

13. Edward Driver, *Indians of North America* (Chicago, 1964).

14. W. D. Hambley, *The History of Tattooing and its Significance* (London, 1925).

CHAPTER VIII

1. See George A. England, *Vikings of the Ice* (London, 1924), for an excellent account.

2. *Ibid.*, p. 174.

3. *Ibid.*, pp. 313–23.

4. Personal collection.

5. England, *op. cit.*, pp. 54–59.

6. *Ibid.*, p. 218.

7. David Thomson, *People of the Sea, A Journey in Search of the Seal Legend* (London, 1965), p. 167.

8. Personal collection. See also David Thomson, *People of the Sea* (London, 1954), pp. 64–65.

9. Thomson, *op. cit.*, p. 167.

10. See A. W. Brógger, *Ancient Emigrants* (Oxford, 1929), p. 5.

11. Karl Blind comes to a similar conclusion, but he bases his feeling on the fact that the Norse incorporated sealskins in their clothing. "Scottish and Germanic Water Tales," *Contemporary Review*, 40:186–208, 1881.

12. John G. Campbell, *Superstitions of the Highlands and Islands of Scotland* (Glasgow, 1900), pp. 283–84.

13. Alexander Carmichael, *Carmina Gadelica, Hymns and Incantations with Illustrative Notes on Words, Rites, and Customs, Dying and Obsolete: Orally Collected in the Highlands and Islands of Scotland* (Edinburgh, 1941), Vol. IV, pp. 14–17.

14. Otta F. Swire, *The Highlands and Their Legends* (Edinburgh, 1963), pp. 265–67.

15. Francis J. Child, *The English and Scotish Popular Ballads* (Dover edition, New York, 1965), Vol. II, p. 494.

16. Personal collection.

17. Thomson, *op. cit.*, pp. 103, 123–27.

18. *Ibid.*, pp. 80–84.

19. *Ibid.*, pp. 81, 131–33.

20. For further detail, see Gwen Benwell, and Arthur Waugh, *Sea Enchantness* (New York, 1965), pp. 163, 180–81, 183–84.

21. J. G. Campbell, *op. cit.*, p. 285.

22. Thomson, *op. cit.*, p. 68.

23. Personal collection.

24. Alexander Hislop, *The Book of Scottish Anecdote, Humorous, Social Legendary, and Historical* (Edinburgh, 1883), p. 524.

25. *Journal of the English Folk Dance and Song Society*, Vol. VI, No. 3.

26. Folklore and Language Archives, Memorial University of Newfoundland.

27. *Ibid.*

28. Natural History, Vol. 89, #3 (March, 1970), pp. 56–63.

29. James Wallace, *An Account of the Isles of Orkney* (London, 1700), p. 60.

30. J. R. Tudor, *The Orkneys and Shetland, Their Past and Present State* (London, 1883), pp. 341–42.

31. Jessie M. Saxby, *Shetland Traditional Lore* (Edinburgh, 1932), pp. 88–96.

32. A. T. Cluness, *The Shetland Isles* (London, 1951), pp. 107–08.

33. Fletcher Bassett, *Legends and Superstitions of the Sea and Sailors* (Chicago and New York, 1885).

34. Richard Henry Dana, *Two Years Before the Mast* (New York, 1947), pp. 35–36.

35. C. S. Forrester, *Commodore Hornblower* (Boston, 1945), pp. 57–58.

36. John Spense, *Shetland Folklore* (Lerwick, 1899), pp. 20–26.

CHAPTER IX

1. Sabine Baring-Gould, *Curious Myths of the Middle Ages* (London, 1868), pp. 48–50.

2. *Ibid.*, p. 258.

3. Dr. A. S. Rappaport, *Superstitions of Sailors* (London, 1928), p. 190.

4. Baring-Gould, *op. cit.*, pp. 230–58.

5. Rappaport, *op. cit.*, pp. 172–73.

6. John Josselyn, *An Account of Two Voyages to New England* (London, 1674), p. 228.

7. Gwen Benwell, and Arthur Waugh, *Sea Enchantress, The Tale of the Mermaid and Her Kin* (New York, 1965), p. 99.

8. *Ibid.*, p. 121.

9. Arthur K. Davis, Jr., *Traditional Ballads of Virginia* (Cambridge, 1929), p. 526 of Child #289.

10. Peter F. Anson, *Fisher Folklore* (London, 1965), p. 43.

11. Rappaport, *op. cit.*, p. 194ff.

12. Robert Hunt, *Popular Romances of the West of England* (London, 1865), pp. 163–83.

13. *Ibid.*, pp. 185–86.

14. *Ibid.*, pp. 187–89.

15. Baring-Gould, *op. cit.*, pp. 206ff.

16. Roger Loomis, "Morgan la Fee and the Celtic Goddess," *Speculum*, Vol. 20, (April, 1945), pp. 183–203.

17. Raphael Patai, "Lillith," *Journal of American Folklore*, Volume 77, #306, (1964), pp. 294–312.

18. Karl Blind, "Scottish, Shetlandic and Germanic Water Tales," *Contemporary Review*, Volume XL (1881), p. 190.

19. For a further consideration of the development of these stories on Shet-

land into the now famous ceremony of the Up-Helly-Aa, wherein a mock ship is burned, see H. R. Ellis Davidson, "The Chariot of the Sun," *Folklore*, Volume 80.

20. One must remember that in Ireland and Scotland "loch" refers to salt-water bays and fresh-water lakes with equal facility.

21. Isabel Cameron, *A Highland Chap Book* (Stirling, Scotland, 1928), pp. 120–28.

22. Helen Drever, *Lure of the Kelpie* (Edinburgh and London, 1937), pp. 66–71.

23. Cary Archives, University of Maryland. See also Cameron, *op. cit.*, p. 126, for an identical tale.

24. Drever, *op. cit.*, pp. 87–89. One cannot help but remark on the similarity of this tale to the ones about the nuggle in the Shetlands.

25. For the complete text, see Francis J. Child, *English and Scottish Popular Ballads* (Boston, 1881–1889), p. 243.

26. Benwell and Waugh, *op. cit.*, p. 176.

27. John F. Campbell, *Popular Tales of the West Highlands*, (Edinburgh, 1860), Volume IV, pp. 330–35.

28. Except, perhaps, in belief held by the Aran Islanders. See Lady Augusta Gregory, *Visions and Beliefs in the West of Ireland*, pp. 15–30.

29. John Gregorson Campbell, *Superstitions of the Highlands and Islands of Scotland* (Glasgow, 1900), pp. 199–200.

30. Martin Martin, *A Description of the Western Isles of Scotland* (Stirling, Scotland, 1934), p. 107.

31. Benwell and Waugh, *op. cit.*, p. 173.

32. Campbell, *op. cit.*, p. 199.

33. David MacRitchie, *Fians, Faeries and Picts* (London, 1895).

34. It has been further suggested that the Picts deliberately sought to control the sea routes between the Outer Hebrides and the mainland. If such was the case, they would be remembered, if at all, as a warlike group. See F. T. Wainwright, *The Northern Isles* (Edinburgh, 1964), pp. 82–83; see also Stuart S. Piggot, *The Prehistoric Peoples of Scotland* (London, 1962).

35. John L. Campbell, *Stories from South Uist* (London, 1961), p. 122.

36. Fletcher Bassett, *Legends and Superstitions of The Sea and of Sailors*, (Chicago and New York, 1885), Chapter IV.

37. Benwell and Waugh, *op. cit.*, p. 74.

38. Bassett, *op. cit.*, p. 184.

39. Hunt, *op. cit.*, p. 157.

40. Rappaport, *op. cit.*, pp. 177–78. Wrens are often associated with faeries and are killed in Ireland on St. Stephen's Day, December 26. The dead birds are put on brooms and kept in the kitchen to drive out faeries.

41. Carey Archives, University of Maryland.

42. Hunt, *op. cit.*, pp. 72–85.

43. John F. Campbell, *op. sit.*, Volume I, pp. 71ff.

44. Horace P. Beck, "Old World Tales Among the Mohawks," *Journal of American Folklore*, July–September, 1950, Vol. 63, #2, pp. 285–308.

45. Personal collection.

46. Fannie H. Eckstorm, *Old John Neptune and Other Maine Indian Stories* (Portland, 1945), pp. 83–89.

47. Abby L. Alger, *In Indian Tents* (Boston, 1897), pp. 65–71. For further references, one should examine *Jesuit Relations*, Volume LVII, and Dwight Kelton, *Indian Names of Places Near the Great Lake* (1888), pp. 34, 52.

48. Samuel B. D. Purchas, *Hakluytus Posthumus* or *Purchas His Pilgrims* (Glasgow, MCMVII, Vol. XIX) p. 439.

49. Fletcher M. Bassett, *op. cit.*, pp. 195–6.

50. Nicholas Denys, *Works* (Ottoman Edition), p. 80.

51. Bassett, *op. cit.*, pp. 196–97.

52. Harriet Beecher Stowe, *The Pearl of Orr's Island* (Boston, 1862), pp. 127–28.

53. Benwell and Waugh, *op. cit.*, p. 145.

54. *Ibid.*, p. 145.

55. *Ibid.*, p. 145.

56. F. H. MacArthur, *Legends of Prince Edward Island* (Charlottetown, n.d.), p. 49.

57. Mary L. Fraser, *Folklore of Nova Scotia* (Toronto, 1932), pp. 92–93.

58. *Ibid.*, pp. 94–95.

59. *Ibid.*, p. 99.

60. Personal collection.

61. Letter from Dr. Donald Hill, Department of Anthropology, Indiana University.

62. G. J. Afolabi Ojo, *Yoruba Culture* (London, 1966), pp. 162–66.

63. Elsie C. Parsons, *Folklore of the Antilles, French and English in Memoirs of the American Folklore Society*, New York, 1933, Volume XXVI, Pt. 1, pp. 83, 247.

64. Personal collection.

65. Parsons, *op. cit.*, Pt. 2, p. 293.

66. H. B. Meikle, "Mermaids and Fairymaids or Water Gods and Goddesses of Tobago," *Caribbean Quarterly*, 5 (1958), pp. 103–08.

67. Personal collection. In still another version of the tale the brother kills the "fish" and the girl is forced to eat her lover Oshun when he is served on the table, after which she dives into the water and turns into a mermaid. One should also note that Oshun is the name of a Nigerian river in which lives a water god similar to a mermaid. See M. G. Smith, *Dark Puritan* (Kingston, Jamaica, 1963), p. 137.

68. Personal collection. Obviously the mermaid has some sort of connection with the darker side of the otherworld, for the two stories called to mind a series of these tales.

69. Newbell N. Puckett, *Folk Beliefs of the Southern Negro* (New York, 1969), pp. 136–37.

70. Alexander Marshack in "The Baton of Montgaudier," (*Natural History*, Volume LXXIX, #3), examined art sketched on a reindeer's horn at least twelve

thousand years old: a great serpent, two seals, a strange animal, a salmon and a small plant. He suggests that we may learn more about ancient peoples through a study of art and stories than through many other more "respectable" media. If this be true, the symbols on that bone may tie in with stories of mermaids, sea monsters, salmon and faeries told here or yet to be revealed.

CHAPTER X

1. Olaus Magnus, *A Compendious History of the Geoths, Swedes and Vanduls, and Other Northern Nations* (London, 1658), *passim*.

2. Heuvelmans' book alone lists at least 525 separate written accounts of sightings between 1634 and 1964. See Bernard Heuvelmans, *In the Wake of the Sea Serpents* (London, 1968), pp. 575–85.

3. It has been suggested by some scholars that this was a hoax (see Heuvelmans, *op. cit.*, p. 202). He also mentions one being sighted in latitude 24° south, longitude 12° east in cloudy, blustery weather.

4. Richard M. Dorson, *America Begins* (New York, 1950), pp. 28–29.

5. Joseph C. Allen, *Tales and Trails of Martha's Vineyard* (Boston, 1938), pp. 229–30.

6. Personal collection.

7. J. F. Campbell, *The Celtic Dragon Myth with the Geste of Fraoch and the Dragon*, translated with introduction by George Henderson (Edinburgh, 1911), pp. 67–69.

8. *Ibid.*, p. 80.

9. *Ibid.*, pp. XXI–XXII.

10. Bernard Heuvelmans, *op. cit.*, p. 66.

11. Alan O. Anderson and Marjorie O. Anderson, *Adomnan's Life of Columba* (London and New York, 1961), p. 551.

12. Anderson, *op. cit.*, pp. 387–89.

13. The Scots take pains to point out the great accuracy of this man's visions.

14. Personal collection.

15. This lake is popularly believed to have underground connections with Loch Ness.

16. See F. W. Holiday, *The Great Orm of Loch Ness* (London, 1968), for complete details; see also Tim Dinsdale, *Loch Ness Monster* (London, 1966).

17. Ivan T. Sanderson, "Don't Scoff at Sea Monsters," *Saturday Evening Post* (March 8, 1947).

18. Heuvelmans, *op. cit.*, p. 465.

19. Carey Archives, University of Maryland. This tale recalls one told by Heuvelmans, wherein a great snake crawled into a boat via the rudder port and coiled itself by the mast before being chased overboard. (Heuvelmans, *op. cit.*, p. 85.)

20. Gershom Bradford, "Sea Serpents? No or Maybe," American Neptune, Vol. XIII (October, 1953), pp. 268–74.

21. Lawrence D. Geller, "Notes on Sea Serpents of Coastal New England," *New York Folklore Quarterly*, Vol. 26, No. 2 (June, 1970), p. 154.

22. *Ibid.*, pp. 158–59.

23. Heuvelmans, *op. cit.*, Ch. II.

24. Lady Augusta Gregory, *A Book of Saints and Wonders* (London, 1920), Book Six.

25. J. W. Van Dervoort, *The Water World* (New York, 1886), pp. 72–73.

26. "A discovery of the Barmudas, otherwise called the Isle of Divils; by Sir Thomas Gates, Sir George Sommers and Captayne Newport, set forth by Fil. Jourdan," in Richard Hakluyt, *Voyages and Discoveries of the English* (London, 1812), Vol. V, p. 556.

27. George G. Cary, *Folk Motifs in the Writings of John Josselyn* (unpublished master's thesis, Indiana University, 1962), Ch. II.

28. See Sabine Baring-Gould, *Curious Myths of the Middle Ages* (London, 1868), pp. 259–65.

29. Bassett, p. 299; Heuvelmans, p. 50.

30. Hugh Marwick, *Orkney* (London, 1951), pp. 110–11. See also Garry Hogg, *The Far Flung Isles, Orkney and Shetland* (London, 1961), p. 27.

31. John Gun, *The Orkney Book* (London, 1909), pp. 393–94.

32. George Carey, "Enchanted Island Traditions of the Sixteenth and Seventeenth Centuries," *American Neptune*, Vol. 29, No. 2 (October, 1969), pp. 275–81.

33. Harry P. Swan, *Highlights of the Donnegal Highlands* (Belfast, 1958), pp. 97–98. It might be added that a similar fate overtook the Irish hero Cuchulainn after his sojourn of four hundred years in Faeryland.

34. Francis Parkman, *Pioneers of France in the New Yorld* (Boston, 1880), p. 173.

35. See Lady Augusta Gregory, *Visions and Beliefs in the West of Ireland* (London, 1920), "Sea Stories," pp. 15–30.

36. P. A. O. Siochain, *Aran Islands of Legend*, 3rd ed. (New York, 1967), pp. 55–57.

37. Parkman, *op. cit.*, pp. 173–75, 202–06.

38. John Josselyn, *An Account of Two Voyages to New England* (London, 1674), p. 218.

39. Stanley Rogers, *Sea-Lore* (London, 1934), p. 185.

CHAPTER XI

1. For a typical statement see C. J. S. Thompson, *The Hand of Destiny* (London, 1932), p. 193.

2. Personal collection.

3. W. Carew Hazlitt, *Faith and Folklore of the British Isles* (New York, 1965), Vol. II, p. 639.

4. Folklore and Language Archives, Memorial University of Newfoundland.

5. Horace P. Beck, *Folklore of Maine* (Philadelphia, 1956), p. 68.

6. Wilbur Bassett, *Wander-Ships* (Chicago, 1917), pp. 122–24.

7. Frank Shay, *A Sailors Treasury* (New York, 1951), pp. 58–59, 167.

8. Jane C. Beck, *Ghostlore of the British Isles and Ireland*, unpublished PhD. dissertation in folklore, University of Pennsylvania (1969), pp. 240–41.

9. *Ibid.*, p. 185.

10. Personal collection.

11. *Ibid.*

12. *Ibid.*; also Folklore and Language Archives, Memorial University of Newfoundland.

13. *Ibid.*

14. H. P. Beck, *op. cit.*, p. 73.

15. Personal collection. Whether this was a local custom or a holdover from old world practice, I have been uable to determine.

16. H. P. Beck, *op. cit.*, pp. 203–04.

17. *Ibid.*, pp. 201–07.

18. Joshua Slocum, *Sailing Alone Around the World* (New York, 1900), pp. 59–62.

19. Helen Creighton, *Bluenose Ghosts* (Toronto, 1957), pp. 135–36.

20. J. C. Beck, *op. cit.*, pp. 283–84.

21. Creighton, *op. cit.*, pp. 130–31. See also H. P. Beck, *op. cit.*, pp. 190–91, for a similar story.

22. Carey Archives, University of Maryland.

23. Personal collection.

24. *Ibid.*

25. *Ibid.*

26. *Ibid.*

27. *Ibid.*; see also D. D. C. Pochin Mould, *West-Over-Sea* (Edinburgh, 1953), pp. 181–83.

28. Personal collection; see also MacEdward Leach, *Folk Ballads and Songs of the Lower Labrador Coast* (Ottawa, 1965), pp. 74–75, for bibliography, discussion and a variant.

29. Personal collection.

30. George Coggeshall, *Voyages in Various Parts of the World* (New York, 1851), pp. 135, 138, 142.

31. Carey Archives, University of Maryland.

32. Folklore Archives, Memorial University of Newfoundland.

33. William F. S. A. Jones, *Credulities Past and Present* (London, 1880), pp. 12–13.

34. *Ibid.*, pp. 12–13.

35. Thomas Henderson, "Traditions and Tales," *Shetland Folk Book*, Vol. 1 (1947), pp. 54–55.

36. Personal collection.

37. *Ibid.*

38. *Ibid.*

39. *Ibid.*; see also Lowry C. Wimberly, *Folklore in the English and Scottish Ballads* (New York, 1928), p. 66.

40. Personal collection.

41. *Ibid.*

42. *Ibid.*

43. For details, see Alexander MacKenzie, *The Prophecies of the Brahan Seer* (Stirling, 1946).

44. Personal collection, from the narration of Captain Paddy O'Halloran, July 1968.

45. Creighton, *op. cit.*, p. 70.

46. Mary L. Fraser, *Folklore of Nova Scotia* (Toronto, 1932), p. 140.

47. Personal collection.

48. John MacInnis, "The Oral Tradition in Scottish Gaelic Poetry," *Scottish Studies*, 12:29–43 (1968), p. 41.

49. Personal collection; also Folklore Archives, Memorial University of Newfoundland.

50. Personal collection; see also J. R. Tudor, *The Orkneys and Shetlands* (London, 1883), p. 167.

51. Personal collection.

52. Charles H. Whedbee, *Legends of the Outer Banks* (Winston-Salem, 1966), pp. 57–63.

53. For discussion and text, see MacEdward Leach, *The Ballad Book* (New York, 1955), p. 697.

54. Personal collection; see also Fletcher M. Bassett, *Legends and Superstitions of the Sea and of Sailors* (Chicago, 1885), pp. 459–61. It is interesting to note that in the West Indies, according to my informants, being born with the caul allows the person to see the future and to see ghosts.

55. Personal collection.

56. George Coggeshall, *History of the American Privateers* (New York, 1861), p. 31.

57. Dunbar M. Hinrichs, *The Fateful Voyage of Captain William Kidd* (New York, 1955), p. 139.

58. Personal collection.

59. Personal collection, from the telling of the late MacEdward Leach.

60. Carey Archives.

61. Personal collection.

62. *Ibid.*

63. *Ibid.*

64. *Ibid.*

65. Carey Archives.

66. Hazlitt, *op. cit.*, pp. 665–66.

67. Bassett, *op. cit.*, pp. 275–76.

68. Personal collection.

69. Martin Martin, *A Description of the Western Islands of Scotland* (Stirling, 1934), p. 107.

70. Personal collection.

71. Folklore Archives, Memorial University of Newfoundland.

72. Personal collection.

73. Folklore Archives, Memorial University of Newfoundland, and Personal collection.

74. Personal collection.

75. *Ibid.*

76. H. P. Beck, *op. cit.*, p. 72.

77. Gerald Averill, *Ridge Runner* (Philadelphia, 1948), pp. 29–40. I heard this identical story during World War II from Robert Davidson. This time it was flank steak instead of shoat and a boiled pumpkin instead of a hot shot.

78. Carey Archives.

CHAPTER XII

1. Captain John Smith, *A Sea Grammar* (London, 1627), pp. 59–62.

2. Edgar S. Maclay, *A History of American Privateers* (New York, 1899), p. 13, a quote.

3. G. W. Allen, *Massachusetts Privateers of the Revolution* (Cambridge, 1927), pp. 3–5.

4. See Maclay, *op. cit.*, pp. 13–16.

5. G. W. Allen, *A Naval History of the American Revolution* (New York, 1962), Vol. I, pp. 45–47.

6. For a more extensive list, see G. W. Allen, *op. cit.*, and William Sheffield, *Rhode Island Privateers* (Newport, 1883).

7. Personal collection.

8. *Ibid.*

9. Folklorists who read this account will recall that identical tactics to those of the Bishop had already been tried successfully by King Canute nearly a millennium before. See also Samuel E. Morison, *John Paul Jones, A Sailor's Biography* (Boston, 1959), pp. 216–19. Here the story is given somewhat differently.

10. George Coggeshall, *History of the American Privateers,* and *Letters-of-Marque, During Our War with England in the Years 1812, '13 and '14, Interspersed with Several Naval Battles Between American and British Ships-of-War* (New York, 1861), pp. 67–68.

11. John P. Cranwell and William B. Crane, *Men of Marque: A History of Private Armed Vessels out of Baltimore During the War of 1812* (New York, 1940), pp. 261–65.

12. Coggeshall, *op. cit.*, p. 108.

13. *Ibid.*, pp. 370–84.

14. *Ibid.*, Chapters VI and X.

15. Cranwell and Crane, *op. cit.*, p. 68.

16. This story was related to the author by the late Captain George Barney Wright of Newport, Rhode Island. See also Ralph D. Paine, *Joshua Barney* (New York, 1924), pp. 98–100.

17. James Fenimore Cooper, *History of the Navy of the United States of America*, 2nd ed. (Philadelphia, 1840), pp. 206–08.

18. Philip Freneau, *The Poems of Philip Freneau*, ed., Fred L. Pattee, Vol. II (Princeton, N.J., 1903), pp. 149–53.

19. Paine, *op. cit.*, pp. 162–88. See also Cooper, *op. cit.*, Vol. I, p. 208.

20. Cooper, *op. cit.*, pp. 217–18.

21. Horace P. Beck, "The Making of the Popular Legendary Hero," in W. D. Hand, ed., *American Folk Legend A Symposium* (Berkeley, 1971), pp. 121–33.

22. Horace P. Beck, *Folklore of Maine* (Philadelphia, 1956), pp. 20–21.

23. For a good account of Morgan, see John Esquemeling, *Buccaneers of America* (London, n.d.), pp. 119–215.

24. Personal collection. See also Joanna Colcord, *Songs of American Sailormen* (New York, 1938), pp. 141–44. The opinions expressed in this song were still espoused by competent historians as late as 1934; see Philip Gosse, *The History of Piracy* (New York, 1934), pp. 175–86.

25. There are numerous biographies of Kidd. For an early account, see Captain Charles Johnson, *A General History of the . . . Pirates* (New York, 1926), pp. 386–96; for his voyage and trial, see Dunbar M. Hinrichs, *The Fateful Voyage of Captain Kidd* (New York, 1955); for his life, see Willard H. Bonner, *Pirate Laureate* (New Brunswick, 1947).

26. Personal collection. Actually, the number was fourteen and all fourteen "danced at the end of a rope"; see Edward Peterson, *History of Rhode Island and Newport in the Past* (New York, 1853), pp. 64–65. For a history of Lowe, see Anon., *The Pirates Own Book* (Philadelphia, 1839), pp. 228–36.

27. Personal collection.

28. *Ibid.*

29. Johnson, *op. cit.*, pp. 130–40.

30. Petrel Fulmar, *Grania Waile* (London, 1895), pp. 11–13.

31. William O'Brien, *A Queen of Men* (Dublin, 1958), p. 13.

32. The two most available sources of information on Granuaile are O'Brien, *op. cit.*, especially pp. 10–17, and Petrel, *op. cit.*

33. H. P. Beck, "The Prince of Spain," *Journal of the Folklore Institute*, Vol. VIII, #1, 1971, pp. 48–56.

34. Points two and three refer particularly to buried or hidden treasure.

35. Rupert Furneaux, *The Great Treasure Hunts* (New York, 1969), pp. 9–23.

36. William Haynes, *Casco Bay Yarns* (New York, 1916), pp. 21–42.

37. Charles B. Driscoll, *Doubloons: The Story of Buried Treasure* (New York, 1930), pp. 3–35.

38. Personal collection.

39. Helen Creighton, *Bluenose Ghosts* (Toronto, 1957), pp. 57–59.

40. Furneaux, *op. cit.*, pp. 38–45.

41. See Chapter XI, herein.

42. Driscoll, *op. cit.*, pp. 42–43.

43. Personal collection.

44. *Ibid.* Note that the first part of this story is almost identical to a story told on Carriacou Island in the Caribbean. Captain MacFarlane of Windward

said a young boy was "forking the land" and discovered a treasure. He took it to the owner who upbraided him for finding it; told him he must not mention it to anyone and kept if for himself. Unlike the Irish story, this man prospered like the proverbial green bay tree.

45. *Ibid.*

46. For a more detailed study of the factual points of this story, see Charles B. Driscoll, *op. cit.*, pp. 1–35; Rupert Furneaux, *The World's Strangest Mysteries* (London, 1961), Chapter 1. The folk material on the treasure was collected in Chester, Nova Scotia, in June 1948, from a family of shipwrights named Stevens.

47. Personal collection.

48. *Ibid.*

49. One is immediately reminded in this case of Stoertebeker cramming his loot into his masts.

50. Creighton, *op. cit.*

51. Mary L. Fraser, *Folklore of Nova Scotia* (Toronto, 1932), pp. 79–81.

52. For an interesting discussion of this attitude, see George Washington Cable, "Jean Ah Poquelan," in *Old Creole Days* (New York, 1937).

53. Hesketh J. Bell, *Obeah; Witchcraft in the West Indies* (London, 1889), pp. 177–85.

54. George Howe, *Mount Hope: A New England Chronicle* (New York, 1959), p. 87. See also Richard B. Morris, *Encyclopedia of American History* (New York, 1953), p. 80.

55. Personal collection.

56. *Ibid.*

57. *Ibid.*

CHAPTER XIII

1. The foregoing definition is intended to distinguish between these two types as they are used within the present work. For a more detailed and general evaluation, see Stith Thompson, *The Folktale: Stories Men Tell from Egyptian Myth to Uncle Remus* (New York, 1946).

2. Wilbur Bassett, *Wander–Ships* (Chicago, 1917), pp. 52, 98.

3. For a detailed study of this material, see T. C. Letherbridge, *Herdsmen and Hermits: Celtic Seafarers in the Northern Seas* (Cambridge, 1950), pp. 140–43, and Reidar T. Christiansen, "The People of the North," Lochlann, *A Review of Celtic Studies*, Vol. II (1962), pp. 137–64.

4. Lady Augusta Gregory, *Gods and Fighting Men* (Gerrands Cross, 1970), p. 141. See also T. W. Rolleston, *Myths and Legends of the Celtic Race* (London, 1911), pp. 252–308, and Eileen O'Faolain, *Irish Sagas and Folktales* (London, 1954), pp. 125–34.

5. John Ryan, *Ireland from the Earliest Times to A.D. 800* (Dublin, n.d.), pp. 130–38.

6. Alan O. Anderson and Marjorie Anderson, *Adomnan's Life of Columba* (New York and London, 1961).

7. Stories about cursing stones are not only popular in Ireland but in Scotland as well. See D.D.C. Pochin Mould, *Irish Pilgrimage* (Dublin, 1955), p. 81.

8. Hence we discover the folk are here using sympathetic magic, a favorite device to ward off evil.

9. For further information and stories, see William Bottrell, *Traditions and Hearthside Stories of West Cornwall, Penzance, 1873*, 2nd Series, pp. 276–79; see also W. Carew Hazlitt, *Faith and Folklore of the British Isles* (New York, 1965), Vol. I, pp. 40–43.

10. Hazlitt, *op. cit.*, p. 42.

11. *Ibid.*, p. 42.

12. William F. S. A. Jones, *Credulities Past and Present* (London, 1880), pp. 12–13.

13. For a complete and detailed account of this occurrence, see Robert F. Marx, *Pirate Port: The Story of the Sunken City of Port Royal* (New York, 1967).

14. Edward R. Snow, *Great Sea Rescues* (New York, 1958), pp. 141–51. For further accounts of wreck and rescue, see Birse Shepard, *Lore of the Wreckers* (Boston, 1961); Cyril Noall and Graham Farr, *Wreck and Rescue Round the Cornish Coast* (Truro, Cornwall, 1965).

15. For a detailed discussion of this story, see Horace P. Beck, "The Prince of Spain," *Journal of the Folklore Institute*, Vol. VIII, #1, June 1971, pp. 48–56.

16. For a good summary, see Roger Jefferis and Kendall MacDonald, *The Wreck Hunters* (London, 1966), pp. 59–74.

17. Bottrell, *op. cit.*, pp. 231–33.

18. The mastiffs' song was considered to be a "bad song" because at one time the hell hounds had tried to prevent a priest from giving absolution to a dead man by attempting to delay him in listening while they sang "Cailín Deas Crúite na mBó." From that day forward it had been known as a "bad song."—Jane C. Beck, *Ghostlore of the British Isles and Ireland*, unpublished PhD. dissertation, University of Pennsylvania (1969), p. 283.

19. Hugh Miller, *Scenes and Legends of the North of Scotland* (Edingburgh, MDCCCLIII), pp. 174–90.

20. This story was told to me by Captain Ben Pine of Gloucester, master of the schooner *Gertrude Thibeault*, in the summer of 1940. See also J. B. Connolly, *Out of Gloucester* (New York, 1902).

21. Edouard A. Stackpole, *The Sea Hunters: The New England Whalemen During Two Centuries 1635–1835* (Philadelphia, 1953), pp. 317–37.

22. Carey Archives, University of Maryland.

23. For a more detailed account of the exploits of Barney Beal, see Richard M. Dorson, *Buying the Wind* (Chicago, 1964), pp. 40–54.

24. Horace P. Beck, *Folklore of Maine* (Philadelphia, 1956), pp. 140–44.

25. This story was told twice. The first time Captain Buchan included the bit about the Russian, the collision and the plans for taking off the crew of the

Alliance. At the second telling into the microphone, he overlooked these items until after he had finished the story. I have taken the liberty of including them in the story as they belonged.

CHAPTER XIV

1. George K. Anderson, *The Legend of the Wandering Jew* (Providence, 1965).

2. *Ibid.*, p. 11.

3. *Ibid.*, pp. 11–31.

4. *Ibid.*, p. 5.

5. Funk and Wagnalls' *Standard Dictionary of Folklore, Mythology and Legend*, Maria Leache, ed., Vol. II (New York, 1949), p. 1177.

6. Benjamin Thorpe, *Northern Mythology*, Vol. III (London, 1852), pp. 294–95.

7. Wilbur Bassett, *Wander-Ships* (Chicago, 1917), pp. 38–45.

8. Dr. Angelo S. Rappaport, *Superstitions of Sailors* (London, 1928), pp. 233–34.

9. It is worth recalling that Ahasuerus always appeared in a long cloak; see Anderson, *op. cit.*

10. Bassett, *op. cit.*, p. 51.

11. For a fairly detailed discussion, see Wilbur Bassett, *op. cit.*, "Dahul," pp. 35–63.

12. Richard H. Dillon, *Shanghaiing Days* (New York, 1961), pp. 66–127.

13. Edward A. Ives, "The Burning Ship of Northumberland Strait: Some Notes on That Apparation," *Midwest Folklore*, Vol. VIII, #4 (1958), pp. 199–203.

14. F. H. MacArthur, *Legends of Prince Edward Island* (Charlottetown, P.E.I.), pp. 69–71.

15. George Coggeshall, *History of the American Privateers and Letters-of-Marque, During Our War with England in the Years 1812, '13, '14, Interspersed with Several Naval Battles Between American and British Ships-of-War* (New York, 1861), p. 125.

16. Personal collection. See also Charles B. Driscoll, *Doubloons* (New York, 1930), p. 31. For an abbreviated account, see Helen Creighton, *Folklore of Lunenburg County, Nova Scotia* (Ottawa, 1950), p. 12.

17. Horace P. Beck, *The American Indian as a Colonial Sea Fighter* (Mystic, Conn., 1959), p. 22.

18. For a complete discussion of the material on the *Palatine*, see George G. Carey, "Folklore in the Writings of John Greenleaf Whittier," doctoral dissertation (Indiana University, 1966), pp. 125–30. See also Ralph Childs, dissertation, "Phantom Ships of the Northeast Coast of North America," *New York Folklore Quarterly*, Vol. II, No. 2, (1946), pp. 160–81; E.C. Ritchie, *Block Island Lore and Legend* (Block Island, 1955), pp. 75–76; Samuel Livermore, *History of Block Island* (Hartford, 1877), pp. 124–25; John Kobler, "The Mystery of the

Palatine Light," *Saturday Evening Post* (June 11, 1900), p. 55; Albert Mathand, "The Word Palatine in America," *Publications of the Colonial Society of Massachusetts*, VIII, p. 217 ff.; Benjamin A. Botkin, *Treasury of New England Folklore* (New York, 1947), pp. 296–97; John Greenleaf Whittier, *Complete Poetical Works* (Boston, 1894), p. 257.

19. Personal collection. See also Ritchie, *op. cit.*, p. 81.

20. Fletcher Bassett, *Legends and Superstitions of the Sea and of Sailors* (Chicago and New York, 1885), p. 372.

21. William Bottrell, *Traditions and Hearthside Stories of West Cornwall*, 2nd Series (Penzance, 1873), pp. 247–49.

22. George A. England, *Vikings of the Ice* (1924), p. 219.

23. Hugh Miller, *Scenes and Legends of the North of Scotland*, 3rd edition (Edinburgh, 1853), pp. 22–23.

24. Personal collection.

25. Horace P. Beck, *Folklore of Maine* (Philadelphia, 1956), pp. 146–51.

26. Edmund Pearson, *Murder at Smutty Nose and Other Murders* (London, 1927), pp. 1–70.

27. Beck, *op. cit.*, pp. 148–52.

28. Frank C. Brown, *North Carolina Folklore* (Durham, 1952), Vol. 1, p. 625.

29. Allen Cunningham, *Traditional Tales of the English and Scottish Peasantry* (London, 1822), p. 288.

30. John Greenleaf Whittier, *op. cit.*, p. 310. For a detailed analysis of the facts, see George Carey, *op. cit.*, pp. 130–33.

31. Wilbur Bassett, *op. cit.*, p. 72.

32. *Ibid.*

33. Henry Wadsworth Longfellow, "The Phantom Ship," in *Complete Poetical Works* (Boston, 1902)), p. 230. See also Cotton Mather, *Magnalia Christi Americana*.

34. Carey Archives, University of Maryland.

35. Memorial University of Newfoundland Folklore and Language Archives.

36. Lady Augusta Gregory, *Visions and Beliefs in the West of Ireland* (Garrands Cross, 1920), pp. 15–31.

37. Ralph Childs, *op. cit.*

38. Henry W. Splitter, "New Tales of American Phantom Ships," *Western Folklore*, Vol. IX (1950), pp. 204–09.

39. *Ibid.*

40. Ralph Childs, *op. cit.*, pp. 160–61.

41. Wilbur Bassett, *op. cit.*, pp. 11–24, 92–105.

42. Memorial University, *loc. cit.*

43. Edward Peterson, *History of Rhode Island* (New York, 1853), pp. 63–64.

BIBLIOGRAPHY

Abbott, John S. C. *Captain William Kidd*. New York, 1878.

Adams, Captain R. C. *On Board the "Rocket."* Boston, 1879.

Alger, Abby L. *In Indian Tents*. Boston, 1897.

Allen, Gardner Wold. *Massachusetts Privateers of the Revolution* (in Massachusetts Historical Society Collections, Vol. 77). Cambridge, Mass., 1927.

————. *A Naval History of the American Revolution*, 2 vols. New York, 1962.

Allen, Joseph C. *Fireside Tales Told on Martha's Vineyard*. Boston, 1934.

————. *Tales and Trails of Martha's Vineyard*. Boston, 1938.

Alpers, Anthony. *Dolphins: The Myth and the Mammal*. Boston, 1961.

Anderson, Alan O., and Anderson, Marjorie O. *Adomnan's Life of Columba*. London and New York, 1961.

Anderson, Captain Alex. *Windjammer Yarns*. London, 1923.

Anderson, George K. *The Legend of the Wandering Jew.* Providence, 1965.

Anderson, Otto. "Seal-folk in East and West; Some Comments on a Fascinating Group of Folk Tales," in *Folklore International, Essays in Traditional Literature, Belief and Custom in Honor of Wayland Hand*, ed. D. K. Wilgus. Hatboro, Pa., 1967.

Anson, Peter F. *British Sea Fishermen*. London, 1944.

————. *Fisher Folklore*. London, 1965.

Armstrong, G. H. *The Origin and Meaning of Place Names in Canada*. Toronto, 1930.

Ashley, C. W. *The Ashley Book of Knots*. Garden City, N.Y., 1956.

————. *The Yankee Whaler*. New York, 1942.

Ashton, John. *Real Sailor Songs*. London, 1891.

Averill, Gerald. *Ridge Runner*. Philadelphia, 1948.

Ayres, J. A. *Legends of Montauk*. New York, 1849.

Babcock, C. Merton. "Melville's Backwoods Seamen." *Western Folklore*, 10:126–33, 1951.

————."Melville's Proverbs of the Sea." *Western Folklore*, 11:254–65, 1952.

Babcock, William. *Legendary Islands of the Atlantic*. New York, 1922.

Baker, William A. "Early Seventeenth Century Ship Design." *American Neptune,* 14:262–77, 1954.

Ballard, Edward. "Geographical Names on a Coast of Maine," *United States Coast Survey* from Coast Survey Report from 1868. Washington, 1891.

Barbeau, Marius. "All Hands Aboard Scrimshawing." *American Neptune,* 12: 99–122, 1952.

Baring-Gould, Sabine. *Curious Myths of the Middle Ages.* London, 1868.

Bassett, Fletcher M. *Legends and Superstitions of the Sea and of Sailors.* Chicago and New York, 1885.

Bassett, Wilbur. *Wander-Ships.* Chicago, 1917.

Bassin, Rose E. "74 Tolmic Manuscripts." *Journal of the English Folk Dance and Song Society,* 4:64, December 1951.

Batchelder, Samuel F. "Some Sea Terms in Land Speech." *New England Quarterly,* 2:625–53, 1929.

Baughman, Ernest. *Type and Motif Index of the Folktales of England and North America.* The Hague, 1966.

Bauman, Richard. "Three Legends from the Ayrshire Coast." *Scottish Studies,* 8:33–44, 1964.

Beazley, Julia. "The Uneasy Ghost of Lafitte." *Publications of the Texas Folklore Society,* III:185–89, 1924.

Beck, Horace P. *The American Indian as a Colonial Sea Fighter.* Mystic, Conn., 1959.

———. *Folklore of Maine.* Philadelphia, 1956.

———. "Sea Lore." *Northwest Folklore,* Vol. 2, #2, 1967.

———. "Tales of Banks Fishermen." *The American Neptune,* 13:125–30, 1953.

———. "The Prince of Spain." *Journal of the Folklore Institute,* 8:48–56, 1971.

———, and Speck, F. G. "Old World Tales Among the Mohawks." *Journal of American Folklore,* 63:285–308, 1950.

Beck, Jane C. *Ghostlore of the British Isles and Ireland.* Unpublished PhD. dissertation, University of Pennsylvania, 1969.

Beckett, W. N. T. *A Few Naval Customs, Expressions, Traditions and Superstitions.* Portsmouth, England, 1931.

Bell, Hesketh J. *Obeah: Witchcraft in the West Indies.* London, 1889.

Benwell, Gwen, and Waugh, Arthur. *Sea Enchantress.* New York, 1965.

Bergen, F. D. "On the Eastern Shore." *Journal of American Folklore,* 2:298–99, 1889.

Berry, James. *Tales of the West of Ireland.* Dublin, 1966.

Bertram, Colin. *In Search of Mermaids.* New York, 1964.

Bertram, James Glass. *The Harvest of the Sea.* London, 1865.

Besson, Maurice. *The Scourge of the Indies.* New York, 1929.

Bishop, W. H. "Fish and Men in the Maine Islands." *Harper's Magazine,* September 1880.

Black, G. F., and Thomas, N. W. *County Folklore III: Orkney and Shetland Islands.* London, 1903.

Black, William G. "Folklore from the United States." *Folk-Lore Record*, 4:92–95, 1881.

Blind, Karl. "Scottish, Shetlandic and Germanic Water Tales." *The Contemporary Review*, 40:186–208, 399–423, 534–63, 1881.

Bone, Captain David W. *Capstan Bars*. Edinburgh, 1931, and New York, 1932.

Bonner, Willard Hallan. "Hudson River Legends of Captain Kidd." *New York Folklore Quarterly*, 2:40–51, 1946.

————. *Pirate Laureate, The Life and Legends of Captain Kidd*. New Brunswick, N.J., 1947.

Bottrell, William. *Traditions and Hearthside Stories of West Cornwall*. Penzance, 1873.

Boughton, Captain George P. *Seafaring*. London, 1926.

Bowen, Frank C. *Sea Slang*. London, 1929.

Bowen, Richard L. "Maritime Superstitions of the Arabs." *American Neptune*, 15:5–48, 1955.

Bradford, Gershom. "Sea Serpents? No or Maybe." *American Neptune*, 13:268–74, 1953.

Bradford, J., and Fagge, A. *Old Sea Chanties*. London, 1904.

Brewington, Marion V. *Chesapeake Bay: A Pictorial Maritime History*. New York, 1956.

————. *Ship Carvers of North America*. Barre, Mass., 1962.

Briggs, Katherine M. *The Fairies in English Tradition and Literature*. Chicago, 1967.

Brogger, A. W. *Ancient Emigrants*. Oxford, 1929.

Brooks, Alfred A. "The Boats of Ash Point, Maine." *American Neptune*, 2:307–23, 1942.

Brown, Frank C. *North Carolina Folklore*, Vol. 1. Durham, N.C.

Buchan, Peter. *Annals of Peterhead*. Peterhead, 1819.

Buchanan, Robert. *The Hebrid Isles*. London, 1883.

Bullen, Frank T. *A Sack of Shakings*. New York, 1901.

————, and Arnold, W. F. *Songs of Sea Labor*. London, 1914.

Bulletin of the Folk-Song Society of the Northeast, Nos. 1–12, ed. Phillips Barry. Cambridge, Mass., 1930–1937.

Burgess, Robert F. *Sinkings, Salvages and Shipwrecks*. New York, 1970.

Burgess, Robert H. *Coasting Captain*. Newport News, Va., 1967.

Burney, William. *A Universal Dictionary of the Marine*. London, 1815. (Original compiled by William Falconer.)

Cable, George Washington. "Jean Ah Poquelon," in *Old Creole Days*, New York, 1937.

Cameron, Isabel. *A Highland Chap Book*. Stirling, 1928.

Campbell, John F. *The Celtic Dragon Myth*, translated and with introduction by George Henderson. Edinburgh, 1911.

————. *Popular Tales of the West Highlands*. 4 vols. Edinburgh, 1860.

Campbell, John F. "A Marine Note of Protest." *American Neptune*, 23:46–55, 1963.

Campbell, John Gregorson. *Superstitions of the Highlands and Islands of Scotland*. Glasgow, 1900.

———. *Witchcraft and Second Sight in the Highlands and Islands of Scotland*. Glasgow, 1902.

Campbell, John L. *Stories from South Uist told by Angus MacLellan*. London, 1961.

———. *Tales of Bara Told by the Coddy*. Edinburgh, 1961.

Campbell, Mary. *Sea Wrack or Long Ago Tales of Rathlan Island*. Ballycastle, 1951.

The Captain of the "Phantom": The Story of Henry Jackson Sargent, Jr., 1834–1862. Foreword by Daniel Sargent. Mystic, Conn., 1967.

Carey, George. "Enchanted Island Traditions of the Sixteenth and Seventeenth Centuries." *American Neptune*, 29:275–81, 1969.

———. *Folk Motifs in the Writings of John Josselyn*. Unpublished master's thesis, Indiana University, 1962.

———. "The Tradition of St. Elmo's Fire." *American Neptune*, 23:29–38, 1963.

Carmichael, Alexander. *Carmina Gadelica, Hymns and Incantations with Illustrative Notes on Words, Rites, and Customs, Dying and Obsolete: Orally Collected in the Highlands and Islands of Scotland*, Vol. IV. Edinburgh, 1941.

Carrington, Richard. *Mermaids and Mastodons*. London, 1957.

Carruth, J. A. *Loch Ness and Its Monster*. Fort Augustus, Scotland, 1967.

Carse, Robert. *The Age of Piracy*. New York, 1965.

Chapelle, Howard I. *The Baltimore Clipper*. Salem, Mass., 1930.

———. *The History of American Sailing Ships*. New York, 1935.

Chaplin, W. R. "The History of Flat Holm Lighthouse." *American Neptune*, 20:5–43, 1960.

Chase, George David. "Sea Terms that Have Come Ashore." *New England Quarterly*, 14:272–91, 1941.

———. *Sea Terms Come Ashore*. Orono, Maine, 1942.

Chase, Owen. *Narrative of the Most Extraordinary and Distressive Ship Wreck of the Whaleship Essex of Nantucket*. New York, 1821.

Child, Francis J. *English and Scottish Popular Ballads*, 5 vols. Boston, 1881–1898.

Childs, Ralph. "Phantom Ships of the Northeast Coast of North America," *New York Folklore Quarterly*, Vol. II, #2, 1946.

Christiansen, Reidar T. "The People of the North." *Lochlann*, 2:137–64, 1962.

Church, Albert Cook, and Connolly, James B. *American Fishermen*. New York, 1940.

Clark, Admont G. "They Built Clipper Ships in Their Back Yard." *American Neptune*, 22:233–51, 1962.

Clark, Arthur Hamilton. *The Clipper Ship Era*. New York, 1910.

Clark, G. E. *Seven Years of a Sailor's Life*. Boston, 1867.

Clark, W. Fordyce. *Northern Gleams: Tales of the Shetland Islands*. Lerwick, Scotland, 1898.

Cluff, John A. "Lobster Fishing on the Marine Coast Past and Present." *American Neptune*, 14:203–08, 1954.

Clyde Cruising Club. *Sailing Directions and Anchorages: West Coast of Scotland.* Glasgow, 1966.

Coggeshall, George. *History of the American Privateers.* New York, 1861.

———. *Voyages to Various Parts of the World.* New York, 1851.

Cohen, Hennig. "Burial of the Drowned Among the Gullah Negroes." *Southern Folklore Quarterly,* 22:93–97, 1958.

Colcord, Joanna C. "Domestic Life on American Sailing Ships." *American Neptune,* 2:193–202, 1942.

———. *Roll and Go: Songs of American Sailormen.* Indianapolis, 1924.

———. *Sea Language Comes Ashore.* New York, 1945.

———. *Songs of American Sailormen.* New York, 1938.

Coleridge, Henry Nelson. *Six Months in the West Indies in 1825.* London, 1832.

Colton, Walter. *The Sea and the Sailor.* New York, 1860.

Connolly, James B. *Out of Gloucester.* New York, 1902.

———. *The Port of Gloucester.* New York, 1940.

Conrad, Joseph. *The Mirror of the Sea.* New York, 1906.

Cooper, James Fenimore. *History of the Navy of the United States of America,* 2nd ed. Philadelphia, 1840.

———. *The Pilot,* New York, 1859.

———. *The Red Rover.* New York, 1896.

Couch, Jonathan. *History of Polperro, a Fishing Town on the South Coast of Cornwall.* London, 1871.

Courtney, M. A. "Cornish Folk-Lore." *Folklore Journal,* 5:85–112, 1887.

Coxhead, J. R. W. *Legends of Devon.* North Devon, 1954.

Cranwell, John P., and Crane, William B. *Men of Marque: A History of Private Armed Vessels out of Baltimore during the War of 1812.* New York, 1940.

Creighton, Helen. *Bluenose Ghosts.* Toronto, 1957.

———. *Folklore of Lunenburg,* National Museum of Canada, Bulletin #117. Ottawa, 1950.

———. "Folklore of Victoria Beach, Nova Scotia." *Journal of American Folklore,* 63:131–46, 1950.

———. *Maritime Folk Songs.* Toronto, 1961.

———. *Songs and Ballads from Nova Scotia.* Toronto and Vancouver, 1933.

———, and Senior, Doreen H. *Traditional Songs from Nova Scotia.* Toronto, 1950.

Crétien, C. Douglas. "Comments on Naval Slang." *Western Folklore,* 6:157–62, 1947.

Cross, Tom P. *Motif Index of Early Irish Literature.* Bloomington, Ind., 1952.

———, and Slover, Clark T. *Ancient Irish Tales.* New York, 1936.

Cunningham, Allen. *Traditional Tales of the English and Scottish Peasantry,* London, 1822.

Cutler, Carl C. *Greyhounds of the Sea: The Story of the American Clipper Ship.* New York, 1930.

———. *Five Hundred Sailing Records of American Built Ships.* Mystic, Conn., 1952.

Dacombe, Marianne. *Dorset Up Along and Down Along.* Dorchester, 1951.

Dana, Richard H. *Two Years Before the Mast.* New York, 1911.

Danaher, Kevin. *Gentle Places and Simple Things.* Cork, 1964.

Daniel, Hawthorne. *The Clipper Ship.* New York, 1928.

D'Arbois de Jubainville, Marie Henri. *The Irish Mythological Cycle,* trans. Richard I. Best. Dublin, 1903.

Davidson, Leverette S. "Two Old War Songs." *Western Folklore,* 4:141–45, 1945.

Davis, Harold. "Shipbuilding on the St. Croix." *American Neptune,* 15:173–90, 1955.

Davis, J., and Tozer, Ferris. *Sailor Songs or 'Chanties.'* London, 1887.

Dean, Michael C. *The Flying Cloud and One Hundred and Fifty Other Old Time Songs.* Virginia, Minn., 1922.

Denys, Nicholas. *The Description and Natural History of the Coasts of North America,* ed. W. F. Ganong. Toronto, 1908.

dePaor, Máire, and dePaor, Liau. *Early Christian Ireland.* London, 1960.

Dillon, Richard H. *Shanghaiing Days.* New York, 1961.

Dinsdale, Tim. *The Loch Ness Monster.* London, 1966.

Dixon, John H. *Gairloch.* Edinburgh, 1886.

Doerflinger, William Main. *Shantymen and Shantyboys.* New York, 1951.

Doering, J. Frederick. "Legends from Canada, Indiana, and Florida." *Southern Folklore Quarterly,* 2:213–20, 1938.

Dorson, Richard M. *Buying the Wind.* Chicago and London, 1964.

———. "Collecting Folklore in Jonesport, Maine." *Proceedings of the American Philosophical Society,* 101:270–89, June 1957.

———. *Jonathan Draws the Long Bow.* Cambridge, Mass., 1946.

———. "The Legend of Yoho Cove." *Western Folklore,* 18:329–31, 1959.

Dow, George Francis. *Slave Ships and Slaving.* Salem, Mass., 1927.

Drever, Helen. *Lure of the Kelpie: Fairy and Folktales of the Highlands.* Edinburgh and London, 1937.

Driscoll, Charles B. *Doubloons: The Story of Buried Treasure.* New York, 1930.

———. *Pirates Ahoy!* New York, 1941.

Driver, Edward. *Indians of North America.* Chicago, 1964.

Dugan, James. *The Great Iron Ship.* New York, 1953.

Dunbabin, Thomas. "The Friendly Mermaid of St. John's." *American Antiquity,* 48:75, January, 1958.

Duncan, Leland S. "Fairy Beliefs and Other Folklore Notes from County Leitnin." *Folklore,* 7:161–83, 1896.

Duncan, Norman. *Dr. Grenfell's Parish: The Deep Sea Fishermen,* 4th ed. New York, 1905.

Duncan, Robert, and Blanchard Fessenden. *A Cruising Guide to the New England Coast.* New York, 1955.

Dyer, Thiselton T. F. *English Folk Lore.* London, 1878.

Eckstorm, Fannie H. *Old John Neptune and Other Maine Indian Stories.* Portland, 1945.

———. *Place Names of Maine.* Orono, Maine, 1941.

————, and Smythe, Mary W. *Minstrelsy of Maine*. Boston, 1927.

Empson, C. W. "Weather Proverbs and Sayings Not Contained in Inwards' or Swainson's Books." *Folklore Record*, 4:126–32, 1881.

England, George Allan. *Vikings of the Ice*. London, 1924.

Esquemeling, John. *The History of the Buccaneers of America Containing Detailed Accounts of Those Bold and Daring Freebooters*. Boston, 1851.

Fahy, Francis A. *The Ould Plaid Shawl and Other Songs*. Dublin, 1945.

Falconer, William. *The Shipwreck: A Poem*. London, 1868.

Falconer, William. *Dictionary of the Marine*. London, 1815.

Fauset, Arthur H. "Folklore from Nova Scotia." *Memoirs of the American Folklore Society*, Vol. XXIV. New York, 1931.

Fermor, Patrick L. *The Traveller's Tree*. New York, 1950.

The Fisherman's Own Book. Gloucester, 1881.

Fitzgerald, Edward. "Seawords and Phrases Along the Suffolk Coast." *Works of Edward Fitzgerald*, 2 vol. New York and Boston, 1887. (Originally published in *East Anglican*, 1869.)

Fitz-Gerald, S. J. Adair. *Stories of Famous Songs*, 2 vol. Philadelphia, 1901.

Folkard, Richard. *Plant Lore Legends and Lyrics*. London, 1892.

Forbes, Athol. *The Romance of Smuggling*. London, 1909.

Forester, C. S. *Commodore Hornblower*. Boston, 1945.

Foster, Jerry. "Varieties of Sea Lore." *Western Folklore*, 28:260–66, 1969.

Fraser, Mary L. *Folklore of Nova Scotia*. Toronto, 1932.

Freneau, Philip M. *Miscellaneous Works Containing his Essays and Additional Poems*. Philadelphia, 1788.

Fulmar, Petrel. *Grania Waile*. London, 1895.

Funk and Wagnall's *Standard Dictionary of Folklore, Mythology and Legend*, ed. Maria Leach, Vol. II. New York, 1949.

Furneaux, Rupert. *The World's Strangest Mysteries*. London, 1961.

————. *The Great Treasure Hunts*. New York, 1969.

Geller, Lawrence D. "Notes on Sea Serpents of Coastal New England." *New York Folklore Quarterly*, 26, No. 2 (June 1970):158–60.

Gillespie, G. J. "Jerome." *American Antiquity*, 48:69–72, 1958.

Gleason, Duncan. *The Islands and Ports of California*. New York, 1958.

Goodrich-Freer, A. *Outer Isles*. Westminster, 1902.

Gordon, Seaton. "Distinguished Scarba and Its Whirlpool." *The Times* (London), November 5, 1966.

Gosse, Philip. *The History of Piracy*. New York, 1934.

Gould, R. T. *The Case of the Sea Serpent*. London, 1930.

Gourlay, George. *Fisher Life: or the Memorials of Cellardyke and the Fife Coast*. Cupar, Fife, 1879.

Granville, Wilfred. *Sea Slang of the Twentieth Century*. New York, 1950.

Greenleaf, Elizabeth Bristol, and Mansfield, Grace Yarrow. *Ballads and Sea Songs from Newfoundland*. Cambridge, Mass., 1933.

Greenough, William Parker. *Canadian Folk-Life and Folk-Lore*. New York, 1897.

Gregor, Walter. *The Folklore of the North East of Scotland*. London, 1881.

——. "Guardian Spirits of Wells and Lochs." *Folk-Lore Journal*, 3:67–73, 1892.

——. "Kelpie Stories," *Folk-Lore Journal*, 7:199–201, 1889.

——. "Kelpie Stories from the North of Scotland." *Folk-Lore Journal*, 1:292–94, 1883.

——. "Some Folk-Lore of the Sea." *Folk-Lore Journal*, 4:7–17, 1886.

Gregory, Lady Augusta. *Gods and Fighting Men*. Gerrards Cross, England, 1920.

——. *Visions and Beliefs in the West of Ireland*. Gerrards Cross, England, 1920.

——. *A Book of Saints and Wonders*. London, 1920.

Greig, Gavin. *Folk-Song of the North-East*. Hatboro, Pa., 1963.

Gudde, Erwin G. *California Place Names*. Berkeley, 1960.

Gunn, John. *The Orkney Book*. London, 1909.

Hadfield, R. L. *The Phantom Ship*. London, 1937.

Hambly, W. D. *The History of Tattooing and Its Significance*. London, 1925.

Hand, Wayland D., ed. *American Folk Legend: A Symposium*. Berkeley, 1971.

Hannan, Thomas. *The Beautiful Isle of Mull*. Edinburgh, 1933.

Harlowe, Frederick Pease. *Chanteying Aboard American Ships*. Barre, Mass., 1962.

——. *The Making of a Sailor*. Salem, Mass., 1925.

Harrington, Michael F. "Newfoundland Names." *Atlantic Advocate*, 1:71–77, 1956.

——. *Sea Stories from Newfoundland*. Toronto, 1958.

Harris, J. Henry. *Our Cove Stories from a Cornish Fisher Village*. London, 1900.

Harris, Reginald V. *The Oak Island Mystery*. Toronto, 1958.

Hartwell, Frank E. *Forty Years of the Weather Bureau*. Bolton, Vt., 1958.

Hatfield, James Taft. "Some Nineteenth Century Shanties." *Journal of American Folklore*, 59:108–13, 1946.

Haverty, Martin. *The History of Ireland, Ancient and Modern*. New York, 1885.

Haynes, William. *Casco Bay Yarns*. New York, 1916.

Haywood, Charles. *A Bibliography of North American Folklore and Folksong*. 2 vols., 2nd revised edition. New York, 1960.

Hazlitt, W. Carew. *Faith and Folklore of the British Isles*, Vols. I and II. New York, 1965.

Healey, Jack. "Fo'c'sle Lingo." *American Speech*, 3 (No. 4):345–46, 1928.

Hemingway, Ernest. *The Old Man and the Sea*. New York, 1952.

Henderson, George. *The Norse Influence on Celtic Scotland*. Glasgow, 1910.

Henderson, Thomas. "Traditions and Tales." *Shetland Folk Book*, Vol. I. Lerwick, 1947.

Henningsen, Henning. *Crossing the Equator*. Munksgaard, Denmark, 1961.

Heuvelmans, Bernard. *In the Wake of the Sea Serpents*. London, 1968.

Higginson, T. W. *Tales of the Enchanted Islands of the Atlantic*. New York, 1898.

Hinrichs, Dunbar M. *The Fateful Voyage of Captain William Kidd*. New York, 1955.

Hislop, Alexander. *The Book of Scottish Anecdote, Humorous, Social Legendary, and Historical.* Edinburgh, 1883.

Hogg, Garry. *The Far Flung Isles, Orkney and Shetland.* London, 1961.

Hole, Christina. "Superstitions and Beliefs of the Sea." *Folklore,* 78: 184–90, Aug. 1969.

Holiday, F. W. *The Great Orm of Loch Ness.* London, 1968.

Holland, Clive. "Some Superstitions of Sea-Faring Folks." *Nautical Magazine,* 143:12–15, 1940.

Hornell, James. *British Coracles and Irish Curraghs.* London, 1938.

Hoskins, W. G. *Devon and Its People.* Newton Abbot, Devon, 1968.

Howe, George. *Mount Hope: A New England Chronicle.* New York, 1959.

Howe, Octavius T., and Matthews, F. C. *American Clipper Ships, 1833–1858.* Salem, Mass., 1926.

Hugill, Stan. *Sailor Town.* London and New York, 1967.

———. *Shanties from the Seven Seas.* London and New York, 1961.

Huguenin, Charles A. "The Figurehead of Hercules at Stony Brook, L.I." *New York Folklore Quarterly,* 11:106–15, 1955.

———. "The Kidd Salvage Project in the Hudson River." *New York Folklore Quarterly,* 15:192–214, 1959.

———. "The Truth about the Schooner Hesperus." *New York Folklore Quarterly,* 16:48–53, 1960.

Hulme, Edward. *Natural History Lore and Legend.* London, 1895.

Hunt, Robert. *Popular Romances of the West of England,* 1st series. London, 1865.

Huntington, Gale. *Songs the Whalemen Sang.* Barre, Mass., 1964.

Hurley, Gerard T. "Buried Treasure Tales in America." *Western Folklore,* 10: 197–216, 1951.

Hutchinson, Percy A. "Sailor's Chanties." *Journal of American Folklore,* 19:16–28, 1906.

Hyde, Douglas. *Legends of Saints and Sinners.* London, n.d.

Igglesden, Sir Charles. *Those Superstitions.* London, 1932.

Inwards, R. *Weather Lore.* London, 1898.

Irish Coast Pilot, 10th edition. London, 1954.

Irish Cruising Club. *Sailing Directions for the East and North Coasts of Ireland.* Dublin, 1965.

———. *Sailing Directions for the South and West Coasts of Ireland.* Dublin, 1966.

Irving, John. *Bends, Hitches, Knots and Splices.* London, n.d.

Ives, Edward A. "The Burning Ship of Northumberland Strait: Some Notes on the Apparition." *Midwest Folklore,* 8:199–203, 1958.

———. "More Notes on the Burning Ship of Northumberland Strait." *Northwest Folklore,* 2:53–54, 1959.

Ives, Ronald L. "The 'Phantom Ship' of the Gulf of California." *Western Folklore,* 18:327–28, 1959.

Jackman, Eugene T. "Efforts Made Before 1825 to Ameliorate the Lot of the American Seamen: With Emphasis on His Moral Regeneration." *American Neptune*, 24:109–18, 1964.

Jackson, Birdsall. *Stories of Old Long Island*. Rockville Center, N.Y., 1934.

Jameson, J. F. *Privateering and Piracy in the Colonial Period*. New York, 1923.

Jefferis, Roger, and MacDonald, Kendall. *The Wreck Hunters*. London, 1966.

Jeffrey, Percy Shaw. *Whitby Lore and Legend*, 2nd edition. Whitby, 1923.

Jenkin, A. K. Hamilton. *Cornish Seafarers: The Smuggling, Wrecking and Fishing Life of Cornwall*. London, 1933.

————. *Cornwall and Its People*. London, 1945.

Jewitt, W. Henry. "The Wild Huntsman." *Folk-Lore*, 18:342, 1907.

Johnson, Captain Charles. *A General History of the Robberies and Murders of the Most Notorious Pirates From Their Rise and Settlement in The Island of Providence to the Present Year*. Ed. Arthur Haywood. New York, 1926.

Johnson, Clifton. *What They Say in New England*. Boston, 1896.

Johnson, James B. *Place-Names of Scotland*. Edinburgh, 1892.

Jones, Herbert G. *The Isles of Casco Bay in Fact and Fancy*. Portland, Maine, 1946.

Jones, William. *Credulities Past and Present*. London, 1880.

————. *The Broad Broad Ocean*. London, 1883.

Jordain, Sylvester. *A Discovery of Bermuda*. New York, 1940.

Josselyn, John. *An Account of Two Voyages to New England*. London, 1674.

————. *New England Rarities*. Ed. E. Tuckerman. Boston, 1865.

Joyce, P. W. *The Origin and History of Irish Names and Places*. Dublin, 1871.

Kay, Frances. *This—Is Grenada*. Trinidad, 1966.

Keightley, Thomas. *The Fairy Mythology*. London, 1905.

Kelton, Dwight. *Indian Names of Places Near the Great Lakes*. Detroit, 1888.

Kerridge, J. B. *Notable Shipwrecks Near Weymouth*. Weymouth, Mass., n.d.

Kinahan, G. H. "Aughisky, or Water Horse." *Folk-Lore Journal*, 2:61–63, 1884.

————. "Notes on Irish Folk-Lore." *Folk-Lore Record*, 4:96–125, 1881.

King, S. H. *King's Book of Chanties*. Boston, 1918.

Kingston, William H. G. *Michael Penguyne or Fisher Life on the Cornish Coast*. London, n.d.

Kittredge, George Lyman. *Witchcraft in Old and New England*. Cambridge, Mass., 1929.

Knight, Frank. *The Sea Story Being a Guide to Nautical Reading from Ancient Times to the Close of the Sailing Ship Era*. London, 1958.

Knowlson, T. Sharper. *The Origins of Popular Superstitions and Customs*. London, 1910.

Krappe, Alexander H. *Balor of the Evil Eye*. New York, 1927.

————. *The Science of Folklore*. New York, 1929.

Kuehl, Warren F. *Blow the Man Down*. New York, 1959.

Laighton, Oscar. *Ninety Years at the Isles of Schoals*. Boston, 1930.

Laing, Alexander. *Clipper Ship Men*. New York, 1944.

Leach, MacEdward. *The Ballad Book*. New York, 1955.

———. "Celtic Tales from Cape Breton." *Studies in Folklore.* Bloomington, Ind., 1957.

———. *Folk Ballads and Songs of the lower Labrador Coast.* Ottawa, 1965.

Leavitt, John F. *Wake of the Coasters.* Middletown, Conn., 1970.

Lee, Henry. *Sea Fables and Monsters.* London, 1883.

Le Guin, Charles A. "Sea Life in Seventeenth Century England." *American Neptune,* 27:111–34, 1967.

LeMoine, James M. *The Legendary Lore of the St. Lawrence.* Quebec, 1862.

Leslie, R. C. *A Sea Painter's Log.* London, 1886.

———. *Old Sea Wings, Ways and Words, in the Days of Oak and Hemp.* London, 1890.

Lethbridge, T. C. *Herdsmen and Hermits: Celtic Seafarers in the Northern Seas.* Cambridge, England, 1950.

Lewis, Charles L. *Books of the Sea: An Introduction to Nautical Literature.* Annapolis, Md., 1943.

Linscott, Eloise H. *Folk Songs of Old New England.* New York, 1939.

Lipman, Jean. *American Primitive Painting.* New York, 1942.

Littlejohn, E. C. "Life and Legends of Lafitte the Pirate." *Publications of the Texas Folklore Society,* 3:179–85, 1924.

Livermore, Samuel T. *A History of Block Island.* Hartford, 1877.

Lloyd, Christopher. *The British Seaman.* London, 1968.

Lockhart, John G. *Peril of the Sea.* London, 1924.

London, Jack. *Jack London: Short Stories,* ed. Maxwell Geismar. New York, 1960.

Long, W. H. *Dictionary of the Isle of Wight, and Provincialisms Used in the Island.* London, 1886.

Longfellow, Henry Wadsworth. *Complete Poetical Works of Henry Wadsworth Longfellow.* Boston, 1902.

Lorenz, Lincoln. *John Paul Jones: Fighter for Freedom and Glory.* Annapolis, 1943.

Loomis, C. Grant. "Sea Serpent." *Western Folklore,* 15:291, 1956.

Loomis, Roger. "Morgan la Fée and the Celtic Goddess." *Speculum,* 20:183–203, 1945.

Lover, Samuel. *Legends and Stories of Ireland,* 2nd series. Westminster, England, 1899.

Lovette, L. P. *Naval Customs, Traditions and Usage.* Annapolis, 1939.

Lum, Peter. *Fabulous Beasts.* Wakefield, Mass., 1951.

Lydenberg, Harry Miller. *Crossing the Line.* New York, 1957.

Lyman, John. "Chantey and Limey." *American Speech,* 30:172–75, 1955.

MacArthur, F. H. *Legends of Prince Edward Island.* Charlottetown, P.E.I., n.d.

MacCormick, John. *The Island of Mull.* Glasgow, 1923.

MacCracken, Henry Noble. "The Lore of the 'Monitor.'" *New York Folklore Quarterly,* 17:116–22, 1961.

MacCulloch, John A. *Celtic Mythology.* Boston, 1918.

———. *The Misty Isle of Skye.* Stirling, 1927.

———. *Religion of the Ancient Celts.* Edinburgh, 1911.

MacDonald, Dr. of Geisla. *Tales and Traditions of Lews*. Stornoway, 1967.

Macdonald, Alexander. *Story and Song from Loch Ness Side*. Inverness, 1914.

MacFarlane, A. M. "Sea Myths and Lore of the Hebrides." *Transactions of the Inverness Scientific Society and Field Club*, 9:360–409, 1918–1925.

MacInnis, John. "The Oral Tradition in Scottish Gaelic Poetry." *Scottish Studies*, 12:29–43, 1968.

MacKenzie, Alexander. *The Prophecies of the Brahan Seer*. Stirling, 1946.

MacKenzie, Sir Compton; Campbell, J. L.; and Borgström, Carl Hj. *The Book of Barra*. London, 1936.

MacKenzie, W. C. *The Book of the Lews*. Paisley, 1919.

MacKenzie, W. Roy. *Ballads and Sea-Songs from Nova Scotia*. Cambridge, Mass., 1928.

MacKinlay, James M. *Folklore of Scottish Lochs and Springs*. Glasgow, 1893.

Maclay, Edgar E. *A History of American Privateers*. London, 1899.

MacLeod, Kenneth. *The Road to the Isles*. London, 1956.

MacRitchie, David. *Fians, Fairies and Picts*. London, 1893.

Macy, William F. *Nantucket Scrapbasket*. Boston, 1930.

Maddock, Llywelyn W. *West Country Folk Tales*. Bath, England, 1965.

Maloney, W. B. *The Chanty Man Sings*. New York, 1926.

Marshall, Logan. *Sinking of the Titanic and Great Sea Disasters*. Princeton, 1912.

Martin, Martin. *A Description of the Western Islands of Scotland*. Stirling, 1934.

Marwick, Hugh. *Orkney*. London, 1951

Marx, Robert F. *Pirate Port: The Story of the Sunken City of Port Royal*. New York, 1967.

Mason, George Carrington. "An Atlantic Crossing of the Seventeenth Century." *American Neptune*, 11:35–41, 1951.

Mason, Thomas H. *The Islands of Ireland*. Cork, 1936.

Mather, Cotton. *Magnalia Christi Americana*. 2 vols. Hartford, 1820.

Mather, Increase. *Remarkable Providences*, ed. George Offer. London, 1890.

Mather, J. Y. "Boats and Boatmen of Orkney and Shetland." *Scottish Studies*, 8:19–32, 1965.

McElory, John William. "Seafaring in the Seventeenth Century in New England." *New England Quarterly*, 8:331–64, 1935.

McFee, William. *The Law of the Sea*. Philadelphia, 1950.

McMechan, Archibald. *Sagas of the Sea*. Toronto, 1924.

McPherson, J. M. *Primitive Beliefs in the North-East of Scotland*. New York, 1929.

Meikle, H. B. "Mermaids and Fairymaids or Water Gods and Goddesses of Tobago." *Caribbean Quarterly*, 5:103–08, 1958.

Meltz, Adrienne. "Why the Sea Waters Taste of Salt." *New York Folklore Quarterly*, 14:59–64, 1958.

Melville, Herman. *Moby-Dick*. New York, 1851.

———. *Redburn*. New York, 1850.

———. *White Jacket*. New York, 1850.

Miller, Hugh. *Scenes and Legends of the North of Scotland*. Edinburgh, 1853.

Moore, A. W. *The Folk-lore of the Isle of Man*. London, 1891.

Moore, R. O. *Some Aspects of the Origin and Nature of English Piracy, 1603–1625*. PhD. thesis, University of Virginia, 1960.

Morison, Samuel Eliot. *John Paul Jones: A Sailor's Biography*. Boston, 1959.

———. *The Maritime History of Massachusetts, 1783–1860*. Boston, 1961.

Mould, D. D. C. Pochin. *Irish Pilgrimage*. Dublin, 1955.

———. *West-Over-Sea*. Edinburgh, 1953.

Murray, Lt. Col. the Honorable Arthur. *St. Columba and the Holy Isle of Garvellachs. The Whirlpool of the Corre Vreckan*. Edinburgh, 1950.

Murray, James. "Sailor's Songs with California Significance." *California Folklore Quarterly*, 5:143–52, 1946.

Murray, Margaret. *The God of the Witches*. London, n.d.

Naish, George. "Decorative Rope and Canvas Work." *Decorative Arts of the Mariner*, Boston, 1966, pp. 205–17.

Newell, W. W. "The Ignis Fatuus, Its Character and Legendary Origin." *Journal of American Folklore*, 17:39–60, 1904.

Nicholson, John. *Restin Chair Yarns*. Lerwick, Scotland, n.d.

———. *Shetland Incidents and Tales*. Edinburgh, 1931.

Noall, Cyril, and Farr, Graham. *Wreck and Rescue Round the Cornish Coast*. Truro, Cornwall, 1965.

Nordhoff, Charles. *The Yankee Windjammers*. New York, 1940.

Nordhoff, Charles. *Sailor Life on Man of War and Merchant Vessels*. New York, 1884.

———. *Whaling and Fishing*. New York, 1895.

O'Brien, William. *A Queen of Men*. Dublin and London, 1958.

O'Faolain, Eileen. *Irish Sagas and Folktales*. London, 1954.

Ojo, G. J. Afolabi. *Yoruba Culture*. London, 1966.

Olds, Nathaniel S. "Square-Rigger Relics in American Speech." *Atlantic Monthly*, 150:383–84, 1932.

O'Rahilly, Thomas F. *Early Irish History and Mythology*. Dublin, 1964.

O Súilleabháin, Séan. *Irish Folk Custom and Belief*. Dublin, 1967.

Pacifique, Père. *Pays des Micmacs*. Montreal, 1934.

Paine, E. J. *Voyages of Elizabethan Seamen*. Oxford, 1900.

Paine, Ralph D. *The Book of Buried Treasure*. London, 1911.

———. *Joshua Barney*. New York, 1924.

Parsons, Elsie Clews. "Ballads and Chanties Sung by May Hoisington." *Journal of American Folklore*, 44:296–301, 1931.

———. "Folklore of the Antilles, French and English." *Memoirs of the American Folklore Society*, Vol. XXVI. New York, 1933.

Parkman, Francis. *Pioneers of France in the New World*. Boston, 1880.

Patai, Raphael. "Lillith." *Journal of American Folklore*, 77:294–312, 1964.

Patterson, George. "Notes on the Folk-Lore of Newfoundland." *Journal of American Folklore*, 8:285–90, 1895.

Pearson, Edmund. *Murder at Smutty Nose and Other Murders*. London, 1927.

Peterson, Edward. *History of Rhode Island and Newport in the Past*. New York, 1853.

Philbrick, Thomas. *James Fenimore Cooper and the Development of American Sea Fiction.* Cambridge, Mass., 1961.

Piggot, Stuart S. *The Prehistoric Peoples of Scotland.* London, 1962.

Pinckney, Pauline A. *American Figureheads.* New York, 1940.

The Pirate's Own Book. Philadelphia, 1839.

Platt, Charles. *Popular Superstitions.* London, 1925.

Poole, C. H. *The Customs, Superstitions and Legends of the County of Somerset.* St. Peter Port, Isle of Jersey, Channel Islands, 1970.

Porter, Kenneth. "Granny Wales." *Western Folklore,.* 13:51, 1954.

Procope, Bruce. "Launching a Schooner in Carriacou." *Caribbean Quarterly,* 4:122–31, 1955.

Proctor Brothers. *Fishermen's Ballads and Songs by the Sea.* Gloucester, Mass., 1874.

Puckett, Newbell Niles. *Folk Beliefs of the Southern Negro.* New York, 1969.

Purchas, Samuel B. D. *Hakluytus Posthumus or Purchas His Pilgrims.* Glasgow, 1907.

Quigley, Carroll. "Certain Considerations on the Origin and Diffusion of Occuli." *American Neptune.* 15:191–98, 1955.

———. "The Origin and Diffusion of Occuli: A Rejoinder." *American Neptune,* 18:25–58, 1958.

Raglan, Lord. *The Hero.* New York, 1956.

Randolph, Norris. "Newport's Forgotten Heroine." *Yankee,* 23:128–31, 1959.

Ransom, J. *Songs of the Wexford Coast.* Enniscorthy, Ireland, 1948.

Rappaport, Angelo. *Superstitions of Sailors.* London, 1928.

Rattray, Jeannette. "Notes on Ship and Shore." *New York Folklore Quarterly,* 12:54–60, 1956.

———. "Rum-Running Tales from the East End." *New York Folklore Quarterly,* 19:3–18, 1963.

Reed's Nautical Almanac, ed. Captain O. M. Watts. London, 1969.

Rhys, John. *Celtic Folklore.* 2 vols. Oxford, 1901.

Richard, W. *Weather Lore.* London, 1893.

Richards, Stanley. *Black Bart.* Llandybythe, Wales, 1966.

Rickaby, Franz. *Ballads and Songs of the Shanty Boy.* Cambridge, Mass., 1926.

Riordan, John Lancaster. "American Naval 'Slanguage' in the Pacific in 1945." *California Folklore Quarterly,* 5:375–90, 1946.

Ritchie, Ethel C. *Block Island Lore and Legend.* Providence, 1967.

Roads, Samuel. *The History and Traditions of Marblehead.* Boston, 1881.

Robertson, R. Macdonald. *More Highland Folktales.* Edinburgh and London, 1964.

———. *Selected Highland Folktales.* Edinburgh and London, 1961.

Robinson, Charles-Napier. *The British Tar in Fact and Fiction.* London and New York, 1909.

Robinson, John, and Dow, G. F. *The Sailing Ships of New England, 1607–1907.* Salem, Mass., 1922.

Rogers, Stanley. *Sea-Lore.* London, Bombay and Sydney, 1934.

Rolleston, T. W. *Myths and Legends of the Celtic Race*. London, 1911.

Rose, H. J. "Ghost Summoning the Drowned." *Folk-Lore*, 55:168–69, 1944.

Rowe, William H. *Shipbulding Days in Casco Bay, 1727–1890*. Yarmouth, Me., 1929.

Ryan, John. *Ireland from the Earliest Times to A.D. 800*. 2 vols. Dublin, Belfast, Cork, Waterford, n.d.

Sampson, John. *The Seven Seas Shanty Book*. London, 1927.

Sampson, William. *History of Ireland*. New York, 1833.

Samuels, Captain S. *From the Forecastle to the Cabin*. New York, 1887.

Saunders, William. "Sailor Songs and Songs of the Sea." *Musical Quarterly*, 14: 339–58, 1928.

Sawtell, C. C. *The Ship Ann Alexander of New Bedford, 1805–1851*. Mystic, Conn., 1962.

Sawyer, E. O., Jr., ed. *Our Sea Saga: The Wood Wind Ships*. San Francisco, 1929.

Saxby, Jessie M. E. *Shetland Traditional Lore*. Edinburgh, 1932.

Scott, Michael. *Tom Cringles's Log*. 2 vols. Philadelphia, 1833.

Scott, Sir Walter. *Letters on Demonology and Witchcraft*. London, 1884.

Sea Stories: Putnam's Library of Choice Stories, vol. 5. New York, 1958.

Sewall, Samuel. "Diary of Samuel Sewall." *Collections of the Massachusetts Historical Society*. 5 vols. Cambridge, Mass., 1880.

Sharp, Cecil J. *English Folk-Chanteys*. London, 1919.

Shaw, Captain Frank. *The Splendour of the Seas*. London, 1953.

Shay, Frank. *American Sea Songs and Chanteys*. New York, 1948.

———. *Deep Sea Shanties*. London, n.d.

———. *Here's Audacity! American Legendary Heroes*. New York, 1930.

———. *Iron Men and Wooden Ships*. New York, 1925.

———. *A Sailor's Treasury*. New York, 1951.

Sheffield, William. *Rhode Island Privateers*. Newport, 1883.

Shepard, Birse. *Lore of the Wreckers*. Boston, 1961.

Short, Bernard C. *Smugglers of Poole and Bournemouth*. Bournemouth, 1969.

Sikes, Wirt. *British Goblins: Welsh Folk-Lore, Fairy Mythology, Legends, and Traditions*. Boston, 1881.

Simmons, Gerald. *Barbarian Europe*. New York, 1968.

Simpson, George G. "Sea Sirens." *Natural History*, 30:41–47, 1930.

Siochain, P. A. O. *Aran Islands of Legend*, 3rd. ed. New York, 1967.

Skinner, Charles M. *American Myths and Legends*. 2 vols. Philadelphia, 1903.

———. *Myths and Legends of Our Own Land*. 2 vols. Philadelphia, 1896.

Slocum, Joshua. *Sailing Alone Around the World*. New York, 1900.

Smith, G. Hubert. "Legend of the Origin of Nantucket Island." *Journal of American Folklore*, 54:83, 1941.

Smith, Captain John. *A Sea Grammar, With the Plaine Exposition of Smith's Accidence for Young Sea-men enlarged*. London, 1627, 1970.

Smith, Laura A. *The Music of the Waters*. London, 1888.

Smith, M. G. *Dark Puritan*. Kingston, Jamaica, 1963.

Snaith, William. *Across the Western Ocean*. New York, 1966.

Snow, Edward Rowe. *Great Sea Rescues*. New York, 1958.

———. *Famous New England Lighthouses*. Boston, 1947.

———. *Storms and Shipwrecks of New England*. Boston, 1946.

Spence, Lewis. *The Minor Traditions of British Mythology*. London, 1948.

Spense, John. *Shetland Folklore*. Lerwick, Scotland, 1899.

Speroni, Charles. "California Fishermen's Festivals." *Western Folklore*, 14: 77–91, 1955.

Splitter, Harry Winfred. "New Tales of American Phantom Ships." *Western Folklore*, 9:201–16, 1950.

Squire, Charles. *Celtic Myths and Legend, Poetry, and Romance*. London, n.d.

Stackpole, Edouard A. *Figureheads and Ship Carvings at Mystic Seaport*. Mystic, Conn., 1964.

———. "Scrimshaw." *Decorative Arts of the Mariner*. Boston, 1966.

———. *The Sea Hunters: The New England Whalemen During Two Centuries, 1635–1835*. Philadelphia, 1953.

Stanchfield, Bessie Mae. "Old Granny Wales." *California Folklore Quarterly*, 4:393–97, 1945.

Standard Dictionary of Folklore, Mythology and Legend, ed. Maria Leach. New York, 1950.

Sternbeck, Alfred. "Sea-Lore and Sea Slang." *Neuphilogische Monatschrift*, 3: 113–33, 1931.

Stewart, George W. *Names on the Land*. Boston, 1969.

Stokes, Samuel. *An Narrative of the Many Unparalleled Hardships, and Cruel Sufferings While in France, of the Crew of the Terrible, Privateer, Commanded by Captain William Death, With the Particulars of that Most Bloody Engagement, and the Cruel Treatment of the Crew, when taken by the Vengeance, a French Privateer*. London, n.d.

Stowe, Harriet Beecher. *The Pearl of Orr's Island*. Boston, 1862.

Swan, Harry P. *Highlights of the Donegal Highlands*. Belfast, 1958.

———. *Romantic Stories and Legends of Donegal*. Belfast, 1965.

Swire, Otta F. *The Highlands and Their Legends*. Edinburgh and London, 1963.

———. *The Inner Hebrides and Their Legends*. London, 1964.

———. *The Outer Hebrides and Their Legends*. Edinburgh, 1966.

———. *Skye: The Island and Its Legends*. London, 1952.

Tait, E. S. "Press Gang Stories." *Shetland Folk Book*, 4:43–69, 1964.

Taylor, A. B. "The Name 'St. Kilda.'" *Scottish Studies*, 13:145–58, 1969.

Teit, J. A. "Water-Beings in Shetlandic Folk-Lore, as Remembered by Shetlanders in British Columbia." *Journal of American Folklore*, 31:180–201, 1918.

Thaxter, Celia. *Among the Isles of Shoals*. New York, 1915.

Thompson, C. J. S. *The Hand of Destiny*. London, 1932.

———. *The Mystery and Lore of Monsters*. London, 1930.

Thompson, Harold W. *Body, Boots and Britches*. Philadelphia, 1939.

Thompson, Stith. *The Folktale: Stories Men Tell from Egyptian Myth to Uncle Remus*. New York, 1946.

———. *Motif-Index of Folk Literature*. 6 vols. Bloomington, Ind., 1955–1958.

Thomson, David. *The People of the Sea*. London, 1954.

Thorpe, Benjamin. *Northern Mythology Comprising the Principal Popular Traditions of Scandinavia, North Germany and the Netherlands*. 3 vols. London, 1851–1852.

Toye, Geoffrey. *Sea Chanties*. London, 1924.

Trevelyan, Marie. *Folk-Lore and Folk-Stories of Wales*. London, 1909.

———. *From Snowdon to the Sea*. London, 1894.

Trevine, Owen. *Deep Sea Chanties*. London, 1921.

Tudor, J. R. *The Orkneys and Shetland, Their Past and Present State*. London, 1883.

Turner, W. *A Complete History of the Most Remarkable Providences*. London, 1697.

Van Dervoort, J. W. *The Water World*. New York, 1886.

Verrill, A. Hyatt. *The Real Story of the Whaler, Whaling Past and Present*. New York, 1916.

The Voyage of Bran. Ed. and trans. Kuno Keyer. 2 vols. London, 1895.

Wainwright, F. T. *The Northern Isles*. Edinburgh, 1964.

Wallace, Captain Frederick William. *Wooden Ships and Iron Men*. Boston, 1937.

Wasson, George S. *Cap'n Simeon's Store*. Boston, 1903.

———. "Our Heritage of Old Sea Terms." *American Speech* 4 (No. 5) 377–83, 1929.

———. *Sailing Days on the Penobscot*. New York, 1932.

Watson, Arthur C. *The Long Harpoon: A Collection of Whaling Anecdotes*. New Bedford, 1929.

———. "Scrimshaw," *Technology Review*, March 1938.

Watson, W. J. *History of the Celtic Place-Names of Scotland*. Edinburgh, 1926.

Webb, J. O. "Lafitte Lore." *Publications of the Texas Folklore Society*, 3:189–91, 1924.

Weightman, A. E. "Figureheads." *Decorative Arts of the Mariner*. Boston, 1966.

Westropp, Thomas J. "A Folklore Survey of County Clare." *Folklore*, 21:180–99, 338–49, 476–87, 1910.

———. "A Study of the Folklore on the Coast of Connacht, Ireland." *Folklore*, 29:305–19, 1918.

Whedbee, Charles H. *Legends of the Outer Banks*. Winston-Salem, 1966.

Whittier, John Greenleaf. *Complete Poetical Works*, Boston, 1894.

Whymper, Frederick. *The Romance of the Sea*. London, 1896.

Whyte, Constance. *More Than a Legend*. London, 1961.

Wilde, Lady. *Ancient Legends of Ireland*. London, 1902.

Wilkins, Harold T. *Captain Kidd and His Skeleton Island*. New York, 1937.

———. *Pirate Treasure*. New York, 1937.

Williams, Gomer. *History of the Liverpool Privateers and Letters of Marque with an Account of the Liverpool Slave Trade*. London, 1897.

Wilmerding, John. *A History of American Marine Painting*. Boston and Toronto, 1968.

Wilson, T. G. *The Irish Lighthouse Service*. Dublin, 1968.

Wimberly, Lowry C. *Folklore in the English and Scottish Ballads*. New York, 1928.

Winship, George Parker. *Sailors' Narratives of Voyages Along the New England Coast, 1524–1624*. Boston, 1905.

Winthrop, John. *Winthrop's Journal*, ed. J. K. Hosmer. 2 vols. New York, 1908.

Wood-Martin, W. G. *Traces of the Elder Faiths in Ireland*. 2 vols. New York, 1902.

Wright, A. R. "Mer-Folk in 1814." *Folk-Lore*, 40:87–90, 1929.

Yelvington, Henry. *Ghost Lore*. San Antonio, Tex., 1936.

Young, Hazel. *Islands of New England*. Boston, 1954.

INDEX